Privatizing the United States Justice System

To our children:
Daniel and Sarah
Liora, Rami and Doron
Mindye, Bob, Terri and Marla

Privatizing the United States Justice System

Police, Adjudication, and Corrections Services from the Private Sector

Edited by

Gary W. Bowman
Simon Hakim
Paul Seidenstat

with a foreword by
JAMES K. STEWART

McFarland & Company, Inc., Publishers
Jefferson, North Carolina, and London

Acknowledgments. This book would not have been possible without the assistance of many people. We would like to thank the Manhattan Institute of New York, which sponsored the project. In particular, we wish to express our appreciation to Lawrence Mone, its director of research, whose advice was extremely valuable.

We would also like to thank Dean William Dunkelberg and the School of Business and Management of Temple University which made funds available for the project.

Our gratitude is also extended to the authors of the chapters for sharing their research and for extending to us their cooperation in the many rounds of editing this book.

British Library Cataloguing-in-Publication data are available

Library of Congress Cataloguing-in-Publication Data

Privatizing the United States justice system : police, adjudication,
   and corrections services from the private sector / edited by Gary
   W. Bowman, Simon Hakim, Paul Seidenstat.
      p. cm.
   Includes index.
   ISBN 0-89950-704-2 (library binding : 50# alk. paper) ∞
   1. Criminal justice, Administration of–United States.
   2. Privatization–United States.   3. Police–United States–
   Contracting out.   4. Corrections–United States–Contracting out.
   I. Bowman, Gary W., 1942– . II. Hakim, Simon. III. Seidenstat,
   Paul.
   HV9950.P75   1992
   338.4'7364973–dc20   91-51002
                                                                     CIP

Manufactured in the United States of America

McFarland & Company, Inc., Publishers
  Box 611, Jefferson, North Carolina 28640

Contents

Foreword. The Justice System and the Private Sector: Time for an Expanded Partnership

James K. Stewart

Prior to the 1970s, there was little or no systematic, objective information available on crime and criminal justice policies. Today, we recognize that the costs of crime to our society are far greater than we realized. Different policies have varied consequences in terms of cost, public safety, and fear. The value of policy-relevant research can be seen in the emerging policies that are making a difference in our ability to safeguard the public and concentrate scarce criminal justice resources where they will do the most good. We have moved far in creating a favorable climate for collaboration—building understanding and respect between those who design and conduct research and those who set and carry out crime policies. Developing new means of cooperation between the public and private sector is one of the emerging issues in law enforcement and criminal justice that research can help illuminate in police, adjudication, and corrections—the three sections of this volume.

Public-private partnerships are one way law enforcement has responded to the challenge of crime in the face of increased demand and leaner budgets. Growing feelings of vulnerability by residents, customers, employees, delivery, and supply personnel have created an increasing demand for protective services—services far beyond a police department's capacity to provide. These security customers are paying an estimated $52 billion for protection. There are now approximately three times as many private security personnel as public police. The U.S. Department of Labor estimates security will be the fastest market of growth in the next decade. Nearly as much money is paid by governments to private security companies as is spent for public law enforcement by federal and state governments combined. Of course, some types of property protection and security tasks are better suited for contracting with private contractors than requiring police agencies to perform them. The chapters in Part 1 include not only how private security has helped and can further help deal with limited police resource problems but also how it can provide better service in some areas.

There are substantial delays in many courts at all levels nationwide. Here too the chapters of Part 2 show how privatization has reduced and can further reduce backlogs and even provide better solutions in some cases. Access to an arbiter in matters of dispute is important in an increasingly heterogeneous society. It is an essential fairness issue that delay corrodes.

The role of private mediation is explored and the use of private prosecution is discussed. The concept of "Rent-a-Judge" to settle disputes is examined as a cost-effective method of resolving conflict.

Jail and prison crowding is the most noted problem. National surveys have indicated that criminal justice officials from all parts of the country have identified jail and prison crowding as the most serious problem facing the criminal justice systems. Some consequences of jail crowding are well known: increased victimization and fear, decreased public confidence that dangerous persons can be locked up, lawsuits, court-imposed limits on the number of prisoners, and damage to facilities and equipment. Crowding increases both tension in the institution and the strain on corrections budgets. Less obvious but equally worrisome are delays in case processing due to cumbersome access to prisoners and the limits put on such necessary judicial options as pretrial release and sentencing.

There is also concern about the escalating costs of operating rapidly expanding correctional facilities. The widely held perception that public correctional agencies have failed to achieve even a modest level of public protection, deterrence, or rehabilitation is another area of dissatisfaction.

A few states already have enacted laws authorizing privately operated correction facilities. Twenty or more firms have entered the "prison market." More than thirty-six states contract with private enterprises for at least one correctional service or program.

The chapters in Part 3 characterize and evaluate the somewhat small current record of privatization in corrections and look at its role as an important source for jail and prison construction, operation, and employment of prisoners.

This volume addresses the question of the role and the performance of private institutions in the administration of justice. The complexity of the issues related to the privatization of police, adjudication, and corrections defies an easy answer to whether privatization will offer a major solution to the problems of the justice system. Questions that need to be examined range from the philosophical to the most practical. Only by pursuing policy research and providing opportunities for public discussion can recommendations be made with confidence. I believe that this volume can help frame the issues and add substance to the public policy debate.

In our society we are gaining empirical evidence that can help inform the decisionmakers. The recent past indicates that emotion and preexisting beliefs are not the most effective basis for policy development. Rather, a careful program of experimentation and pilot studies to provide measurable results will help us progress as a just society advancing our principles.

1. Introduction

Gary W. Bowman
Simon Hakim
Paul Seidenstat

The term privatization has been loosely used for reduced government involvement in the marketplace. The trend accelerated in the 1980s during the tenure of Ronald Reagan in the United States and Margaret Thatcher in Great Britain. It runs the whole gamut from the sale of government assets and businesses to the relaxation of government regulation of private corporations.

The present volume focuses on transfer of police, adjudication, and correction activities from governments to private corporations or volunteer groups. Why and when should government transfer responsibilities to the private sector? Much depends upon the values of the society in question. Often the same service is provided in one country or state by a government agency and in another by a private agency. This may reflect differences in societal values and long-term established practices, but there are some conceptual guidelines that can assist in making such decisions.

Economists have determined that efficient allocation of resources is reached under perfect competition. When there are many buyers and sellers for any good or service, and a free market price is established, then capital and workers will be employed where their productivity is maximized. Hence, introduction of competition (where possible) is expected to improve the performance of the existing public monopoly justice system. However, there are some situations in which the competitive marketplace may generate inefficient allocations of resources. Government intervention may be required in order to correct such situations.

Economic theory suggests that one can view the following conditions as "justifications" for government intervention in the marketplace. However, when the conditions do not exist, then the private market should be allowed to operate. The degree of intervention should be minimal so as to correct for the imperfection.

1. Economies of scale which extend for a significant part or the entire market demand: In this situation it is less expensive to have one producer (as opposed to two or more) supply the entire market. If a private company supplies the market as with public utilities, then the government may regulate the price to a level where it is at or near cost. Market forces keep prices at (marginal) cost where competition exists.

1

2. Zero marginal cost: The optimal amount (from society's viewpoint) of any good or service is that which people wish to purchase when the price is equal to marginal cost. For example, if more people are visiting a park and if this imposes no additional costs, (i.e., zero marginal cost) then the number of visitors should not be restricted by charging an admission fee (i.e., zero price).

3. Nonexclusion: Here it is impossible or very costly to exclude those who do not purchase the product or service from consuming it.

4. Significant level of externalities which are not captured by the price system: Externalities can be defined as "by-products" of production or consumption that escape being included in the price of the product.

Properties 3 and 4 are relevant for some justice services. It may be impossible or very difficult to exclude anyone from consuming police patrol; thus nonpurchasers may become "free riders." Everyone in the district enjoys the benefits of patrol even if they do not share its expense.

Externalities can be positive or negative. An example of negative externality which requires government intervention is a noisy party late at night. The homeowner gains utility from the party; however, the neighbors who attempt to sleep suffer disutility. The consumption of party services yields the negative externality of noise. Government may be needed to control for the disruption of peace.

Why should a publicly provided service be shifted to the private sector? The reason for private provision is more efficient use of resources. Private production motivated by profit is expected to be more efficient than public provision. For example, economic theory and experience suggest that the same level of service provided by a county correction institution will be provided less expensively by a private company that needs to compete with others in order to win a contract to run the facility. In 1986 Corrections Corporation of America saved the state of Kentucky $400,000 a year by managing the Marion Adjustment Center in St. Mary. While the cost to the state was estimated at $40 per inmate per day, CCA charged per diem only $25, while maintaining the same quality of service.

In order to decide whether and how a justice service can be shifted from the public domain, we need to observe each of the activities of the justice organizations separately. We need not consider complete privatization of police, adjudication, or corrections. Rather, we can analyze separately each output or task of an agency, such as police, and examine its relation to the other outputs provided by the police. Only then a decision can be made regarding whether to privatize and what is the appropriate form of privatization.

Figure 1.1 illustrates when public provision may be required. The vertical dimension measures the degree of common consumption while the horizontal axis shows the size of the interacting group. Common consumption refers to a situation where a given unit of the same service is consumed by more than one individual or household.

Police services are used as examples. Guarding a housing project is limited to a small part of the locality; however, it provides for the residents in the project a high degree of common consumption since they all enjoy the entire level of the provided security. Such a service can be easily provided privately and initiated by the

Figure 1.1 Typology of Private and Public Security Services

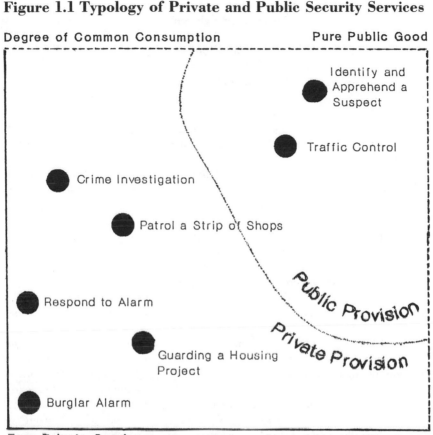

Degree of Common Consumption   **Pure Public Good**

Identify and Apprehend a Suspect

Traffic Control

Crime Investigation

Patrol a Strip of Shops

Public Provision

Private Provision

Respond to Alarm

Guarding a Housing Project

Burglar Alarm

Pure Private Good   **Size of Interaction Group**

small number of residents. Traffic control, on the other hand, is provided to most residents of the locality (most drivers), and they all enjoy equally the entire level of service. Thus, traffic control cannot be easily supplied privately because there is no incentive for any individual(s) to initiate such a service.

A boundary line separates private and public service provision. Similar schemes can be employed for adjudication and correction. Clearly, the exact path of the boundary line depends upon the values of the particular society. The focus in this book is upon the transfer of police, adjudication, and correction activities from the public to private entities. The transfers which are relevant to these three sectors can be of various forms which can be overlapping.

There are two factors which determine the distinction among types of transfers between the public and private sectors. One factor is the primary source of funding; that is, public or private. The second factor involves which sector actually performs the service.

Public contracting among governmental agencies is the only public-public configuration. In this case smaller public agencies can contract with larger ones in order to achieve greater efficiency through economies of scale or economies of scope. An example would be a local police department contracting vertically with the county or state police for crime lab services, communications, or the investigation of serious crimes.

Public funding but private operation can take the form of direct contracting with private firms to perform a particular function. One example of such contracting is for the financing, construction, or operations of prisons or jails. Franchises for prison food services operations are another option. Grants or subsidies to private agencies to perform such services as parole supervision or job training can also be utilized.

A middle position would be a joint public-private venture. Businesses in the community and the government join forces for a particular purpose in order to increase the public awareness and involvement in enhancing security provision. Joint provision can be maintained for a significant period of time.

User charges or fees involve private funding but public provision of service. The government charges users of services directly for the service. The policy usually applies when the service is provided to a small share of the jurisdiction's population. An example would be police response to burglar or fire alarm activations. False activations involve users' fees. Some police departments require all alarm owners to pay annual fees. In this case the financial burden is placed upon the users of the government service.

If reliance is completely on the private sector, then this is called load shedding. Load shedding is where government turns over to a private firm the responsibility for both the financing and provision of service. This is the most extreme form of privatization. An example is the operation of a business-financed private security firm to patrol a downtown business area.

These various types of transfers or privatization methods are discussed and case studies illustrating them are presented in this volume.

In an historical overview (Chapter 2) Robert McCrie from John Jay College of Criminal Justice reveals that most security functions have indeed been privately provided over much of the last one thousand years in Great Britain and later in the United States. In the nineteenth century the public sector gradually assumed almost full responsibility for policing and correction services. The evolution of the private-public-private genesis is presented, reasons for change are discussed, and the current status of the privatization efforts is summarized.

Privatization of Police

Chapters 3 to 14 present several efforts to transfer security services from local governments to private security companies. They indicate that monetary savings can be achieved with no sacrifice of security. There are three stumbling blocks to wider application of private security: the lower quality and training of guards in comparison to sworn police officers, high insurance costs associated with liabilities from armed guards and the lobbying efforts of unions. The training quality of private guards is improving and many companies use the police academies to train their recruits. Better quality manpower with private security companies and good experiences with underwriting armed guards will lower insurance premiums and, in turn, boost private guards services to replace police. As more positive experiences accumulate with private security, the blocking efforts of labor unions may become less effective.

The late Philip Fixler, Jr., and Robert Poole, Jr. (Chapter 3), set the stage for the police section. They categorize police services by funding and delivery functions in order to determine the degree of private provision possible. Their association with the Reason Foundation which specializes in privatization efforts enables them to provide a unique insight into such efforts. No current efforts to privatize police services fully are known. However, the authors present examples of limited transfers involving users fees, contracting out, and load shedding by such means as deputization or the award of arrest power.

A basic question is whether private security is indeed a substitute for police. Edwin Zedlewski, who is a scientific adviser to the director of the National Institute of Justice, has used data of 124 metropolitan areas in the United States in order to investigate this question (Chapter 4). He found that security is a "normal" good in that as income rises more security is demanded. Interesting questions that the chapter addresses include whether increased cost of private security causes a greater demand for public police, and whether more visible private security causes displacement of crime to neighbors.

In Chapter 5 Ronald Boostrom and Corina Draper from San Diego State University expand Zedlewski's analysis by introducing the voluntary sector. They examine the triangular relationship of police, private enterprise, and self-interest voluntary sector directed toward reducing crime and the public fear of crime. The police usually organize and oversee the operations, and corporations help in training police managers while volunteers and community groups assist in the coproduction of community security.

Stephen Mehay and Rodolfo Gonzales from the Naval Postgraduate School and the University of California at San Jose investigate in Chapter 6 a vertical, intergovernmental contracting arrangement for Lakewood County Sheriff Department in California. They analyze the possible cost savings resulting from economies of scale and the extent of spillover benefits.

Dolores Martin from the University of Nebraska, and Robert Stein from Rice University in Chapter 7 have empirically analyzed contracting out from a public choice perspective. They address the key question of whether savings are generated by the contracting out. Other related questions are whether departments reduce their expenses as a result of savings attributed to the contracting out, or do they use the available resources to increase other expenditures? Further contracting out public safety services by localities is hypothesized to depend upon the interests of public managers and their decisionmaking process.

Roland Dart, a member of the Department of Public Administration at California State University at Sacramento, has many years of police experience, including those as chief of a large department. In Chapter 8 he presents a public administration model which defines the environmental conditions that are crucial to deciding whether private security could successfully replace the police. Dart reviews and evaluates one commercial and three residential examples of possible privatization of security. The chapter suggests four levels of privatization ranging from alarm monitoring and response to contracting out services.

In Chapter 9 Mike Freeman, a city manager previously associated with the International City Managers Association, discusses the process of how to actually contract out police responsibilities to a private company. Freeman discusses labor problems, how to prepare the bidding for the contractor, and introduces the municipality's fiscal concerns.

Chapters 10 to 12 provide three successful examples of actual privatization experiences. All three cases satisfy Dart's criteria for private policing. The private and the public sectors appear to successfully complement each other in all cases, thus providing a good prospective for the expansion of police privatization efforts.

One area where private security can readily assist local police departments is the response to burglar alarm activations. Local police departments are overwhelmed with such activations.

In large cities across the United States it may take up to two hours for the police to respond to residential activations. Jerry Usher is a pioneer in both owning and managing a rapidly growing private company that responds to alarms in Los Angeles. In Chapter 10 he shares his experience in a field that could become the fastest growing privatization effort in the police area.

In Chapter 11 Thomas Windham of Forth Worth, Texas, discusses his experiences with a large private security company in the city. It proves that with responsive management on both sides, police and private security can complement each other.

William Walsh and Edwin Donovan from Pennsylvania State University and James McNicholas present in Chapter 12 a detailed evaluation of a privately secured housing development of a self-contained community in New York City. It appears to be a nearly crime-free community which is fully supported by its residents and provides relief to the police department.

Starting in 1984, we have been witnessing greater cooperation between public law enforcement agencies and the large American corporations. Successful training and practices of corporate America are shared with law enforcement agencies under various forums initiated by the International Association of Chiefs of Police. Michael Shanahan from the University of Washington Police Department discusses these efforts in Chapter 13.

Richard Neely, chief justice of the Supreme Court of West Virginia, analyzes in Chapter 14 problems with both the police and the court systems. Most police activities are oriented toward public services and less than 5 percent is devoted to crime prevention. The court system deals with both civil and criminal cases and is so overburdened that civil cases do not get resolved for years. Neely finds that the self-interests of the people in these systems make real change unlikely; one solution suggested is to rely more on voluntary community policing.

Privatization of Adjudication

Larry Ray, the director of the Standing Committee on Dispute Resolution of the American Bar Association, discusses alternatives to courts in Chapter 15. The juvenile court started on a very moderate scale in the 1950s with the development of community dispute resolution centers. In the ten years since 1980, fifty "for profit" dispute resolution firms have come to exist with 60,000 members in the American Arbitration Association. They offer a range of civil dispute resolution services which are compatible with the public courts system, including negotiation, mediation, arbitration, and adjudication—a hearing before private judges. The rent-a-judge concept which is often used by businesses and corporations in order to expedite the process of resolving civil dispute was created in 1976 in San Diego and has been expanding since then to many other states of the nation.

Bruce Benson, an economist from Florida State University, analyzes the adjudication system in Chapter 16. He argues that public provision should be avoided if the private sector can efficiently and equitably "do the job." Neither system is perfect, but introducing competitiveness to the system will yield a noncumbersome service.

U.S. Congressman Tim Valentine introduces us in Chapter 17 to the interesting notion of private prosecution even in criminal cases. He argues that in many criminal cases the district attorney does not have the time nor the resources to provide services comparable to those of the defense attorney. Fair, timely trials can be enhanced with private assistance to the prosecution.

Michael Gillie, of the U.S. Arbitration and Mediation Service, heads one of the major private adjudication firms in the United States. In Chapter 18 he discusses alternative dispute resolution and answers some of the criticisms leveled against the practice.

David Strawn, with Dispute Management, also has extensive experience in dispute resolution. In Chapter 19 he profiles the ideal private mediator and discusses some of the legal and practical issues in mediation.

Privatization of Correctional Institutions

The area of justice privatization which is the fastest growing and where the need to change appears most urgent is that of corrections. However, at the same time it arouses emotional debate. Each year about 625,000 people are arrested in the United States for violent crimes and 2.3 million more for serious property crimes. As of October 1990 local jails held 400,000, state prisons housed 700,000 inmates, and federal institutions held 60,000 prisoners. The annual increase is approximately 10 percent.

The U.S. correctional system has the largest number of inmates in the world. The demand for prison beds is growing at a rate of 1,000 per week. New laws that require minimum sentencing and longer incarceration of serious criminals have substantially increased prison populations. The prisons and jails suffer from enormous overcrowding. Due to lack of prison space, judges release convicted criminals who pose a threat to the public. Correctional institutions cannot provide decent living conditions for many inmates owing to limited budgets. In the 1980s county and state governments lost many lawsuits for violating the civil rights of both inmates and guards (Eshelman, 1990). In 1985 there were pending or recently settled lawsuits in all fifty states.

Correctional institutions fail in their prime obligation to correct criminals. Instead, correctional institutions appear to be schools for criminals and places where criminals cultivate associations for future illegal initiatives. Judges who avoid imprisonment commit criminals to parole. Parole officers are scarce and they are overwhelmed with the number of cases assigned to them. In most cases, as criminals admit (Rengert and Wasilchick, 1985), for all practical purposes parole is a meaningless sentence which allows them to continue their normal, illegal routines.

Adjudication and correction urgently require attention. Both areas have had limited private involvement. Private firms have played a role in the management of juvenile correctional housing for most of the twentieth century. However, in adult correction private firms' involvement has been limited to the delivery of education, medical services, limited prison industry, vocational preparation, and management of nonsecure centers. Logan (1990), in a most comprehensive description and evaluation of private corrections, outlines the rapid growth since mid–1985 where local, state, and federal agencies have shifted to private firms the full-scale operation of correctional facilities. He estimated that in 1989 the value of contracts exceeded $250 million a year. By 1990 over forty sizable correctional facilities were completely managed by private contractors.

Samuel Jan Brakel, of DePaul University in Chicago and a staff member of the Isaac Ray Center in Chicago, in Chapter 20 presents a comprehensive view of the major issues in privatization. They include construction, financing, cost and quality of management, and legality of the public sectors' delegation of authority to the private sector. He then analyzes the impact privatization has on the various interest groups, including the taxpayers, prisoners, the contractors, and politicians.

From the practitioner's perspective Richard Kiekbusch, the superintendent of Prince William–Manassas Regional Adult Detention Center in Virginia, concentrates his discussion on jail management objectives, priorities, and constraints. In Chapter 21 he presents guidelines to jurisdictions which consider private management of their jails.

More concrete guidelines for public administrators who consider possible privatization are provided in Chapter 22 by Robert Gemignani, the president of the National Office for Social Responsibility in Alexandria, Virginia. Gemignani suggests a step-by-step approach which includes data collection on costs, assessment of the existing system, the legal and liability issues, and other relevant environmental issues. He then provides useful information on the preparation of the Request for Proposal, the negotiation phase, and the monitoring of the contractor.

An accounting perspective which compares the construction costs of private and public sectors is offered by Robert Guzek, a certified management consultant with the Hill organization of Willingboro, New Jersey. In Chapter 23 he analyzes three alternatives of facility ownership, financing, and manangement under the private and or the public sectors, and suggests the optimal privatization scheme, explicitly recognizing how tax considerations can affect financial feasibility.

Canadians Daniel Hawe, Howard Sapers, and Paulette Doyle give a Canadian perspective in Chapter 24. They detail the history of Canada's experience with privatization in general and with the John Howard Society in particular. They examine the mission and operation of the society in dealing with criminal offenders.

The concluding two chapters of the book deal with allowing private-sector industry programs in prisons. George Bronson of the Carl Robinson Correctional Institution of Enfield, Connecticut, and Claire Bronson, Michael Wynne, and Richard Olson in Chapter 25 discuss the barriers to entry as posed mostly by labor unions, like AFSCME, and the National Sheriff's Association, which are expected to lose their monopolies on corrections.

The last chapter expresses the famous sentiments of the Honorable Warren Burger, retired chief justice of the United States, on whether to build more "warehouses" for inmates or rather to construct factories with fences around them. The chief justice stresses the moral obligation to rehabilitate the person put behind bars so that he or she, when released, can become a productive member of society.

References

Eshelman, Y. (1990). *Privatization: Part II. A Private Sector Solution to Pennsylvania's Prison Crisis.* Harrisburg, PA: Commonwealth Foundation.

Logan C. (1990). *Private Prisons: Cons and Pros.* New York: Oxford University Press.

Rengert, G., and J. Wasilchick (1985). *Suburban Burglaries: A Time and Place for Everything.* Springfield, IL: Charles C. Thomas.

Part 1 : Police

2. Three Centuries of Criminal Justice Privatization in the United States

Robert D. McCrie

In capitalistic societies people have been expected to provide for themselves many services and requirements, and to do so to the greatest extent possible. However, many services are not ordinarily furnished to individuals or groups by themselves but are provided for the public by government. The reason for this may be due to historical, philosophical, and practical factors. One such category of services commonly provided by contemporary governments is reflected in a widely used and current expression, the criminal justice system.

Allen and Simonsen point out that several elements make up this collective group of services as encountered in the United States:

> The American criminal justice system is, in fact, many separate systems of institutions and procedures. The thousands of American villages, towns, cities, counties, states—and even the federal government—all have criminal justice "systems" of sorts. Though they may appear similar in that all function to apprehend, prosecute, convict, and sentence lawbreakers, no two are exactly alike. . . . The criminal justice system is composed of three separate subsystems—police, courts, and corrections—each with its own tasks.

Currently, American criminal justice services are widely perceived as traditional, essential, and, in many respects, inextricably parts of the government's obligation to the public. However, interest in privatization of public services has spread to criminal justice activities, spurred by private and public initiatives (Report of the President's Commission, 1988; Donahue, 1989). A review of the origins of the three subsystems to criminal justice reveals that in some ways the private provision of such services antedated their being provided by government; in other ways privatization features coexisted with or were suppressed by the growth to public institutions. Therefore, the current waxing of interest in aspects of criminal justice services privatization has roots in American colonial times, which themselves originated in the Anglo-Saxon legal tradition and date from the period before laws were written (Hawes, 1979).

What follows is a review of some of those historical economic and political antecedents. Separate consideration is given to policing, the courts, and prisons and correctional services. Attention will be devoted primarily to institutions in the United States; however, references also will be made to pertinent developments abroad. Why and when some of these developments occurred also will be considered.

Privatization, as a term, covers five formal arrangements: sale of government-owned assets; abolition or relaxation of monopolies held by nationalized industries; the Build-Operate-Transfer agreement under which a private company agrees to build a major project and to operate it for an agreed-upon length of time; financing by customer fees—"pay for use"—rather than by taxes; and the contracting out of public services to the private sector (Lipman, 1989). I shall concentrate on the contracting out of private security services to supplement or, in rare cases, replace public law enforcement. A similar mechanism is used for the emergence of private courts. Prisons for profit reflect a combination of contracting-out and build-operate-transfer for the penal facility itself.

Policing: The Struggle to Satisfy Pressing Needs

Policing and security are critical features of urban civilizations. Primitive rules of clan and kinship to protect against animals and raiding tribes gave way over time to organized military forces that provided both internal security (protective) and attacking or defensive capacities. However, the military eventually came to be regarded as inadequate for protective purposes. Soldiers were trained to close in on enemies and destroy them. Excesses in killing and maiming the enemy and stealing (appropriating) and destroying enemy property were highly regarded as conventional features on battlefields through most of history.

However, in the cities the soldierly mentality was out of place. Governments depended upon military forces to protect an area from external attack. During lengthy periods in which no external attacks occurred, soldiers might be impressed to concentrate on serving internal protective needs. By training, temperament, and purpose, soldiers were inappropriate agents to maintain the peace. Caesar Augustus created centralized protective services apart from the military; hence, recognizing the separate importance of policing—or internal—protection from the need to provide defense against external attacks (Schnabolk, 1983).

Even prior to the Norman Conquest of 1066, England had established a system of Tens, whereby this many members of family units would be responsible to each other for protective purposes. The Tens were bound together in groups of ten to make the Hundreds. Groups of Hundreds occupied a territory called a shire. The monarch or a surrogate appointed a reeve to oversee a shire. This shire-reeve in time was called sheriff (Lipson, 1988). Under William of Normandy other officers were elected or appointed to patrol the Hundreds, called constables. By Norman custom, a constable would serve for one year without pay, except for small fees and allowances. All able-bodied men were expected to take their turns in this office. Lipson (1988) writes, "By the end of the thirteenth century, by royal decree, the number of constables per Hundred was increased to two. Each citizen was required to join in the catch of those who broke the law. . . . In the cities, standing watch was a duty, along with the others, that growing guilds used in order to regulate the master and apprentice system."

The *gegilden*, later to be the crafts guilds, had been given police duties before Norman times and came to be important sources of personnel for the watch. Constables might have assistants for their duties, which were largely conducted during the day. At night, community watches were instituted, initially and only briefly on a voluntary basis, next on a mandatory service basis, and still later as a semivocational activity. The watch formally reported to the constables.[1]

Civil institutions in the Colonies were adopted from procedures previously in place and apparently functioning well in England. The first community watch system was established in Boston in 1636. New York was next in 1658. Over the following generations, other growing urban areas in the United States instituted their own watch systems (Schnabolk, 1983).

The level of criminality in the seventeenth through the nineteenth centuries in the United States cannot be accurately compared to contemporary levels. Criminal statistics collection and analysis in the United States did not emerge until the mid-nineteenth century (Robinson, 1969). Justice often was dispensed summarily. Criminal records had little utility when people could be arrested, charged with crimes, arraigned, tried in court, and sentenced, and, if found guilty, punished—all in a brief period of time. Draconian measures such as branding, mutilation, or amputation sometimes served as adequate enough indication of criminality, lessening the need for records.

Nonetheless, the level of crime in the eighteenth and nineteenth centuries in urban North American communities was probably higher than that of their contemporary counterparts. This crime and the fear and losses that accompanied it over the years accounted for the growth of policing. The constable provided the focal point for such organization.

Constables were agents of government. They were appointed and charged to perform certain specific duties by government. However, compensation for constables was inadequate or nonexistent. For much of its history the office of constable was forced volunteerism, with severe penalties to the officer for wrongful arrest or escape of prisoners from custody (McLynn, 1989). It was understood that constables would earn their keep by charging fees to the private sector for performing duties. In effect, the private sector underwrote the services of the constable. Elected or appointed officials could remove constables from their office for malfeasance, nonfeasance, and with changes in political fashion.

In theory, constables could work at night to protect the peace, but had little incentive to do so. They had adequate work during the day when the courts and jails were open and when legal papers normally were served. Constables' staffs were organized into units often based on geography and population density in larger urban areas. Staffs were fairly small in part because the chief constable would have to pay for any additional workers. The staffing levels were not adequate for twenty-four-hour service; therefore, protection at night was assumed by other means: the public night Watch. In early American communities, the Watch began as a replication of European efforts to control arson, theft, muggings, vandalism, and other crimes that plagued early cities after dark. Generally, citizens on the Watch were expected to arrive at a meeting post at a designated hour. In one conventional arrangement, half of the contingent would rest there while the other half would go on designated patrols. Later during the Watch they would switch roles and the first group of patrollers would rest. If citizens on patrol made arrests for criminal violations, the Watch would hold the detainees until the morning when they would be turned over to the constables.[2]

The Watch embodied structured public service surveillance of all nocturnal activities within a geographic area. However, commercial and maritime business owners required additional protection to what was afforded by the Watch. Consequently, specialized private security units were created — merchant and maritime police, for example — that in many ways are analogous with the later private security guards. In addition, the local parishes in English urban centers were organized to provide protective services: the parochial police.

English society had discovered that the Watch had severe limitations as urban areas grew in size. In his popular history of police and crime in London, Wade (1972) described the "ludicrous mistakes frequently committed by watchmen, constables and patrols, from ignorance of their most ordinary duties." The Watch had served its purpose in England as well as in Holland and other continental countries where similar protective organizations existed. Rife with amateurism and cronyism, the Watch system became the target of mounting criticism. Similar observations and criticisms were soon to be made in America.

The Watch never fully satisfied public requirements and goals. Franklin noted his frustration with these paid volunteers:

> The city Watch was one of the first things I conceived to want regulation. It was managed by the constables of the respective wards in turn; the constable warned a number of housekeepers (i.e., homeowners) to attend him for the night. Those who chose never to attend paid six shillings a year to be excused, which was supposed to be for hiring substitutes, but was, in reality, much more than was necessary for the purpose and made the constableship a place of profit; and the constable for little drink often got such ragamuffins about him as a Watch that respectable housekeepers did not choose to mix with. Walking the grounds, too, was often neglected, and most of the nights spent in tippling [Franklin, 1941].

The Watch, which had begun as a private sector service with support from the electorate, was ripe for reorganization. Further, the constable–Watch system had serious gaps in service. The day patrol, headed by the constable, came on duty at 9 A.M. and remained on duty until 7 P.M. The nightly watch did not overlap. Thus, cities were left with in some cases eight and in no case less than four hours out of twenty-four in which the city would be entirely without protection (Wade, 1972). Employers, industrialists, and wealthy individuals depended on physical security, the presence of numerous employees and servants (some of whom served as guards), and constant alertness to prevent losses during this period of time.

The great turning point was the creation of the Metropolitan Police Department of 1822 in London. This signaled the demise of the Watch, replacing it with a twenty-four-hour protective force. Headed by Sir Robert Peel, the "Peelian revolution" brought a philosophy and structure to the London police force which has remained unchanged in many ways since then.

The first police department in the United States was established in New York City in 1844. Within a few years the Ward system disappeared in urban America with the establishment of modern police departments. By 1856 police departments had supplanted the Watch in Chicago, Cincinnati, Detroit, Los Angeles, Philadelphia, San Francisco, and elsewhere (Schnabolk, 1983).

The presence of organized police departments in the United States did not fully meet the need of the rapidly growing urban sector even from the beginning. Private organizations continued to provide for their own protection in the urban environment.

On the frontier, crime and its prevention often exceeded the ability of government to control it. For example, money could be printed by the government or issued by private banks. The bank notes could be confusing to early Americans as to their genuineness. Counterfeiting became a common crime. Arresting counterfeiters and bringing them to justice was not easy for a law enforcement structure in which policing agencies were sorely inadequate to effect controls.

Similarly, the theft of goods in transportation represented a serious threat to organizations. Bandits might stop a train carrying gold or cash. The presence of armed guards on the train did not always deter well-planned attackers. The costly network of transcontinental trains was vulnerable to attack. If the crime occurred near a city with police, a posse might be organized to search for the train robbers. But by the time the posse came together to pursue the now long departed thieves, prospects for recovery were poor. The robbers merely had to get a good head start and they could outrun a pursuing sheriff and posse. Further, the robbers might enter a new jurisdiction which could complicate arrest and return of the robbers if they happened to be caught (Seng and Gilmour, 1959).

These opportunities served as the basis of a private business for a barrel maker (cooper) who serendipitously encountered counterfeiters and confederates in a wooded clearing and later aided in their arrest. The cooper, Alan Pinkerton, was living in the Chicago area and seemed to feel bringing counterfeiters to justice was part of his civic duty. That may have been because his father was a policeman in Glasgow. His success as a private citizen in helping police find and arrest counterfeiters earned him the reputation as an extraordinary operative. He soon accepted the modestly paid and largely volunteer position of deputy sheriff of Cook County, Illinois (Horan, 1962).

By 1850 Pinkerton decided that private security services could be a more profitable and interesting career than making barrels. His business was established with six railroads as initial clients. Thus, with his private business, Pinkerton had initiated the private investigative services industry which sought to find the sources of losses and make recoveries. His company also provided private guarding services to avail the railroads of additional security officers (McCrie, 1988).

By 1860 the Civil War had commenced and like so many commercial enterprises, Pinkerton's business was suspended. The urge to participate in the great national crisis was strong. Pinkerton provided personal protection briefly to President Lincoln early in the conflict. Lincoln apparently did not care for Pinkerton and rejected his services, preferring to depend on local police officers and soldiers for his protection when he traveled (Morn, 1982).

Still seeking to be of service in the national conflict, Pinkerton created an intelligence network for the Union which sought to provide military and political intelligence for Lincoln and his generals. Consequently, Pinkerton also established by this means a private military intelligence network working for Lincoln's beleaguered government.

Alan Pinkerton's company was the precursor of the private guard and investigative industry in the United States. This industry was able to emerge because public law enforcement could not or would not provide the level of security demanded by the private sector. Within a few years after the end of the Civil War, Pinkerton's company and its rapidly increasing competitors' guard services came to be more important than investigative services in terms of total revenues (Horan, 1962). It was to be that way from then on.

By the early 1980s the employment of federal, state, and local law enforcement personnel totaled about 650,000, according to the Hallcrest Report. Similarly, employment of private security guards and investigators reached 1.1 million. The authors of the Hallcrest Report believe their analysis may be too modest and that the private sector might be more than twice the size of public law enforcement. Private employment included over 640,000 for contract security firms and almost 450,000 as proprietary (i.e., employed) personnel of organizations. The Hallcrest authors estimated that growth in the public sector for the decade 1980 to 1990 would be approximately 16.3 percent. By comparison, employment in the private security sector would grow 31.9 percent—almost twice as fast (Cunningham and Taylor, 1985). Are these private security guards in actuality *private police,* as referred to in references in the United Kingdom (Shearing and Stenning, 1987) or in the United States (Cameron, 1964; Cunningham and Taylor, 1985)? Security guards are private people protecting private property. They can make citizens' arrests and may carry weapons; however, both qualities are incidental and supportive to the primary responsibility of deterring crime and providing a variety of support services to the employer or client. The existence of such formidable corps of security personnel is only possible because the private sector in this century wants more security than government can or will supply, much as their counterparts did in the past.[3]

The presence of a robust policing-for-profit industry from private security guard and investigative companies may have some deleterious effects for the public. Selection, training, supervision, licensing, and civil rights violations are a few of the risks society as a whole conceivably could face from a vigorous and unregulated private security enterprise (South, 1988). Yet private security companies occasionally even have explored providing services for government to supplement or replace those being provided by sworn police officers. In 1980 the town of New Paltz, New York, sought to disband the joint town-village police department and hire a private security firm to provide police services. The proposal was made by a member of the local board of police commissioners who was also a criminology professor. He argued that extensive savings would be realized and that a private security company would be able to do all the police work except serve warrants and make arrests in cases in which they did not personally witness a crime occurring. The professor said a titular, unsalaried police chief could be appointed to deputize the officers to carry out those additional duties as he claimed was widely done in the Southwest and Texas (Muise, 1980). The proposal was blocked in part by action of the police officers' union which claimed the proposal would violate the Taylor Law under which a public service could not be eliminated and subcontracted to a private company to provide it.

Efforts by cost-cutters to reduce conventional police expenses appear to have met stiff opposition based on legal and political challenges. However, private security companies are constantly exploring the means by which they might serve the public sector by providing services. An example might be Eastgate Security and Investigations, which provides community crime prevention in conjunction with Nassau County (New York) Police. The town of East Hills, Long Island, employs thirty unarmed, uniformed security officers to patrol the town twenty-four hours a day. If security officers see a problem, they call Eastgate's base station and police (*Security*, 1989).

New, planned communities offer the opportunity of providing a private security patrol which operates in effect as a private police department for the community. Wynstone, a housing development in North Barrington, Illinois, provides twenty-four-hour access control, traffic control, emergency response, loss prevention, and rule enforcement by private security officers. Costs are passed on to residents in the development's monthly assessments (*Security*, 1989).

Such incursions of the private sector into a domain often considered public are uncommon at present. Still, the opportunity for further growth of limited, private police-type services may be possible in urban environments. Hair proposed that private security officers could replace sworn law enforcement officers in selected situations:

> [H]aving been assigned to numerous parades, stadium activities, and other special events in New York City, where large numbers of police were taken from their communities to police the special events, I am well aware that this procedure resulted in less protection for the communities from which they came. Consideration should be given to studying the feasibility of developing a program whereby private security officers could be hired to police such special events and be supervised by police personnel [Hair, 1979].

Closer and more productive cooperation between the private security and public law enforcement sectors was advocated in 1975 by the Private Security Task Force, an analysis group sponsored by the Law Enforcement Assistance Administration. This task force was one of many interactions between the public and private sectors in which an environment of growing cooperation was engendered.

More recently, as an example, a program in New York City, Area Police-Private Security Liaison (APPL) was created in three police precincts and later expanded into other areas of the city. Police officers canvas their precincts to determine the depth and strength of private security personnel and to seek means of mutual cooperation. Following the survey police captains might share data on drug dealers, whereabouts of unlicensed street vendors, thefts and assaults, and other matters of mutual concern. Private security apprised of police concerns are able to contact police immediately with special phone numbers and radio links. Training of private security personnel in the New York City Police Department's academy has been part of the program ("Police and Security," 1990).

Similarly, City Center Security assigns 50 guards to patrol a twenty-four-block area between and surrounding an office complex in Fort Worth, Texas. The unit has assembled a high-tech system of computers and 150 hidden video cameras to monitor buildings and streets. An escort service is provided for visitors returning to their cars. Security personnel have on occasion made citizen's arrests, such as during two bank robberies in 1987. The Fort Worth police chief Thomas Windham has been quoted as saying, "They do not police the public area in the same sense that the Fort Worth Police Department does, but they do perform a tremendous public service" (*Privatization*, 1989).

The private-public interface is further illustrated at the Starrett housing complex in Queens, New York. The self-contained residential community is located in one of the area's most crime-ridden sections, the Seventy-Fifth Precinct. Nonetheless, the comprehensive measures of the Starrett security force has made that part of the community one of the safest in the city by any measure. Researchers have determined that the security force minimizes the requirements and costs for public law enforcement, in effect protecting investment values by permitting an otherwise marginal real estate location to be profitable for the investors and taxpayers in the city, while simultaneously minimizing protective costs.

Safety and protection of one's self, family, and friends from fear and harm, and safeguarding one's possessions from loss reflect a deep human need (Maslow, 1970). It is not surprising that even the most competent and fully staffed police departments will fail to meet these requirements and create a need for outside security or "private police." On the other hand, government managers facing pressures on costs, flexibility, and other issues may explore the use of private sector security workers to mitigate problems.

For the past three centuries in America public law enforcement has coexisted with private protective measures. It is probable that the private sector will seek to offer support services to law enforcement. No evidence exists that the private sector currently envisions playing a future role as a for-profit policing service in competition with the public police. However, further experimentation is bound to occur. The private sector, therefore, may not displace police so much as they may absorb less challenging activities such as guarding, reference checking, and routine patrols. The largest employer of security guards in the United States is a federal agency (McCrie, 1985). Those positions could just as easily have been provided by sworn officers, but at higher cost and less flexibility.

The Courts: Tentative Responses to Clogged Calendars

Courts emerging from antiquity seem to be an inherent part of government's responsibility to the public. A judge and jury are incontestably linked to the traditional and conventional concept of what government should provide, though the concept of government itself is intrinsically unsettled. Nonetheless, courts are indelibly near the core of government.

Judges represent the central government as the English judges on assizes represent the king (Surrency, 1987). From the establishment of the First Judiciary Act by the Congressional Committee through the Judiciary Act of 1801, activities of the courts appear to be exclusively in the domain of government, certainly on a federal level. Yet the American colonial experience had taught the framers of the Constitution that the exercise of public power was dangerous when unrestrained. Dargo (1983) states:

> Americans were more comfortable with private decision making, and they regarded the enhancement of private power as a necessary check on potential governmental abuse. This predilection resulted in the *privatization* of American law. Privatization presupposes that all individuals are equal before the law, that the law is neutral, and that the good of all is best promoted by shifting power from public bodies to private (preferably individual) actors.

American jurisprudence in post–Revolutionary times emphasized great activities in private law concerning the distribution and use of economic resources (Dargo, 1983). The legal disputations, analyses, and decisions were made by judges and in courtrooms of governmental control. As America grew into a nation, the court in growing regions emerged as an integral part of life in most communities. Courts were often built before churches, so they served as the location for local dances, meetings, and town assemblies.

The local justice of the peace might handle minor issues; less often, on "court day," a judge of higher authority might arrive to deal with issues. Nonetheless, the growth of demands on the court system encouraged the development of nongovernmental dispute-resolving mechanisms such as arbitration. Existing as a not-for-profit private service, professional arbitration has been practiced in the United States since the nineteenth century.

In recent times a new phenomenon has emerged: the creation of for-profit private courts. These services employ former judges or others competent at deciding complicated issues and are able to render judgments far faster than what could be possible by a clogged court calendar (Greene, 1988; Lacayo, 1988; Gest and Hawkins, 1988). Such private services handle only a tiny fraction of legal disputes at the present time, and almost all of these concern private disputes. Nonetheless, the existence of this nongovernmental court option represents an original response to an unfulfilled need, permitting the emergence of such services.[4]

Prisons and Correctional Programs

Albeit small in numbers, private prisons and correctional programs have been the recipient of extraordinary public attention in recent years (Donahue, 1989; Keating, 1985; Press, 1987; Uchitelle, 1988). However, in many ways this current social phenomenon is firmly rooted in earlier privately operated forms.

Excluding the consideration of jails and prisons for military purposes, the evolution of such institutions for the commission of crimes followed a pattern that increasingly reflected the growth of urbanization. In the seventeenth century as the new nation grew, the requirements for jails and prisons increased.

> Crimes which in the Old World depended upon anonymity for their success were impossible in the American wilderness. Everyone knew everyone else; in fact, most were related by blood or marriage. Identification of criminals (or strangers who were watched for illegal behavior) was a simple matter, and flight to avoid prosecution meant living a precarious existence among compassionate Indians or being tortured to a slow death by tribes less friendly to white settlers [Johnson, 1988].

By contrast, urban centers tended to deal with criminals by rapid dispatch: death, whippings, brandings, financial restitution, public humiliation, transportation, and similar punishments. Jails were where the Watch detained prisoners until magistrates could hear the complaints. In the seventeenth century periods of incarceration became an increasingly acceptable form of punishment in America.

The Marquis de Beccaria's *Essay on Crimes and Punishments* (1766) emphasized the value of deterrence as a factor in prison confinement. Both English and American observers saw the limitations to harsh penalties that could not be associated with crime reduction.

One common reason for incarceration was personal debt (Johnson, 1988). The individual imprisoned for failure to meet his or her financial obligations faced dire circumstances. Jailers demanded payment for their services in addition to costs borne by prisoners for food, clothing, firewood, and other necessities. Clearly, the prisoner incarcerated for debt faced a distressing situation of likely going deeper into debt for the very reason he or she was there.

Philadelphia in post–Revolutionary times developed a "solitary system" of prison discipline espoused by Quakers. Prisoners were brought to the Walnut Street Prison in silence and were expected to remain quiet. Prisons were reluctantly constructed by public funds in an era in which incarceration took hold as penal fashion. The operating of these institutions had many laissez-faire qualities in which private enterprise operated the facilities.

While appointed by government, head jailers could be construed as independent operators of for-profit enterprises which each operated as a sole source government contractor. The jailers provided craft employment for prisoners. The resulting products were sold by the jailers with a small amount paid to prisoners. By these prison industries, prisoners might earn enough to buy their way out of debtors' prison or to have sufficient money to exist briefly after being released from confinement.

By contrast, wealthy prisoners could command a different ambiance: the best foods could be brought in; the prisoner might have a private bedroom with fine furnishings and ample heat; prostitutes, friends, and business or professional contacts could arrive or leave as they wished. For all of these accommodations a price had to be paid to the jailer as independent contractor.

In the latter nineteenth century in America, the concept of the jailer as an independent contractor subsided in urban prisons. Prison administration was reformed following the establishment of police departments and their early changes. Similar treatment for all became the pattern for the administration of state prisons. Wardens and staff were paid salaries set by government and the institutions sought to be as fully self-supporting as possible, providing their own food, clothing, and furniture. This pattern of government providing as many services as possible by its own personnel became the norm and still is in many ways in state and federal prisons.

However, a generation ago a trend began for the out-contracting of services by jails and prisons. These facilities had long contracted out for medical, dental, and psychological services. Now the facilities were seeking outside sources for food preparation and educational services. More recently, governments have been willing to contract out for an increasing part of the incarceration program, including total facility construction and management.

Today, the prison-for-profit industry remains small, representing perhaps only twenty or thirty private correction facilities depending on the definitions of *private* and of *correctional* facility (Donahue, 1989). The most notable company is the Corrections Corporation of America (cca), based in Nashville, Tennessee, and founded in 1983 by founders and investors in Kentucky Fried Chicken (cca Annual Report, 1988). This corporation reported its first profit in the fourth quarter of 1989 and now owns or operates four county jails, two juvenile detention centers, two penal work camps, two alien detention units, and two minimum security state prisons (Donahue, 1989). Pricor, also based in Nashville, operates five correctional facilities and issued shares to the public in a stock offering floated in 1989. Other major corporations interested in the prison-operating industry include Wackenhut, a publicly held security guard company, and Bechtel, a privately held contractor, which seek to construct and operate two Texas prisons.

Juvenile facilities often have been operated bynot-for-profit institutions such as church and other charitable groups since the early eighteenth century in America. Facilities for juveniles that are operated by the private sector tend to be small, residential, education-oriented, and flexible in programming (Fox, 1985). Such facilities may be better operated by private initiatives than by government; many government managers currently underwrite such programs. Pricor seeks to expand its juvenile correctional management programs following its public offering of stock in 1989 (Pricor, 1989).

Conclusion

In the late seventeenth century much security and incarceration provided for early urban communities was supplied by the private sector in one guise or another. Police departments and government-operated correctional facilities emerged in the mid-eighteenth century as a firmly established service of states and urban communities. Elements of private policing, however, continued as the security guard industry emerged and began to flourish in post–Civil War economic expansion. Such growth continued until present times. Prisons initially were constructed by governments but operated by jailers who, until the latter part of the eighteenth century, had the characteristics of independent contractors in managing the facilities. In contemporary times prisons for profit have emerged as an intriguing alternative to state-provided incarceration facilities. The courts have always been part of the essence of government. Nonetheless, resolution of disputes has always occurred outside the court systems. Arbitration and for-profit private courts represent contemporary responses to perceived limitations of traditional courts.

Notes

1. The constable's assistant in London was the beadle, who "implemented the Poor Laws, acted as town crier, kept order in churchyards, and, most important, supervised the parish Watch." The beadle was immortalized in Dickens' Mr. Bumble (McLynn, 1989).
2. The Watch has been described as a volunteer group with quasi-public features concerned with vandalism, theft deterrence, and the maintenance of public law and order. However, the most important function of the Watch certainly was to serve as an early fire spotting and response service. Fires had been a devastation to earlier urban centers. To cite a few examples: London was destroyed by fire in 798, 982, 1212, and 1666. Venice was devastated by fire in 1106, and again in 1577. Edinburgh was nearly destroyed in 1700. Lisbon was burned in 1707. Lyons was burned in 1759 (Bugbee, 1971).

Early American fires included nearly every building in Jamestown in 1608; one-third of Boston in 1653, and again devastating fires there in 1673, 1679, 1711, and 1760; New Orleans was almost gutted twice by fire in a seven-year period, 1788–94; almost all of Detroit was burned in 1806; and the Great New York Fire of 1835 destroyed seventeen blocks of lower Manhattan in "the most destructive non-military fire the world has known since London was turned to ashes in 1666" (Smith, 1978).

England had set the pattern for dealing with fire in the seventeenth century: volunteerism supported by public subscriptions characterized fire suppression methods from the sixteenth century onward. In London the insurance industry helped create a firefighting presence by supporting business entities such as the Friendly Society of 1684, the General Insurance Office of 1685, and the Amicable Contributors for Insurance from Loss by Fire in 1694. This latter company's badge came to be called a Hand-in-Hand and survived as a separate company for over 200 years, being finally absorbed into the Commercial Union in 1905 (Blackstone, 1957).

Similarly, colonial America depended on volunteerism for much of its early firefighting ability. Like England, insurance companies encouraged the establishment of for-profit firefighting groups or operated them on their own. However, "city governments justified their entry into firefighting in the mid-nineteenth century as a response to market failure in the private sector: the inability to control violence by competing fire fighters" (McChessney, 1986). Salvage groups continued as private businesses until the twentieth century in England and the United States (Anderson, 1979; Dehmer, 1987).

Again in the past generation, private firefighting companies have emerged in the United States where they mostly serve new communities in preference to the extension of public fire departments from nearby communities.

3. Growth of privatization is not limited to security guards performing less skilled and easily terminated services for government. Such services may include undercover investigations and specialized consulting services (McCrie, 1990).

4. The concepts of criminal justice privatization need not be limited to the three subunits discussed in this chapter. Travis (1990) believes that recent developments in victims' rights may be considered indicative of trends toward privatization of justice. "There is recognition that private individuals are harmed by crimes, and that private individuals must be involved in solving the problem of crime." An example is the growth of Crime Stoppers programs as one expression of private crime control. Other examples include neighborhood watch programs, dispute resolution, and programs for victims.

References

Allen, H. E., and C. E. Simonsen (1989). *Corrections in America: An Introduction*. New York: Macmillan.

Anderson, A. G. (1979). "The Development of Municipal Fire Departments in the United States." *Journal of Libertarian Studies* 3 (Fall): 331–59.

Appleton, C. (1983). "Operating Private Prisons." *Venture* (August), 17–18.

Behavioral Systems Southwest (1984). Prospectus. Pomona, CA.

Blackstone, G. V. (1957). *A History of the British Fire Service*. London: Routledge and Kegan Paul.

Browning, F., and J. Gerassi (1980). *The American Way of Crime*. New York: G. P. Putnam's Sons.

Bugbee, P. (1971). *Man Against Fire*. Boston: National Fire Protection Association.

Cameron, M. O. (1964). *The Booster and the Snitch*. New York: Free Press of Glencoe.

Camp, C. G., and G. M. Camp (1984). "Private Sector Involvement in Prison Services and Operations." Project report. Washington, DC: National Institute of Corrections.

Corrections Corporation of America (cca) (1989). Annual Report 1988.

Cunningham, W. C., and T. M. Taylor (1985). *The Hallcrest Report: Private Security and Police in America*. Portland, OR: Chancellor.

Dargo, G. (1983). *Law in the New Republic: Private Law and the Public Estate*. New York: Alfred A. Knopf.

Dehmer, W. A. (1987). "Private-Sector Fire Brigades." Letter in the *Wall Street Journal* (April 6).

Donahue, J. D. (1989). *The Privatization Decision: Public Ends, Private Means*. New York: Basic Books.

Foltz, K. (1984). "The Corporate Warden." *Newsweek* (May 7), 80.

Fox, V. (1985). *Introduction to Corrections.* Englewood Cliffs, NJ: Prentice-Hall.

Franklin, B. (1941). *The Autobiography of Benjamin Franklin.* New York: Walter J. Black.

Gest, T., and S. L. Hawkins (1988). "Slug It Out in the Privacy of Your Own Courtroom." *US News and World Report* 105 (December 5): 56.

Ginsberg, S. F. (1968). "The History of Fire Protection in New York City, 1800–1842." Ph.D. dissertation. New York University.

Greene, R. (1988). "Try It, Settle It or Dismiss It." *Forbes* 41 (May 30): 266.

Gumpert, D. (1977). "Civilian Cops: Private Guards Assume Many Police Functions but Problems Emerge." *Wall Street Journal* (May 2), 1.

Hair, R. A. (1979). "Private Security and Police Relations," 113–23. J. T. O'Brien and M. Marcus (eds.), *Crime and Justice in America: Critical Issues for the Future.* New York: Pergamon.

Hawes, J. M. (1979). Introduction, 3–5. J. M. Hawes (ed.), *Law and Order in American History.* Port Washington, NY: Kennikat.

Henderson, D. F. (1971). *Courts for a New Nation.* Washington, DC: Public Affairs.

Horan, J. D. (1962). *The Pinkertons.* New York: Bonanza Books.

Johnson, H. A. (1988). *History of Criminal Justice.* Cincinnati: Anderson.

Keating, J. M., Jr. (1985). "Seeking Profit in Punishment: The Private Management of Cor rectional Institutions." Washington, DC: AFSCME.

Lacayo, R. (1988). "Tell It to the Rent-a-Judge." *Time* 132 (August 29): 50.

Larson, F. (1988). "Captive Company." *Inc.* (July).

Lipman, I. (ed.) (1989). "The Global Trend Toward Privatization." *Lipman Report* (December 15), 2.

Lipson, M. (1988). "Private Security: A Retrospective." *Annals, AAPSS.* 498 (July): 11–22.

McChesney, F. S. (1986). "Government Prohibition on Volunteer Fire Fighting in Nineteenth-Century America: A Property Rights Perspective." *Journal of Legal Studies* 15 (January): 69–92.

McCrie, R. D. (1988). "The Development of the US Security Industry." *Annals, AAPSS* 498 (July): 23–33.

McCrie, R. D. (ed.) (1985). "US General Services Administration Bringing Managerial Standards to Guard Operations." *Security Letter* 15 (June 1): 2.

_____. (1990). *Security Letter Source Book: 1990–1991.* Stoneham, MA: Butterworth.

McLynn, F. (1989). *Crime and Punishment in Eighteenth-Century England.* Boston: Routledge and Kegan Paul.

Marks, G. T. (1987) "The Interweaving of Public and Private Police in Undercover Work." 172–93. C. D. Shearing and P. C. Stenning (eds.) *Private Policing.* Newbury Park, CA: Sage.

Maslow, A. H. (1970). *Motivation and Personality.* New York: Harper and Row.

Matthews, R. (1989). "Privatization in Perspective," 1–23. R. Matthews (ed.) *Privatizing Criminal Justice.* London: Sage.

Morn, F. (1982). *The Eye That Never Sleeps.* Bloomington: Indiana University Press.

Muise, J. (1980). "Private Police Force Opposed by Official." *Times Herald Record* (October 30).

"Police and Security: New York Partnership" (1990). *National Foremen's Institute Security Management. Bureau of Business Practice* 1902 (January 25): 1–5.

Press, A. (1987). "A Person, Not a Number: Slowly, Private Prisons Are Finding Their Niche." *Newsweek* (June 24), 63.

Pricor (1989). Common Stock Prospectus.

Private Security: Report of the Task Force on Private Security (1976). National Advisory Committee on Criminal Justice Standards and Goals. Washington, DC: Government Printing Office.

Privatization (1989). "Case Study B: Fort Worth, Texas and Tacoma, Washington—Private Security Patrol." *Third Annual Report on Privatization.* New York: Reason Foundation.

Report of the President's Commission on Privatization (1988). *Privatization—Toward More Effective Government.* Washington, DC: Government Printing Office.

Robinson, L. N. (1969). *History and Organization of Criminal Statistics in the United States.* 1911, reprint ed. Montclair, NJ: Patterson Smith.

Schnabolk, C. (1983). *Physical Security: Practices and Technology.* Stoneham, MA: Butterworth.

Security (1989). "Private Security Takes to the Streets." 26 (September): 19.

Selz, M. (1989). "Wackenhut Goes to the Slammer." *Florida Trend* (July), 32–34.

Seng, R. A., and J. V. Gilmour (1959). *Brink's the Money Movers.* Chicago: Lakeside.

Shearing, C. D., and P. C. Stenning (1987). *Private Policing.* Newbury Park, CA: Sage.

Smith, D. (1978). *History of Firefighting in America: 300 Years of Courage.* New York: Dial.

South, N. (1988). *Policing for Profit: The Private Security Sector.* London: Sage.

Sullivan, H. J. (1989). "Privatization of Corrections and the Constitutional Rights of Prisoners." *Federal Probation* 53 (June): 36–42.

Surrency, E. C. (1987). *History of the Federal Courts.* Dobbs Ferry, NY: Oceana.

Tolchin, M. (1985). "Private Guards Get New Role in Public Law Enforcement." *New York Times* (November 29), D27.

Travis, II, L. F. (1990). *Introduction to Criminal Justice.* Cincinnati: Anderson.

Uchitelle, L. (1988). "Public Services Found Better If Private Agencies Compete." *New York Times* (April 26), 1.

U.S. Department of Justice (1985). *Private Sector Involvement in Prison-Based Businesses: A National Assessment.* Washington, DC: National Institute of Justice.

Van Gieson, J. C. (1988). "Private Jail a Boon to Bay County." *Central Florida Business* (February 15–21), 21.

Wade, J. (1972). *A Treatise on Police and Crimes of the Metropolis, 1829.* Reprint ed. Montclair, NJ: Patterson Smith.

Weiss, R. P. (1989). "Private Prisons and the State," 26–51. R. Matthews (ed.) *Privatizing Criminal Justice.* London: Sage.

3. Can Police Services Be Privatized?

Philip E. Fixler, Jr., and
Robert W. Poole, Jr.

One of the most significant developments in state and local government over the past decade has been the "privatization revolution." Numerous public services, from ambulances to zoning, have been shifted, in part or in whole, into the private sector. Public safety and criminal justice functions have shared in this privatization trend. There are hundreds of for-profit emergency ambulance firms and several dozen private fire protection and jail/prison operators. There has also been extensive use of private, voluntary alternatives to civil court proceedings, and a growing amount of contracting with private organizations for work-release programs, juvenile rehabilitation, and the like. But policing has generally been considered a service which cannot and should not be privatized.

How coherent is this point of view? Are there inherent characteristics of the police function which render it so inherently governmental that it ought not even to be considered for privatization? If this widespread view is mistaken, how do we account for its persistence among public policy analysts? This chapter will seek to answer those questions.

Analysis of the Police Function

When analysts refer to certain types of services as being inherently governmental, what they generally mean is that the services in question have the characteristics of *public* goods, as opposed to *private* goods. In simplest terms, a public good is one which is provided collectively and from whose benefits nonpayers cannot be excluded. The classic example of a public good is national defense. If an organization provides defense of a given territory, everyone within that territory receives the benefits, whether or not they pay the costs. Thus, clearly identified public goods are generally produced in the public sector and paid for via taxation.

Policy analyst (and privatization expert) E. S. Savas (1982:29–51) has developed a somewhat more sophisticated typology of public and private goods. Savas looks at two basic criteria—exclusion and joint consumption—to categorize

Figure 3.1 Types of Goods and Services

Consumption

	Individual	Joint
Feasible	private goods	toll goods
Infeasible	common-pool goods	collective goods

various services. A service which is consumed privately and only available to those who pay for it is a private good. Savas points out that some goods which are consumed collectively may still be charged for individually in proportion to use: for example, cable television, water and electricity service, and toll roads. Savas terms them "toll goods." The classic public good is one which is consumed collectively and for which nonpayers cannot be excluded. Savas also notes that there are goods and services for which nonpayers cannot be excluded but which are consumed individually: for example, water drawn from an underground aquifer or fish caught from a (publicly owned) lake or ocean. These he terms "common-pool goods." Thus, instead of a simple alternative of public versus private goods, the Savas typology gives us a two-by-two matrix shown in Figure 3.1.

The key question for our analysis of police privatization is thus: what is the proper way to categorize police services? The key to answering that question correctly is to realize that policing is not a single service. Police departments perform a number of functions, some of which have the characteristics of private goods, some of which are toll goods, and some of which are, in varying degrees, collective goods. This being the case, it is clear that there is at least some theoretical scope for privatization in police services.

Some police department functions are essentially of a security-guard nature— providing specific protective services to a specific client. Examples include surveillance of a vacant house when the owner is on vacation, police escorts to a funeral, or providing traffic direction at a construction site which blocks a lane of traffic. In Savas' typology, these are basically private goods, which could be provided by a private firm. Some police departments charge for such services.

Other aspects of security-related police work are less private in nature. If a neighborhood, a shopping center, or even a specific block receives regular police patrol, those who live and work there will feel safer than otherwise. In such cases the consumption of the service is joint, and the key privatization question is whether funding can be provided voluntarily, rather than by taxation. This type of police service falls between a toll good and a collective good.

Once we move beyond preventive functions of law enforcement, the picture becomes even more complex. When the police identify an actual or suspected criminal and take him or her into custody, they are generally doing so in response to the complaint of a specific victim, based on a specific crime. Thus, in such a case it would be possible to charge the victim for the services of the police in thereby following through on the victim's complaint. We do not do so, presumably because of a shared judgment that *everyone* is better off from having criminals apprehended, even though someone else has been the victim in this particular case. But the

Figure 3.2 Types of Service Delivery

Funding

	Public	Private
Public	conventional	user fee
Private	contracting out	service shedding (e.g., franchise)

presumption that all of society benefits equally – and therefore that all should bear the costs – should at least be given careful scrutiny. When it comes to insuring against the risks of crime, we find that insurance companies tend to group people and businesses into specific categories – homeowners, renters, liquor stores, department stores, etc. – rather than assessing the risks (and therefore the charges) solely on some sort of neutral criterion (such as the square footage of the property or number of persons on the premises each day). Thus, smaller units than an entire city might be considered in financing the police's crime-response functions.

The purpose of this brief discussion has been to identify the mixture of private goods, toll goods, and collective goods inherent in the policing function as it has evolved in American society. We cannot make intelligent decisions about privatization without taking account of this mix of services and functions.

The other essential ingredient in a privatization analysis is an understanding of the possible forms of privatization. As in the case of Savas' two-by-two matrix of the characteristics of goods and services, we need to look at two key dimensions of public service delivery: who pays for the service and who delivers it. The classic form of public service (and the common assumption for all police functions) has the government providing the funding via taxes and producing the service directly, using government employees. But private mechanisms may be used in either or both of these areas, as shown in Figure 3.2 (for a similar breakdown see Feinstein, 1986:10).

Thus, if government retains the funding responsibility, collecting taxes to provide the funds, but hires the provider in the marketplace, we have the form of privatization known as contracting out. Note that the service provider in this case might be either a for-profit firm or a nonprofit organization. On the other hand, if government produces the service but charges individual users in proportion to their use, the funding (but not the delivery) of the service has been privatized via user fees. Finally, if both the funding mechanism and the service delivery are shifted into the private sector, we have the most complete form of privatization, referred to as service shedding or load shedding. Government may retain some degree of control over the terms and conditions of service, as in the case when it issues an exclusive franchise. Government may simply bow out (other than for ordinary business licensing), leaving the service to be handled entirely by the marketplace.

How do these various forms of privatization apply to police services? As noted earlier, some municipalities do charge the users of certain specialized police services. The scope for police-service user charges is wider than is commonly imagined (as will be discussed shortly), once it is realized how close many such services come to being private goods. Contracting out is applicable to a great number of police services, ranging from crime lab analyses to parking meter enforcement to full-fledged general police patrol. All of these functions have been successfully contracted out in selected communities. Finally, even the "pure" form of privatization, in which both funding and service delivery are provided privately, can and does exist, in the form of deputizing and or licensing fully trained private security officers who offer patrol services to private clients.

The following section discusses our empirical observations on the extent to which the various forms of police privatization have been utilized in the United States (and, to a limited degree, in Europe). After reviewing this evidence, we will then attempt to assess why privatization has proceeded only to the limited extent we have described.

Extent of Police Privatization

As previously indicated, a useful taxonomy for analyzing the extent of police privatization is the financing/service delivery model in Figure 3.2. For the purposes of this discussion, partial police privatization may be defined as the private financing of (some) police services through user fees, with public employees actually providing the service; or public financing of police services through taxation, with private contractors actually providing the service. Full police privatization (service shedding) may be defined as the private financing and provision of police services, ranging from the exercise of limited, quasi-police powers on private property to regular police powers on public and or private property.

User-Financed Police Services

While many jurisdictions have traditionally charged special fees for some types of services, such as parade and special events security, one of the most common user fees is a charge for responding to burglar alarms. Oftentimes these charges are for responding to false alarms, usually after a certain threshold point.

The growing number of homeowners who have contracted out for alarm services has placed an increasing burden on public police departments, even with the imposition of charges for responding to false burglar alarms. As a result, some police departments have permitted alarm companies to provide response services to answer their subscribers' alarms. For example, the city of Amarillo, Texas, authorized Allstate Security to respond to subscribers' alarms beginning in 1982. The result, as reported in *Police Chief*, was that this procedure relieved the police department of the time-consuming responsibility of answering an average of eight alarms per day and saved the department approximately 3,420 man-hours, or the equivalent of adding 1.75 men per year to the police department. All of this was at no cost to the taxpayer (Pancake, 1983:35).

Although more of a probation than police activity, San Bernardino, California, has even implemented a user fee for juvenile supervision and victim restitution (*Reason*, 1985).

Another, more comprehensive form of user-financed police services is exemplified by the arrangement negotiated between the Montclair Plaza shopping center and the Montclair (California) Police Department. The arrangement came about as a result of increasing calls for police service by the shopping center. The burden became so great that the department considered designating the center as a new, separate beat. However, limited budget resources precluded the establishment of such a beat. The department then proposed that the shopping center pick up 50 percent of the beat officer's salary and benefits (Moulton, 1983:43–44). The arrangement proved to be mutually beneficial to the department and the shopping center. The department was able to accommodate the new service demand, while the shopping center and its security staff achieved greater liaison with the department.

A similar concept was implemented in Oakland, California, where private developers entered into an agreement with the police department to fund special downtown patrol services to attract more shoppers. According to James Stewart, director of the National Institute of Justice, "Fear is down in the inner-city areas and development is thriving" (Stewart, 1985:760).

Another example of private funding for municipal police patrol is in one of the largest enclosed shopping malls in the world, King of Prussia, which is located in Upper Merion, Pennsylvania, a Philadelphia suburb. The high rate of shoplifting and burglaries of stores induced the tenants to request a police station within the mall. Funded by the shopping mall, a twenty-four-hour-a-day police shift is assigned to the mall.

Contracting Out: Private Provision of Police Services

As with a number of other public services, contracting out police services began with support services and later certain auxiliary services. For example, police departments in many parts of the nation contract out for vehicle maintenance.

In some cities the towing of illegally parked vehicles is also a police responsibility. New York City has privatized this function using two different methods. First, New York contracts with private firms to tow these vehicles. In addition, the city charges reclaimants a fee to cover the police department's costs (Diebold, 1984:161).

Some departments contract out for laboratory and communication services (Institute for Local Self-Government [ILSG], 1977:14). Of course, contracts for these last two services can involve confidential information and must include requirements and procedures for strict confidentiality.

The contracting out of support services has occurred even in connection with more sensitive custodial responsibilities of police and sheriffs' departments. Some jurisdictions contract out for food provision and medical care for jail inmates. (See, for example, McCarthy, 1982:6–17.)

Contracting out has even been applied to dispatch services. For example, the municipality of Woodland, Maine, contracts out its dispatching services to Wallace Security of Portland, Oregon (Fixler, 1986a:3).

Traffic control and parking is another police responsibility that has been contracted out in some jurisdictions. Companies such as Wackenhut and Pinkerton's provide special event security, and other companies provide such mundane services as school crossing guards. The city of Los Angeles, for example, once contracted out for school crossing guards until political pressures ended the experiment. Private firms furnish parking lot enforcement services for the Eastern Idaho Medical Center, Arizona Department of Transportation, and the University of Hawaii, Hilo (Fixler, 1986a:3).

Contracting out line law enforcement activities is an obvious second level of police services contracting. For example, San Diego, Los Angeles County, and Norwalk, California; and St. Petersburg, Florida, have contracted out some public parks patrols (Poole, 1980:40; Fixler, 1986a:3). Private security guards also provide protective services in Candlestick Park in San Francisco and the Giants Stadium in New Jersey (Tolchin, 1985). Other jurisdictions have contracted for private patrol of crime-ridden housing projects including San Diego, Lexington, Kentucky, and New York (Poole, 1980:40; Fixler, 1986a:2). The Suffolk School District in New York contracts for school security services (ILSG, 1977:14). Fresno, California, recently began to contract with private security firms for the patrol of its convention center. In Munich, Germany, private police patrol the subways (Poole, 1980:41).

Many U.S. local governments contract for public buildings and grounds security. Among them are Boston; Denver and Fort Collins, Colorado; Houston, Texas; Los Angeles County and San Francisco; Pensacola, Florida; New York City; Seattle; and the states of California and Pennsylvania (Poole, 1980:40; Fixler, 1986a:2). Many U.S. executive branch departments contract for private security guards, and U.S. federal courts in many parts of the nation contract out for court security officers and bailiffs who are sworn in as U.S. deputy marshals (Wackenhut, 1984:1, 4).

In Britain within the last several years, the British Transport Police stationed at the port of Southampton (public employees since 1820), and at Sealink (the cross-channel ferry line), have been replaced with private security personnel (*Reason*, 1985:13; Leppard, 1989). In several other countries some licensed security personnel are authorized to exercise police-like powers (Shearing and Stenning, 1981:231, citing Magnusson, 1979). In one country a private SWAT team was formed (McQuillan, 1984).

Another major police activity that has been turned over to contractors by some jurisdictions relates to prisoner custody. For many years the transportation of prisoners has been contracted out in parts of Maryland and California (Fixler, 1986a:3). Santa Barbara County, California, contracts with Security Air Transport of Visilia, California, for some of its prisoner transport (Fixler, 1986a:3). Private police have also been hired for other specialized custodial services, such as guarding prisoners who are being transported and or treated in public hospitals (Fixler, 1986a:3). For example, several Alabama prisons, including the West Jefferson, St. Clair, and Hamilton facilities, contract with private firms to guard prisoners receiving hospital treatment (Joynt, 1986). Pinkerton's has transported prisoners in New York City to and from the hospital for treatment (Fixler, 1986a:3).

The application of contracting out for custodial care has moved beyond these special situations. At least six U.S. counties now contract with private organizations to manage local prisons, including Hamilton County, Tennessee; Bay County, Florida; Butler County, Pennsylvania; Hennipin County, Minnesota (Fixler, 1986b:2–3); and Aroostock County, Maine (*Boston Globe*, 1986). In 1986 two states contracted out for the management and operation of state prison facilities—California and Kentucky. California's contract is for a minimum-security, return-to-custody facility for parole violators in Hidden Hills (Fixler 1986b:3). Kentucky has gone a step further by contracting with a firm that owns its own site (*State Government News*, 1986).

Even the contracting out of a basic line police service such as investigation has had precedent. Some U.S. government agencies contracted with Pinkerton's Detective Agency and others for many investigative services up until about 1909 (O'Toole, 1978:28). About twenty years ago the governor of Florida had a short-lived arrangement to contract out with the Wackenhut Corporation for investigative services for which payment was from private contributions (O'Toole, 1978:32–34). Some police departments in the Midwest contract out for special narcotics enforcement, for example, with Multi-State Unit (O'Toole, 1978:13). Several U.S. cities, including Allentown, Pennsylvania, and Tacoma, Washington, have formed special downtown assessment districts that have employed private security personnel to provide patrol services (Fixler, Poole, and Scarlett, 1989:2).

A third level of police privatization is contracting for regular or full police services in a given jurisdictional area. The federal government has contracted for full police services at its Mercury test site operated by the Energy Research and Development Administration in Nevada and at NASA's Kennedy Space Center in Florida (O'Toole, 1978:31).

However, it is the several examples where local governments have contracted for regular police service and even their entire police force that have attracted the most attention. Probably the first local government to contract out for what are considered regular police services in modern times was the city of Kalamazoo, Michigan. In the mid–1950s Kalamazoo contracted for about 3.5 years with Charles Services for street patrol and apprehension of traffic law violators (Wooldridge, 1970:122). In order to ensure that the activities of the private police were fully in accordance with the law, Charles' patrol personnel were sworn in as full deputy sheriffs (Wooldridge, 1970:122–23).

One of the advantages of the arrangement was that Charles Services' patrolmen could be put on at peak hours and released during slow periods. Employing them by the hour may have been more economical than adding men to the local police force (Wooldridge, 1970:123).

Unfortunately, a court case (involving a technicality relating to an arrest) led to the demise of the arrangement, even though the decision was in favor of Charles Services. This resulted from a virulent attack by one of the dissenting judges (Wooldridge, 1970:123).

In 1981 the village of Reminderville, an Ohio municipality, went further than Kalamazoo by contracting with a private firm for full, comprehensive police service. When the county withdrew its patrol from Reminderville and some of the surrounding, unincorporated Twinsburg township territory for budgetary reasons, Reminderville and Twinsburg first explored the possibility of recontracting with the county for continued service. After a thorough analysis, however, Reminderville and Twinsburg began giving serious consideration to an offer to provide police services submitted by a private firm, Corporate Security, headed by a former Ohio police chief. The Corporate Security offer came in at $90,000 per year, about half that required by the county. Moreover, Corporate Security agreed to provide two patrol cars rather than one, and to reduce emergency response time from forty-five to six minutes. As part of the arrangement, Corporate Security also agreed to select trained, state-certified candidates for the police positions, leaving the village to make the final choice. In fact, village officials "would have full autonomy in hiring, firing, disciplining, and organizing the police force" (Gage, 1982:24). The arrangement worked well for two years, surviving threats of a lawsuit by the Ohio Police Chiefs' Association. An attack in *Newsweek* and other skeptical publicity disturbed Reminderville officials and in 1983 they ended the contract and set up their own conventional city police department at a higher cost.

Another example, which involved an even greater degree of privatization, was that of the small town of Oro Valley, Arizona. In 1975 Rural/Metro Corporation, as part of a comprehensive public safety protection package (including fire protection and ambulance service), agreed to additionally provide full police services, including management and operations (Gage, 1982:25). It furthermore "agree[d] to establish a police headquarters and keep all records according to state guidelines for police departments" and to supervise and assume all liability for the conduct of its employees (Gage, 1982:25). Oro Valley, however, would fully control and have responsibility for the police force and would be able to override Rural/Metro's authority at any time. The force would thus be under the control of the town marshal (Gage, 1982:25). Rural/Metro would decide what equipment and how many officers were needed to do the job and what their salaries should be (Gage, 1982:25). The price for full police service was substantially lower than what it would have cost the town to set up its own public police force (Gage, 1982:25).

Again, however, the contracting out arrangement was undermined when the Arizona Law Enforcement Advisory Council refused to accept Rural/Metro employees in its training and accreditation program, and this council is the only organization licensed to award accreditation in Arizona (*Arizona Territory*, 1976). This was followed by a state attorney general opinion that Oro Valley could not commission Rural/Metro employees as police officers. In the face of anticipated high court costs, Rural/Metro decided to discontinue the arrangement for the provision of police services, although the Rural/Metro representative who originally signed the contract and acted as the police chief (and who later left the company) indicated that it was his belief that Rural/Metro would have prevailed in court (Gage, 1982:26).

Several other small American towns have contracted for private police services for as long as five years, including Buffalo Creek, West Virginia; Indian River, Florida; and several other small Florida (Poole, 1980:41–42) and Illinois jurisdictions (Cunningham and Taylor, 1985:186). Sometimes these contracts were an interim measure until the jurisdiction could form its own police force.

The only other country in which there has been any significant amount of contracting for regular police services is Switzerland. Some thirty Swiss villages and townships contract with a firm called Securitas. According to the Swiss Association of Towns and Townships, contracts offer substantial savings over what it would have cost these small towns to operate their own police forces. The typical contract calls for foot and vehicle patrol, building security checks, night closing of bars and restaurants, and ticket validation at special events. (*Urban Innovation Abroad*, 1980:1).

Deputization and Special Powers:
Private Financing and Provision of Police Services

The extent of privately financed and provided police services ranges from situations where private security personnel are given special arrest powers beyond that of citizen's arrest to be exercised in certain limited areas to being given almost full police powers and jurisdiction-wide authority.

A study by the RAND Corporation for the Department of Justice defined deputization as "the formal method by which federal, state, and city governments grant to specific, named individuals the powers or status of public police [or "peace officers"] — usually for a limited time and in a limited geographic area — " (Wildhorn and Kakalik, 1971:4). As one student of the history of private police in the United States observed, "Certain classes of private police such as railroad detectives, campus security guards, and retail security guards may be granted special powers concerning arrest and search" (Becker, 1974:446).

According to a 1985 study for the Department of Justice, approximately 25 percent of medium and large police departments deputize special officers or give them special police powers, probably more often to proprietary (i.e., in-house) than contract (i.e., an outside firm) security agencies (Cunningham and Taylor, 1985:40, 324). Also 29 percent of proprietary security managers and 14 percent of contract security managers surveyed in 1984 indicated that their personnel had special police powers.

One of the most limited forms of this type of privatization occurs in New York City where the hard-pressed New York Police Department has authorized retail security officers in some establishments to "provide surveillance, make arrests, transport suspects to police holding facilities, complete records checks, and enter criminal history information" (Stewart, 1985:761). Private security personnel exercising these powers must be trained in the apprehension of suspects and various legal issues. Private security officers in Washington, DC, may also be awarded certain police powers of arrest. Those licensed to carry weapons are designated as "special police officers" (Knight, 1980). As of the early 1970s DC had about 2,500 such officers. In the 1970s Boston passed an ordinance to establish training and clothing requirements as well as guidelines for the use of firearms for "special officers" who have the power of arrest on the employer's premises (Schlesinger, 1978:43). In Maryland the governor may appoint "special policemen" with full police power on the premises of certain private businesses," and North Carolina has a similar law (O'Toole, 1978:10). Security guards in Las Vegas are able to be appointed as special deputy sheriffs (O'Toole, 1978:10).

In Oregon the governor can appoint "special policemen" in the railroad and steamboat industries (O'Toole, 1978:10). Texas permits its Department of Public Safety to commission Special Rangers who may work for private employers and "who have the full arrest and firearms powers of an official policeman and are empowered to enforce all laws protecting life and property" (O'Toole, 1978:10–11).

Another form of fully privatized police service occurs on the campuses of some private universities and colleges. Some forty states have passed legislation giving some degree of police authority to campus security personnel (Hess and Wrobleski, 1982:276), including private universities in some states. And a survey in the early 1970s found that seven states have statutorily granted some degree of police authority to security personnel on private campuses (Kakalik and Wildhorn, 1971:39, citing survey described in Gelber, 1972). In some states private campus police may receive police powers via deputization by governors, courts, law enforcement agencies, or city governments. Campus police at the University of Southern California have been given certain powers of arrest under California Penal Code, section 830.7, pursuant to a memorandum of understanding with the Los Angeles Police Department. These powers grant the USC campus police the same arrest powers as a California "peace officer," while they are on duty and within their jurisdiction and while responding to calls off-campus in the area surrounding the university (conversation with Lieutenant William Kennedy, USC Campus Police, 1987).

Probably one of the purest forms of full police privatization is that of railroad police in a number of states. Enabling legislation was originally based on problems of interstate operation and the lack of public police protection in some areas. "In many parts of the country, the railroad police provided the only protective services until government and law enforcement agencies were established" (Hess and Wrobleski, 1982:13).

One Pennsylvania study (conducted in the 1930s) cited an 1865 state law that authorized railroad companies to employ security personnel who were also commissioned with full police powers in the county or state. If appointed by the state, railroad officers in Pennsylvania and New York, for example, had and exercised full police powers both on and off railroad property (Shallo, 1933:25). In fact, they were obligated to do so as sworn peace officers. Shallo also indicates that Philadelphia at one time had hundreds of deputized, private security personal providing police patrol services (Shallo, 1933:208). One researcher indicated that the Pennsylvania legislation was still in effect (Wooldridge, 1970:118).

Privately financed and provided police services also exist on Paradise Island in the Bahamas. Virtually all island police activities are supplied by Security Services, a firm employed by the island's hotels and resorts. The firm employs sixty or seventy guards and several vehicles, plus three or four administrative personnel and a captain. Security Services has responsibility for protecting twenty-five to thirty firms and the island territory. One analyst concluded that "since [Security Services took] responsibility for protective services of the island, they have had one of the best records for low incidence of theft, rape, and assault in the area." This is in contrast to major incidences of theft and assault on the main island of New Providence which has similar tourist attractions (Gallagher, 1985:95–96).

Another example of privately financed private police patrol is in Fort Worth, Texas, where private corporate interests under the control of the Bass brothers started City Center Security to provide downtown patrol and high-tech security services for a twenty-four-block downtown area. The Bass brothers own a number of buildings in this area (Fixler, Poole, and Scarlett, 1989:36).

Perhaps the foremost U.S. example of privately financed and provided police is that of the Patrol Special Police in San Francisco. Patrol Specials are private individuals who undergo extensive training (440 hours of classroom instruction) at San Francisco's police academy or elsewhere and are sworn as full-fledged "peace officers" (one step below "police officers") (Wallace, 1984a). Once licensed, they are permitted to bid on one or more of some sixty-five private beats, with their salaries paid by merchants or residents along their beats. On the more lucrative beats, Patrol Specials hire assistants (who must also complete the same training) and in some cases even hire security guards and administrative staff—thus, in effect, becoming mini-police departments. They are legally members of the San Francisco Police Department (like reservists) and are required to respond to police calls in their area (Wallace, 1984b; Dorffi, 1979:26, 27).

Recently, however, the Patrol Specials have had to undertake a lawsuit to mandate California's Police Officers Standards and Training Commission to continue their certification as sworn peace officers. (See Case No. 866532, Superior Court of California, City and County of San Francisco, 1986.)

Why Police Privatization Is Particularly Difficult

There are several reasons that make applying privatization to police services much more difficult than in the case of other services. These include such factors as cultural norms or attitudes, the "public goods" problem, administrative concerns for control and accountability, union opposition, and legal constraints.

In the Anglo-American tradition, ample precedent for the private provision of police services certainly exists. In Britain local assignees, volunteers, or deputies were hired by wealthy individuals (who were required to provide such services as part of the noblesse oblige tradition). (See Becker, 1974:444.) Oftentimes, the private law enforcement personnel were partially paid from fees based on the recovery of stolen goods (Hess and Wrobleski, 1982:9).

In London some individuals eventually organized private patrols as a deterrent to crime and as a more formal means of pursuing criminals. During the 1700s and early 1800s the British people were quite skeptical of a tax-supported government police for fear that it would provide political leaders with a means of oppression (Critchley, 1978:29).

The British system of requisitioning watchmen or using volunteers was transported to America. Gradually social attitudes and norms accepted the institution of public police forces in major U.S. urban areas as occurred in London. With the advent of the first public police department in New York in the 1840s, other major cities quickly adopted public police departments. For over one hundred years most police protection in the United States has been publicly provided. Thus, it is not surprising that many people now find it difficult to accept the notion of private police, despite their long history.

Another attitudinal factor is that some of the duties and activities undertaken by the police are qualitatively different than most other public services. The police have the right and obligation to use force, even deadly force, in the pursuit of their duties and receive special state authorization to do so.

A further barrier to police privatization is the difficulty of arranging for individuals to privately finance and use police services in contrast to other public services. Moreover, even if a number of individuals in a neighborhood employ a private agency for patrol services, it is difficult to force those who do not wish to voluntarily finance these services to pay for the benefits they receive. One approach to dealing with this public goods problem is the deed-based (mandatory membership) homeowners association, in which security services are funded from (mandatory) membership dues. For example, in Los Angeles neighborhoods such as Bel-Air and Beverlywood, a major fraction of the annual association dues goes to pay for the contract services of the Bel-Air Patrol. This commercial firm provides twenty-four-hour-a-day armed vehicular patrol, by nonsworn security officers.

Another major barrier to police privatization is that of control and accountability. Understandably, people have serious concerns that those who are authorized to use deadly force be held accountable and under the control of the law. It certainly seems reasonable to require that all police personnel be properly trained and certified at the level of responsibility required by their particular duties. Moreover, as with any agency enforcing laws, strict quality-control regulation is appropriate, either through detailed contract provisions or regulatory oversight.

In addition to the public's natural apprehension, perhaps the greatest political barrier to privatizing police services is that of union opposition. As shown in the Reminderville and Oro Valley cases, public police officers' associations will strongly react to any local jurisdiction which attempts to privatize police services. In light of today's budgetary constraints, it is shortsighted to permit special interest political pressures to override the public's interest in cost-effective public services.

The final barrier to police privatization is legal restrictions. Upon close examination, however, this may not be as much of a problem as one might think. The attorney for Reminderville, Ohio, found that there was no state law preventing the contracting out of police services. In the case of Troutman, North Carolina, the state deputy attorney general indicated that it was not technically illegal for the city to contract out its law enforcement, as long as the private police were sworn in as official police officers (Associate State Attorney, Eddie Caldwell, March 6, 1984). Perhaps, as in the Oro Valley Case, it is more the political fight or potential legal costs that constitutes the barrier.

Conclusion

In a sense the findings of this study are paradoxical. On the one hand, there has been indeed little progress in privatizing full or regular police services by U.S. local governments. To our knowledge, there is currently no city or county that is contracting for regular police services.

On the other hand, there does seem to be an increasing acceptance of more limited forms of privatization. The concept of special fees on beneficiaries to finance specialized police services, such as burglar alarm response, is increasingly accepted as fair and reasonable. Contracting out police support and ancillary services is growing steadily as well.

There are also signs of a gradual load shedding of certain police services to the private security industry, often through deputization or the award of special police powers. With continued fiscal constraints on local governments and continued high levels of crime it can be expected that police departments will gradually turn over more and more responsibility for law enforcement on private property to security organizations protecting that property.

References

Arizona Territory (1976). "Oro Valley Must Hire Own Police" (February 19).

Becker, T. (1974). "The Place of Private Police in Society: An Area of Research for the Social Sciences." *Social Problems* 21, 3: 438–53.

Boston Globe (1986). "Jail Goes Private" (December 18).

Commonwealth Review (1989). "Foundation Ideas Are Having a Statewide Impact." Harrisburg, PA: Spring.

Critchley, T. A. (1967; 1978). *A History of Police in England and Wales.* London: Constable.

Cunningham W. C., and T. M. Taylor (1985). *The Hallcrest Report: Private Security and Police in America.* Portland, OR: Chancellor.

Diebold, J. (1984). *Making the Future Work: Unleashing Our Powers of Innovation for the Decades Ahead.* New York: Simon and Schuster.

Dorffi, C. (1979). "San Francisco's Hired Guns." *Reason* (August), 26–29, 33.

Feinstein, C. (1986). *Privatization Possibilities Among Pacific Island Countries.* Research Report Series No. 2. Honolulu, HI: East-West Center.

Fixler, P., Jr. (1986a). "Private Prisons Begin to Establish Track Record." *Fiscal Watchdog* 116 (June): 1–4.

———. (1986b). "Which Police Services Can Be Privatized?" *Fiscal Watchdog* 111 (January): 1–4.

Fixler, P., Jr. and R. Poole (1988) "Can Police Services Be Privatized?" *Annals of the American Academy of Political and Social Science* 498: 108–18.

Fixler, P., Jr. R. Poole, and P. L. Scarlett (1989). *Privatization 1989: Third Annual Report on Privatization.* Santa Monica, CA: Reason Foundation.

Gage, T. (1982). "Cops, Inc." *Reason* (November), 23–28.

Gallagher, J. (1985). "The Case for Privatizing Protective Services," 93–96. L. K. Samuels (ed.), *Facets of Liberty: A Libertarian Primer,* Santa Ana, CA: Freeland.

Gleber, S. (1972). *The Role of Campus Security in the College Setting. Report for Law Enforcement Assistance Administration and National Institute of Law Enforcement and Criminal Justice.* Washington, DC: Government Printing Office.

Hess, K., and H. Wrobleski (1982). *Introduction to Private Security.* St. Paul, MN: West.

Institute for Local Self-Government (ILSG) (1977). *Alternatives to Traditional Public Safety Delivery Systems: Civilians in Public Safety Services.* One of six reports of the Institute's Public Safety Delivery Systems Project. Berkeley, CA: ILSG (September).

Joynt, S. (1986). "Private Companies Hired to Guard Hospitalized State Prisoners." *Birmingham Post-Herald* (May 22).

Kakalik, J., and S. Wildhorn (1971). *Special-Purpose Public Police.* Volume 5 of five-part report by the Rand Corporation for the Department of Justice (R-873-DOJ). Santa Monica: Rand Corporation (December).

Knight, A. (1980). "'Rent-a-Cops' Pose Problems for District." *Washington Post* (November 10).

Leppard, D. (1989). "Transport Police Lose Ferry Deal." London *Sunday Times* (January 29).

McCarthy, J. J. (1982). "Contract Medical Care." *Corrections* (April), 6–17.

McQuillan, S. (1984). "Our Own A-Team," *Sunday Star* (October 7).

Magnusson, D. (1979). "The Private Police." J. Kuhlhorn and Albert Reiss, Jr. (eds.), *Police and the Social Order, Report No. 6.* Stockholm: National Swedish Council for Crime Prevention.

Moulton, R. (1983). "Police Contract Service for Shopping Mall Security." *Police Chief* (June), 43–44.

O'Toole, G. (1978). *The Private Sector: Rent-a-Cops, Private Spies, and the Police-Industrial Complex.* New York: W. W. Morton.

Pancake, D. (1983). "Cooperation Between Police Department and Private Security." *Police Chief* (June), 34–36.

Poole, R., Jr., (1980). *Cutting Back City Hall.* New York: Universe Books.

"Public Police Singing the Blues." *Reason* (February, 1985) 16, 9:13–19.

Rehnke, G. (1989) "Private Security Supplements Public Police." *Privatization Watch* (September).

Savas, E. S. (1982). *Privatizing the Public Sector: How to Shrink Government.* Chatham, NJ: Chatham House.

Schlesinger, T. (1978). "Rent-a-Cops, Inc." *Student Lawyer* (December), 18–20, 43–44.

Shallo, J. P. (1983). *Private Police (w/ special reference to Pennsylvania).* Academy of Political and Social Science, Monograph no. 1. Concord, NH: Rumford.

Shearing, C., and P. Stening (1981). "Modern Private Security: Its Growth and Implications," 193–245. M. Tonny N. Morris (eds.), *Crime and Justice: An Annual Review of Research.* Volume 3. Champaign-Urbana: University of Illinois Press.

State Government News (1986). "Frankfort, Kentucky: Commonwealth of Kentucky" (December 30).

Stewart, J. (1985). "Public Safety and Private Police." *Public Administration Review* (November), 758–65.

Superior Court of California (1986). "San Francisco Patrol Special Police Officers and Robert J. Hart (petitioners) vs. State of California, Commission on Peace Officer Standards and Training." Case no. 866532.

Tolchin, M. (1985). "Private Guards Taking the Place of Police." *Rutland Herald* (November 29).

Urban Innovation Abroad (1980). "Private Firms Take Over Public Functions: Germany, Switzerland." Volume 4, no. 9 (September).

Wackenhut Corporation (1984). "Court Officers Now in 21 States." *Wackenhut Pipeline* (December), 1, 4.

Wallace, B. (1984a) "The Patrol Specials—Salesman with Badges." *San Francisco Chronicle* (July 30).

_____. (1984b) "Unique San Francisco Private Cops and How They Operate." *San Francisco Chronicle* (July 30).

Wildhorn, S., and J. Kakalik (1971). *The Law and Private Police.* Volume 4 of five reports by the Rand Institute for the National Institute of Law Enforcement and Criminal Justice, LEAA (R-872-DOJ). Washington, DC: Government Printing Office.

Wooldridge, W. C. (1970). *Uncle Sam, the Monopoly Man.* New Rochelle, NY: Arlington House.

4. Private Security and Controlling Crime

Edwin W. Zedlewski

The exploration of the public-private nature of safety investments is important to an understanding of private security and crime control in today's world. A number of questions can be raised. What factors induce communities to buy the mix of police and private services that they do? Are there qualitative differences in safety produced by these alternative forms of security? How do these investments fight crime?

The study draws upon data from large metropolitan areas across the United States to address the issues. Because the relationships among crime, the demand for safety, and the provision of safety are complex, it was necessary to construct a model of the process. The model specified the interactions through a group of interrelated eequations which were then estimated by appropriate methods. The elements of the model appeal in the overview. Subsequent sections of the chapter discuss results relating to each of the issues raised.

Overview

Watchdogs and alarm systems no doubt differ technologically from a police-man in a patrol car. They are restricted to monitor fixed areas and they cannot make arrests. However, unlike police, they protect their designated area twenty-four hours each day.

The exclusive ownership of private security is one of its most attractive features. Protection is ever present and unshared. Police services, in contrast, are shared by all members of the community. Their benefits are also enjoyed by everyone in the sense that arrested criminals no longer victimize any member, and would-be criminals who are deterred by police spare the entire community from their crimes.

Investing in police protection clearly produces qualitatively different crime control than investing in guards and alarm systems. A key question is whether these qualitative differences translate into quantitative differences in levels of safety. It is useful to consider the diagram in Figure 4.1, where each block represents a theme in this article.

42

Figure 4.1 Community Safety Dynamics

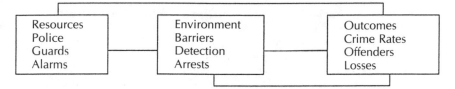

Resources	Environment	Outcomes
Police	Barriers	Crime Rates
Guards	Detection	Offenders
Alarms	Arrests	Losses

Individual safety purchases perform readily understandable functions. Deadbolt locks, for example, impede a burglar's ability to enter a building. Alarm systems notify police and guards of an unauthorized presence and police make arrests.

When these purchases are aggregated over an entire community, they create the safety environment that determines the profitability of crime. Key environmental parameters are the risk of detection and the risk of arrest.[1] They determine state of the world for offenders: how frequently they will be forced to flee a premise and how much time they will spend in prison.

It seems plausible that increases in private security investment should increase the probability of detection and that investment in police response should increase the probability of arrest. The investments interact, however. Police on patrol make some arrests simply by discovering crimes in progress, but others result from calls by guards and alarm systems (including neighbors). Increasing the number of police increases the probability that a crime in progress will be discovered and thus suppresses crimes through increased police presence.

The process by which arrest risk affects community crime rates is deterrence. It has been studied extensively, the general finding being that greater arrest rates are associated with lower crime rates.[2] Relatively little is known about the effects of private security on the safety environment and offender decisionmaking. A critical question is whether the threat of discovery discourages offenders from subsequent crime or simply forces them to look for more vulnerable targets. If detection risks and other signs of formidable protection discourage offenders from committing as many crimes, then private security produces community-wide benefits. If it serves only to displace crime to less protected households and businesses, then it is a cause for public concern.

The data used to investigate the issues were measures of crime, safety resources, and other socioeconomic characteristics of 124 Standard Metropolitan Statistical Areas (smsas) of the United States in 1977. They came from a variety of government statistical series which are listed at the end of this chapter under Data Sources. The measures were used to estimate a set of interrelated equations: demands for police and private security, production of detection and arrest risks, and community crime relationships.

A unique aspect of the analysis was the use of two independent measures of victimization risk. Crimes reported to the Federal Bureau of Investigation (fbi) by local police have appeared frequently in the study of community crime. Crimes recorded by the National Crime Survey (ncs) have appeared infrequently, and

Table 4.1 Descriptions of Key Variables (N = 124)

Variable	Mean	Min	Max	StdDev
Population (millions)	1.02	0.13	9.39	1.37
Police per thousand population	2.33	1.21	4.37	0.57
Pri. Sec. Emps per thousand pop.	1.59	0.21	7.04	1.03
Property crimes per capita (FBI)	0.05	0.02	0.12	0.02
Property crimes per household (NCS)	0.45	0.08	1.11	0.17
Arrests per property crime (FBI)	0.18	0.09	0.41	0.05
Arrests per property crime (NCS)	0.06	0.02	0.22	0.03
Failures per attempted theft	0.14	0.03	0.39	0.06
Reports to police per theft/attempt	0.34	0.13	0.70	0.08

almost never in direct comparison with FBI statistics. Each equation was estimated with both crime measures. The results sometimes supported each other but other times conflicted. Descriptive information on key study variables is presented in Table 4.1.

Because of the interactions between variables determined within the framework, simultaneous equation estimation techniques were used to eliminate possible biases in parameter estimates. All equations were estimated by two-stage least-squares method (Intriligator, 1978). All variables were represented in natural logarithmic form.

Safety Purchases

Among the factors influencing purchases of police and private security are surely the costs of these services and a community's ability to pay. Local victimization risks and the magnitudes of potential losses should also enter into the decision (Bartel, 1975; Ehrlich and Becker, 1972). Measures of these factors were included in the safety purchase equations.

Two dependent variables measured the demand for safety: the number of police officers per thousand population (POLICE) and the number of private security employees per thousand population (PRIVATE). While additional measures of expenditures on private security goods and services were sought, none were available on a cross-sectional basis.

Prices of services were measured by average costs. Police prices (COPPR) were obtained by dividing police expenditures by the number of sworn officers employed; private security prices (GRDPR) were obtained by dividing private security sales by the number of employees. Ability to pay, or income, was measured by the average annual pay (AVGPAY) for workers in each SMSA. Community wealth (WEALTH) was measurued by time deposits in banks and savings and loan associations per capita. It was used as a surrogate for the size of potential losses because greater wealth implies greater cash and property holdings.

The crime threat was measured by property crimes (THEFTS). One measure was the number of property crimes per capita reported to police, as published by the

FBI. It includes all thefts and attempted thefts reported to the police by citizens except robberies. The second measure was *actual* victimizations per *household*, as estimated by the NCS. Since reporting rates can vary between 13 and 70 percent (Table 4.1), the survey is a useful alternative to police statistics. Its estimates are derived from a sample of about 60,000 households throughout the United States and cover the same crimes defined in the FBI statistics. Its limitations are its sampling error and the fact that it does not survey commercial establishments.[3]

Two control variables were included in each demand equation: the percent of housing owner-occupied (OWNER) and SMSA population (POP). Homeowners often bear disproportionate shares of public sector expenditures through property taxes. They also have greater flexibility than renters to buy and install private security systems. Population was included to test for scale economies in police services. Results for public-sector and private-sector demand are given in Table 4.2 for both measures of crime risk. Standard errors of the estimates are in parentheses.

Table 4.2 Safety Personnel per 1,000 Population

| Variable | FBI Crime Rates | | NCS Crime Rates | |
	POLICE	PRIVATE	POLICE	PRIVATE
Constant	-0.92	-0.21	-2.35	-3.65
	(1.53)	(5.35)	(1.61)	(5.46)
THEFTS (FBI)	0.28**	0.64*	0.19*	0.56
	(0.10)	(0.34)	(0.10)	(0.36)
COPPR	-0.05	-0.30	-0.06	0.48
	(0.11)	(0.39)	(0.15)	(0.50)
GRDPR	0.28**	-0.29	0.35**	0.28
	(0.08)	(0.29)	(0.08)	(0.28)
AVGPAY	-0.17	0.21	0.21	0.27
	(0.19)	(0.67)	(0.22)	(0.75)
WEALTH	0.14**	0.32**	0.23**	0.56*
	(0.05)	(0.19)	(0.07)	(0.25)
OWNER	-0.21**	0.30	-0.23**	0.24
	(0.08)	(0.30)	(0.09)	(0.32)
POP	0.07**	0.24**	0.07**	0.25**
	(0.02)	(0.08)	(0.02)	(0.08)

*Statistically significant at 0.05 level of confidence.
**Statistically significant at 0.01 level of confidence.

The results indicate that consumers of safety products consider both the costs and benefits of protection. Potential losses (WEALTH) were significant determinants of demand: a 1 percent increase in potential losses implied between a 0.14 to 0.23 percent increase in police officers per 1,000 population and a 0.32 to 0.56 percent increase in security personnel per 1,000 population.

Victimization risk (THEFTS) was a signficant determinant of demand in three of the four equations. A 1 percent increase in reported crime rates implied a 0.28 percent increase in police employed per capita and a 0.64 percent increase in private security personnel per capita. A 1 percent increase in true victimization rates implied a slightly lesser reaction to the crime threat. These estimates of reactions to crime lay in the midst of Clotfelter's (1978) estimates of a variety of specific reactions to victimization risk. He found that a 1 percent increase in victimization risk implied a 0.18 percent increase in households that locked their doors when leaving home and a 0.91 percent increase in the number of households buying window bars. A logical explanation for its lack of significance in the private security equation using NCS data is the fact that the survey does not include commercial firms (or apartment managements), the predominant purchasers of private security services.

Neither police nor private security demand was sensitive to its own price, but police demand was influenced by the price of its substitute. A 1 percent increase in GRDPR elicits a 0.28 to 0.35 percent increase in police per capita. Owner occupancy (OWNER) was associated with lower demand for police services, probably explained by the tax liabilities incurred by homeowners for increases in public services and the adaptability of their dwellings to private security systems. Clotfelter (1977) found a similar relationship between owner occupancy rates and *relative* demand for police: higher owner occupancy rates implied a reduction in the ratio of police to private security employees.

Population elasticities[4] estimated in the study of public-sector goods have been interpreted as measures of scale economies (Borcherding and Deacon, 1972; Bergstrom and Goodman, 1973). A population elasticity of 0.07, as found, would suggest slight diseconomies of scale in policing; that is, slightly greater numbers of officers per capita are needed to produce equivalent levels of services as the population increases. In the case of private-sector security, a population elasticity of 0.25 simply means that people living in highly populated areas prefer more private security than those living in less populated areas, other things being equal.

Safety and the Environment

It is relatively easy to describe how any security device or service prevents crime. Locks and window bars impede entry; cameras and guards perform surveillance; and store detectives apprehend shoplifters. It is quite difficult to describe how these devices combine with police services to produce an environment that is favorable or hostile to criminals.

Two aspects of the urban environment are of interest to would-be offenders and are theoretically influenced by investments in safety. The probability of arrest brings with it the threat of imprisonment. The probability of detection may or may not lead to arrest, but it will lead to a loss of an offender's time and increase the total time he spends per successful theft. If offenders fail often enough, they may be discouraged from further attempts because of the low return from their efforts.

It seems logical that increases in police or private security investment would increase both probabilities, but the limited empirical evidence available on the subject fails to confirm this relationship. Authors have found extremely weak associations between resources and arrest risk (Ehrlich, 1973), negative associations (Pogue, 1975), and sometimes positive associations (Zedlewski, 1983). One reason

Table 4.3 Risks of Arrest and Detection

Variable	FBI Statistics		NCS Statistics	
	P(A)	P(F)	P(A)	P(F)
Constant	-1.80	-2.12	-2.40	-3.75
	(1.35)	(2.21)	(1.06)	(1.24)
POLICE	0.24	-0.01	-1.33	1.67
	(1.86)	(2.99)	(2.15)	(2.50)
PRIVATE	0.36	-1.17*	-0.46	-1.29*
	(0.34)	(0.56)	(0.46)	(0.56)
COPSQ	-0.18	-0.28	0.83	-1.16
	(1.05)	(1.69)	(1.27)	(1.48)
GRDSQ	0.02	-0.18*	-0.02	-0.15*
	(0.06)	(0.09)	(0.07)	(0.09)
COPGRD	-0.36	1.27*	-0.40	1.40*
	(0.37)	(0.61)	(0.50)	(0.61)
THEFTS(FBI)	-0.13	0.32	-0.23	0.02
	(0.23)	(0.37)	(0.19)	(0.24)
DENSITY	-0.07**	0.22**	0.05	0.20
	(0.04)	(0.07)	(0.06)	(0.07)

*Statistically significant at 0.05 level of confidence.
**Statistically significant at 0.01 level of confidence.

for such disappointing results is that arrest is only one of many police functions and that increases in resources are distributed over these many services, dissipating the potential increase in arrest risk. Another possibility is that increases in resources act perversely with respect to arrest risk.

Consider a city with police at every street corner and security guards at every store. Would the probabilities of arrest and detection be greater there than in a more typical city? As police and guard visibility increases, theft attempts would decline but the effect on arrest and detection *rates* is indeterminate. Thieves might plan more thoroughly or act more recklessly when faced with reduced opportunities. They would not all be deterred from attempts.

The safety environment was modeled flexibly in anticipation of potentially perverse results. The output variables were the probability of arrest P(A), measured as the fraction of property crimes cleared by arrest, and the probability of failure P(F), measured as the number of unsuccessful attempts at theft divided by total attempts. The latter variable was computed from victim reports in the National Crime Survey. The P(A) was measured from FBI statistics and alternatively from the NCS. In the latter case, the numerator—crimes cleared by arrest—was taken from FBI statistics, while the denominator—total property crimes—was estimated from the survey. As before, two equations were estimated for each set of measures.

Primary resource variables were police officers and private security personnel per 1,000 population. The squares of these variables, COPSQ and GRDSQ, and an interaction term COPGRD were included to enhance the flexibility of the estimation function.[5]

Prevailing crime rates (THEFTS) were included as a possible drain on resources. If the volume of thefts is large relative to the levels of safety resources, one would expect those resources to become overloaded and police arrest productivity to decline. The FBI and NCS measures of thefts corresponding to the arrest rates were used. The final variable included was population density (DENSITY).

The arrest risk equations performed poorly, as other researchers have discovered. Does this necessarily mean that safety resources have no effect on arrest rates? That possibility must certainly be considered, but there are other interpretations.

One possibility, already mentioned, is that police presence discourages attempts. The result may be either lower or higher arrest rates but at lower crime levels. A second possibility is that safety resources increase arrest risks for certain types of property crimes but not others. Zedlewski (1983) found, for example, that greater numbers of police per capita (to a point) improved arrest rates for burglaries but not for larcenies (purse snatching, shoplifting, etc.). The negative findings here and elsewhere for property crime may result from a masking of effects through aggregation of crime groups.

The findings for failure rates were more intriguing. Increases in guards per capita were associated with significant decreases in failure rates. The total effect, because of the quadratic and cross product terms in the equation, depends upon the levels of both police and private security personnel per capita.[6]

A possible explanation for the negative relationship found is that the visibility of protection produces a "scarecrow effect." Offenders, upon seeing guards or alarm systems, may gauge their chances of successful theft as very low and look elsewhere for targets with less patent signs of protection. If so, then private protection has distributional consequences in that it displaces thefts from those who can purchase protection to others who cannot afford protection. Whether the community enjoys a lower overall victimization risk as a result of high levels of private security investment is discussed in the next section.

The other significant determinant of failure rates is population density. It implies that densely populated areas have more potential witnesses to a crime and that these witnesses produce a higher probability of detection.

Crime Control

The overview section suggested a causal relationship between the environment resulting from safety investments and community crime rates. This section elaborates on that relationship and presents the evidence resulting from the data.

Offender behavior – and consequently crime rates – is influenced by probabilities of arrest and failure. This notion is derived from theories that crime is not deviant behavior but an occupational choice much like plumbing or carpentry. People discover over time what legal and illegal opportunities they have to earn money, their relative distastes for steady work and punishment, and their physical and mental capabilities. These discoveries channel them into a set of occupational choices.

Many will work entirely in legitimate jobs or entirely in crime, but others will perform in both areas.

A critical determinant of the decision is the relative amount of income that can be earned in legal and illegal activities. Legal wages are determined by the kinds of jobs a person can obtain and the frequency of unemployment. Illegal wages depend on several factors: the value of loot taken, monetary and psychological consequences of imprisonment, and the hours required to acquire and dispose of the "take." Ignoring psychic costs and benefits, theft wage rates can be represented by a combination of these factors: $W_T = (R - p_a S)/H(p_f)$. R is the gross take from a successful theft. Costs of imprisonment are $p_a S$, where p_a is the probability of arrest and imprisonment and S is the income loss associated with arrest and subsequent imprisonment for a given period. The hours per successful theft $H(p_f)$ depends on the probability of failure in two ways. Failures are time lost and add to the labor devoted per successful theft. The offender's subjective estimate of the probability of failure also influences the time he spends casing targets. If he sees visible signs of protection such as guards, police, or alarms, he must either spend time planning to avoid their detection or looking for better prospects.

How these parameters affect crime rates is depicted in Figure 4.2. H(W) depicts how many hours an individual is willing to work for a given hourly wage W. It indicates that individuals are willing to work more hours at higher wage rates.

Figure 4.2 Theft Wages and Crime Rates

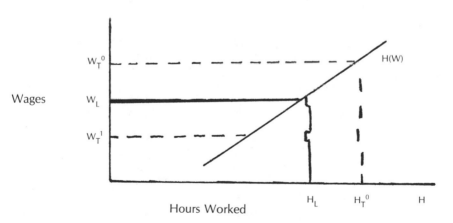

The relationship as drawn assumes that an individual is indifferent between legal and illegal work (otherwise two separate curves would be needed) and chooses his occupation solely on the basis of hourly returns. This simplification causes individuals to specialize in either crime or legal work but illustrates the basic points of this paper.

If thefts net the individual a wage rate of $W_T{}^\circ$, he will devote $H_T{}^\circ$ hours to theft. If instead the probability of arrest were greater or the probability of failure were greater, the hourly wage for theft would fall to W_T' below his best legal wage W_L. The individual would leave crime and spend H_L hours at a legal job.

In reality, of course, individuals may be basically honest or dishonest and have clear preferences for one form of work over the other. The key point is that reducing theft wages through P(A) and P(F) should cause some reduction in the hours spent stealing and, consequently, the number of crimes committed. Data are not available to calculate actual theft wages, so the analysis used P(A) and P(F) as its wage surrogates.

Both FBI-based and NCS-based measures of crime and arrest rates were used in Table 4.4. Other variables in the crime equation are related to labor returns and opportunity: the average annual pay (AVGPAY) for legal work in the SMSA; WEALTH as a measure of potential returns from theft; unemployment rates (UNEMP) and labor force participation rates (LFPR) as measures of legal opportunities; and the percentage of the population receiving welfare (AFDC) as a measure of need.

Two demographic variables, percentage of nonwhite population (NONW) and percentage of male population, aged 15 to 24 (YOUTH), were used to control for the presence of populations that might face below average legal wage rates and opportunities, either through discrimination or lack of experience. The absolute value of

Table 4.4 Community Crime Control

Variables	Thefts (FBI)	Thefts (NCS)
Constant	9.57	10.80
	(4.73)	(7.94)
P(A) (FBI)	-0.67	-1.92*
	(1.37)	(0.96)
P(F)	0.42*	0.32
	(0.24)	(0.48)
AVGPAY	-1.09*	-1.26
	(0.57)	(0.81)
WEALTH	0.17	-0.40
	(0.28)	(0.29)
UNEMP	0.16	0.08
	(0.22)	(0.32)
LFPR	1.30*	1.37
	(0.65)	(0.91)
AFDC	0.01	-0.08
	(0.11)	(0.16)
NONW	0.15**	0.24**
	(0.04)	(0.10)
YOUTH	1.26**	0.23
	(0.38)	(1.09)
NETMIG	0.08*	0.06
	(0.04)	(0.06)

*Statistically significant at 0.05 level of confidence.
**Statistically significant at 0.01 level of confidence.

net migration (NETMIG) in the SMSA between 1970 and 1977 was included to capture upheaval, or lack of neighborhood stability.

The equations varied in which variables were significant, but they agreed for the most part over the signs of the relationships to property crime rates.

Legal wage rates (AVGPAY) and demographic variables (NONW and YOUTH) are significant and have the signs predicted by theory using the FBI data. That labor force participation is positively associated with crime is less surprising than it appears. Jacob and Lineberry (1982) found a similar relationship and interpreted it as a "guardianship" effect. High labor force participation rates typically mean greater numbers of working women in the community. This implies a reduction in the number of dwellings occupied during the day, when half of all residential burglaries occur.[7] It also implies a reduction in the supervision of children under eighteen years old, who account for 38 percent of burglary arrests and 33 percent of larceny arrests.[8]

Both equations indicate that high population turnover (NETMIG) is associated with high crime rates. There are a variety of theories as to why high turnover should lead to higher crime rates: lack of trust of one's neighbors, lack of commitment to protect the neighborhood, in-migration by a new socioeconomic class, etc. Which of these are most compelling is beyond the scope of this present work.

Estimations using FBI data indicate negligible deterrence through arrest risk and a positive association between failure rates and crime rates. Interpreted in isolation, this positive association suggests that high failure rates are symbolic of high rates of attempted theft. Taking into account the negative association between private security resources and failure rates found earlier, the association here suggests that greater levels of security personnel are associated with reduced levels of community crime. It suggests that investment in private security produces spillover benefits to the community at large. Crime is not only displaced; it is somewhat discouraged.

The NCS-based equation leads to different conclusions. It finds that arrest risk exerts powerful deterrent effects on property offenders, and that failure rates are a negligible influence on crime rates. A 1 percent increase in arrest rates would produce a nearly 2 percent decrease in property crime rates, other factors held constant. The results suggest that private security produces no significant spillover benefits and may only displace crime to the more vulnerable.

The results underscore some fundamental issues in community crime control and the privatization of safety. If arrest is indeed a powerful deterrent, then communities should make investments, either public or private, that increase arrest rates. Unfortunately, the preceding section indicates that police manpower increases will not affect arrest rates greatly, so the most obvious investment is likely to be unprofitable. Arrest rates may depend on departmental skill or policy, but the aggregate data used in this analysis cannot suggest how to increase them.

An inability to produce predictable increases in arrest rates, coupled with demonstrably effective private security systems, indicates that safety investment in private security will grow more rapidly than investment in police (beyond what is dictated by population growth).

Conclusion

This chapter has examined a variety of issues related to investment in private security as a partial substitute for police. The question was asked why people might prefer one form of protection over another; we have explored what safety investments have produced and how they have produced it; and we have also asked whether these investments affected crime rates. The data used provided clearer answers to some questions than others, partly because of the aggregate nature of the data and partly because experience has shown that some of the questions are inherently more difficult.

A significant asset to the inquiry was alternative measures of crime and arrest rates, each with different limitations. The FBI-based statistics capture only reported crimes. The NCS-based statistics capture unreported crimes as well as reported, but cover only personal and household offenses. Results from these different sources were sometimes quite similar, adding credibility to findings. Even when results were apparently dissimilar, awareness of the data characteristics offered plausible explanations for the differences.

The first investigation found that people invested in police and private security for a variety of logical reasons. They wished to protect their property, and the more property they had the more they were willing to spend. Investments rose with victimization risk and wealth. Relative costs were important. As the cost of private security rose, people demanded more police. The question of who would pay for police was also important. Homeowners, who frequently bear a disproportionate share of municipal costs through property taxes, were less supportive of increased police employment.

How investments alter the environment facing offenders is less clear. The data indicate that arrest rates are not affected significantly by changes in police manpower, at least over the range observed in large SMSAs. Failure rates, which are based on NCS household interviews, were negatively associated with changes in private security resources. This relationship is consistent with an hypothesis that visible security protects its owner by displacing crime to neighbors with either less or less visible security. Whether crime in the aggregate remains constant, private security systems have distributive consequences that communities may wish to address, possibly by alignment of police patrol routes. If total crime is reduced, then private security systems produce social benefits beyond protecting the owner.

The two data sources used come to different assessments of that issue. The FBI-based results found that low failure rates (high visible security) were associated with significantly lower crime rates and that arrest risk was only weakly related to crime rates. The NCS-based results held the opposite view: arrest risk was a powerful deterrent to crime and failure rates were a negligible influence.

Variable Definitions

Variable	Definition	Source Codes*
POLICE	Police employees per 1,000 pop.	2, 3
PRIVATE	Security employees per 1,000 pop.	2, 4
P(A)	Fraction of thefts cleared by arrest	7
P(F)	Fraction of theft attempts failing	6
THEFTS	Property crimes per 1,000 pop.	7
COPPR	Average cost of police employee	3
GRDPR	Average cost private-security employee	4
AVGPAY	Average annual pay	9
OWNER	Fraction of dwellings owner-occupied	6
POP	SMSA population in 1977	2
WEALTH	Time deposits per capita	1, 2
UNEMP	Unemployment rate	9
LFPR	Labor-force participation rate	2, 5, 8
AFDC	Welfare recipients per capita	1
NONW	Fraction of population nonwhite	5
YOUTH	Fraction of population male, 15–24	5
NETMIG	Absolute value net migration 1970–77	2
DENSITY	Population per square mile	1

All variables expressed in natural logarithms.

* Refer to data source list.

Data Sources

1. U. S. Department of Commerce, Bureau of the Census (1978). *County and City Data Book 1977*, Washington DC.
2. U. S. Department of Commerce, Bureau of the Census (1979). *Current Population Reports: Estimates of the Population of Counties and Metropolitan Areas: July 1, 1976 and 1977* (Series P-25, No. 810), Washington, DC.
3. U. S. Department of Commerce, Bureau of the Census (1980). *1977 Census of Governments, Vol. 5: Local Government in Metropolitan Areas*, Washington, DC.
4. U. S. Department of Commerce, Bureau of the Census (1980). *1977 Census of Service Industries* (SC77-A-1 through SC77-A-50), Washington, DC.
5. U. S. Department of Commerce, Bureau of the Census Estimates Research Branch. "Population Distributions in Counties by Age [5-year intervals], Race [white or nonwhite], and Sex: 1971–1977" (unpublished).
6. U. S. Department of Commerce, Bureau of the Census, Crime Surveys Branch (1980). "Household Interviews Extract, 1977 National Crime Surveys" (unpublished).
7. U. S. Department of Justice, Federal Bureau of Investigation (1978). *Uniform Crime Reports for the United States: 1977*, Washington, DC.
8. U. S. Department of Labor, Bureau of Labor Statistics (1979). "Local Area Unemployment Statistics" (August 28 extract, unpublished).

9. U. S. Department of Labor, Bureau of Labor Statistics (1979). Press Release USDL-79-803, "Annual Pay by State" (November 15), Washington, DC.

Notes

1. Risk, probability, and likelihood are used interchangeably in this article. Some authors (e.g., Heineke, 1978) distinguish between risk and probability of arrest in the study of offender decisions.

2. Virtually every study of deterrence effects can be criticized for severe methodological shortcomings. There is considerable disagreement about the magnitude of deterrence effects and even whether they exist. The National Academy of Sciences, in their assessment of the limitations to deterrence research, summarized their position: "Our reluctance to draw stronger conclusions does not imply support for a position that deterrence does not exist, since the evidence certainly favors a proposition supporting deterrence more than it favors one asserting that deterrence is absent" (Blumstein and Cohen, 1978).

3. Commercial establishments were dropped in 1976. See Garofalo and Hindelang (1977) for a description of the survey's history and sampling design.

4. An *elasticity* is the percentage change in one variable associated with a given percentage change in another variable. A population elasticity is the percentage change in police or private security personnel associated with a 1 percent change in population. Commonly mentioned elasticities in consumer demand studies are price (percentage change in demand as price changes) and income (percentage change in demand as income changes) elasticities.

5. Since all variables were in logarithmic form, the squared logs of the variables were used. The resultant specification is the transcendental logarithmic (translog) production function, a popular and flexible form. See, for example, Intriligator, 1978.

6. The total effect on $P(F)$ of a change in resources is given by:

$$\frac{d \ln P(F)}{d \ln x} = b_1 + b_2 \ln x + b_3 \ln y$$

where $\ln x = $ PRIVATE, $\ln y = $ POLICE, b_1 is the coefficient of PRIVATE, b_2 is the coefficient of GRDSQ, and b_3 is the coefficient of COPGRD. Taken at the sample means, a 1 percent increase in security personnel per capita implies a 0.23 percent decrease in $P(F)$.

7. *Sourcebook of Criminal Justice Statistics*, 1983. Estimated number of personal and household incidents by time of occurrence. Half of burglaries for which approximate time of occurrence is known occur between 6 A.M. and 6 P.M. (p. 335).

8. FBI, *Crime in the United States (1985)*, Table 33. Washington, DC, July 1986.

References

Bartel, A. (1975). "Analysis of Firm Demand for Protection Against Crime." *Journal of Legal Studies* 3 (June): 433–78.

Bergstrom, T., and R. Goodman (1973). "Private Demands for Public Goods." *American Economic Review* 63 (June): 280–96.

Blumstein, A., D. Nagin, and J. Cohen (1978). *Deterrence and Incapacitation: Estimating the Effects of Criminal Sanctions on Crime Rates.* Washington, DC: National Research Council.

Borcherding, T. E., and R. T. Deacon (1972). "The Demand for Services of Non-Federal Governments." *American Economic Review* 62 (December): 891–901.

Clotfelter, C. (1977). "Public Services, Private Substitutes, and the Demand for Protection Against Crime." *American Economic Review* 67 (December): 371–86.

————. (1978). "Private Security and Public Safety." *Journal of Urban Economics* 5 (July): 338–402.

Ehrlich, I. (1973). "Participation in Illegitimate Activities: A Theoretical and Empirical Investigation," *Journal of Political Economy* 81 (May–June):531–67.

Ehrlich, I., and G. S. Becker (1972). "Market Insurance, Self-Insurance, and Self Protection." *Journal of Political Economy* 80 (July–August): 632–48.

Garofalo, J., and M. Hindelang (1977). *An Introduction to the National Crime Survey.* U.S. Department of Justice, National Criminal Justice Information and Statistics Service (SD-VAD-4), Washington, DC.

Heineke, J. M. (1978). "Economic Models of Criminal Behavior: An Overview," 1–33. J. M. Heineke (ed.), *Economic Models of Criminal Behavior.* New York: North Holland.

Intriligator, M. D. (1978). *Econometric Models, Techniques, and Applications.* Englewood Cliffs, NJ: Prentice-Hall.

Jacob, H., and R. L. Lineberry (1982). *Governmental Responses to Crime: Crime and Governmental Responses in American Cities.* Washington, DC: U.S. Department of Justice, National Institute of Justice.

Pogue, T. F. (1975). "Effect of Police Expenditures on Crime Rates: Some Evidence." *Public Finance Quarterly* 3 (January): 14–44.

U.S. Department of Justice, Bureau of Justice Statistics (1983). *Sourcebook of Criminal Justice Statistics, 1983,* Washington, DC.

Zedlewski, E. W. (1983). "Deterrence Findings and Data Sources: A Comparison of the Uniform Crime Reports and the National Crime Surveys." *Journal of Research in Crime and Delinquency* (July), 262–76.

5. Community Policing, Problem-Oriented Policing, Police-Citizen Coproduction of Public Safety, and the Privatization of Crime Control

Ronald L. Boostrom
Corina A. Draper

Experimentation with various efforts to privatize criminal justice services has been encouraged in the past decade by the antigovernment, probusiness ideology espoused by the Reagan administration in the United States and by the Thatcher government in Great Britain. In addition, the Bush administration has continued to emphasize volunteer citizen involvement in the provision of public services. This can be seen as an effort to operationalize the ideology of privatization. Experiments have included attempts to create a partnership between the public sector, private enterprise, and citizen self-help efforts which affect the provision of services in the areas of crime prevention, policing, victim services, legal services, corrections, and juvenile justice.

Crime prevention efforts and the provision of police services have been profoundly influenced by the transformations in social relationships signified by the recent growth of private policing (Shearing and Stenning, 1981, 1987) and the increasing involvement of citizens groups in crime prevention efforts to improve community safety (Rosenbaum, 1988). The police role in society is being reconceptualized in theory and practice due to the philosophy of "Community Policing" which fosters the idea of partnership between the public and private sectors and citizen self-help to improve public safety and the quality of life in our communities.

This reconceptualization led to an erosion of the idea that the state should monopolize the delivery of police services and the administration of justice. The emphasis on private alternatives to state-controlled justice was encouraged by a critique of the state-sponsored criminal justice system. Dissatisfaction with traditional approaches was encouraged by the research revolution in this field during the past three decades (Walker, 1989). The state-monopolized criminal justice system was found to be inefficient and ineffective in many respects, to be over-centralized, and discriminatory in its provision of services (Hall et al., 1978; Quinney, 1977; Ryan and Ward, 1989).

Research conducted during the 1970s tended to indicate that traditional police strategies which kept police officers distant from citizens led to ineffective crime prevention and control efforts. By the early 1980s it was being demonstrated that police tactics that emphasized increased police-citizen interaction could pay off in reducing crime and public fear of crime. At the same time, research into the improvement of management techniques and organizational effectiveness was having an impact on police agencies. For instance, Houston Chief of Police Lee Brown began to place his key managers in internships with private sector corporations with a reputation for management excellence.

A partnership between the public and private sectors, including citizen self-help groups, was promoted as an antidote to the failure of state-monopolized criminal justice. Crime prevention had been conceptualized as a public good to be provided by public agencies. It is increasingly thought of as a shared responsibility to be shouldered by public, private, and volunteer agencies and community groups (Boostrom and Henderson, 1988; Clarke, 1987; Lavrakas, 1985; Rosenbaum, 1987; Skogan, 1987; Smith and Uzhida, 1988).

The concept of "mixed economy" has been used to describe this reconceptualization of state, private enterprise, voluntary sector, and informal community-based agencies sharing responsibility for the delivery of community services, including crime prevention, public safety, and the administration of justice (Mawby, 1989).

The privatization of criminal justice services can be conceptualized as a movement to demonopolize and decentralize services formally provided exclusively by government agencies and to encourage shared responsibility for the maintenance of public safety and the administration of justice. Savas (1982:57–58) states that there are at least nine different arrangements possible for delivering collective goods and services. These range from private contracting to self-help. Most discussions of privatization have emphasized the first type of arrangement; we will emphasize efforts to promote a partnership between government police agencies and citizen self-help efforts.

The literature of public administration has used the concept of coproduction to describe various public–private-sector partnerships for the delivery of collective goods and services. Brundy and England (1983) have reviewed this literature analyzing the concept of coproduction. Differing perspectives on this concept are provided by Dunn and Rohr (1984), Ferris (1984), and Levine (1984). The concept has also been adopted to describe police-citizen partnerships in the coproduction of community safety (see Bish and Neubert, 1977; Ostrom and Ostrom, 1977; Percy, 1979; Rich, 1977). For the purpose of considering future policy directions in policing, this meaning of coproduction and privatization—promising improved police-citizen interaction and partnerships in crime prevention, and control—seems to be the most promising.

Police-Citizen Coproduction of Public Safety

The concepts of a mixed economy to deal with issues of crime prevention and public safety and police-citizen coproduction of crime control are consistent with a new role for the police in our society. This new role, which implies a partnership with law-abiding citizens to improve the quality of life in our communities, is promoted under the rubric of "Community Policing." Community policing has been characterized as a revolutionary change in police organizational strategy (Brown, 1989; Trojanowicz and Bucqueroux, 1990). The new organizational strategy attempts to forge a partnership between public police agencies, community businesses, and private self-help citizen groups for more effective problem-solving and social control.

Community policing is a philosophy which "rests on the belief that law-abiding people in the community deserve input into the police process, in exchange for their participation and support" (Trojanowicz and Bucqueroux, 1990:xiii). Brown (1989:5–8) stresses several interrelated components of this philosophy which distinguish it from traditional policing:

> 1. Community policing is oriented to problem-solving and focuses on results. It encourages techniques such as problem identification, problem analysis, and problem resolution.
> 2. Community policing demands that police departments organize to incorporate citizen involvement and citizen input in matters that affect the safety and quality of neighborhood life. Police-citizen partnerships and power sharing in crime control efforts are encouraged. Police are expected to be accountable to the community for their actions and results.
> 3. Decentralization is encouraged. Beats are drawn to coincide with natural neighborhood boundaries to encourage responsibility for shared "turf." Beat officers are given permanent beat assignments and are encouraged to become actively involved in the affairs of the community and to initiate creative solutions to neighborhood problems. The patrol officer becomes the "manager" of their assigned beat.
> 4. Performance evaluations are based on problem-solving ability and success in involving citizens in crime fighting efforts. The criterion for success becomes an absence of incidents such as criminal offenses, traffic accidents, and repeat calls for service.
> The basic mission of the police is defined as preventing crime and disorder.

The philosophy of community policing implies that greater organizational autonomy be given to line patrol officers in police agencies consistent with an approach to police professionalism emphasizing community relations, community service, and creative problem-solving. Continuous positive contact with law-abiding people in the assigned beat area is expected. Community policing officers would be expected to act as community ombudsmen, linking individuals and groups to public and private agencies; long-term solutions to problems of community safety would be sought; traditional reliance on arrest and prosecution would be supplemented with other types of regulatory measures to improve the quality of community life; and decentralized, personalized, and creative joint problem-solving efforts should be emphasized.

More than 300 police departments nationwide have reported that they have incorporated some form of community policing in their organization (Trojanowicz and Bucqueroux, 1990:4). This movement has begun to reverse a past trend toward police isolation from the community.

Community policing entails basic changes in police organizational structure and mission. Therefore, this approach to policing will be resisted by some police and public comfortable with methods and philosophies which have defined policing throughout most of this century in our society. It will be misunderstood by many if it is seen as a limited tactic to be incorporated into traditional police organizational structure rather than a new philosophy of policing.

This philosophy of community policing revives a traditional emphasis in American society on participatory democracy and "popular justice" (Walker, 1980). This philosophy of policing proposes that public police agencies and other law-abiding members of the community act as coresponsible agents of social control. Regulatory measures which go beyond criminal judicial punishment methods are explored as long-term problem solving mechanisms.

Community Policing: Revolutionary or Evolutionary?

If we view the responsibility of government for policing the community in a long-range historical context, the philosophy of community policing does not appear so revolutionary. Perhaps we only got off track in our society in our definition of the policing function in the short term and we are returning to a more realistic perspective on the idea of a shared responsibility for policing the community.

Chapman (1970) points out that the Polizeistaat in eighteenth-century Prussia had three purposes: protection of the population, welfare of the state and its citizens, and the general improvement of society. This way of viewing the policing function had been developing in European societies since the responsibilities of government to the citizens of the state had been defined in ancient Greek civilization. Police authorities had both repressive functions and positive welfare functions. The police powers of the state included the detection of crime, apprehension of the offender, and prosecution of criminal offenses. However, these police powers also included an administrative function involving the maintenance of public order, public morality, and the public welfare. A responsibility for the coordination of public and private functions to promote overall public safety and welfare was taken for granted as part of the community policing responsibility of government.

The community policing responsibility in early American society was a shared responsibility between government officials and private citizens (Walker, 1980). This responsibility was gradually turned over to uniformed, full-time specialists as urbanization, industrialization, and a division of labor became the norm and changed social relationships in our nation. However, the British police system, from which we took our basic model of policing, emphasizes that the primary purpose of the police is to prevent crime and disorder. It is the job of law enforcement officers to secure the cooperation and respect of the community, and they must view themselves as a part of that community. The police are paid to help maintain the quality of life in cooperation with the other citizens of the community, and they must judge their performance and be accountable to the public for reducing crime and disorder in the community. These guidelines, known as "Peel's principles" have formed the basis of policing philosophy since the introduction of the London police model in 1822 by Sir Robert Peel (Hunt, 1989). They also serve as the basis of today's "revolutionary" philosophy of community policing (Brown, 1989).

An effort to depoliticize the police in our society had led to a reform movement to professionalize the police by militarizing and centralizing police agencies and narrowing their functions to fighting crime. The police began to aspire to professional crime fighter status with the encouragement of police reformers such as August Vollmer and J. Edgar Hoover. Police administrators began to decry the breakdown of community order and morality in the 1930s as the effects of the depression devastated parts of American society. Influential police leaders saw themselves as "standing armies of American civilization, charged with the protection of all American ideals from within" (Jordan, 1972:40). They were the "thin blue line" saving our civilization from itself and from the weakness, sloth, and ignorance of evil forces which characterized most of the citizenry.

On the other hand, the public reveled in entertainment picturing the police as buffoons and or corrupt, ineffective "flat-foots." Thus, the police developed a defensive posture and an estrangement from the rest of the community. This was enhanced by technology such as automobile patrol and the telephone which removed the police from continuous, face-to-face contact with most of the public. A police subculture developed which emphasized internal loyalty, a code of secrecy, social isolation, and an attitude that only other police officers could be trusted (Shernock, 1988). The police came to view most of those in the community as the enemy, rather than as potential partners in crime prevention.

Because of historical circumstance, the "community context" of policing had been temporarily lost for much of the twentieth century in American society. The philosophy of community policing and the strategies that follow from it attempt to recapture this context. They are an attempt to review policing as community service and to recapture the linkages which the professional police agencies must forge with other community resources to create crime prevention, public safety, and social order.

Problem-Oriented Policing: Operationizing the Community Policing Philosophy

One effort that was used by many police departments in the past decade to incorporate the public into the coproduction of crime control was known as "civilianization." This involved the hiring of civilians for many of the routine housekeeping, analysis, and public contact positions formerly filled by sworn officers. Theoretically, uniformed police officers could then concentrate on investigation and patrol (Skolnick and Bayley, 1986).

In Santa Ana, California, for instance, civilians are hired for a special unit of "Police Service Officers" (PSOs). Their duties are community service oriented and include: follow-up contacts with citizens and completing reports on crimes not in progress, liaison to various minority groups in the community, collecting and analyzing crime statistics, coordinating meetings on crime prevention issues, and distributing crime data to community groups. These PSOs are nonsworn officers defined by the department as paraprofessional community social workers operating under a "crime control philosophy" (Skolnick and Bayley, 1986:25–28).

These PSOs are seen by the department as a great public relations tool because they seem to have an orientation toward community service, an attitude of caring about the plight of victims and potential victims in the community, and commitment to the welfare of their community.

However, the characteristics attributed to the PSOs should be common to the department as a whole if the community policing philosophy is to guide normal police operations. Otherwise, those operating with this philosophy will be denigrated by some as mere social workers, will have second-class status, and in a budget crunch they will be the first group to be eliminated.

A new strategy now being implemented at five test sites throughout the country attempts to implement this community service philosophy as a true organizational philosophy of policing for police departments in general. The term "problem-oriented policing" (POP) was coined by Herman Goldstein to summarize an approach to policing which is an outgrowth of twenty years of research into police operations and police effectiveness. It proposes to directly attack underlying community problems that give rise to incidents that consume patrol and detective time. It is based on cultivating reliance on the expertise and creativity of line patrol officers to study problems and develop innovative solutions, and on cultivating closer police involvement with the public to ensure than the police are addressing the needs of neighborhood residents who form the law-abiding, orderly majority of a community (Spelman and Eck, 1987).

Problem-oriented policing also proposes to implement a four-step decisionmaking model to be used by patrol officers on their assigned beat. This is known as the SARA model (Scanning, Analysis, Response, Assessment).

    1. Scanning: Instead of responding to discreet incidents as law-related incidents such as burglary or robbery, officers are trained to group incidents that come to their attention into problems and patterns.

    2. Analysis: Officers working on a defined problem collect information from a variety of public and private sources — not just internal police data — to attempt to discover underlying causes of the problem and options for possible problem resolution.

    3. Response: Officers tailor a strategy of problem resolution suitable to the

characteristics of the problem. They work with citizens, businesses, and public and private agencies that are appropriate to problem resolution. They are encouraged to go beyond traditional criminal justice system remedies and to include other organizations and groups in community problem-solving.

4. Assessment: The impact of these efforts are evaluated to determine if the problem was solved or alleviated. Effectiveness can be judged, for instance, by factors such as reduced calls for service, resident satisfaction, and less complaints to policymakers about department performance [McPherson, 1989].

Ideally, the patrol officer applying a community policing philosophy using the problem-oriented, decisionmaking model would combine the characteristics of a community organizer, problem solver, social service provider, local politician, crime prevention specialist, expert in community resources, and law enforcer. Where traditional police officers have been trained to emphasize reactive strategies to criminal law violation, problem-oriented officers need to be trained in human resource management, communication and human interaction skills, problem-solving and mediation skills, and knowledge of a broad range of available community resources for problem-solving.

The San Diego Experience in Implementing Problem-Oriented Policing

The San Diego Police Department was chosen as one of the test sites for the implementation of the problem-oriented decision strategy in early 1988. Area captains and Nancy McPherson, a coordinator for the POP program, have worked together to encourage supervisors to allow patrol officers to define and to solve their own beat problems with minimal control. The department has attempted to develop a philosophy of trusting subordinates to uncover, diagnose, and plan strategies for problem solutions on their assigned beats. Patrol officers are encouraged and allowed to initiate and apply this model to situations that they have defined as appropriate for this purpose.

Patrol officers who utilize problem-oriented policing are required to keep a log documenting steps they take in applying the SARA decisionmaking model. They have not attempted to replace, but to supplement, traditional law enforcement techniques with this approach.

Some examples of attempts to implement the SARA problem-oriented approach in the San Diego Police Department are:

1. Scanning: In the southeast area of San Diego two residences were identified as long-standing breeding grounds for illegal drug activities. Hundreds of arrests in the past had not eliminated these ongoing problems. Numerous complaints and calls for service had been received by the department related to illegal drug and criminal activity at these residences. A number of search warrants were executed providing further documentation of a pattern of criminal activity and an ongoing problem.

2. Analysis: Officers began to conduct a series of interviews with neighbors to determine the underlying problem. After conducting the interviews the officers went to the housing commission, the special assistant to city councilman for that area, and city zoning and building inspection offices to determine what options they could apply. Other agencies contacted were marshalls, the city attorney, the joint San Diego Abatement Task Force, and the county narcotic task force. A major contributing factor at this stage of the process was establishing a working relationship between the police department and the owners of the property.

3. Response: The first step in eliminating the problem was a thirty-day eviction notice served by the owner to the tenants. The owner contacted the marshall's office to file the appropriate legal documentation to remove the tenants. The San Diego Police Department in conjunction with their communication division and narcotic street team started compiling information such as the number of calls for service, the number of search warrants executed, and the number of arrests at this location for the purpose of building a concrete case. Officers took tenants' arrest reports and criminal histories to the city attorney's office to have court cases expedited. The housing commission initiated a new policy to inform property owners of their responsibilities for screening tenants and ensuring that illegal activity would not take place on their property. A private senior citizen group was contacted to help give support to the owner.

4. Assessment: The problem was eliminated through eventual eviction of the tenants. This outcome was possible because of the cooperation established between the agencies listed above and the owner's willingness to monitor activities taking place on the property. Utilization of the SARA model made possible continuing cooperation and sharing of information between these agencies. To date, there have been no complaints to the police department regarding illegal drug and criminal activities at this location.

The Promise of POP

Attempts to operationalize the philosophy of community policing through the application of POP strategies appear to hold promise at this time in reorienting an approach to police professionalism which had become too narrow and estranged from a community context. These efforts to institutionalize a "mixed economy" and coproduction approach to public safety and crime prevention appear positive thus far, judged by experiences in San Diego which we have been studying recently.

Patrol officers who have used the POP approach to decisionmaking and problem-solving were surveyed and report networking with the following examples of public agencies to solve community problems such as those documented above: the welfare department, Housing and Urban Development, the city attorney's office, U.S. military commands, City Litter Control, the fire marshall, building inspection agencies, the fire department, and other criminal justice agencies. Private agencies with which working relationships were established to solve problems include: hotels, convenience stores, general contractors, property owners, property management groups, private security services, and individuals and neighborhood groups in the immediate vicinity of the defined community problem.

Many patrol officers have reported that they appreciate the opportunity this gives them for exercising independent judgment and report satisfaction with long-term problem-solving as opposed to only temporarily removing a problem individual from the situation through arrest. However, some also report that it has increased paperwork, it has increased frustration waiting for other agencies to take action, and that it increases the opportunity for citizens to get involved in voicing complaints against the police department and individual patrol officers.

It appears that opportunities for police-citizen interaction and police-private enterprise interaction are increased with this approach. Citizen-directed policing is consistent with the philosophy of community policing and the POP strategy. Joint responsibility for public safety and a community context for policing seem to be a characteristic of this approach in both theory and practice.

It also appears that, to a great extent, this approach to policing codifies and institutionalizes many of the techniques used by experienced, community-oriented police officers even under traditional agency structures. Even now, with the publicity and support given to the community policing philosophy and POP strategies, some officers adapt better than others to its opportunities and demands. Perhaps officers should be screened for this willingness and ability to adapt and should then be assigned to community policing units, rather than to the traditional 911 patrol response so that they can chart community trends and follow up on long-term planning for community problem-solving efforts.

It appears to us that the opportunities for productive community networking among public agencies, private enterprise, and citizen self-help groups provided by this approach may be its most important legacy. To some extent, this constitutes a privatization effort, as the police are no longer able to monopolize problem definition and solution. Whether they are the appropriate agency in the long run to act as brokers and ombudsmen to further this approach to public safety remains to be seen. If they are, perhaps the approach could better be characterized as network-oriented policing.

References

Bish, F., and N. Neubert (1977). "Citizen Contributions to the Production of Community Safety and Security." M. Rosentraub (ed.), *Financing Local Government: New Approaches to Old Problems.* Western Social Science Association.

Boostrom, R., and J. Henderson (1988). "The Ideology of Community Crime Prevention." *Journal of Security Administration* 11 (1):53–66.

Brown, L. (1989). "Community Policing: A Practical Guide for Police Officials." *Perspectives on Policing,* no. 12. Washington, DC: National Institute of Justice.

Brundy, J., and R. England (1983). "Toward a Definition of the Coproduction Concept," *Public Administration Review* 43: 59–65.

Chapman, B. (1970). *Police State.* New York: Praeger.

Clarke, M. (1987). "Citizenship, Community and the Management of Crime." *British Journal of Criminology* 27 (4):384–400.

Dunn, W., and J. Rohr (1984). "Adapting Theories of Public Administration to the Emerging Role of Citizens." *Public Administration Review* 6:190–91.

Ferris, J. (1984). "Coprovision: Citizen Time and Money Donations in Public Service Provision." *Public Administration Review* 44:324–33.

Greene, J., and S. Mastrofski (1988). *Community Policing: Rhetoric or Reality?* New York: Praeger.

Hall, S. et al. (1978). *Policing the Crises.* New York: Macmillan.

Hunt, D. (ed.) (1989). *PC 832 II: Peace Officer Required Training.* Tappan, NY: Customback.

Jordan, K. (1972). "Ideology and the Coming of Professionalism: American Urban Police in the 1920s and 1930s." Unpublished Ph.D. dissertation, Rutgers University.

Lavrakas, P. (1985). "Citizen Self-Help and Neighborhood Crime Prevention Policy." L. Curtis (ed.) *American Violence and Public Policy.* New Haven, CT: Yale University Press.

Levine, C. (1984). "Citizenship and Service Delivery: The Promise of Coproduction." *Public Administration Review* 6:187–89.

McPherson, N. (1989). "The Problem Solving Model." Internal memo, San Diego Police Department.

Matthews, R. (1989). *Privatizing Criminal Justice.* London: Sage.

Mawby, R. (1989). "The Voluntary Sector's Role in a Mixed Economy of Criminal Justice." R. Matthews (ed.) *Privatizing Criminal Justice.* London: Sage.

Ostrom, V., and E. Ostrom (1977). "Public Goods and Public Choices." E. Savas (ed.) *Alternatives for Delivering Public Services: Toward Improved Performance.* Boulder, CO: Westview.

Quinney, R. (1977). *Class, State, and Crime.* New York: Longman.

Percy, S. (1979). "Citizen Coproduction of Community Safety." R. Baker, and F. Meyer (eds.), *Evaluating Alternative Law Enforcement Policies.* Lexington, MA: Lexington Books.

Rich, R. (1977). "The Roles of Neighborhood Organizations in Urban Service Delivery." Working Paper W77-17. Workshop in Political Theory and Analysis, Indiana University of Pennsylvania.

Rosenbaum, D. (1987). "The Theory Behind Neighborhood Watch: Is It a Sound Fear and Crime Reduction Strategy?" *Crime and Delinquency* 33(1):103–35.

_____. (1988). *Community Crime Prevention: Does It Work?* Beverly Hills, CA: Sage.

Ryan, M., and T. Ward (1989). "Privatization and Penal Politics." R. Matthews (ed.), *Privatizing Criminal Justice.* London: Sage.

Savas, E. (1982). *Privatizing the Public Sector.* Chatham, NJ: Chatham House.

Shearing, C., and P. Stenning, (1981). "Modern Private Security: Its Growth and Implications." M. Tonry and N. Morris (eds.) *Crime and Justice: An Annual Review of Research.* Volume 3. Chicago: Chicago University Press.

Shearing, C., and P. Stenning (eds.) (1987). *Private Policing.* Newbury Park, CA: Sage.

Shernock, S. (1988). "An Empirical Examination of the Relationship Between Police Solidarity and Community Orientation." *Police Science and Administration* 16 (3) 123–42.

Skogan, W. (1987). "The Impact of Victimization on Fear." *Crime and Delinquency* 33(1):135–55.

Skolnick, J., and D. Bayley (1986). *The New Blue Line: Police Innovation in Six American Cities.* New York: Free Press.

Smith, D., and C. Uzhida (1988). "The Social Organization of Self-Helf: A Study of Defensive Weapon Ownership." *American Sociological Review* 53:94–102.

Spelman, W., and J. Eck (1987). "Problem Oriented Policing." Research in Brief. National Institute of Justice.

Trojanowicz, R., and B. Bucqueroux (1990). *Community Policing: A Contemporary Perspective.* Cincinnati: Anderson.

Walker, S. (1980). *Popular Justice.* New York: Oxford University Press.

————. (1989). *Sense and Nonsense About Crime: A Policy Guide.* Monterey, CA: Brooks/Cole.

Note: In addition to those reports mentioned above, further evaluative information on the philosophy of community policing and on the strategy of problem-oriented policing may be found in the series of occasional papers published by the National Institute of Justice in their Perspectives on Policing, Research in Action, and Research in Brief series.

6. Direct and Indirect Benefits of Intergovernmental Contracting for Police Services

Stephen L. Mehay
Rodolfo A. Gonzalez

Municipal governments have experienced a period of adjustment and retrenchment as taxpayers have demanded that taxes be reduced without sacrifices in service quality. Various arrangements have evolved over time to provide local government services. A survey by the International City Management Association (Shulman, 1982) identifies nine alternative institutional arrangements for providing local services: (1) the traditional method of government (in house) provision; (2) intergovernmental agreement, which includes intergovernmental contracting, the focus of this chapter; (3) contract purchase of a service from a private provider; (4) franchising of a private provider; (5) grants; (6) vouchers; (7) free market; (8) voluntary service; and (9) self-provision. Some communities use multiple arrangements in providing any given service. Most prior studies have focused on contracting for services from private, profit-seeking firms and estimating the cost differential between that structure and producing services in-house (Savas, 1982; Bennett and Johnson, 1980; Stevens, 1978). Little attention has been devoted to agreements between governments for providing services. Our focus is the Lakewood intergovernmental contracting plan in California, a highly developed example of nonprofit contracting of public services. Under the Lakewood system municipalities purchase basic public services from *county* government departments rather than provide the services in-house. Prior research on intergovernmental contracting has found that municipalities participating in the Lakewood Plan tend to benefit by obtaining services at a lower cost than when the service is provided in-house. Mehay (1979), for example, found that per capita spending for police services by contract cities located in Los Angeles County was 29 percent lower on average than per capita spending by in-house production cities. Similarly, Deacon (1979) found that total police expenditures were about 50 percent lower in California contract cities.[1]

These cost savings appear to be due in part to the greater efficiency of the county agency that supplies the services—the sheriff's department. Kirlin (1973) found that, compared to most municipal police departments, the Los Angeles County Sheriff's Department tended to use a greater proportion of one-man patrol cars in contract cities. Mehay (1979) observed that contract cities devote a larger fraction of their manpower to patrol activities, while noncontract municipalities tend to allocate a higher percentage to nonpatrol (overhead-type) functions. The substantial cost differential between contract and noncontract cities appears to be explained by the combination of these factors plus the scale economies of the county sheriff's department.

Our purpose is to examine the economic benefits of the Lakewood Plan to public agencies and taxpayers in jurisdictions other than the municipalities that directly contract with the county. Insofar as these secondary benefits exist, they must be added to the direct cost savings from the Lakewood system to estimate the total social impact of intergovernmental contracting.

The Niskanen (1971) theory of bureaucracy is used to model public-sector supply decisions. This model provides several implications about potential spillover benefits of the Lakewood system to other public-sector agencies. In particular, the model suggests that intergovernmental contracting generates "outside" information on the actual production cost for a service, which breaks the asymmetric bargaining pattern assumed by Niskanen. Since this cost information is available to other "trustees" who must evaluate similar budget requests from police agencies producing similar police services, it therefore shares the characteristics of a pure public good. The hypothesis advanced here is that this cost information will tend to spill over to adjacent jurisdictions, which may assist trustees in controlling the rent-seeking tendencies of public bureaus.

The analysis proceeds as follows. First we provide the basic theoretical framework for analyzing the effects of Lakewood on other public agencies. The next section undertakes an empirical analysis of the effect of Lakewood on the county sheriff's department, while the following section examines the effect on noncontracting municipalities.

An Economic Model of the Effects of Contracting

The starting point for the analysis is the Niskanen (1971) model of bureaucracy, in which public bureaus confront legislative overseers ("trustees" or "sponsors") with the equivalent of all-or-nothing output and budget offers and, as a consequence, extract all consumer surplus from the trustees. Niskanen posited that bureaus maximize budget size and concluded that bureau expenditures will absorb the benefits that trustees receive from the bureau's services.[2]

Later studies questioned this conclusion, pointing out that the superior bargaining power of the bureau in the exchange relationship with trustees is based largely on the absence of information on the bureau's true cost function.[3] Spencer (1980), for instance, demonstrates that if trustees have "the minimal information that the average cost curve intersects the demand curve," then they can limit the bureau's power to that of a simple, nondiscriminating monopoly. Furthermore, under certain conditions—constant cost and a bureau that maximizes output—this information allows trustees to exercise full control over the resulting budget.

It is not obvious, however, that this information is available without cost in most institutional settings. At a practical level, Savas (1979) cites evidence that the budgeted cost of municipally provided refuse collection is far below—30 percent on the average—the actual (per household) cost. He also finds that in municipal refuse collection cities, the user charge is well below the actual cost, whereas in contract (private) collection cities user charges tend to be aligned fairly closely with actual cost. From this and other evidence he concludes that public officials generally are ignorant of the actual cost of municipal services. This evidence seems to support the Niskanen model of bureaucracy; namely, even at the local government level, asymmetric cost information appears to characterize the budgetary process.

We shall test the hypothesis that the availability of outside cost information provides trustees with a control device that reduces the superior bargaining position of public bureaus. Not all institutional settings generate sufficient (Spencer's "minimal") information on cost and production functions to minimize bureaucratic power. However, the Lakewood system of intergovernmental contracting appears to be an institutional environment in which significant cost information is generated and which is freely available to trustees, at least in the immediate surrounding area. Thus, we hypothesize that the information generated by intergovernmental contracting will tend to reduce budget levels for municipal police departments located in the same geographical areas where contracting is widespread.

A simple model of bureaucracy, reproduced in Figure 6.1, demonstrates the major arguments.[4] For simplicity it is assumed that bureaus maximize either output or excess budget (defined as revenue in excess of the minimum necessary cost of production) and that costs are constant. In Figure 6.1, q represents output, and $C(q)/q$ represents per unit cost. The trustees' demand curve is the marginal benefit curve, labeled $A'(q)$, while the average benefit (or all-or-nothing demand) curve is $A(q)/q$. The curve labeled M is the marginal revenue curve corresponding to the per unit demand curve, $A'(q)$. With full information, the trustees instruct the bureau to produce at q_2, where marginal cost intersects marginal benefit. In exchange, the bureau receives a budget indicated by area $Ob_2P_2q_2$, and the trustees derive net benefits equal to area $b_2b_0P_2$.

In the no-information case, an output-maximizing bureau produces where average cost and benefit are equal, at point q_3, yielding a budget of $Ob_2P_3q_3$. This output-budget combination leaves zero net benefits for trustees. A bureau that maximizes excess budget will produce at q_2, the same output the trustees would choose under full information. In this case output is not excessive, but production inefficiency generates an excess budget of $b_2b_3P_4P_2$ and a total budget of $Ob_3P_4q_2$, leaving zero net benefits for trustees.

Spencer (1980) claims that both of these extreme results are unlikely since they require the trustees to "believe that average cost is decreasing in such a way that it does not cut the demand curve and moreover is tangent to $A(q)/q$" (tangent at P_3 if the bureau maximizes output, and at P_4 if it maximizes excess budget). If trustees have only the minimal necessary information that average cost intersects demand, they can ensure that at least one per unit price and output combination on their demand curve is feasible; consequently, they will not allow a bureau to set

Figure 6.1 Demand and Supply in a Bureaucracy Model

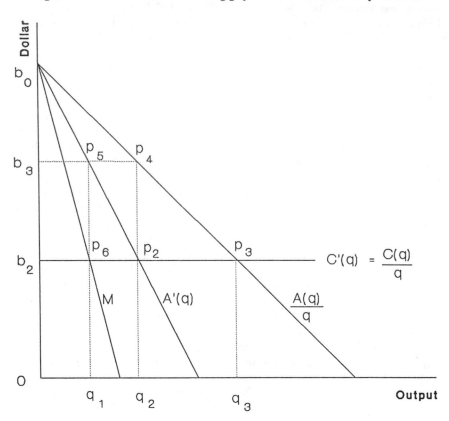

both the output and budget levels. Instead, trustees will require the bureau to quote a per unit price, at which *they* will choose the desired output level. If the bureau maximizes output, it will quote a price based on the per unit cost, Ob_2. This ensures the same result as in the full information case.[5] If the bureau maximizes excess budget, it will quote per unit price Ob_3, and will obtain excess budget $b_2b_3P_5P_6$ since the trustees will choose output q_1.[6] In this case the bureau still exploits the trustees, but not to the same extent as in the Niskanen model.

No prior studies have identified mechanisms or institutional arrangements that will generate outside information on average cost. Spencer, for example, simply asserts that trustees would have to be extremely naive to believe there is no output that yields a positive net benefit. Presumably, bureau heads who persistently misinform trustees will simply be dismissed. Despite the intuitive appeal of this argument, however, there is nothing to prevent a bureau from manipulating its output and expenditures in such a way as to persuade trustees that average cost is decreasing, that it lies above $A'(q)$, and that the best feasible output budget will yield only a small surplus. More important, even if the minimal information is available, it will not be sufficient to fully control a bureau that attempts to maximize excess budget rather than total budget.

In practice, the availability to the trustees of the minimal necessary information will depend on the institutional setting. When institutions exist that generate outside information on per unit cost, trustee control of bureau bargaining power will tend to be greater and budget levels smaller; when such information is absent or very costly to acquire, trustee control will be weaker and budget levels higher. A comparison of institutional settings forms the basis for the empirical analysis in this chapter. In particular, we argue that the Lakewood contracting system generates the necessary cost information in counties where the system is widespread.

In normal budgetary settings a county bureau provides services only to its own trustees (the county board of supervisors in California) in exchange for an annual lump-sum appropriation. In contrast, a Lakewood county department that sells services on contract is forced to "cost out" and sell each service at a per unit price that covers cost.[7] Once the contract price is determined, the same price must be charged to all municipalities who then purchase the quantity desired at the quoted price. Assuming county departments seek to retain existing customers and attract new ones, the price must be set below what it would cost the purchasing city to produce the service in-house. This constraint on the price creates an incentive for county departments to control the production cost of the contracted service,[8] so that the price charged may approximate the minimum per unit cost of production.

Once available, the quoted price becomes a pure public good in the form of valuable information on the true cost of producing a given service. This information is freely available to other trustees who must evaluate similar budget requests by police departments; furthermore, the information places these trustees in a position to choose their desired output level at the per unit contract price, ensuring that they receive a positive net benefit.[9]

There are two sets of trustees who stand to benefit from the cost information generated by the Lakewood Plan. One group is the county board of supervisors who oversee the county sheriff, whose operation includes the unincorporated areas of the county as well as the contracting cities. In evaluating the sheriff's request for funds to operate in the unincorporated areas, the trustees will be guided by the cost information generated in the market-like interaction between the sheriff and the contract cities. The general implication is that the noncontract (unincorporated area) portion of the sheriff's budget in counties that contract will tend to be below the sheriff's budget in unincorporated areas in counties that do not contract.[10]

The second set of trustees affected by the cost information consists of those cities providing police services in-house and located in geographical areas where contracting is practiced. The trustees of these cities also will receive (or have ready access to) the per unit cost and budget information generated by the Lakewood system. Although this information is unlikely to mirror each city's actual cost of production, it will at least represent Spencer's "minimal necessary information" to control appropriation of net benefits by bureaus. If so, the Lakewood Plan will generate a spillover benefit (of information) to municipalities that are not participants in the contracting process.

Thus, the general hypothesis to be tested in this chapter is that the police budgets of noncontracting cities and the sheriff's budget in unincorporated territories will benefit from the cost information produced by the plan when these agencies are located in areas where the Lakewood Plan exists. We test this hypothesis with two data sets, one for the unincorporated area operations of county sheriff's departments in California (Tables 6.1 and 6.2) and one for noncontract (independent) cities in California (Tables 6.3 and 6.4). It remains an empirical question, however, whether the "outside" cost information in Lakewood counties is sufficient to significantly constrain the bargaining power of Lakewood Plan departments, or whether non–Lakewood jurisdictions also possess a (different) channel of outside information. If the necessary information is readily available to trustees in all institutional settings, then we would observe no significant difference in budget levels across county departments differing only by contract structure.

An Empirical Analysis of County Sheriff Expenditures

A reduced form expenditure equation is specified for county sheriff's departments to estimate the impact of contract structure on expenditures (see Table 6.1). The dependent variable, EXP, is measured as the sheriff's annual operating outlays per capita in the unincorporated area. The expenditures are measured net of the revenue earned from supplying contract cities. County contract status is captured by a dummy variable, CONTRACT, which equals unity for those counties that supply law enforcement services on contract to incorporated cities; in addition, the supplying agency must receive compensation for the service, and the rate charged must include departmental overhead.[11] The sample consists of fifty-three of California's fifty-eight counties, fifteen of which were classified as contract counties.[12]

The reduced form expenditure equation includes both supply and demand factors in the specification. To measure the effect of police output (Q) on unit cost, the number of major felony crimes recorded in the jurisdiction of the respective sheriff's department is included in the specification. The number of major felony crimes is used, rather than the felony crime rate, to capture the effect of total output volume on per unit cost.[13]

While most previous studies have adopted either the rate or volume of felony crime as a direct output measure (McPheters and Stronge, 1974; Swimmer, 1974), other indicators also have been used: clearance rates (Carr-Hill and Stern, 1973); conviction rates (Votey and Phillips, 1975); arrest rates (Chapman et al., 1975); the number of subactivities performed (Schmandt and Stephens, 1960); and a weighted index of offenses cleared, accidents investigated, and police vehicle miles (Walzer, 1972). We have adopted felony crimes as the major output measure because most alternative police output indicators represent *intermediate* measures of police activity, rather than *final* output measures. However, for purposes of comparison we also employ the volume of juvenile and adult felony arrests as a second

Table 6.1 Variable Definition and Descriptive Statistics: County Sheriff Sample

Variable Name	Description	Mean (Standard Deviation)
EXP	Net annual sheriff expenditures per capita, 1980–81*	$64.64 (43.46)
CONTRACT	=1 for counties that supply law enforcement to incorporated cities†	0.26 (0.44)
WAGE	Average monthly earnings for full-time county employees, 1982§	$1089.53 (140.37)
POP	Population of unincorporated county area, 1980**	110015.0 (165907.0)
CRIME	Total felony crimes, 1980††	17520.0 (51400.0)
VALU	Assessed property value per capita, 1980–81	16544.0 (13893.0)
AGE	Median age of population, 1980§§	30.8 (3.1)
DENSITY	Population per square mile, 1980§§	258.1 (463.6)
GROWTH	Population growth rate, 1970–80§§	0.34 (0.21)
ARRESTS	Total adult and juvenile felony arrests††	28908.0 (72292.0)

Sources: *California State Controller (a).
       **Census Bureau (a).
       †Santa Clara County.
       ††California Bureau of Criminal Statistics.
       §Census Bureau (b).
       §§County and City Data Book, 1983.

measure of police output. All output proxies are squared in their respective equations to test for scale effects.

The specification of the reduced form spending equation follows that of previous expenditure studies (Gonzalez and Mehay, 1985). Since the underlying model is based on bureau supply considerations, a median voter framework is not specified. In the specification, community wealth—measured by the per capita assessed value in the unincorporated area (VALU)—captures the effect of the budget constraint on police spending. Median population age (AGE) is included to reflect community factors that affect the demand for police services. The estimated coefficient of VALU is expected to be positive, but the sign of the coefficient for AGE is ambiguous. If youth tend to commit more offenses, a youthful population may increase the demand for police protection. On the other hand, an older population may increase the demand for police services due to higher wealth levels and increased vulnerability.

Population density (DENSITY) also has opposing effects on spending. On the demand side, denser areas are characterized by more crime and greater congestion, which increase the demand for police services; on the cost side, economies of density may reduce spending.

The county population growth rate from 1970 to 1980 (GROWTH) is included in the specification to account for the effect of rapid growth on the demand for public facilities. Rapid growth rates normally are positively correlated with public spending. However, local outlays may lag behind population growth, in which case the coefficient of GROWTH could be negative or zero. Finally, following Borcherding and Deacon (1972), public employee earnings (WAGE) are included to capture differences in the cost of public services.

Definitions of the variables, means, and data sources are displayed in Table 6.1. The final expenditure equation is specified as follows:

$$\text{EXP} = a_0 + b_1 \text{ (CONTRACT)} + b_2 \text{ (Q)} + b_3(Q^2) + b_4 \text{ (VALU)}$$
$$+ b_5 \text{ (AGE)} + b_6 \text{ (DENSITY)} + b_7 \text{ (GROWTH)} \tag{1}$$
$$+ b_8 \text{ (WAGE)} + e$$

The results of estimating this equation by ordinary least squares are displayed in Table 6.2.

Column 1 in Table 6.2 displays the results of estimating the police spending equation using total crime as the output measure; column 2 uses total arrests. The estimated coefficients in Table 6.2 generally have the expected signs. One noteworthy result is that both output measures suggest the presence of scale economies.

While the coefficient of DENSITY is consistently negative—which suggests that economies of density may play a significant role in police services—the coefficient is not statistically significant at usual levels in either equation. The coefficient of GROWTH also is insignificant. It may be that the growth rate for the entire county does not accurately capture the growth pattern of the county's unincorporated areas.

The coefficient of CONTRACT is negative and significant in both estimations in Table 6.2, lending some support to the hypothesis that the information advantages of contract supply can influence bureau bargaining power and bureau costs. The coefficient of CONTRACT indicates that annual sheriffs' operating outlays per capita in unincorporated areas are approximately 9 percent lower (estimated at the mean) in counties where the Lakewood Plan is widespread than in counties where the plan is not in effect.[14]

Table 6.2 Sheriff Expenditures in Unincorporated Areas (Dependent Variable = EXP)

Variable	Equation 1	Equation 2
Constant	41.21	45.32
	(0.76)	(0.84)
CONTRACT	−20.49	−20.35
	(2.15)	(2.18)
CRIME	−0.005	−
	(1.43)	−
CRIME^2	0.17×10^8	−
	(1.94)	−
ARREST	−	−0.0003
	−	(1.71)
ARREST^2	−	0.89×10^9
	−	(2.43)
VALU	0.003	0.003
	(9.45)	(9.60)
AGE	−1.48	−1.65
	(1.23)	(1.37)
DENSITY	−0.041	−0.042
	(0.84)	(0.90)
GROWTH	9.58	10.11
	(0.55)	(0.59)
WAGE	0.03	0.03
	(0.71)	(0.75)
R^2	0.77	0.78
F-statistic	18.70	19.06
(d.f.)	(8,44)	(8,44)

Note: Absolute t-statistics in parentheses.

An Empirical Analysis of Noncontract Cities

To test for the impact of intergovernmental contracting on expenditures in non-contract cities, a sample is constructed of all California municipalities exceeding 25,000 population. The original sample contained 162 cities, but omitting the contract cities and cities with missing data reduced the final sample to 138 noncontracting communities. To test for the effect of outside information a new dummy variable is constructed, PROXIM, which equals unity for noncontracting cities that are contiguous to a contract city.

The assumption of this variable is that a noncontracting community must be adjacent to a contracting city in order to observe the maximum impact of the information flow from the plan. That is, even though two cities—one a contracting city and one a noncontracting city—may be located in the same county, if they are not

Table 6.3 Variable Definition and Descriptive Statistics: Noncontract City Sample

Variable Name	Description	Mean (Standard Deviation)
POLPC	Police expenditure per capita, 1980	$ 61.17 (15.25)
PROXIM	Dummy variable=1 for cities contiguous to contract cities	0.25 (0.41)
CRIME	Total felony crimes, 1980	7360.1 (2181.0)
HOUSE	Median house value, 1980	$90,078.0 (27,309.0)
AGE	Median age, 1980	29.65 (3.78)
DENSITY	Population per square mile, 1980	4858.4 (2628.9)
GROWTH	Percent population change, 1970–80	29.06 (38.4)
WAGE	Average monthly wage, city government employees, 1981	$ 1863.32 (224.92)
AID	Intergovernmental revenue per capita	$ 355.49 (131.75)

Source: Census Bureau, *County and City Data Book, 1983.*

adjacent the cost information generated in the contract city is assumed to provide no benefit to the noncontract city. Noncontract cities are not influenced by cost information from the Lakewood Plan unless they are contiguous to a contracting city.

There are two reasons for this assumption. First, in some counties the cities that contract with the sheriff are very small. These cities are unlikely to influence their larger neighbors, no matter how accurate the cost information that is generated by the contracting process. Neighboring cities are unlikely to judge that the production environment in small communities is equivalent to their own. Second, the majority of contract cities in California are located in Los Angeles County, which is very large in terms of geographical size, population, and the number of incorporated municipalities (77). Portions of Los Angeles County are still rural and it is unlikely that the experiences of the urban areas will translate to communities in the rural sections. Of the 138 noncontracting cities in the sample, 25 percent were contiguous to a contract city. All data were taken from the Census Bureau's *County and City Data Book, 1983.*

The specification of the reduced form expenditure equation is similar to that

Table 6.4 Municipal Police Expenditures in Noncontract Cities (Dependent Variable = POLPC)

Variable	All Cities (N = 138)	Cities 50,000 (N = 74)	Cities 50,000 (N = 64)
Constant	−7.514	21.13	−43.93
	(0.48)	(0.97)	(1.53)
PROXIM	−8.628	−8.507	−8.889
	(2.58)	(2.20)	(1.56)
CRIME	−3.771	-7.3×10^{-5}	0.008
	(1.92)	(0.35)	(0.66)
CRIME^2	1.3×10^{-9}	3.9×10^{-10}	7.5×10^{-7}
	(2.00)	(0.57)	(0.39)
HOUSE	4.9×10^{-5}	8.3×10^{-5}	1.1×10^{-4}
	(0.83)	(1.09)	(0.71)
AGE	0.334	−0.277	0.501
	(0.73)	(0.41)	(0.85)
DENSITY	-3.9×10^{-6}	-6.3×10^{-4}	.001
	(0.01)	(0.90)	(1.39)
GROWTH	−0.062	−0.115	−0.019
	(1.53)	(2.08)	(0.37)
WAGE	0.021	0.022	0.016
	(3.32)	(2.87)	(1.71)
AID	0.066	0.035	0.093
	(7.82)	(3.43)	(6.69)
R^2	0.56	0.51	0.75
F-statistic	17.35	7.50	16.67
(d.f.)	(9,125)	(9,65)	(9,50)

Note: Absolute t-statistics in parentheses.

in equation (1), with two exceptions. The amount of aid received from higher levels of government has an obvious effect on a city's budget constraint and is captured by including intergovernmental aid per capita (AID). This variable was omitted from the analysis of county sheriffs' departments because aid received by the county could not be apportioned to the unincorporated areas on any reasonable basis. Second, since assessed property value data was unavailable for all California cities, median house value (HOUSE) was used instead. This will be an accurate proxy for assessed property value to the extent that residential property constitutes a significant share of the municipal tax base. Descriptions of the variables and their means for this sample are presented in Table 6.3.

The results of estimating the police spending equation for the noncontract cities are presented in Table 6.4. The spending equation is estimated in column 1 for the full sample of cities. However, an F-test (Chow Test) for structural differences rejected the null hypothesis of identical coefficients for cities in different population groupings. Therefore, the sample was partitioned into two size groups: those below and those above 50,000 population. The results of reestimating the spending equation for the two subsamples are presented in columns 2 and 3 of Table 6.4.

The results in Table 6.4 are consistent with those in Table 6.2. In particular, the coefficients of the crime (output) variables once again support the existence of economies of scale in police services, at least for the full sample. The scale effect seems to be due entirely to differences in city size rather than output volume, since the scale effect is not observed in the two subsamples. One difference between Tables 6.2 and 6.4 is that the coefficient of GROWTH is negative in Table 6.4 and is statistically significant in the large-city sample; however, the coefficient of GROWTH is not significant in the small-city sample. Also, economies of density do not appear to be important in these communities. The coefficients of both AID and WAGE are positive and significant in Table 6.4.

The coefficient of PROXIM is negative and significant in the full sample and in the large-city sample, but is significant only at the 12 percent level in the small-city sample. For all three samples the coefficient of PROXIM indicates that noncontract cities located adjacent to contract cities spend approximately 12 percent less on police services (at the mean) than noncontract cities that are not adjacent to a contract city. This estimate of the cost savings is consistent with that observed in the county sheriff sample.

It remains for future research to improve our understanding of the nature of the information flow between contract and noncontract cities and between other provision types. Certainly case studies are one technique to identify the nature of the interaction between these two or any other types of governmental provision structures. In addition, an improved econometric specification of the model offered here is warranted. Nonetheless, the empirical results obtained here are remarkable, given the preliminary nature of the test; in both empirical tests a pronounced spillover effect of contracting on other jurisdictions is observed.

Summary and Conclusions

The Niskanen theory of bureaucracy relies on the assumption that trustees react passively to a bureau's output/budget offers. Our results suggest that this is not the case in all local service production environments. In institutional structures where information is available at a sufficiently low cost, trustees appear to be in a position to limit the rent-seeking tendencies of local public bureaus. However, the empirical tests do not permit a determination of whether public bureaus still are able to manipulate their sponsors to some extent, even when some information on bureau cost function is available. That is, these results suggest that bureaucratic rents are less than they would be in the absence of fee-for-service contracting, but do not indicate whether contracting induces least-cost production.

What can be concluded is that the Lakewood system of intergovernmental service agreements offers important spillover benefits to other government jurisdictions located in proximity to the system. These spillover benefits must be added to any direct cost savings that accrue to purchasing cities in order to determine the total efficiency improvement associated with the Lakewood system.

One suggested strategy for reducing the inefficiency associated with monopoly bureaus is to set up two bureaus to compete for the trustees' budget (Niskanen, 1971). Interbureau competition would generate the necessary cost information for trustees to accurately evaluate budget requests. The Lakewood contract system appears to create this desired outcome without introducing the transactions costs associated with the duplication of bureaus. By generating a flow of information on production cost for a given service, the Lakewood system eases the trustees' task of monitoring departmental performance and increases the overall efficiency of local production.

Notes

1. Deacon noted that the *spending* differential, which is actually observed, could be due either to demand or cost differences. Although no sophisticated tests were performed, Deacon concluded that the difference was mainly due to lower cost rather than to simply lower output.

2. In Niskanen's simple model the output levels tend to be excessive, indicating allocative inefficiency. More general models (see Tullock, 1974; Migue and Belanger, 1974; Niskanen, 1975) have assumed that bureaus maximize excess budget (revenue in excess of the minimum cost of production) and concluded that production inefficiency is also a characteristic of bureau operation.

3. Breton and Wintrobe (1975) maintain that trustees will not react passively to the bureau's output/budget offers but will invest in output-control and shirking-control devices. These devices include direct monitoring, overlapping bureaus, duplication of services, and purchasing information from alternative sources, including lower levels within the bureau itself. Toma and Toma (1980) describe several methods trustees can use to acquire the necessary cost information.

4. The graphical analysis follows that in Spencer (1980). Maximizing output is the same as maximizing total budget, so long as marginal benefit of output is positive.

5. If per unit cost is rising rather than constant then the output-maximizing bureau will still exercise some power.

6. Since the bureau is restricted to sell at a per unit price, it maximizes excess budget by behaving like a nondiscriminating monopoly.

7. Contract prices are based on a formula that, by state law, must include recovery of divisional and department overhead expenses, as well as the direct expenses of the service (Sonenblum et al., 1977).

8. Kirlin (1973) indicates that a major goal of the Los Angeles County Sheriff's Department has been to minimize the contract price charged for general law enforcement. He also shows that, in order to keep contract prices low, the sheriff's department has attempted to improve internal efficiency.

9. Toma and Toma (1980) note that information on the *actual* cost will control output maximization but not shirking, which requires information on *least* cost of production. In the

Lakewood structure the information generated will allow trustees to control both shirking and excess output, assuming that the department's goals of attracting and maintaining contract customers creates a sufficient competitive incentive to minimize production cost.

10. This conclusion rests in part on the assumption that the demand for county services is price inelastic. However, the bulk of prior research supports this assumption (Inman, 1979).

11. The classification of counties is based on a 1970 survey (Santa Clara County). A recent telephone survey by the authors confirmed that this classification scheme was still valid.

12. The omitted counties included four small rural counties and San Francisco, the state's only consolidated city-county government.

13. The expenditure equation was also estimated using crime rates (per 100,000 population) and arrest rates. This substitution did not alter the basic results (in Table 6.2), although the estimated scale effects were somewhat weaker.

14. Public bureaus often are assumed to be interested in expanding their overall size and clientele. Given that participation in the Lakewood Plan offers county agencies the opportunity to expand, an unanswered question is why the system is not more widespread? One rationale is offered by the authors. County officials may be well aware of the public good characteristics of the cost information generated by the plan. If so, since their contract operations are only a small portion of their total revenue, the cost of engaging in contracting may be a reduction in revenues from their unincorporated area operations and a reduction in discretionary revenue that may exceed any small gains from the contract operation. Of course, the fact that intergovernmental contracting is not widely adopted may be explained simply by a lack of demand for this service delivery system rather than a lack of supply incentives.

References

Ahlbrandt, R. (1973). "Efficiency in the Provision of Fire Services." *Public Choice* 16:1–15.

Bennett, J., and M. Johnson (1980). "Tax Reduction Without Sacrifice: Private Sector Production of Public Services." *Public Finance Quarterly* 8:363–96.

Borcherding, T., and R. Deacon (1972). "The Demand for the Services of Non-Federal Governments." *American Economic Review* 63:891–901.

Breton, A., and R. Wintrobe (1975). "The Equilibrium Size of a Budget Maximizing Bureau: A Note on Niskanen's Theory of Bureaucracy. "*Journal of Political Economy* 83 (February): 195–207.

California, Bureau of Criminal Statistics (1980). Criminal Justice Profile.

California, State Controller (1980–81a). Financial Transactions Concerning Counties of California, Annual Report.

_____. (1980–81b). Financial Transactions Concerning Streets and Roads of Cities and Counties of California, Annual Report.

California, State Department of Finance (1981). California Statistical Abstract. Sacramento.

Carr-Hill, R., and N. Stern (1973). "An Econometric Model of the Supply and Control of Offenses in England and Wales." *Journal of Public Economics* 2:289–318.

Chapman, J., et al. (1975). "Crime Prevention, the Police Production Function, and Budgeting." *Public Finance* 30:197–215.

Deacon, R. (1979). "The Expenditure Effects of Alternative Public Supply Institutions." *Public Choice* 34:381–97.

Gonzalez, R., and S. Mehay (1985). "Bureaucracy and the Divisibility of Local Public Output." *Public Choice* 45:89–101.

Inman, R. (1979). "The Fiscal Performance of Local Governments: An Interpretative Review." P. Mieszkowski and M. Straszheim (eds.), *Current Issues in Urban Economics.* Baltimore: Johns Hopkins University Press.

Kemper, P., and J. Quigley (1976). *The Economics of Refuse Collection.* Cambridge, MA: Ballinger.

Kirlin, J. (1973). "Impact of Contract Services Arrangements Upon the L.A. Sheriff's Department and Law Enforcement in Los Angeles County." *Public Policy* 21:553–84.

McPheters, L., and W. Stronge (1974). "Law Enforcement Expenditures and Urban Crime." *National Tax Journal* 27:633–44.

Mehay, S. (1979). "Intergovernmental Contracting for Urban Police Services." *Land Economics* 55:59–72.

Migue, J., and G. Belanger (1974). "Toward a General Theory of Managerial Discretion." *Public Choice* 17:27–42.

Niskanen, W. (1971). *Bureaucracy and Representative Government.* Chicago: Aldine.

—————. (1975). "Bureaucrats and Politicians." *Journal of Law and Economics* 18:617–43.

Santa Clara County, Office of the County Executive (1970). "Contract Law Enforcement: A Survey of California Counties." Mimeo.

Savas, E. C. (1979). "How Much Do Government Services Really Cost?" *Urban Affairs Quarterly* 15 (September): 23–42.

—————. (1982). *Privatizing the Public Sector.* Chatham, NJ: Chatham House.

Schmandt, H., and G. Stephens (1960). "Measuring Municipal Output." *National Tax Journal* 13:369–75.

Shulman, M. (1982). "Alternative Approaches for Delivering Public Services." *Urban Data Service Reports,* Vol. 14, No. 10. Washington, DC: International City Management Association.

Sonenblum, S., et al. (1977). *How Cities Provide Services.* Cambridge, MA: Ballinger.

Spencer, B. (1980). "Outside Information and the Degree of Monopoly Power of a Public Bureau." *Southern Economic Journal* 47:228–33.

Stevens, B. (1978). "Scale, Market Structure, and the Cost of Refuse Collection," *Review of Economics and Statistics* 60:438–48.

Swimmer, E. (1974). "Measurement of the Effectiveness of Urban Law Enforcement." *Southern Economic Journal* 40:618–30.

Tiebout, C. (1956). "A Pure Theory of Local Public Expenditure." *Journal of Political Economy* 56:416–24.

Toma, M., and E. Toma (1980). "Bureaucratic Responses to Tax Limitation Amendments." *Public Choice* 35:333–48.

Tullock, G. (1974). "Dynamic Hypothesis on Bureaucracy." *Public Choice* 19:127–31.

U.S. Bureau of the Census (1980a). Census of Population.

—————. (1980b). Census of Governments.

—————. (1980c). County Business Patterns.

U.S. Department of Justice, FBI (1980). Uniform Crime Reports.

Votey, H., and L. Phillips (1975). "Crime Control in California." *Journal of Legal Studies* 4: 327–49.

Walzer, N. (1972). "Economies of Scale and Municipal Police Services." *Review of Economics and Statistics* 54:431–438.

7. An Empirical Analysis of Contracting Out Local Government Services

Dolores Tremewan Martin
Robert M. Stein

Local government good and service delivery has always been characterized by a highly complex set of interrelationships between governmental units and private-sector actors. As early as 1900 cities contracted with private-sector producers; thus use of private-sector delivery mechanisms is not radically new. What is new is the increasing use of such devices to produce the output of the local government market. A 1982–83 representative sample of U.S. cities with 10,000 or more population shows that 92 percent of the cities contract out all, or part of, at least one of their functional responsibilities (see Figure 7.1).

It is argued that the shifting of government functions to the private sector will make governmental service delivery systems more cost effective by opening up competing channels of information and introducing competitive pressures (Sonenblum, Ries, and Kirlin, 1977; Bish and Ostrom, 1973; Ostrom and Ostrom, 1971). Considerable research efforts examined the efficiency aspects of contracting out particular services in local government markets in the United States, Canada, Britain, and West Germany. The vast amount of the empirical evidence suggests that indeed the restructuring of delivery mechanisms can lead to substantial reductions in the cost of providing a given good or service (Bennett and Johnson, 1981; Hamer, 1983; Straussman, 1981; Savas, 1982).

Alternatively, an extensive body of literature draws attention to the deficiencies of political institutions, bureaucratic organizations, and regulatory/legal processes that limit the efficiency with which governments respond to citizens' preferences (Niskanen, 1971; Buchanan, 1967; Tullock, 1970). Thus, it is important to investigate under what conditions governments are likely to alter service arrangements and shed activities that truly can be provided or produced more efficiently by the private sector.

Advocates of local government restructuring argue that the efficiency gains generated by the introduction of alternative producers will lead to net reductions in the size of the public sector via reduced expenditures and lower tax levies (Butler, 1985; Pirie, 1985; Savas, 1982; Bennett and Johnson, 1981). Shifting functions to private entities is seen as a mechanism to make government expenditure both smaller and more efficient. Restructuring government, either federal, state, or

Figure 7.1
Proportion of Municipal Functions Contracted: 1982–83

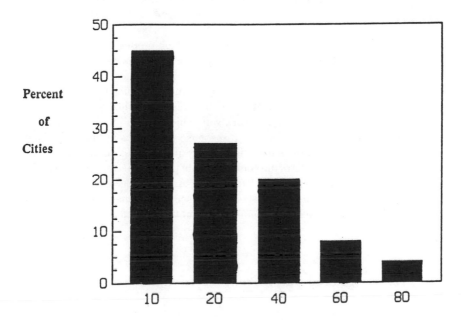

Percent

of

Cities

Percent of Functions Contracted

Source: Local Government Data Base, U.S. Advisory Commission on Intergovernmental Relations, Washington, DC 1986.

local, to make it more efficient is clearly desirable; however, it does *not* follow that more efficiency in government delivery systems will be translated into smaller levels of public expenditures.

There are numerous alternative strategies that a governmental decisionmaker might adopt when reaping efficiency gains from a nontraditional delivery mechanism. For example, the gains could be passed on to the citizen/taxpayer in the form of lower taxes or reduced fees, permitting individuals to receive the same or a better bundle of services at a lower net cost. Alternatively, the gains might be redirected toward providing more or different goods and services for residents. In this case the total cost of government would remain the same or increase, with citizens receiving a larger quantity and or better quality of the service "privatized" or more of other goods and services.

Contracting out is the most common form of privatization employed by localities (Ferris and Grady, 1986; ICMA, 1983) and is the focus of the following analysis. A comprehensive examination of contracting out must address at least two related issues: first, why do public-sector managers choose to alter their government's cur rent delivery mechanisms, and secondly, what determines the distribution of any resulting efficiency gains? These questions can only be addressed within a theoretical framework that models public-sector behavior and seeks to provide clues as to the likely response of public-sector managers and politicians to alterations in institutional arrangements.

The research presented here focuses exclusively on production decision questions. Our intention is to first model the aggregate decision process, and then focus our empirical analysis on a specific functional area – public safety. If our model accurately reflects the determinants of local government contracting decisions, we expect that the results of empirical tests at both levels will be highly consistent.[1]

Section one will develop a framework with which to analyze the behavior of public sector managers and politicians in response to changes in the institutional arrangements for service production. Section two presents an outline of the empirical specification of a model of the contracting out process. Section three explains our research design and operational measures. An empirical estimation of the model is tested in section four and the concluding section summarizes the empirical findings with respect to the determinants of the contracting out process and poses questions for further inquiry.

The Process of Local Government Decisionmaking

For purposes of modeling the local government contracting decision process, we chose as a referent decisionmaker in this interactive process the chief administrative officer (city manager, city councilman, county commissioner, or mayor). We are most interested in the effect the position of chief administrative officer (CAO) has on the decision to contract out. Of course the CAO's discretion varies, given the set of political and economic constraints he faces.

The CAO sets an agenda containing alternatives, consisting of a bundle of tax and expenditure components for representatives of the electorate; these representatives then choose some bundle of public goods and some production mechanism. Within this decisionmaking framework, it is the CAO's utility function which tends to be most important. Thus, we must examine the benefits our referent decisionmaker can expect to receive from changes in the mechanism of public-sector production. Budget preferences of the electorate tend to be effective only indirectly through testimony at public hearings before county or city councils, citizen committees, or voting directly on initiatives and referendums, and by turning representatives "out" at the polls.

A growing body of literature devoted to the investigation of output-pricing policies of public-sector decisionmakers asserts that CAOs behave analogously to private-sector entrepreneurs, with the same incentive to restrict competition and extract monopoly profits (Breton, 1974; Wagner and Weber, 1976; Martin and Wagner, 1978). As a general case, it is argued that the primary difference between the two classes of entrepreneurs is that in the public sector, entrepreneurs do not have residual claimant status. Therefore, they cannot directly take home any monetary rewards from making their agency more efficient or from their monopoly position as the sole supplier of a good or service. If, however, the financial rewards of public-sector management are tied to the size of the budget managed, then it is clearly in a manager's interest to expand the size of the budget. Niskanen (1971) has argued quite persuasively that this is a very common behavioral pattern for government bureau managers at the federal government level, while Staaf (1977) found evidence of similar behavior among local school administrators.

Given the institutional structure, CAOs, in pursuit of their own self-interest, and salary levels associated with their office (Tullock, 1970) rather than pursue low-cost production of public-sector output. It is argued that the ability of the public-sector employee to obtain these financial advancements and perquisites of office primarily depends on the size and composition of the budget he controls; thus, it is clearly in his best interest to manipulate the public budget (Klatzky, 1970; Staaf, 1977; E. Ostrom and Parks, 1982).

The local government decisionmaker, like any other member of the community, pays taxes and enjoys benefits from the provision of the collective goods bundle. Unlike other members of the community, he also benefits directly from either an expansion of public spending levels or an alteration in budget composition in terms of his utility and personal income. When compared to the median voter, the CAO, for the same level of utility, will select a goods mix that contains more public goods and less private, as the relative price of the public goods bundle is lower for the CAO (Martin and Schmidt, 1981). The CAO agenda setters will want higher levels of government expenditure, not because preferences are necessarily different from those of the median voter but because they face a different constraint. The price differential exists because a portion of the CAO's income is determined by the level of the public spending.[2]

While the budget level is no doubt an important factor in the determination of the CAO's present income, the individual may not strictly seek to maximize public spending. Varying the composition of the total budget may also increase or decrease a decisionmaker's real income. Ostrom and Parks (1982) found that police chiefs derive considerable satisfaction from specialized personnel and staff that reduce their administrative load while Lee (1972) found that the status of hospital administrators is defined in part by the "inputs" the hospital employs to produce its services. Conversely, the service mix may lead to increased management problems. Certain services, for example, may be a source of taxpayer/consumer dissatisfaction due to irregular delivery or nonuniformity of quality. In these instances, CAOs may constantly have to field citizen complaints about public services. Contracting out or load shedding the services may well increase the "real income" of the CAO by making his job less stressful and more pleasant (see McGuire, Oshfeldt, and Cott, 1987).

This view of the service bundle provides one explanation why CAOs may voluntarily reduce their control. In general, it is very difficult for citizens to monitor the quantity or quality of local public goods due to the lack of close correspondence between benefits received and tax prices (Brainard, Dolbear, and Trenery, 1967).

It is more likely that citizen complaints would generate a delivery change response from the CAO for services where it is possible to monitor poor performance, governmental shirking, or when alternative production costs are observable. These characteristics most generally apply to local government activities where private goods are funded publicly — toll goods — such as swimming pools, golf courses, and garbage collection.

The Decision to Contract Out

Even if the self-interested actor model of local government decisionmaking reflects social reality, there are several important forces at work in the local government market that will shape the response of CAOs in their pursuit of financial advancements and perquisites of public office. Any decision to contract out will be shaped by the complex legal, legislative, economic, and political arrangements that exist in the local government market in any particular state. In predicting which jurisdictions will utilize the alternative delivery mechanism of contracting out, a number of factors would appear to have important explanatory value:
1. the degree of competition among local units;
2. the degree of competition among potential alternative producers;
3. the "fiscal health" of the jurisdiction;
4. the upward mobility of political decisionmakers;
5. the method of financing service provision;
6. the composition of the work force;
7. the institutional structure imposed by the state.

Supply Side Competition

Competitive pressures play an important role in constraining the ability of the CAO to extract any fiscal surplus from the residents of the given jurisdiction.[3] The availability of large numbers of government units providing a wide variety of public goods and services reduces the power of any single CAO to pursue policies that the taxpayer consumer is unwilling to support. In a metropolitan area for example, consumers not only have the choice of alternative cities, they also have easier access to information concerning the relative cost of public goods. Recent research (Bish, 1984) suggests that the single most important economic variable in explaining the cost saving from contracting out is the presence of a competitive environment. Obviously, unless alternative producers are available, neither the governmental manager or consumer taxpayers have a viable means to replace self-production; therefore, we predict that jurisdictions located in areas with a large number of producers — either public or private — will engage in more contracting out, *ceteris paribus*. Previous studies of local government functional responsibility find that larger jurisdictions engage in more functional responsibilities. Therefore, we expect that the size of the governmental unit will be positively related to the number of functions provided (Stein, 1982). The empirical analysis will provide a mechanism to separate these two effects. Both the number of producers – public and private – and city and county population should be positively related to the degree of contracting out.

Fiscal Viability

Increasing the budget size may not always be an alternative available to the CAO, given spending lids or taxpayer resistance to increased levies. Alternative production strategies may provide a mechanism to rearrange the public spending to produce a more preferred bundle of goods, given the CAO's utility function. Consider a typical case. When faced with rising costs, citizen taxpayers are unwilling to accept either a decrease in the local government services or a tax increase. The level of public spending of the jurisdiction is effectively constrained and the CAO may come under increased public scrutiny with respect to his management record. Further, if self-production, financed out of general taxation, is the predominant mode of service delivery for the community, the referent decisionmaker is faced with the constraint that to add to the perquisites of office, he must somehow free up committed resources. If private production via contracting out actually leads to cost savings, the CAO will have an incentive to alter the production mode if he can capture any or all of the cost savings for some more preferred budget mix.

Given the current environment of fiscal stringency, CAOs may face very slim prospects for budget expansion without some demonstration that efficiency goals have been pursued and gains exhausted. We predict, therefore, that the longer a fiscal constraint has been binding on a locality the more likely it is to employ contracting out as a method of service production. Further, the type of fiscal constraint (debt limit versus tax ceiling) may have differential impacts. We have constructed an index of fiscal stringency in an attempt to capture the degree of fiscal discretion across localities.

The Market for Managers

While it is true that the CAO is not a residual claimant, it may well be the case that an individual administrator can, under certain circumstances, reap a portion of the profits or losses from his management activities. It is not uncommon for a set of fiscal consequences to be associated with a specific public-sector actor. Further, at the local government level this may have important efficiency consequences as there exists a highly organized market for local government management – the professional city manager or county administrator. A cursory examination of the advertisements in the professional manager market suggests that cost saving techniques – either contracting out or more efficient self-production – appear to be important factors of the hiring decision.

Elected local officials can, of course, use their management record to increase their permanent income – that is, mayors capturing governorships – however, upward mobility appears to be almost exclusively limited to a given geographic area, the state. Given the greater employment opportunities for professional local government managers and the existence of a highly organized labor market, we would expect that something akin to residual claimancy might arise in the management of localities. The ability of a nonelected CAO to increase his salary depends in part upon his alternative employment opportunities. For example, if he can demonstrate that his administration of the city or county has increased services and concurrently tax rates have fallen, he is better able to retain his current job and may become more marketable if these attributes are prized by competing jurisdictions. Obviously, the extent to which the market for managers reduces production costs depends directly on the incentives of the employers. For example, a private-sector entrepreneur has an incentive, *ceteris paribus*, to hire the most productive worker, as this increases the entrepreneur's returns from the business. When evaluating the same process of a city council to hire a manager, it is clear the incentive structure is markedly different. We predict that the more mobile the government manager—generally the county executive or city manager—the more likely the jurisdiction is to use contracting out. This production mode, if efficiency enhancing, allows the manager the advantages of residual claimancy. If significant, the form of government variable will allow us to predict the impact of these managerial differences.

Production Mixes

Contracting out a portion of a jurisdiction's activities may provide a mechanism for the CAO to improve his overall credibility with taxpayers while reducing the burdens of his job. Table 7.1 presents the typical range of services provided by local governments sorted into seven functional categories.

The CAOs will have every incentive to maintain activities that raise the level of net revenues available for their discretion; however, many local goods may have negative impacts on the budget. For example, consider a municipal bus system operating at a loss. It may well be that the system has several highly profitable routes, that is, routes that return more in user fees than operating costs. The CAO may be very willing to devise a test of the private sector by dividing up the transit system and contracting out the unprofitable routes.

This is a must win situation for the referent decisionmaker—if the private sector fails to run the routes at a profit, this can be taken as evidence of the necessity of public production. However, if private firms are successful, the CAO can take the credit for making the city more efficient while not reducing any of his positive residual. Thus, we might well expect to find *adverse selection* in the activities that CAOs willingly turn over to the private sector either via contracting or by load shedding.

A related strategy might find privatization actually leading to an increase in public-sector budgets. Should the CAO select for contracting those services that seem to be good candidates for whatever reason, this may well provide him with a case for future budget expansion on the grounds that all the fat has been trimmed from the jurisdiction's budget and unless budget increases are provided essential services will be cutback. Table 7.2 presents data on the degree of contracting by functional area.

Table 7.1 Service Activities by Functional Category

Functional Category	Service Activity
Public Safety, Corrections	Police patrol
	Police, fire communications
	Fire prevention
Public Works, Utilities	Street and bridge maintenance
	Solid waste disposal
	Sewage disposal
	Street lighting
	Water supply
	Traffic signal installation
Health, Welfare, Hospitals	Public health clinics
	Hospitals
	Sanitary inspections
	Drug rehabilitation
	Emergency services
	(ambulance services)
	Mental health services
	Child welfare
	Day care facilities
	Elderly care programs
	Public housing maintenance
	Animal control
	Insect, rodent control
Transportation	Mass transit system
	Airport operation
	Paratransit operation
Parks, Recreation	Parks
	Recreational facilities
Cultural, Education	Museums
	Libraries
General Government and Finance	Computer and data processing
	Building and grounds
Maintenance	Tax assessing
	Tax, utility processing
	Fleet management
	General support services
	(legal, personnel)

Thus contracting out provides the CAO a means to demonstrate his concern for efficiency at the same time as he rids himself of difficult management chores.

Financing Mode

Potential gains from contracting out may well depend upon the current mode of financing the local public good. As a general rule, managers prefer the status

Table 7.2 Percentage of Cities
Contracting by Functional Activity

Functional Category	Contracting for One or More Services	Contracting for Two or More Services
General Government	41.6	21.6
Parks and Recreation	13.1	5.3
Health and Welfare	63.3	44.9
Transportation	33.9	13.2
Education and Culture	25.0	6.3
Public Safety	29.2	12.1
Public Works	64.8	40.5

Source: Local Government Data Base, U.S. Advisory Commission on Intergovernmental Relations, Washington, DC, 1986.

quo. The introduction of an alternative production mode will, by its very nature, generate uncertainty and additional work. The costs of self-production must be determined, new arrangements entered into, and production monitoring undertaken on a continuing basis. The willingness to incur these additional management costs may depend upon whether or not he can capture a substantial portion of the gains for himself. The current financing method appears to impact upon the degree of potential managerial discretion.

Financing production via a user fee arrangement increases the probability that consumers get the benefit of a better production arrangement but produces incentives which tend to reduce the potential gains to consumers. Alternatively, general fund financing, which produces greater incentives to maximize the gains from contracting, carries a reduced probability that the gains will be distributed to consumers. It appears that the incentive to drive the least cost bargain depends directly upon the lack of direct benefits to the taxpayer consumer.

Given the available data set, a direct measure of the impact of alternative financing modes on the contracting out process is not possible. One possible proxy is to test whether or not the use of user fee financing is related to the degree of contracting out.

Governmental Labor Force

Spann (1976) argues that the government bureaucrat does not normally benefit financially from cost reductions; therefore, municipal workers are likely on average to receive higher salaries for comparable work than their private-sector counterparts. In addition, the size of the public-sector work force should be greater due to the relatively smaller rewards from monitoring (Mehay and Gonzalez, 1986). These effects should be magnified by the unionization of the municipal work force. Compared to other regions of the United States, the relatively high unionization of

Table 7.3 Contracting for Public Safety by Population Size, Form of Government, and Region

Measure	Percentage Contracting
Population Size	
1,000–9,999	20.0
10,000–24,999	27.0
25,000–49,999	28.9
50,000–99,999	28.9
100,000–249,999	26.0
250,000	33.0
Government Form	
City manager	30.0
All other	24.2
Region	
Northeast	20.5
North-central	28.2
South	22.0
West	40.2

Source: Local Government Data Base, U.S. Advisory Commission on Intergovernmental Relations, Washington, DC, 1986.

the Northeast is reflected in above average municipal labor forces and salary levels. In the early 1970s Muller's (1976) study of the New York region found there were approximately 40 percent more municipal workers per capita than the national average. These workers received wages 10 to 15 percent higher than private-sector workers in similar occupations. As illustrated in Table 7.3, public safety contracting is lowest in the heavily unionized northeastern corridor of the United States.

In many localities the governing coalition is composed of individuals who have strong ties to the organized labor movement; thus, the incentives for the CAO to adopt an alternative production mechanism may depend in a very direct way on how politically powerful employee unions may be affected. For example, a number of cities, including Detroit, Philadelphia, New Orleans, and Milwaukee, have clauses in their agreements with public-sector unions whereby the city agrees not to contract out public works services (Fisk, Kiesling, and Muller, 1978).

While a CAO's salary is an increasing function of the size of the organization managed, it does not appear that contracting out reduces salaries. This occurs, in part, due to the obligation of the CAO to monitor contract performance; thus, CAOs can reduce the size of their bureaucracy and not adversely affect their remuneration. We predict that the greater the degree of unionization in the locality's labor force, the more resistance there will be to contracting out. Further, the level of unionization of all workers in the jurisdiction, a measure of general union strength, may adversely impact on the contracting out decision.

Institutional Constraints

Contracting out must be seen as a mere instrument or tool which may or may not be available to the local government decisionmaker. The contracting mechanism may be restricted in use to a small subset of local public goods production or it may cover the full range of local government activities as in the case of California's contract cities. The legal structure imposed on cities and counties by their state will define to a large extent the latitude for independent action. For example, New York statutes require that all cities provide and produce jail facilities. Such regulations clearly limit the use of contracting out. Composite indices that attempt to capture the degree of independent action of cities and counties have been constructed with respect to centralization, annexation, consolidation, home rule, and functional scope. We expect that, as the degree of state control increases, jurisdictions will be more constrained with respect to production choice so greater centralization might work to increase the amount of contracting while home rule provisions could be expected to have the opposite effect. These measures should permit us to gauge the impact of varying state institutional structures on the production decision.

The Decision Process in the Aggregate

The rational, self-interested, utility-maximizing CAO will seek to increase both his salary and his job-related perquisites. But the long-term tenure of the CAO is far from assured. Security of tenure is a function of many different factors, only some of which he can influence by way of strategic behavior. One of the more important of these margins of influence involves his relationship with the agency heads under his authority.

Agency heads generally have significant power to affect the future job tenure of a CAO. By exercising discretionary authority over their employees and the operations they oversee, agency heads can often affect perceptions of the efficiency of the CAO as a manager of government operations. To the extent that agency heads directly control the disbursement of funds to client groups or the allocation of services within the community, they can influence political support for the CAO. Further, agency employees may constitute a well-organized, vocal, and highly motivated political interest group in their own right, able to express their dissatisfaction with a CAO through union as well as political activity of various sorts—including, but not necessarily limited to, voting. For these reasons, it will generally be in the CAO's interest to attempt to placate agency heads. Given that they are, as a group, competitors with one another—the budgetary allocation to the police department represents funds unavailable for allocation to the transportation department—it is unlikely to be either feasible or necessary for the CAO to consistently protect department head interests; however, by and large CAOs will try to secure the support of their agency heads.

The CAO must manage the competing claims of his many agency heads so that, in the aggregate, he can provide himself with security of tenure given his limited discretionary authority. The CAO's ability to purchase the support of agency heads by means of increased budgetary allocations all around is limited, either by voter resistance to tax increases, express state or local limitations on spending levels and or revenues (e.g., Proposition Thirteen in California), or other factors. Contracting provides the CAO with a potentially attractive option which presents a means to significantly increase the support he receives from his agency heads. Numerous studies have found that the contracting out of government services is often associated with significant efficiency gains by comparison with own government provision of the same services. In other words, the same level of public service quantity and quality can be provided to taxpayers at lower cost. These efficiency gains are potentially available to CAOs to distribute in ways that maximize benefit to themselves. If we assume that the opportunities for actual corruption are relatively rare, a choice available to a CAO which meets this criterion is to allocate those efficiency gains not to voters and taxpayers but to agency heads. It is relatively unimportant whether the CAO accomplishes this by actually redistributing the gains to particular agencies, or simply allows agencies to retain those gains resulting from the contracting out by the local government of activities within their purview. As a rule, we expect CAOs will tend to pursue the latter course of action as it minimizes transaction costs. Further, agency heads may have some ability to partially disguise the true magnitude of any gains associated with the contracting process.

Therefore, we predict that when contracting out occurs at the local government level, the theoretically expected contracting gains are unlikely to be reflected in lower public spending levels. This is not because the gains are actually illusory, but simply because the CAO will allow his agency heads to keep whatever efficiency gains result. In short, while contracting out may tend to reduce levels of *employment* in the contracting government, it is expected to have little or no effect on overall *spending* levels.

Research Design and Operational Measures

Our research objective is twofold. First, to discover how contracting *per se*, as well as the type of contracting arrangement employed, affects the behavior of CAOs as reflected in local government public safety employment and spending levels. And second, to explore whether or not this relationship is consistent with the effects of contracting activity on these variables both at a higher level of aggregation (i.e., with respect to total government employment and spending), and in the case of other forms of publicly provided goods.

In order to test for the latter relationships, we must construct a model of total municipal spending and employment levels for specific service areas. Our empirical study involves some relatively complex problems; thus, we explain our estimation procedure in some detail.

Analysis of a single functional category alone is likely to provide a very different, and potentially misleading, perspective on the problem of local government contracting than would a more comprehensive analysis of the jurisdictional budget process. An example drawn from the recent privatization literature should suffice to make our point. A recent study of California cities conducted by Barbara Stevens (1986) demonstrated that cities which contracted for asphalt overlay services produced the same quality of street coverage as noncontracting cities but at 189 percent less cost. In such a case, it might seem superficially plausible to suppose that in the aggregate, cities that employed relatively more extensive contracting would exhibit lower levels of per capita government expenditures in addition to reductions in total expenditures for public works, holding other expenditures equal. Our hypothesis is that neither expenditure effect is, in fact, likely to result. The model specification is reported in Table 7.4.

Table 7.4 Determinants of Municipal Spending (PCTOTEXP) and Employment (PCFTE)

Concept/Measure	Hypothesized Relationship	Data Source	Mnemonic
Per capita income	+	Census (1976)	PCINCOME
Per capita intergovernment aid	+	Census (1982)	TOTIGR
Per capita own source taxes	+	Census (1982)	PCOWNTAX
Taxes paid as a percentage of personal income	+	Census (1982)	TAXBURD
State imposed spending limits[1]	+	ACIR (1982)	EXPLIM
Municipal authority to annex and consolidate with adjacent areas[2]	+	ACIR (1972)	CONSOL/ANNEX
State centralization[3]	+	Stephens (1982)	CENT
Population size	+	Census (1982)	POP
Functional responsibility	+	ICMA (1982, 83)	RESPON
Contract for public services[4]	−	ICMA (1982, 83)	CONTRACT
Contracting for 25% or more of total services[5]	−	ICMA (1982, 83)	OVER25
Interaction of CONTRACT and TAXBURD	−	ICMA (1982, 83)	INTER1
Interaction of TAXBURD and over25	+	ICMA (1982, 83)	INTER2

[1]1 = no limits, 2 = limits since 1978, 3 = limits since 1974, 4 = limits since 1970.

[2]Scale score ranging from 1 = limited local authority to 5 = maximum local authority.

[3]State spending as a percentage of total state and local spending.

[4]1 = Contract for one or more services, 0 = no service contracts.

[5]1 = Contract for 25 percent or more of total services, 0 = Contract for less than 25 percent of total services. The excluded category is 10–25 percent of functions contracted.

The independent variables are those reported in the literature as major determinants of municipal employment and spending (Bahl, 1984). Our analysis proceeds in two stages. Spending and employment equations were estimated for each of our seven functional categories (see Table 7.5) using a dichotomous dummy measure of contracting (i.e., 0 = no services contracted, 1 = at least one service contracted). Two separate sets of equations for total municipal spending and employment are estimated. Two dummy measures of contracting are included in both sets of equations; CONTRACT and OVER25. The CONTRACT dummy variable differentiates between cities that do not contract for any of their service responsibilities (CONTRACT = 0) and those cities that have at least one service contract (CONTRACT = 1). The OVER25 dummy variable distinguishes between those cities that contract less than 25 percent of their service responsibilities (OVER25 = 0) and those cities that contract for 25 percent or more of the service responsibilities (OVER25 = 1). The inclusion of both dummy measures allows us to assess the linear/nonlinear effects of contracting on spending and employment levels. Substantively, the coefficients for these dummy variables are interpreted as the mean level of spending and employment for cities by contracting experience, controlling for other independent regressors. The sign for each coefficient indicates whether the mean value for cities contracting some or more than 25 percent of their services is larger or smaller than cities that do not contract or contract for less than 25 percent of their service responsibilities.

The second set of equations estimates policy outputs with the addition of two interaction terms; INTER1 (CONTRACT*TAXBURDEN) and INTER2 (OVER25*TAXBURDEN). These two interaction terms allow us to test the proposition that service contracts are most likely to have a negative effect on spending and employment levels when cities are most fiscally stressed. It is expected that the coefficients for the interaction terms will be negative and more significant than the coefficients for the individual dummy measures of service contracting. Finally, the inclusion of the interactive terms should clarify the effect tax burden has on spending levels by increasing the significance and magnitude of the tax burden coefficient.

Findings

Table 7.5 reports the regression estimates for per capita spending and employment by function and the mean spending and employment levels by contracting experience. As hypothesized, contracting has a negative and significant effect on employment levels. Employment levels in six of the seven functional categories are significantly and negatively affected by the use of service contracts. Employment levels for health and welfare services are unrelated to the incidence of contracting. Cities that contract for these services do not experience a significant reduction in their own work force. In part, this finding can be explained as a function of policy content. The primary output produced by health and welfare agencies is a nondurable, interpersonal service. Unlike clean streets, trimmed trees, and balanced accounts, the effort required to monitor and oversee service contracts for health and welfare services may be motivated by a desire to extend the scope and improve the quality of these services rather than simply cutting production costs through labor reductions (DeHoog, 1984; Nelson, 1981).

Contracting within a specific functional area has no consistent effect on spending levels. The contract coefficient in five of the seven spending equations is statistically insignificant. Only spending levels for public works are negatively impacted by service contracting. Cities contracting for these services experience

Table 7.5 Regression Estimates and Means for Per Capita Spending and Employment by Functional Activity

(N=877)

Function	Mean FTE Contract	Mean FTE Noncontract	β	R^2	Mean Per Capita Spending Contract	Mean Per Capita Spending Noncontract	β	R^2
Health and Welfare[1]	0.80	0.80	0.053 (0.239)	35.9	19.76	19.10	0.839 (0.839)	35.2
Public Safety	3.60	3.90	-0.256 (2.48)*	33.2	92.78	93.48	-1.03 (0.690)	50.8
Public Works	2.80	3.80	-0.370 (2.78)*	42.5	231.88	412.09	-68.18 (2.61)*	39.3
Transportation	0.09	0.11	-0.051 (2.31)*	45.9	5.54	4.19	1.52 (1.68)	47.9
General Government	1.38	1.40	-0.026 (2.68)*	10.5	36.27	34.78	0.225 (0.153)	22.5
Parks and Recreation	0.001	0.015	-0.052 (2.04)*	17.8	32.25	25.25	3.15 (2.11)*	33.3
Education and Culture	0.342	0.488	0.043 (2.43)*	55.6	6.88	6.90	-0.609 (1.11)	55.5

*P .05.

** = Full-time equivalent workers per 1,000 population.

Note: Regression estimates were derived from an equation which included the following independent regressors: per capita personal income, per capita intergovernmental revenues (i.e., state and federal), own source revenue (net of user fees and charges), state spending limits, consolidation and annexation authority, population size, tax burden, and state centralization score. The number of full-time equivalent employees was included in the equation for per capita spending and per capita spending was included in the equation for full-time equivalent employment. A dummy measure of contracting (1 = one or more service contracts, 0 = no service contracts) was included in each spending and employment equation by functional area. See Table 7.1 for a full description of each independent variable.

[1] Only cities with service responsibility for the functional activity were included in the analysis. The number of observations varies with the equation estimated, producing a different threshold for the significance of t-statistics in each question.

significantly lower per capita expenditures than their noncontracting counterparts. In the only other spending equation with a significant contracting effect – parks and recreation – the coefficient is positive, indicating that contracting is associated with a significantly higher spending level. This finding is particularly surprising given the significant and negative effect contracting has on public employment levels for parks and recreational services. This slightly anomalous finding can be explained by disaggregating the spending variable. A significant component of municipal outlays for park and recreational services is capital expenditures for the acquisition and development of land. Cities that contract for these services spend a significantly greater amount of their total outlay on land acquisition ($15.75 per capita) than their noncontracting counterparts ($7.85 per capita). When spending for parks and recreation is limited only to outlays for current operations, the contracting coefficient is positive, but statistically insignificant. Though only speculative, it would seem that cities that contract for park and recreational services are engaged in more extensive programs of land acquisition and development, skewing total spending for this service toward capital rather than operating outlays.

The findings in Table 7.5 confirm that contracting has a significant and negative effect on employment levels by function but no appreciable effect on spending for the same functions. These findings may seem inconsistent with previous research and require some further explanation before proceeding with the balance of our analysis. Previous work on the effects of contracting has identified significant savings from the contracted provision of certain public services. The variance between the findings in these studies and our own may reflect the aggregate nature of our spending and employment measures.[4]

Table 7.6 reports the regression estimates for our model of total spending and employment levels. Columns 1 and 3 report the model estimated with the two dummy measures of service contracting; CONTRACT and OVER25. Columns 2 and 4 report the same equations with the addition of the interaction between each dummy measure of contracting and tax burden (i.e., INTER1, INTER2).

Contracting for public services has an unexpected strong effect on both spending and employment levels, albeit in a curvilinear fashion. Though contracting for public services is negatively related to employment levels, this effect is only significant for those cities which contract 25 percent or more of their service responsibilities. The CONTRACT coefficient is negative but not statistically significant, suggesting that a minimum threshold of service contracting must be attained before service contracting is significantly associated with lower levels of public employment. A curvilinear relationship between contracting and spending level is also observed; however, in this instance the threshold is observed at a lower rather than higher level of contracting. The significant and negative CONTRACT coefficient indicates that cities which contract for any portion of their service repertoire have significantly lower per capita outlays than their noncontracting counterparts. The OVER25 coefficient, though negative, is not statistically significant. Cities which contract for 25 percent or more of their services do not have significantly lower spending levels than cities contracting for less than 25 percent of their services. Contracting is significantly related to lower levels of spending, but the savings from

Table 7.6 Regression Estimates for Total
Per Capita Spending and Full-time Equivalent
Public Employment (per 1,000 Population) (N=877)

Variable	Total per capita spending full-time equivalent employment			
	Model 1	Model 2	Model 1	Model 2
	(1)	(2)	(3)	(4)
INTERCEPT	121.69	327.37	−5.31	−10.67
RESPON	8.78*	8.53*	0.025*	0.202*
	(3.05)	(2.86)	(4.27)	(4.28)
PCOWNTAX	0.664*	0.690*	0.007	0.006
	(2.03)	(2.12)	(1.41)	(1.17)
PCINCOME	−0.013	−0.014	−0.053*	−0.047*
	(1.01)	(1.12)	(2.41)	(2.16)
TOTFTES	17,514*	18,440*	−	−
	(8.84)	(9.22)		
PCTOTEXP	−	−	0.004*	0.005*
			(4.14)	(3.82)
TOTIGR	0.807*	0.797*	0.011*	0.011*
	(7.31)	(7.24)	(6.20)	(6.08)
TAXBURD	−3,101*	−9,913*	−86.1*	−268.50*
	(2.04)	(3.27)	(3.39)	(5.40)
EXPLIM	106.25*	105.62*	1.01*	0.974*
	(3.94)	(3.92)	(2.22)	(2.16)
CONSOL/ANNEX	−37.81*	−37.53*	0.619*	0.599*
	(4.07)	(4.05)	(3.96)	(3.89)
POPULATION	0.0623	0.0643	−4.46−3E*	−4.35−3E*
	(0.507)	(0.525)	(2.61)	(2.14)
CONTRACT	−217.40*	−390.44*	−0.876	−3.46*
	(4.11)	(3.71)	(0.977)	(1.97)
OVER25	−9.86	−71.66	−1.11*	1.10
	(0.362)	(1.41)	(2.47)	(1.36)
INTER1	−	−5,631*	−	−141.20*
		(2.04)		(3.08)
INTER2	−	−1,584	−	−56.0*
		(1.56)		(3.33)
R²	0.409	0.416	0.580	0.597
F-RATIO	28.33	25.34	58.43	54.10

*p .05.

additional contracting is insignificant after a city contracts for more than 25 percent of its services.

The regression estimates reported in columns 2 and 4 provide a test for the interaction effect of contracting and the tax burden on spending and employment levels. Substantively the coefficients for each of the interaction terms can be interpreted as real slopes for the nonzero value of each dummy contract variable.

The inclusion of the interaction terms in our second model does not significantly alter any of the coefficients for noncontracting independent regressors. This allows us to place greater confidence in the stability of our estimates for various contracting effects on spending and employment levels. There are, however, notable differences in the estimates for our independent measures of contracting. The coefficients for both INTER1 and INTER2 are negative and statistically significant, indicating that any level of contracting (CONTRACT) as well as higher levels of contracting (OVER25) in cities with higher tax burdens is significantly related to smaller public work forces. In model 1 we observed a curvilinear relationship between the incidence of contracting and spending and employment levels. With the inclusion of the interaction terms we obtain a negative and nonlinear relationship between contracting and employment levels. The coefficient for INTER1 (-141.20) is considerably larger than the estimate for INTER2 (-56.0), indicating that a 1 percent change in tax burden among cities contracting more than a 25 percent of their service responsibilities is associated with a much smaller but significant and negative change in employment.

Opposite the results in model 1, the estimate for CONTRACT is significant, while the coefficient for OVER25 is statistically insignificant. Any level of service contracting has a negative though modest effect on employment. This effect, however, is not linear beyond the 25 percent rate of service contracting. Only when cities are fiscally pressed by large tax burdens do contracting rates in excess of 25 percent have a significant and negative effect on public employment levels. The independent effect tax burden has on public employment is significantly altered by the inclusion of the interaction terms. As hypothesized, given the size of the tax burden coefficients between models 1 and 2, we can attribute the increased magnitude and significance of the tax burden coefficient to the influence of the interaction terms.

The inclusion of the two interaction terms in the expenditure equation provides moderate support for our thesis. The coefficient for CONTRACT and INTER1 are both significant and negative. Neither OVER25 nor its interaction with tax burden (INTER2) have significant effects on spending levels. Consistent with the results obtained in model 1 there is a curvilinear relationship between the incidence of contracting and spending levels. A higher incidence of contracting (i.e., above the 25 percent rate) is not significantly associated with reduced spending levels, even when this sustained rate of contracting occurs in cities with high tax burdens. High tax burdens accentuate the effect nominal levels of contracting have on spending.

Consistent with our findings for employment levels, the tax burden coefficient for spending is larger and more significant in model 2 than model 1.

Summary and Conclusions

The literature on privatization and government contracting of services is expanding rapidly. Much of this corpus is empirical in nature and most research concentrates on the efficiency of provision of a single service. While the bulk of these contributions are interesting and worthwhile in their own way, until recently they

have consistently neglected the problem of the determinants of the decision to contract out from the perspective of rational, self-interested local government political
decisionmakers. In short, how do caos gain in either utility or income, or both, from
the decision to contract out? This chapter represents our effort to fill this public
choice gap, at least partially.

Our main thesis receives strong support from the empirical analysis. To avoid
raising taxes, mayors and city managers appear willing to allow their bureaus to
retain all of the savings from service contracting. Evidence of this is found in the
significant negative relationship between contracting and total spending and the insignificant relationship between the same variables for functionally specific—
bureau level—services. An independent and significant CONTRACT coefficient for
total spending was not hypothesized, though it was not unexpected. The magnitude
and significance of the interaction between the incidence of contracting and tax
burden, however, provides supporting evidence for our principal-agent explanation
of the fiscal effects of service contracting. Higher rates of taxation provide a strong
incentive for caos and bureau heads to employ service contracts as a cost saving
device.[5]

The caos attempt to maximize their own income (pecuniary and nonpecuniary),
subject to two distinct political constraints. The first is the need to promote voter
satisfaction by minimizing tax increases. The second is to placate the bureau and
agency chiefs and their employees. In this environment, contracting out of services
can be a useful stratagem. Contracting can be presented to voter-taxpayers as cost-
consciousness evidence by the cao, and may actually result in a measurable improvement in the quality of services delivered to consumers. A reduction, even if
slight, in the size of the public bureaucracy can be employed as further tangible
evidence of the cao's concern with tax-minimizing efficiency. In reality, contracting
appears to have little effect on either aggregate government spending levels or the
budgets of government agencies charged with the provision of a particular public
good. For example, in the case of public safety, contracting appears to reduce the
number of employees but to have little or no effect on the budgets of police departments and other public safety bureaus. Presumably, the public safety head utilizes
the contracting gains the cao allows him to increase the average salary of the remaining employees, thus compensating for the negative effect (to the cao and the
bureau chief) of the employment reduction. The actual distribution of these gains
at the level of the agency head or bureau chief seems a fruitful topic for future empirical investigation.

Appendix

Definitional and Operational Properties of Municipal Contracting

Service contracting is a readily identified procedure for producing any good and or service. Under a service contract the governmental unit is removed from the production and
delivery process, while retaining control over the content of the policy output through the

conditions outlined in a written service agreement. The vendor can be any entity, including another government.

Generically, contracting represents an alternative to direct municipal service provision. Cities continue to ensure that their citizens receive specific goods and services; however, the means of service provision and delivery are removed from the municipality. A service contract has the following characteristics:

1. A contract is a formal written document between a local government and a specific service vendor.

2. A contract can be entered into with either a for-profit or nonprofit firm, a neighborhood association, or another governmental unit.

3. Local governments can contract for services that are directly provided to consumers (e.g., solid waste disposal) as well as for activities that are necessary for the operation of the local government (e.g., janitorial services).

4. A local government can contract for either part or all of a public service.

5. Local governments can contract with more than one vendor for the same service.

The number of municipal service contracts is a function of the number of goods and services for which the city has responsibility. Thus, the incidence of contracting, expressed as the total number of contracts awarded by a single city (ACIR, 1983; ICMA, 1983), does not accurately measure this policy activity. The appropriate measure is one which examines contracting as a proportion of all services provided by a local government. Since functional scope is strongly related to population size, a measure of contracting, unadjusted for functional scope, will produce an artificially strong relationship with population size and bias our estimates of spending and employment levels.

Data on municipal contracting was collected from two separate surveys of municipal governments for the period 1982–83 (ICMA, 1982, 1983). Both surveys were conducted by the International City Management Association. The samples for both surveys were selected from the same universe of communities; all cities with populations over 10,000 and a one-eighth sample by geographical region of cities with populations under 10,000. The 1982 study surveyed local governmental units about their use of private-sector service contracts for 64 functional activities. The 1983 study queried a comparable sample of governments on their use of intergovernmental and joint service agreements for the provision of 42 functional activities. Data from both surveys were merged, producing a sample of 890 communities who responded to both surveys. The merged data set provides information on intergovernmental and private (profit and nonprofit) service contracts for 34 functions in seven functional areas (see Table 7.1). The distribution of cases for the merged sample on measures of region location, population size, form of government, and metropolitan status show them to be representative of the universe of all cities with over 10,000 population. The sample of cities under 10,000 (N = 13) in the merged data set is too small to allow us to make any meaningful generalizations about this class of cities and they were excluded from our analysis, reducing our sample to 877 cities.

Separate measures of service contracting were constructed for services in each functional area and total contracting including intergovernmental, private for-profit contracts. It is not uncommon for a community to award multiple contracts for the same service activity. For example, cities might contract for garbage collection on a geographical basis, awarding individual contracts for different sections of the city. Though this is not a frequent practice among our sample of cities, our measure of service contracting includes multiple contracts for individual services. All measures of contracting are expressed as the ratio of contracted services (total and by function) to municipal functional scope.

The distribution of total contracting and contracting by function (see Figure 7.1 and

Table 7.2) is asymmetric and skewed toward an infrequent incidence of contracting. A majority of cities lack any service contracts in five of the seven functional areas. Given these empirical properties of municipal contracting, we have employed an ordinal and nominal measure for total and service-specific contracting respectively. The measure of total contracting is trichotomized; 0 percent to 10 percent of provided services contracted; 11 percent to 25 percent of provided services contracted; and 26 percent to 100 percent of provided services contracted. Measures of contracting by function are dichotomized—no contracts and one or more service contracts in the functional area.

Notes

1. This research on the impact of alternative delivery systems on local governments is being conducted in conjunction with the Local Government Project of the U.S. Advisory Commission on Intergovernmental Relations, Washington, DC. See Stein, 1990, for a more complete analysis of the incidence and impact of alternative delivery systems.

2. Several studies have examined ways in which public-sector managers can increase their income via rearrangement of the public budget. See for example Lentz, 1981.

3. An extensive body of research has developed concerning the competitive nature of local government market. For a summary see Sjoquist, 1982.

4. Our definition of functional contracting is based on whether one or more services are contracted in a functional area. It may be unrealistic to expect that contracting for one service will have a significant effect on employment and spending levels for all services in that functional category. This procedure may have biased our test and increased the probability of rejecting a significant effect for contracting. The obvious remedy would be to conduct a disaggregate analysis (i.e., by single activity) of contracting effects. This procedure would be theoretically inconsistent with our explanation of the budgetary effects of contacting, and directed at a different research question.

The aggregation of spending and employment by functional area allows us to examine budgetary effects of contracting at the appropriate level of municipal organization—the bureau or agency. Arguably, the assignment of these 34 services among municipal agencies varies across cities. We believe our categorization of these services resembles the actual distribution of services among city agencies. We do not take issue with those studies which have demonstrated savings from the use of service contracts. Rather, we are interested in knowing how these savings affect agency and total spending and employment levels.

The aggregation of functionally related expenditures provides us with a more realistic setting in which to assess the budgetary effects of service contracting. We cannot assume that savings from service contracting will be translated into aggregate reductions in employment and or spending levels. The missing link here is the relationship between various actors in the budgetary process. As noted earlier, the decision to employ potentially cost saving production technologies (e.g., contracting) is not automatic and is at least dependent upon an agreement between relevant actors in the budgetary process.

A potential problem arises in our analysis of contracting effects by functional category. The explanatory power of our model for spending and employment is at best modest and for some functions (e.g., parks and recreation and general government) extremely low. Our estimates for spending levels by function are particularly modest, possibly undermining our confidence in the estimates obtained from these equations. The specific threat posed by the modest R^2 for our model is that we may have rejected a significant contracting effect where one actually exists (i.e., type 1 error). We assess the likelihood of a type 1 error as extremely improbable. The inclusion of additional variables in our model may improve its overall fit with the observed data but it is statistically unlikely to increase the t-value of any single coefficient. To the contrary, assuming no colinearity problems, the inclusion of additional independent regressors is more likely to reduce rather than increase the t-value for any single coefficient. In light of this explanation, our test of the contracting hypothesis for functionally specific spending and employment levels is more susceptible to accepting than rejecting a significant contract effect. This represents a more stringent test of our hypothesis, providing us with greater confidence in our findings.

5. The independent relationship between contracting, spending, and employment is curvilinear with different thresholds for employment and spending. The inclusion of the interaction between contracting and tax burden straightens the curvilinear employment relationship, but accentuates the curvilinear spending effect of service contraction. The substantive meaning of these relationships has been discussed earlier. There is, however, another interpretation of these nonlinear findings. The absence of a strong and significant linear effect for contracting may reflect the variation in the functional content of a city's contracting activities across different levels of service contracting. Research on the incidence of contracting shows a differential rate of service contracting across functional areas (ACIR, 1983; Ferris, Ferns and Graddy, 1986, Stein, 1990), a condition which our data corroborates (see Table 7.2). This variation has been explained by a number of factors, including the absence of competitive markets for contract vendors and diseconomies of scale in the production function of certain service activities (i.e., labor-intensive social services). Contracting for certain services may not result in any savings. As noted earlier, the motivation for service contracting may not always be to reduce outlays. Improved service quality and program coverage are often cited as reasons for contracting for many human services (DeHoog, 1985). DeHoog (1984) and Nelson (1981) suggest there is a limited number of services which can produce significant savings from service contracting. Beyond these services, savings from contracting are less certain and are achieved at a smaller return on the production dollar. Cities contracting more of their service responsibilities may have exceeded the optimal number and mix of service contracts, producing the nonlinear relationships between contracting and policy outputs observed in our data. Future research should examine the functional composition of service contracts and the potential for achieving maximum aggregate savings through an optimal mix of service contracts.

References

Advisory Commission on Intergovernmental Relations (ACIR) (1963). *The Performance of Urban Functions: Local and Areawide.* Washington, DC: Government Printing Office.
_____. (1974). *Sub-State Regionalism and the Federal System,* Vols. 1–4. Washington, DC: Government Printing Office.
_____. (1982). *State and Local Roles in the Federal System.* Washington, DC: Government Printing Office.
_____. (Update 1983). *Intergovernmental Service Arrangements for Delivering Local Public Services: Update 1983.* Washington, DC: Government Printing Office.
Alnoso, W. (1966). "Cities, Planners, and Urban Renewal." James Q. Wilson (ed), *Urban Renewal.* Cambridge, MA: MIT Press.
Anderson, W. (1925). *American City Government.* New York: Henry Holt.

104   P O L I C E

Bahl, R. (1984). *Financing State and Local Government.* New York: Oxford University Press.
Bennett, J. T., and M. H. Johnson (1981). *Better Government at Half the Price.* Ottawa, IL: Caroline House.
Bish, R. L. (1971). *The Public Economy of Metropolitan Areas.* Chicago: Markham.
————. (1975). "Assumption of Knowledge in Policy Analysis." *Policy Studies Journal* 3:256–62.
————. (1977). "Economic Theory, Fiscal Federalism and Political Federalism." Paper delivered at the annual meetings of the American Political Science Association.
————. (1978). "Intergovernmental Relations in the United States: Some Concepts and Implications from a Public Choice Perspective." *Intergovernmental Policy Making: Limits to Coordination and Central Control.* Beverly Hills, CA: Sage.
————. (1984). "Productivity Increasing Arrangements for Providing Government Services: The Role of Contracting Out." Prepared for the Royal Commission on Economic Union and Development Prospects for Canada. Victoria, BC: University of Victoria, School of Public Administration.
Bish, R. L., and V. Ostrom (1973). *Understanding Urban Government.* Washington, DC: American Enterprise Institute for Public Policy Research.
Bish, R. L., and R. Warren (1972). "Scale and Monopoly Problems in Urban Government Services." *Urban Affairs Quarterly* 8:97–120.
Brainard, W. C., F. Dolbear, and G. Trenery, Jr. (1967). "The Possibility of Oversupply of Local 'Public' Goods: A Critical Note." *Journal of Political Economy* 75 (February): 91–92.
Breton, Albert (1974). *The Economic Theory of Representative Government.* Chicago: Aldine.
Buchanan, J. M., and G. Tullock (1962). *The Calculus of Consent.* Ann Arbor, MI: University of Michigan Press.
Butler, S. M. (1985). *Privatizing Federal Spending: A Strategy to Eliminate the Deficit.* New York: Universe Books.
DeHoog, R. (1984). *Contracting Out for Human Services: Economic, Political and Organizational Perspectives.* Albany, NY: State University of New York Press.
————. (1985). "Theoretical Perspectives on Contracting Out for Services." George Edwards Jr. (ed)., *Public Policy Implementation.* Greenwich, CN: JAI Press, 227–59.
Ferris, J. and E. Grady (1986). "Contracting Out: For What, with Whom?" *Public Administration Review* 46 (July/August): 331–44.
Fisk, D., H. Kiesling, and T. Muller (1978). *Private Provision of Public Services: An Overview.* Washington, DC: Urban Institute.
Hamer, E. (1983). *Privatizing Services and Property.* Berlin: Institute für Kommunalwissenschaften der Konrad-Adenauer-Stiftuing E.V.
Hatry, H. P. (1983). *A Review of Private Approaches for Delivery of Public Services.* Washington, DC: Urban Institute.
International City Management Association (ICMA) (1982). "Alternative Approaches for the Delivery of Public Services." *Urban Data Services* 14:10–22.
————. (1983). "Intergovernmental Management for the Delivery of Public Services." *Urban Data Service Report,* 15:10.
Klatzky, S. R. (1970). "Relationship of Urbanization Size to Complexity and Coordination." *Administrative Science Quarterly* 15 (December): 428–38.
Lee, M. L. (1972). "Interdependent Behavior and Resource Misallocation in Hospital Care Production." *Review of Social Economy* 30 (March): 84–96.
Lentz, B. (1981). "Political and Economic Determinants of County Government Pay." *Public Choice* 36:253–63.

McGuire, R. A., R. L. Oshfeldt, and T. N. van Gott (1987). "The Determinants of the Choice Between Public and Private Production of a Publicly Funded Service." *Public Choice* 54:197–210.

Martin, D. T. and Schmidt J. R. (1981). "Expenditure Effects of Metropolitan Tax Base Sharing: A Public Choice Analysis." *Public Choice* 36:253–63.

_____, and R. E. Wagner (1978). "The Institutional Framework for Municipal Incorporation: An Economic Analysis of Local Agency Formation Commissions in California." *Journal of Law and Economics* 21 (October):409–25.

Mehay, S. L., and R. A. Gonzalez (1986). "The Relative Effect of Unionization and Interjurisdictional Competition on Municipal Wages." *Journal of Labor Research* 7 (Winter): 79–93.

Muller, T. (1976). *Growing and Declining Urban Areas: A Fiscal Comparison.* Washington, DC: Urban Institute.

Nelson, B. (1981). "Purchase of Services." George Washnis, (ed.), *Productivity Improvement Handbook for State and Local Government.* New York: John Wiley.

Niskanen, W. A. (1971). *Bureaucracy and Representative Government.* Chicago: Aldine-Atherton.

Ostrom, E. (1972). "Metropolitan Reform: Propositions Derived from Two Traditions." *Social Science Quarterly* 53 (December): 474–93.

_____. (1978). *Patterns of Metropolitan Policing.* Cambridge, MA: Ballinger.

_____ and R. Parks (1982). "Let's Watch Our Language: Or, a Methodological Critique of the Effort to Civilize the Jungle of Local Government in Metropolitan Areas Through the Imposition of Models of Simplicity on Systems of Organized Complexity." Unpublished paper, Workshop in Political Theory and Policy Analysis, Indiana University.

_____, R. Parks and G. Whitaker (1973). "Do We Really Want to Consolidate Urban Police Forces? A Reappraisal of Some Old Assertions." *Public Administration Review* 33 (September–October): 423–32.

Ostrom, V. (1969). "Operational Federalism: Organization for the Provisions of Public Services in the American Federal System." *Public Choice* 6 (Spring): 1–18.

_____. (1973). *The Intellectual Crisis in American Public Administration.* University: University of Alabama Press.

_____. (1977). "Public Goods and Public Choices." *Alternatives for Delivering Public Services.* E. S. Savas (ed.). Boulder, CO: Westview.

_____, and E. Ostrom (1971). "Public Choice: A Different Approach to the Study of Public Administration." *Public Administration Review* 21 (March/April): 203–16.

_____, E. Ostrom, C. Tiebout, and R. Warren (1961). "The Organization of Government in Metropolitan Areas." *American Political Science Review* 55 (December): 831–42.

Pirie, M. (1985). *Dismantling the State: The Theory and Practice of Privatization.* Dallas: National Center for Policy Analysis.

Savas, E. S. (1974). "Municipal Monopolies Versus Competition in Delivering Urban Services." (ed.), *Improving the Quality of Urban Management.* W. D. Hawley and D. Rogers Beverly Hills, CA: Sage.

_____. (1982). *Privatizing the Public Sector: How to Shrink Government.* Chatham, NJ: Chatham House.

Scott, S. L. Keller, and J. C. Bollens (1972). *Local Governmental Boundaries and Areas.* Berkeley: University of California Press.

Sjoquist, D. (1982). "The Effect of the Number of Local Governments on Central City Expenditure." *National Tax Journal* 35 (March): 79–87.

Sonenblum, S., J. Ries, and J. Kirlin (1977). *How Cities Provide Services: An Evaluation of Alternative Delivery Structures.* Cambridge, MA: Ballinger.

Spann, R. M. (1976). "Public *vs.* Private Provision of Governmental Services." Borcherding (ed.). T. E. *Budgets and Bureaucrats: Organization of Government Growth.* Durham, NC: Duke University Press.

Staaf, R. J. (1977). "The Public School System in Transition: Consolidation and Parental Choice." *Budgets and Bureaucrats.* Durham, NC: Duke University Press.

Stein, R. (1982). "The Political Economy of Municipal Functional Responsibility." *Social Science Quarterly* 63:530–48.

_____. (1990). *Urban Alternatives: Public and Private Markets in the Provision of Local Services.* Pittsburgh: University of Pittsburgh Press.

Stevens, B. (1986). "Contracting Out for Municipal Service Delivery." A report prepared for the U.S. Department of Housing and Urban Development, Washington, DC.

Stigler, G. (1971). "The Theory of Economic Regulation." *Bell Journal of Economics and Management Science* 2 (Spring): 220–35.

Straussman, J. D. (1981). "More Bang for Fewer Bucks? Or How Local Governments Can Rediscover the Potentials (and Pitfalls) of the Market." *Public Administration Review* 41:150–57.

Tiebout, C. M. (1966). "A Pure Theory of Local Expenditures." *Journal of Political Economy* 64 (October): 416–24.

Tullock, G. (1970). *Private Wants, Public Means: An Economic Analysis of the Desirable Scope of Government.* New York: Basic Books.

Wagner, R. E. (1971). *The Fiscal Organization of American Federalism.* Chicago: Markham.

_____. (1980). "Institutional Constraints and Local Community Formation." *American Economic Review* 80:352–64.

Wagner, R. E., and W. E. Weber (1976). "Competition, Monopoly, and the Organization of Government in Metropolitan Areas." *Journal of Law and Economics.*

Warren, R. O. (1964). "A Municipal Services Market Model of Metropolitan Organization." *Journal of the American Institute of Planners* 30 (August).

_____. (1966). *Government in Metropolitan Regions: A Reappraisal of Fractionated Political Organization.* Davis: University of California Institute of Governmental Affairs.

Wood, R. C. (1959). "A Division of Powers in Metropolitan Areas." Arthur Maas (ed.), *Area and Power.* Glencoe, IL: Free Press of Glencoe.

8. Police Privatization Ventures as Strategies to Maintain and Enhance Public Safety

Roland C. Dart, III

One of the most serious problems in America today is that the demand for police services by the public is increasing at a rate greater than the ability of local government to generate the revenue to pay for the cost of personnel resources needed to meet this demand. It is contended that the imbalance between demand for police services and available economic resources will increase in the future. If this imbalance is to be effectively addressed, police administrators will have to look for solutions beyond the bounds of their organizations. Opportunities exist to minimize the imbalance of demand for protection and escalating public costs by adopting police privatization strategies.

Our objective is to illustrate how police privatization ventures can enhance the level of public safety in a cost-effective manner. The following are addressed to illustrate this premise:

1. A brief examination of the underlying causes of the imbalance and why intra-organizational management strategies have not been sufficient to correct the imbalance.

2. An examination of several actual situations that involve different levels of privatization at the local level. These include the identification of several within policing environments that appear to offer a greater opportunity to develop and implement privatization ventures.

3. An illustration of why police administrators at the local level of government must become more actively involved in the growth management process by fostering, developing, and implementing privatization strategies and ventures.

4. Concluding comments and consideration of the future of police privatization at the local level.

The Emergence of an Imbalance Between the Demand for Police Services and Available Police Resources

The imbalance between the demand for police services and resources available to respond to public demand has developed over the last twenty-five to thirty years.

Although it could be argued that the growth of law enforcement in the United States began with the Industrial Revolution and development of our early transportation technology, local law enforcement had a relatively narrow role in American society during these eras as compared to today. Local police activities were substantially confined to crime suppression and the enforcement of laws. Organizational specialization was very low compared to that of contemporary police organizations. There were five key historical events, however, that significantly altered the role of local law enforcement in America and will continue to do so in the future.

The first historical event was the availability of television to virtually all Americans by the late 1950s. Up to this time, news of national events was disseminated by theater newsreels, newspapers, and magazines. The news was usually filtered to reflect regional interests and untimely occurrences. With the advent of television, however, news was introduced into family living rooms shortly after occurring or, in some cases, at the time of occurrence. The second major historical event was the Civil Rights Movement. Prior to the 1950s and 1960s, racial clashes and riots had occurred sporadically throughout our history. They were soon forgotten and faded into history. This was not the case once television vividly depicted violent clashes between ill-trained and ill-supervised police and large crowds of citizens angry about continued racial discrimination. During the early 1960s there was a popular reaction that focused upon local law enforcement. This reaction involved two factions. Although these two factions were polarized, their concerns produced the same outcome. The conservative faction focused upon a concern that the police were ineffective in controlling riots, looting, and crowd violence. The liberal faction focused upon the suppressive and violently reactionary nature of local police. Both factions demanded police reform. This was the third event leading to our present dilemma.

For local law enforcement, the period between the early 1960s and late 1970s could be considered a renaissance. President Johnson created the President's Commission on Law Enforcement and the Administration of Justice in 1967. This commission and its many task forces examined in detail numerous facets of our state and local criminal justice community. The reports of these task forces prompted Congress to pass the Omnibus Crime Control and Safe Streets Act in 1968. This act provided for the establishment of the Law Enforcement Assistance Administration (LEAA) within the U.S. Department of Justice. The LEAA was the mechanism whereby millions of dollars were transferred to local government for the improvement of the police, courts, and corrections. The lion's share of all this money went to the police, and the money paid for extensive research into law enforcement improvement strategies and their implementation.

Perhaps the most significant LEAA program to bring about qualitative change in local police was the Law Enforcement Education Program (LEEP). This program paid for college educational costs for peace officers in undergraduate and graduate programs across the United States. As local law enforcement took advantage of new technology in policing and as the average education of peace officers increased dramatically, so did policing costs.

This renaissance period had a companion movement that was to have an additional effect upon policing costs. This fourth historical event concerned the unionization of the police. Prior to the 1960s, only a few Eastern police agencies were unionized. Police strikes were isolated events. Although there were other socioeconomic and political reasons for the unionization of the police during this era, a prime factor involved the social unrest and turbulence of the 1960s and 1970s. The conservative elements of local law enforcement saw unionization as a means of self-protection against the liberal forces of reform. This spread quickly into the Midwest and Western United States. In 1968 the police in Vallejo, California, went on strike for several weeks. State legislation allowed for collective bargaining of public employees, and some cities and counties went so far as to adopt binding arbitration as a part of their charters.

As all these historical forces unfolded, the net effect was an escalation of public service costs—especially policing. Taxes increased proportionately to increasing local government costs. The fifth historical event that brings us to our present dilemma in local public safety concerned large, popular movements to combat efforts of local government to raise taxes. The primary tax that supported local government costs was private property taxes. The public reaction was substantial. This era, the Taxpayer's Revolt, resulted in legislation being passed in states throughout the country that restricted the taxing authority of government. The most notable occurred in California with the passage of Proposition Thirteen, which served as a model for other states.

During the unfolding of these historical events, police administrators tried desperately to maximize the effectiveness of available resources. The most notable strategies involved the reduction of costs by civilianizing functions formerly performed by more costly sworn positions and a greater reliance upon science and technology.

Initial Responses to the Imbalance

Police administrators responded to this challenge for more effective and efficient utilization of resources with the implementation of a number of cost-saving strategies in an effort to channel more resources into the primary police tasks of crime suppression and prevention. It is important to understand that these strategies addressed the restructuring of internal resources as opposed to an attempt to manage the external environment within which the agency operates. These strategies include: (1) the civilianization of certain tasks performed by sworn officers; (2) elimination of certain noncrime related tasks; (3) prioritizing the calls for service requiring that an officer be dispatched; and (4) greater reliance upon science and technology in the management of human resources.

These intra-organizational strategies contributed to greater police efficiency but, in most cases, they were not adequate to substantially correct the imbalance between demand for police service and the costs of meeting the demand. This was especially true of most municipalities and counties because of their heavy reliance upon private property taxes.

Exploration of Alternative Strategies: Privatization

As a police chief in California both before and subsequent to the passage of Proposition Thirteen, I attempted to maintain an adequate level of service in an environment of serious economic scarcity. Vallejo, California, was sharply affected by Proposition Thirteen. All of the management strategies previously described were employed but they were not enough. Our level of service deteriorated like many other jurisdictions that had a high reliance upon property taxes. The topic of privatization of certain governmental services was developing in the literature of public administration. The services being discussed, however, focused mostly in the area of garbage collection, parking control, and similar activities.

We began to speculate about whether or not privatization might be a useful strategy in local law enforcement. We attempted to gain an understanding of the term "privatization of public services."

Choosing Private Police Settings for Examination

My search for existing examples of private policing resulted in a number of different situations that involved varying types of policing. It was decided that these situations would be examined by conducting site visits. We became physically involved in observing the actual operations and conducted interviews with key personnel involved in the services being performed. These settings, all in California, included the Exxon Oil Refinery in Benicia, the Mare Island Shipyard in Vallejo, and the private community of Pebble Beach. Each of these situations involved varying levels of private policing. They were created, for the most part, by the private entities as opposed to a formal effort upon the part of the local governments within which they existed.

My objective was to examine how they came into existence, their relationship and impact on the local government's provision of police services, and to discover any social, economic, or political factors in the environment that affected their creation. In other words, a search for any environmental patterns that might be common to each of these arrangements was conducted. Before these arrangements or situations are examined, however, it is important to discuss what is meant by the term "privatization of police services." As will be seen, the line that distinguishes what is considered public and what constitutes private service is not as sharp as some would believe. This required the development of a conceptual framework to provide a means of understanding real world situations (see Figure 8.1).

A Conceptual Framework to Examine Private Policing

Many different policing environments were visited and examined. A typology of three types of settings was adopted that represents a continuum of settings called "closed," "mixed," and "open." A pattern emerged concerning the nature of these

Figure 8.1 Public-Private Security Continuum

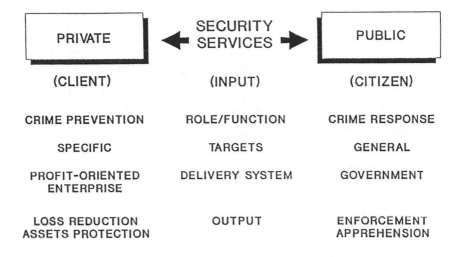

Source: National Advisory Committee on Criminal Justice Standards and Goals, Report of the Task Force on Private Security (Washington, DC: GPO, 1976), p. 7.

environmental settings expressed by five variables. Figure 8.2 is an illustration of these three settings and the intensity of the five variables within each setting. The "closed" setting was noted to exhibit a high level of controlled access, very homogeneous population, singleness of purpose, dense demographics, and a high level of environmental stability. As the settings shift toward a "mixed" and "open" environment, the variables shift as well. Figure 8.3 is an example of the settings within which policing occurs.

The next task was to search for a conceptual framework to further examine the nature of these environmental settings and how they affect the characteristics of the organizations that conduct policing services within the settings. The approach that appeared best suited for the task of examining and comparing policing environments was to employ environmental typologies. Typologies were used as a frame of reference when questions were posed about the nature of police organizations that existed and operated within the environments examined. Generally, there are three approaches in the use of typologies in the study of organizations. These three are: (1) environment-input typologies reflected in the studies of persons such as Burns, Woodward, Stalker, and Emery and Trist; (2) environment-output typologies produced by Parsons, Katz and Kahn, and Blau and Scott; and (3) typologies based upon interorganizational factors proposed by Etzioni, Clark and Wilson, Barnard, and Simon (Silverman, 1978:171).

All were considered, but the one most useful for our purposes was what could be termed an environmental-input typology. This approach to the study of organizations was proposed by James Thompson.

Figure 8.2
A Typology of Environmental
Settings in Which Policing Occurs

VARIABLES	ENVIRONMENTAL SETTING		
	Closed	Mixed	Open
Constraints To Access	High	Moderate	Low
Homogeneity of Population	High	Moderate	Low
Singleness of Purpose	High	Moderate To High	Low
Demographic Density	High	Moderate To High	Low
Level of Stability	High	Moderate	Low

Figure 8.3 Closed, Mixed, and Open Police Settings

CLOSED	MIXED	OPEN
MILITARY BASES	LIMITED ACCESS RESIDENTIAL COMMUNITIES	CITIES
	AMUSEMENT OR RECREATION CENTERS	
PUBLIC AND PRIVATE RESEARCH CENTERS	REGIONAL SHOPPING CENTERS	COUNTIES
	AIRPORTS	
INDUSTRIAL COMPLEXES (Oil Refineries or Chemical Plants)	EDUCATIONAL INSTITUTIONS	
	GOVERNMENT BUILDINGS	STATES

Thompson's *Organizations in Action*

Thompson suggests a typology involving three forms of technology: long-linked, mediating, and intensive. He maintains that as the type of technological demands upon the organization changes, corresponding changes can be seen in the characteristics of the organization (Thompson, 1967:15–16). Some of the characteristics include: (1) levels of specialization; (2) how the organization relates to clients; and (3) the skill level of employees.

Another valuable part of Thompson's study concerned the boundary-spanning characteristics of the organizational structures as they related to adapting or adjusting to the complexity of the environment. He borrowed from March and Simon and from Dill and Coleman the idea that the dimensions of homogeneity and degree of stability are the most useful in the analysis of organizations and their environments. There is a logical connection between Thompson's three typologies and the three types of policing environments. Thompson's three typologies and the three types of policing environments. Thompson's long-linked form of technology equated to police organizations in closed environments, mediating technology to organizations in mixed environments, and intensive technology to organizations in open environments.

Several additional variables proposed by Joan Woodward's work, entitled "Management and Technology," were added to the analysis (Woodward, 1978). The model that resulted from the combing of the variables suggested by Thompson and Woodward's work is illustrated in Figure 8.4. Each of the variables will be briefly defined as they relate to the three types of environmental settings in the continuum. Each of these sites mentioned were visited and inspected.

CONTINGENCY AND SPECIALIZATION. An important dynamic of the organization and the environment concerns the level contingency in the environment and the level of specialization in the organization. Thompson links the level of specialization of an organization with the level of contingencies of the environment external to the organization (Thompson, 1967:70). Specialization is a product of adapting or adjusting to the environment. The level of contingency in closed environments, such as oil refineries, is very low in police security. Consequently, specialization is also low. At the other end of the continuum, contingency faced by police is very high in open settings, such as cities, and specialization is high. Between the two extremes, contingency is moderate and so is organizational specialization.

INTERNAL DEPENDENCE. According to Thompson (1967:54), there are three types of internal dependence. Pooled interdependence, as found in closed police settings, is described as the situation where each part of the organization depends upon the whole. If one part fails, the whole fails. If one shift of a plant security fails, the whole system fails in its mission. An example of pooled interdependence in a city police department would be when the central communications system fails. Officers cannot be dispatched to calls for service.

Sequential interdependence occurs when the organizational parts are linked in a serial fashion. Failure in one part of the organization requires another to be adjusted to accommodate the failure. If the gate security fails to adequately screen

Figure 8.4
Comparison of Organizational Variables by Police Setting

ORGANIZATION TYPE ＼ VARIABLE	CLOSED Oil Refinery	MIXED Private Community Shopping Center	OPEN City County State
Degree of Specialization	LOW	MODERATE	HIGH
Type of Interdependence	POOLED	POOLED & SEQUENT-IAL	POOLED SEQUENT. RECIPRO-CAL
Type of Coordination			
Range of Planning	SHORT	MEDIUM	LONG
Skill Level of Organizational Members	LOW	MODERATE	HIGH
Number & Nature of Policy Decisions	FEW & SIMPLE	BECOMING COMPLEX	MANY & COMPLEX
Level of Discretion by Organizational Members	LOW	MODERATE	HIGH

persons entering the area, the patrol force must adjust its efforts or shift its resources to accommodate the failure.

Reciprocal interdependence, in addition to pooled and sequential interdependence, is exhibited in instances where the output of one part of the organization becomes input for other parts of the organization. An example is when a police patrol force saturates a high crime area and makes numerous arrests. This is an output. This output then becomes an input to other organizational elements such as fingerprinting, jail confinement, bail processing, and the like.

THE REMAINING FIVE VARIABLES. With regard to the remaining five variables, changes in these variables depend upon where the organization exists within a continuum of simple to complex environments (Woodward, 1978:190–206). Each will be discussed briefly in terms of the relative position within the continuum of environmental settings.

There are three types of coordination: standardization, plan, and mutual adjustment. Standardization is found in closed environments. Organizational coordination is achieved through standardization where situations are stable, repetitive, and relatively few in number. Thompson states, "Standardization involves the establishment of routines or rules which constrain each unit or position into paths consistent with those taken by others in the independent relationships" (Thompson, 1967:56). Woodward parallels this concept when she indicates that organizations which operate in simple environments engage substantially in short-range planning with decisions that are few and simple (Woodward, 1978:190–206). Contingencies are few and, if they occur, they are of the same type. Consequently, organizational planning is confined to immediate action. Routines can be standardized due to the environment being highly predictable, certain, and stable. This situation approximates that found in the closed setting of an oil refinery or military installation. The police organizations that operate within these settings reflect these characteristics. The main task of police organizations in settings of this type is to control access to the interior of the facility.

Virtually all contingencies are covered in written procedures. When a situation arises which is not a part of the routine, the gate is simply not opened or the persons not allowed access until a supervisor resolves the problem. Coordination by standardization works well in this environment; however, this is not the case when the environment shifts toward instability and becomes more dynamic.

To illustrate what occurs within organizations in situations of this nature, Thompson borrows from March and Simon's concept of "coordination by plan." He states, "Coordination by plan does not require the same high degree of stability and routinization that is required for coordination by standardization, and therefore, is more appropriate for more dynamic situations, especially when a changing task environment impinges on the organization" (Thompson, 1967:56). This situation is similar to that described by Woodward when the task environment shifts from the simple to the complex. The environment is not as stable as previously described but it is not totally uncertain. Prediction is still relatively high but, because the level of contingency is increasing, not all situations can be accounted for in routinized procedures or rules. Planning becomes mid-range in an attempt to anticipate where contingencies may occur. The number and complexity of decisions begin to increase and policies become more open to allow for expanded limits of discretion. This description of organizations and their environments resembles those observed of policing organizations operating in limited access residential settings and large, regional shopping complexes.

In limited access residential settings control over access is still an important objective of the organization. The nature of the people entering and leaving the setting, however, is more heterogeneous than that found in an oil refinery or military installation. In addition to the residents leaving and entering the setting, persons providing services to the residents also enter and leave at a high frequency. Consequently, controls must be relaxed. A regional shopping center is a similar situation, but control is maintained by monitoring or observing the visitors and site and the persons on the site either electronically or visually. Observations of settings of this type disclosed that the type of coordination included elements of both standardization and plan. Because the organizations had the additional task of patrolling their areas and being available to respond to any need of the population, they faced increased contingency. Although the contingencies could be predicted to occur within certain narrow categories such as family disputes, intoxication, and the like, procedures for handling such contingencies cannot be totally covered by standardized rules.

Further, the potential for other unpredictable contingencies exists as well. As a result, communications between operating units occur frequently and a broader range of discretion in decisionmaking occurs than that in closed situations. The environment demands more from the organizations. But, because of the foregoing environmental variables, the organization reflects the mixed characteristics of both open and closed types.

The third type of coordination identified by Thompson is called coordination by mutual adjustment. In instances where organizations engage in this form of coordination, it is in response to highly shifting, dynamic, and unpredictable environments. Contingency is high. Coordination by mutual adjustment involves the transmission of new information during the process of action. It may also involve communication across hierarchial lines (Thompson, 1967:56).

This environmental situation is analogous with Woodward's complex technological environment. The process of planning becomes centralized and removed from the level of execution or the organization's primary tasks. In addition, because of the relatively unstable or shifting nature of the environment, elements of long-range planning appear. Although the organization employs coordination by standardization and plan, mutual adjustment occurs in the form of feedback mechanisms and communications across hierarchial lines.

Police organization operating within environments of this type have been labeled open organizations. They employ elaborate reporting and management information systems to coordinate their activities. Decisionmaking often involves group processes. The level of contingency is such that not all eventualities can be anticipated and covered by a standardized plan. Organizational members have broad discretionary powers. Policy becomes an important element in coordinating the many units of the organization as compared to the closed or mixed organizations. Municipal, county, and state law enforcement agencies best reflect this situation.

Privatization as a Linkage Between Public and Private Policing: A New Perspective

After all of this analysis, privatization of public policing functions simply means the transfer of certain functional activities to organizations which exist to make a profit or organizations which are nonprofit in nature. Further, it is proposed that the situations best suited for privatization exist in the mixed environmental settings because of the nature of the variables exhibited by the settings.

We found that privatization of police services is best described as the formation of formal linkages between the public and private sectors where prevention of crime is the primary objective to be achieved in the linkage. There are three important factors to understand in our meaning of privatization of police services in the foregoing definition:

1. Privatization means that certain security and crime prevention activities are to be delegated to the private sector. Privatization of police services does not mean a wholesale transfer in the provision of police services to the private sector. There will continue to be an ongoing linkage between the private entity and the parent public entity.

2. Although privatization is viewed as a means to maintain primary crime prevention and security services in an era of economic scarcity, it is not suggested that the arrangements be temporary. So long as the environment retains all the characteristics of a mixed environment, the arrangement can endure. If the environment shifts, then the arrangement must be reexamined. As will be illustrated later, one such situation occurred when the joint venture was terminated and the public agency resumed its full scope of law enforcement activities. In this case, the mixed environment shifted to an open environment over approximately eight years.

3. There are two fictions that exist about public policing. Just because a setting has elements of a public nature, it does not follow that the settings must be policed by a public agency. Airport terminals, shopping centers, recreational complexes, and limited access residential communities are examples of private settings that have substantial public elements. In some cases, settings of these types are policed by public agencies while other very similar settings are policed by private agencies. The second fiction concerns the level of skill required to perform certain police tasks. Highly skilled and costly personnel are not needed to perform certain police tasks. As we will see, levels of skill are closely related to the level of decisionmaking and contingencies being faced in the setting.

A Practical Basis for the Examination of Privatization Opportunities

A search of examples of private policing that approximated the mixed environments was made. Numerous personal and professional associates were contacted in the Western states. A number of examples were located. When policing environments exhibiting the characteristics of mixed settings were explored, however, there were numerous varieties that could not be classified into categories. Consequently, the list had to be narrowed in a focused fashion so that the analysis could be kept within workable limits. We will focus upon those instances where a local government would be faced with commercial or residential growth which would have a direct consequence upon the effective delivery of public police services. Where other appropriate opportunities for privatization occur, however, they will not be ignored.

The review of examples of different forms of police privatization will involve one commercial and three residential examples. Although these settings qualify as mixed settings, the commercial example will have to be examined on a somewhat different basis from that of the residential examples. This is due to the fact that each type of setting generates different policing problems and that the independent variables associated with these situations vary.

The objective of the subsequent part of this chapter is an indepth examination of linkages that have occurred between private- and public-sector policing organizations. The unique residential settings are Rossmoor, California; Sun City, Arizona; and Carefree, Arizona. Brief comments will be made concerning two other settings in Maricopa County, Arizona, and Pebble Beach, California. The commercial setting selected for examination is the Sunvalley Regional Shopping Complex in Concord, California.

It should be noted that all of these examples of private policing in a public environment evolved or came into existence with varying levels of involvement with the government having primary jurisdiction of the area. Carefree, Arizona, was a creation of the developer with little or no involvement by Maricopa County. On the other hand, the Maricopa County Sheriff's Department played a substantial role in the development of security in Sun City. In California the Concord Police Department took an active role in the creation of the Sunvalley Regional Shopping Center. In Rossmoor, however, the Walnut Creek Police Department did not participate in the development of this community's private guard force.

Each of these examples of private policing will be examined in terms of (1) organization and demography; (2) governing structure; (3) personnel resources; (4) interorganizational relationships; and (5) the reciprocal implications between the private policing venture and the police agency having primary jurisdiction.

Rossmoor, California

The Rossmoor development is within the city limits of Walnut Creek, California. Walnut Creek encompasses thirteen to fifteen square miles and has a population of 62,600 (California Department of Finance, 1989). Rossmoor is within the incorporated area of Walnut Creek. Economically the city has a high mix of residential and commercial properties. Although Proposition Thirteen had a serious impact upon the city, the impact was not as severe as many other cities that relied almost entirely upon private property taxes as opposed to sales taxes.

The Rossmoor complex covers seven square miles with fifty-two acres set aside for future development. Development of the community began in 1964 and several small expansions are planned now. Housing is of the cluster type. The older structures are single-story apartment type in appearance while the newer structures have the appearance of condominiums. Interspersed among the clustered housing complexes are landscaped open spaces, walkways, and recreational facilities. To qualify to live in the area, a person must be forty-five years or older. Children are only allowed on a short-term, visiting basis. The population of Rossmoor was estimated to be 7,800 in 1980 and 8,300 in 1989. Housing can range from $80,000 to $400,000. There is only one entrance which is controlled by a guard post. Golf carts are a popular mode of transportation. A bus and shuttle service also provides transportation within the complex.

A board of directors serves as a governing body of Rossmoor. The board appoints a business manager in much the same manner as a city council hires a city manager. For all intents and purposes, Rossmoor resembles a medium-size city (Gasman, 1979).

The Rossmoor security force consists of twenty-two officers, including the supervisors. There are two full-time and two part-time dispatchers. The officers are not armed. Their annual operating budget is approximately $900,000. This is almost double the $555,000 cost in 1979. The officers of the security force are members of a union which negotiates wages and benefits annually.

Security services operate twenty-four hours a day and respond to approximately 900 calls for service a month. This is a moderate increase of 23 percent over the 8,800 calls for service responded to in 1979. If this were a city police department, the size of the Rossmoor Security force would approximate the size of a city handling the same number of calls for services. The vast majority of their calls are for first aid and CPR, persons locked out of the homes, vacation checks, escorting visitors, and the like. Although there are few motor vehicle accidents because of a twenty-five m.p.h. limit, emergency medical calls are high. This, of course, is due the age of the residents.

Both the Rossmoor security staff and Walnut Creek Police Department felt their agencies worked well together. Since the Rossmoor security force do not have police powers and their right to arrest is the same as a private citizen, the policy is that when a crime occurs, the security staff stand by until a Walnut Creek officer can respond. In 1979 there were 150 minor criminal incidents reported by the Rossmoor police. The Walnut Creek Police Department responded to approximately twenty-five of these incidents. There were no exact statistics available for 1989. It was estimated, however, that there had been no significant increase. It should be noted that the residents of Rossmoor pay property taxes for all the services that are provided for other Walnut Creek citizens. In addition, they must pay monthly charges for living in Rossmoor, which include security services. It appears, however, that the residents are willing to pay the extra costs for the level of safety and security they enjoy (Schillinger, 1989).

The economic implications for Walnut Creek in the event that Rossmoor terminated its private police arrangement would be substantial. Rossmoor comprises about 14 percent of Walnut Creek's population and about 25 percent of its land area. Absorbing Rossmoor would entail the creation of at least two additional patrol beats to be staffed around the clock, seven days a week. A conservative estimate of the cost to provide this service today by the city of Walnut Creek is $1.5 million (Murray, 1980). This condition continued over the next nine years (Gould, 1989).

The physical and demographic environment of Rossmoor exhibits all the characteristics of the mixed environment. This particular type of public-private police linkage has important potential implications for cities and counties facing similar types of development in the future.

Carefree, Arizona

Another example of a private-public police linkage, but with an environment slightly different from Rossmoor, is a community north of Scottsdale, Arizona. Carefree was first developed in 1971. The development consisted of large lots that would accommodate homes in the $100,000 to $300,000 range at that time. The lots were purchased from the developer and a number of contractors were available for custom home construction. Unlike Rossmoor, there were no physical boundaries nor a formal governing structure. At the beginning of the development in 1971 the owner organized a private patrol force and home alarm monitoring service. The construction sites were patrolled by guards and homes were constructed with alarm systems as a part of their design. The alarms were monitored by the security force.

When the development was completed in 1974, the developer sold the security and alarm monitoring service to the Sun Bird Security and Management Company. Sun Bird employed eighteen persons who engaged in either alarm monitoring and dispatching or uniformed patrol. Alarms were installed in 500 of the 800 homes built in Carefree (Withers, 1979).

Carefree was a part of Maricopa County and law enforcement was a primary service of the sheriff's department, so the area became a part of a larger patrol zone of that sheriff's department. No public services operated on a full-time basis in Carefree. As a consequence, response by the sheriff's department could take as much as forty-five minutes. The sheriff's department operated a part-time office in Carefree consisting of one investigator assisted by a reserve deputy. It was the custom and practice of the Sun Bird Security Force to respond to incidents and stand by until sheriff's deputies could arrive and take over the situation. The security force patrolled the area in marked vehicles and in uniform (Deputy Bob Barrett, 1979).

In all respects, this community approximated all the characteristics of the mixed policing environment. The level of contingency was relatively low, but not as low as Rossmoor. In Carefree we see a greater daily interaction between the public and private police.

Between 1979 and 1989, however, a significant shift occurred in the environment. Business grew and the area became more populated. Shopping centers and higher density housing were constructed. Today, Sun Bird Security monitors 1,000 alarms and employs 20 guards. Their activities, however, are alarm and facility security as opposed to patrol (Stewart, 1989). Although Carefree remains a very wealthy residential setting with increased commercial enterprises, the policing environment shifted to an open setting. As a consequence, the sheriff's department responded to the environmental shift by increasing its on-site resources. Carefree now has a sheriff's substation consisting of fifteen deputies who patrol the area of

Carefree and the adjoining community of Cave Creek on a twenty-four-hour, seven-day-a-week basis (Nelson, 1989).

There are important implications for public-private police linkages in the history of Carefree, Sun Bird Security, and the Maricopa County Sheriff's Department. This was an environment in transition from a mixed to open setting that took twenty years. As a model, the informal relationship that evolved in Carefree between the private and public sectors of policing could offer a strategy to manage policing in similar situations over a long period of transition.

Sun City, Arizona

Sun City, like Carefree, is an unincorporated residential area of Maricopa County. Also, Sun City approximated the mixed environmental setting of Carefree but in a different manner. Unlike Carefree, however, its mixed nature has not changed and the unique private and public policing arrangement continues today. Sun City's uniqueness is that it is a residential community for retired persons. Unlike Rossmoor, there are no physical boundaries and, for all intents and purposes, resembles a middle- to upper-middle-class community that can be found throughout the United States.

Sun City was the creation of one developer. Construction began 1974 and was completed in 1980. Sun City encompasses an area of about eighteen to twenty square miles with a population estimated to be 45,000 to 48,000. There are seven recreation centers that provide facilities for swimming, tennis, and crafts. There are nine golf courses and two bowling alleys. Although there is a homeowner's association, a taxpayer's association, and other special interest groups, none are involved in the policing arrangement that will be described (White, 1980).

Like Carefree, Sun City is patrolled by the Maricopa County Sheriff's Department. Sheriff's patrol services operate out of the Westside Substation located in Glendale, Arizona. Although Sun City, if incorporated, would constitute a fair-sized city, the public police resources committed to patrol the area are considerably less than what would be required for a police department in a city of this size. The reason for this condition is the existence of a volunteer police organization directed by the sheriff's department.

Although this volunteer group is supervised by the sheriff, it is a nonprofit, tax exempt private corporation organized in accordance with the laws of the state of Arizona. It has a board of officers and functions as a private corporation. The limited police powers of the group, however, are delegated by the sheriff in compliance with the state law governing the appointment of deputies. This force was organized when Sun City was under development. The retired residents, many from the military, formed a volunteer organization to assist in the patrol of the area. By 1980 the Sun City Crime Prevention Posse numbered 250 men and women. The sheriff's department provided training in first aid, CPR, firearms use and safety, and basic laws of arrest (Blankenship, 1980).

The posse has a considerable budget. In 1980 it raised $120,000 to pay for operating expenses, supplies, and liability and medical insurance. None of the posse members are compensated — it is a totally volunteer organization. The posse patrols the community on shifts, checks homes while residents are on vacation, and administers a "Crime Stop" program. This program reports suspicious circumstances or persons to a central reception facility for response by the sheriff's department. Other suspicious circumstances noted by patrolling posse members are relayed to the sheriff's department through their communications center.

Today, the annual budget continues to be approximately $80,000 to $120,000. The posse just moved into a new facility paid for by the volunteers and donations. This 12,400-square-feet facility cost over $1.2 million and contains a modern communications and complaint reception center. Classrooms, locker areas, and other facilities are provided. For all intents and purposes, this facility resembles a modern police department that would be the envy of any city of a similar size. The posse averages 5,569 hours of volunteer work and 15,118 miles of patrol a month. This private-public policing model is estimated to save the sheriff's department over $1 million a year (Page, 1989). Since 1980 several other retirement communities have been built in Maricopa County. Again, posses similar to Sun City's have been organized to assist in policing these communities. Sun City West and Sun Lakes are examples (Nelson, 1989).

The mixed environmental police setting has endured in Sun City and has been replicated in two other communities. It should be noted that the volunteer corporation of Sun City was an outgrowth of the residents' desire for greater protection. Later, the sheriff began to foster encouragement for other communities, but the organizations remain private in nature. This unique arrangement has rich implications for cities or counties facing the development of similar settings. Linkages of this type could be planned in advance of the development as cost-reduction measures while still enhancing the quality of life in the development.

Sunvalley Regional Shopping Center, Concord, California

Like the special purpose residential settings of Rossmoor, Carefree, and Sun City, some shopping complexes exhibit certain environmental variables that make them amenable to alternative modes of policing. Further, like the residential settings, shopping complexes are viewed as the most likely forms of commercial growth adversely affecting the provision of local police services. Without exception, the large, regional shopping complexes pose the greatest threat to increased demand for police services.

In the exploration of ways to mitigate the impact of these forms of commercial growth upon local government, the Sunvalley Regional Shopping Center in Concord, California, was selected for examination. This complex lies within the city limits of Concord. The shopping complex is policed by a private patrol service twenty-four hours a day, seven days a week.

Construction of Sunvalley began in 1965 and was completed in August 1967. The center is located on a 106-acre tract of land with an original development cost of $30 million. The shopping portion of the center encompasses 1.35 million square feet of space with a parking area that can accommodate 9,000 vehicles. Sunvalley has 130 stores, 17 eating establishments, an ice rink, and a motion picture theater. Depending upon the season of the year, the average number of employees is 3,000. The center attracts shoppers from a radius of twenty to twenty-five miles (the Taubman Company, 1980).

The Taubman Company owns Sunvalley and employs a security force supervised by a director of security. Originally, the Taubman Company contracted with a private security firm to supply guard personnel. The effectiveness of this arrangement was not as high as the management wished. As a consequence, they formed their own security force (George Kelly, 1980). According to Assistant Director of Security Bruce Dostie (1989), the guard force numbers twenty—including one full-time and two part-time radio dispatchers. According to Dostie, the security force is allocated within three shifts, with the bulk of personnel assigned to periods when the shopping center is open. The primary functions of the guard force are crime prevention and public assistance. Crime prevention is provided by scooter and foot patrol by unarmed officers equipped with a baton, tear gas, and a portable radio.

It should be noted that at the time the Sunvalley shopping complex was being built in 1965, the area was patrolled by the Concord Police Department. At this time the Concord Police Department consisted of 118 sworn officers and 70 civilians (U.S. Department of Justice, *UCR*, 1968, Table 60, 236). The area of Sunvalley fell within one patrol beat. At the time of Sunvalley's construction, the Concord Police Department had concerns about the impact of the center upon policing and traffic in the area. Unlike the other examples in Arizona and Rossmoor, there was an effort to control the impact by the police department. A study was initiated which resulted in a series of recommendations. These recommendations stated:

1. Double the manpower on the present beat which encompasses Sunvalley and Park and Shop, during the day shift and swing shift hours;
2. That the present citizen's arrest policy be amended, revised or rewritten to provide for a more efficient method of handling this service;
3. Establishment of police records exclusive to Sunvalley center;
4. A staff grade officer to be designated as liaison officer with the center and be responsible for coordinating activity between the police department and Sunvalley; and
5. Tactical plans be instituted for answering alarms or other emergencies at the center [Burns, 1967:24–25].

These recommendations were made in 1967. During the next twenty-three years, all of the recommendations were implemented except for the tactical emergency plan. The importance of an emergency plan which had failed to be implemented was highlighted when a twin-engine, private plane crashed into the mall roof of the center in 1984.

The Concord police study, however, showed foresight and identified that a key aspect in the effective provision of police service at a shopping complex of this magnitude concerned the interorganizational relationship between the public and private police. The Concord police study examined shopping complexes in other communities and stated:

Relationships between the Mayfield Mall and the Mountain View Police Department are strained to the point of nearly no cooperation, due to a series of misunderstandings with both sides. The shopping center management feels the Police Department has not shown sufficient interest in its problems, and the Police Department feels the shopping center has unreasonable demands for service. This relationship has deteriorated to the point that bickering occurred over the design of the badge worn by the shopping center security agents [Burns, 1967:6].

The Concord study, in its examination of this problem, identified the necessity of a close interorganizational relationship between the public police department and the private security forces of the shopping center. The report went on to state, "The importance of maintaining a close relationship with the shopping center and the various security agents employed there will be rewarded with a minimum demand for service, management sympathetic to police problems, an exchange of information between all security units and a generally more efficient accomplishment of the police task at the center" (Burns, 1967:6).

Summary

The examination of these four examples of private policing has disclosed a pattern with regard to the form and structure of the type of policing and some key aspects of their working environment. It appears that as the degree of heterogeneity of the environment and the level of physical access increases, the complexity of the policing tasks increase along with the level of contingency. This interrelationship is illustrated in Figure 8.5.

The implications of this interrelationship are that it provides a basis for local government to evaluate different types of growth and the level of impact the growth might result in for policing. Further, this information can offer an insight into appropriate opportunities to consider privatization ventures to mitigate the adverse impact of the development upon the provision of police services.

Another important factor to consider in the examples examined is how they came into existence and their interrelationship with the public policing organizations in their area. Both Rossmoor and Carefree came into existence because of a conscious effort upon the part of the private organizations that created the developments. Later, however, an informal relationship evolved with the local law enforcement agencies. In the case of Sunvalley and Sun City the local law enforcement agency played an active role in the establishment of private policing resources.

Privatization Ventures as a Strategy to Mitigate the Adverse Impact of Growth

Cities and counties faced with residential and commercial growth in a climate of scarce economic resources should consider privatization of police services as a

Figure 8.5 Level of Contingency Based Upon Degree of Heterogeneity and Physical Access

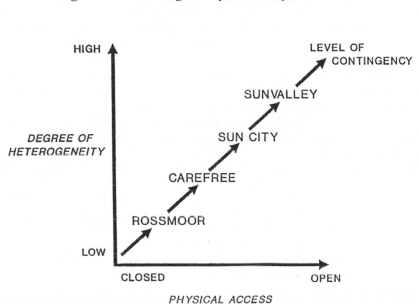

mitigation measure. To accomplish this objective requires that the city or county police assume an active role in the review of proposed developments for the purpose of considering privatization ventures as mitigation measures.

It is recognized that this will be no simple task. There are serious barriers or impediments to this process that must be overcome. Police unions fear privatization because of a loss of membership and other concerns. Developers wish to reduce their costs to increase profit. These factors, however, can be overcome. It can be demonstrated that the public police can play a much more proactive role in the suppression and prevention of major crime in high crime areas of a city or county by being relieved of time-consuming patrol of areas traditionally without major crime problems. Secondly, developers will find that the people are seeking a higher quality of life by living in relatively crime-free environments and will pay for the additional level of protection.

It is suggested that opportunities to create private policing ventures should be viewed in terms of three levels of application: (1) level one—alarm monitoring and response services; (2) level two—volunteer police; (3) level three—private guard forces; and (4) level four—private contracting. The consideration of any one or a combination of these alternatives should be based upon a careful analysis of proposed developments.

Police Planning and Environmental Impact Assessment

Local law enforcement agencies that have no formal planning person or unit that devotes a considerable amount of time to the planning process will, in most cases, be reactive and poorly administered agencies. Fortunately, most of these agencies are not strangers to the planning process. They tend to be the most proactive of the various local government service organizations. They have not, however, extended their influence into the general plan process of cities and counties. It is my contention here that local law enforcement agencies must become an active member of the growth management process of local government.

The police agency should evaluate a proposed development and, based upon the environmental nature of that development, draw conclusions about the impact of it upon the continued provision of police services. The concern should be to maintain a high level of response to serious community crime problems and resist residential or commercial developments that will drain or dilute police resources. The police agency should look at the nature of the development in terms of income level, housing density, the age of the inhabitants the development is intended for, its multiple or single purpose character, and the like. Based upon these factors, an environmental impact report should result with proposed mitigation measures.

Each state has legislation allowing for control of growth and the imposition of mitigation measures when there is an adverse impact upon public safety. Most states have the ability to create special tax districts or mandated homeowner groups.

Level One: Alarm Monitoring and Private Response

Where a development is relatively open and heterogeneous and the task environment has a high level of contingency, the use of alarm monitoring of residential and commercial developments is appropriate. Because of its open nature, greater first line policing by the public agency is necessary. Developers can be required to include medical, fire, and intrusion alarms in residential developments and monitoring conducted through fees collected from homeowner associations or a protection district. Alarm monitoring agencies can forward medical or fire alarms to appropriate departments. In some cities alarm companies provide the first response to intrusion alarms while robbery alarms require first response by police.

Several years ago police communications personnel would monitor hundreds of commercial alarms. The false alarm rate was about 97 percent. This posed a serious threat to police resources. As a consequence, most local law enforcement agencies have not allowed private alarms to terminate in police communications centers, with the possible exception of financial institutions. Local police reserve their alarm monitoring and response to publicly owned facilities.

Level Two: Volunteer Police Ventures

This policing alternative is reserved for developments that approximate Sun City and the other special purpose developments that have evolved around the country. The level of contingency is less than an open environment. The development is becoming more socially homogeneous. The opportunity to develop private police ventures in the form of volunteer groups is very high. Because the task environment still has a measure of contingency, the local police will play a leadership role in the daily supervision and management of the venture.

Communities that face the development of special living environments that approximate Sun City should take the opportunity to make site visits to these examples. The volunteer police groups are very cooperative and proud of their efforts and tours are routinely conducted.

Level Three: Private Guard Forces

Privatization by the use of guard forces is reserved for large, regional shopping complexes like Sunvalley and highly homogeneous and closed environments like Rossmoor. There are many similar developments across the country. In addition, increasingly popular recreational living centers in mountain communities or lake areas are another form of development where private guard forces could be a valuable mitigation measure for local law enforcement.

In these settings the local police should continue to maintain liaison with the guard force. The local police could provide training, communications, and general direction during instances of major or serious crime. Private guard forces can be trained to prepare police reports, make citizen's arrests, and perform CPR and first aid. The police agency could assist in the background investigation process in states that have no strict legal provisions for private security.

Another example of the development of a semiprivate policing venture occurred in Crofton, Maryland, in 1969. Crofton is an unincorporated residential subdivision built as a special living environment for persons working in the Washington, DC, metropolitan area. The Anne Arundel County Police Department could not provide a level of police protection that met the expectations of the residents of Crofton. As a result, the Crofton Homeowners Association decided to finance a private security force. This force performed twenty-four-hour security patrol. When suspicious circumstances or criminal activity was detected, the county police responded and handled the incidents. The costs associated with the security force were shared by the members of the association.

Level Four: Contracting

The Level Four alternative is proposed because of an increase in a relatively new form of privatization. Police personnel are a high cost public resource. Traditionally, police work often included tasks that required a relatively low level of skill. As a consequence, local government leadership advocated civilianization of certain police tasks as a means to reduce personnel costs. These tasks included records management, dispatching, property and evidence processing, data processing, and the like. These tasks are internal to the police organization and generally require public civilian employees as opposed to private contractors.

There are, however, a number of external tasks that police perform that also require a low level of skill and constitute a waste of highly skilled police resources. These activities include parking enforcement, animal control, abandoned vehicle abatement, facility security, service of subpoenas, and the like. Governments at all levels should consider contracting these and similar services to the private sector where they can be done at a considerably reduced cost. In the city of Vallejo, California, a police reserve unit was organized as a nonprofit, tax-exempt corporation. Vallejo is a city of 90,000 with a police department of 140 employees. The police department contracted with the reserve unit to perform many of the services mentioned previously at an annual savings of $250,000.

Summary and Conclusions

The following quote by Florestano and Gordon in their 1980 article continues to be relevant:

> The public versus private debate in local government administration is an old and emotional issue that has occasionally disappeared from view only to surface, inevitably, once again. In recent years, the debate has attained renewed saliency as many local governments, faced with increased demands for new and better service but constrained by constituency pressures to limit the growth of government, have increasingly turned to the private sector for services.

The complexion of our society is under constant change. Science and technology offer new and improved ways of providing quality public safety services. Public costs, however, continue to be a major problem in the provision of police services. As the public becomes more and more involved in restricting revenue through legislation and allocating tax dollars to primary services, local government must become more creative and innovative in how it provides those public services.

Law enforcement leadership must recognize the existing social and economic pressures that can render their agencies incapable of performing their primary crime control responsibilities. Strategic and future-oriented planning and research are vital to maintain present and future police services. These strategic plans should always consider privatization as a possible mitigation measure to growth or maintenance of services in an environment of scarce economic resources.

We recognize that there are numerous social, political, and economic implications associated with privatization ventures in policing. Each state has its own procedures for local control of commercial and residential growth. Regardless of these differences and socioeconomic factors, there are several conditions where privatization venture conditions offer rich, strategic opportunities to maintain a high level of police service at reasonable costs.

References

Burns, R. (1967). "Sunvalley Center Staff Study." Concord Police Department (July 12) (Unpublished Mimeograph).

Due, J. F., and A. F. Friedlaender (1977). *Government Finance.* Homewood, IL: Richard I. Irwin.

California Department of Finance (1989). Demographic Research Unit. *Population of California Cities and Counties, January 1, 1988–January 1, 1989.* Sacramento, CA: State Printing Office (May).

California State Controller's Office (1979). *Annual Report.* "Financial Transactions Concerning Cities of California." Sacramento, CA: State Printing Office.

California State Office of Criminal Justice Planning (1977). *The Impact of Proposition 13.* Sacramento, CA: State Printing Office.

Florestano, P., and S. B. Gordon (1980). "Public vs. Private: Small Government Contracting with the Private Sector." *Public Administration Review* 1 (January–February): 29.

Hudzik, J. K. and G. W. Cordner (1983). *Planning in Criminal Justice Organizations and Systems.* New York: Macmillan.

International City Management Association (1988). *Municipal Year Book.* Washington, DC: ICMA.

National Advisory Committee on Criminal Justice Standards and Goals (1976). *Report of the Task Force on Private Security.* Washington, DC: Government Printing Office.

Silverman, D. (1978). *The Theory of Organizations.* New York: Marcel Dekker.

Thompson, J. D. (1967). *Organizations in Action.* New York: McGraw-Hill.

U.S. Department of Justice. FBI (1979). *Uniform Crime Reports* (UCR). Washington, DC: Government Printing Office.

U.S. Department of Justice. Federal Bureau of Investigation (1989). *Uniform Crime Reports* (UCR). Washington, DC: Government Printing Office.

Wilson, O. W. (1950). *Police Administration.* New York: McGraw-Hill.

Woodward, J. (1978). "Management and Technology." Shafritz, Jay M., and Whitbeck, Philip H. (eds.), *Classics of Organizational Theory,* 190–226. Oak Park, IL: Moore.

Interviews

Barrett, Bob. Deputy Sheriff, Maricopa Sheriff's Department. Interview, September 21, 1979.

Blankenship, Don. Sergeant, Maricopa County Sheriff's Department, Crime Prevention Section, AR. Interview, February 22, 1980.

Dostie, Bruce. Assistant Director of Security, Sunvalley Regional Shopping Center, Concord, CA. Interview, October 13, 1989.

Gasman, Thomas. Chief of Security, Rossmoor, CA: Interview, August 13, 1979.

Gould, Rodney, Assistant City Manager, Walnut Creek, CA. Interview, October 13, 1989.

Kelly, George. Director of Security, Sunvalley Regional Shopping Center, Concord, CA: Interview, January, 1980.

Murray, Robert. Assistant City Manager, Walnut Creek, CA. Interview, March 6, 1980.

Nelson, Marc. Sergeant, Maricopa County Sheriff's Department, AR. Interview, October 16, 1989.

Page, Eldon. Commander, Sun City Crime Prevention Posse, Maricopa County Sheriff's Department, AR. Interview, October 13, 1989.

Schillinger, Ralph. Chief of Security, Rossmoor, Walnut Creek, CA. Interview, October 13, 1989.

Stewart, Richard. General Manager, Sun Bird Security, Carefree, AR. Interview, October 16, 1989.

Taubman Company, 1980.

White, James A. Commander, Sun City Crime Prevention Posse, Maricopa County Sheriff's Department, AR. Interview, April 26, 1980.

Withers, Elmer. Vice President and Chief of Security, Sun Bird Security and Management Company, Inc., Carefree, AR. Interview, September 19, 1979.

9. Contracting Out: The Most Viable Solution

Mike Freeman

Local governments have been driven—by the reduction of revenue sharing from state and federal governments and pressure from citizens to curtail tax increases—to find alternative methods to provide inexpensive and efficient public services. Government agencies have experimented with privatization in a variety of forms, including the use of volunteers, the sale of assets, contracting out with the private sector, vouchers, and subsidy arrangements. The form that privatization takes depends largely upon the type of service being delivered. In the 1980s the most popular form was contracting with the private sector for services and the increased use of volunteers. The benefits gained from privatization are primarily the cost savings and the perception that public services are efficiently provided.

With the increased use of contracting between local governments and the private sector, private firms are responding much more aggressively in pursuing new opportunities. Included in the new areas that are being privatized is the provision of public safety services from the private sector.

Subsequently, the law enforcement community has responded to the use of contracting out by striving to protect the interests of the public. The law enforcement profession is against many of the forms of privatization where it relates to public safety. Therefore, they have determined that "only selected functions of police and sheriffs' departments are going to be transferred to the private sector and the practice of contracting or privatizing does not realistically present a threat of total takeover of entire police agencies" (Chaiken and Chaiken, 1987:1). Other types of services in public safety for which contracting is being done are termed support services and include towing, private security, clerical assistance, data processing, and communications. Because communities "differ substantially in terms of fiscal management, need for services and legal restraints" (National Association of Counties Research Foundation, 1985), the extent to which a community privatizes is a highly individual process.

Service Delivery Approaches for Volunteers

Volunteers work without pay for a local government, although they may receive reimbursement for out-of-pocket expenses. Volunteers can lower service costs and

131

expand service levels. Given that labor costs can represent more than 75 percent of the total budget for public safety services, savings may be significant when volunteers take on staff responsibilities. Volunteers can be used to supplement paid staff during peak demand periods.

Purchase of Service Contracting

Purchase of a service contract is a binding agreement under which a local government pays a private or nonprofit organization to provide all or a portion of a specified service. Citizens pay taxes or user fees to the local government, which in turn pays the contractor. For many smaller jurisdictions the availability of private service providers may restrict the availability of choosing the best firm to handle the service.

On the other hand, there are several examples of smaller communities who have seen new firms develop in response to business opportunities. Local governments can encourage local or small providers by dividing large contracts into service components or large geographic areas into smaller service areas (Farr, 1989:80).

What Public Safety Services Are Appropriate for Privatization?

Contracting for public safety services is often undertaken when a smaller suburban community will contract with a larger city or county to handle calls for service after a certain time when the community's police officers are not in full force, such as late at night; this is known as an intergovernmental agreement. The city of Orono, Minnesota, has been providing law enforcement services to neighboring municipalities by written contract since 1967. This type of intergovernmental contracting is a common method that smaller jurisdictions often have used to meet their law enforcement needs at an affordable price.

The current agreement and contract for law enforcement between Orono and the surrounding municipalities is an eighteen-page written contract covering all insurance costs, including the Minnesota Public Employees Retirement Program, Worker's Compensation, and all salaries and fringe benefits. These types of contracts are very common and are a clear example of how police departments cooperate to provide services between jurisdictions.

The rise of the private security industry has caught the law enforcement community's interest. Employees of these security firms are often uniformed, armed, and typically are required to carry out the same duties as sworn police officers. These private security officers are not as well trained, which is a major concern of law enforcement officials who see the public as misconstruing the real power and duties of the security officer, and suffering as a result. "In 1980 an estimated $3.3 billion was paid by government officials to private security companies, over four-fifths of the $4.1 billion spent by the federal and state governments on public law enforcement" (Chaiken and Chaiken, 1987:17).

This trend is of great concern to sworn officers who feel that their occupational territory is being invaded by the private sector—people who have no legal or moral obligation to hold the public's trust. Police officers are very concerned that contracting for private security will upset the delicate balance that has been achieved between interjurisdictional agreements for the provision of police services. There is a level of cooperation that exists among sworn officers that may not exist between sworn officers and private security firms. Some police officers argue that the crucial transference of information—which is essential in solving many crimes—will not take place in the case of contracted security forces and sworn employees interacting and working on criminal cases together.

The most common duties that are being passed on to the private sector are support functions (see Table 9.1). With local governments spending $27.4 billion on combined police services, judicial services, and corrections in 1985, it is evident that private firms interested in new markets will attempt to become more involved in the overall provision of police services, particularly in the support areas (see Table 9.2).

Fiscal limitations and the overall growth of private-sector security and support services are not the only factors to consider when analyzing the growth of the private provision of police services. Citizen demands have played a crucial role in the development of current thinking on the entire privatization issue. The public has demanded that the police exist outside of the political domain of city and county government, making the police respond to service calls in the order of importance not through the preferential treatment of influential citizens. This situation, in which taxpayers demand equal services despite income levels, has added to the public scrutiny on police programs, because the citizens have increased their awareness of how tax dollars are being spent on public safety programs. Therefore, the attractiveness of intergovernmental contracting, contracting for support services, and the use of volunteers is particularly useful as a public relations tool for police management in convincing police unions and concerned citizens that contracting is an effective means for managing police funds.

Contracting for Support Services: Current Issues

Police administrators are very concerned about retaining civilian personnel for their work force, since many tasks associated with police work do not require the skills and training of uniformed officers. In departments where there is a large contingency of civilian employees, the police administrators retain a greater degree of flexibility in shifting relatively unskilled civilian personnel among tasks in response to changing work requirements. This method allows officers to concentrate on more traditional law enforcement tactics and frees them from performing menial and often tedious tasks.

On the other hand, police administrators must be concerned about losing too many tasks to the civilian labor forces and private firms. The ability to assign sworn officers to less demanding tasks on occasion is a priority that allows administrators

Table 9.1 Alternative Service Delivery Approaches for Public Safety Functions

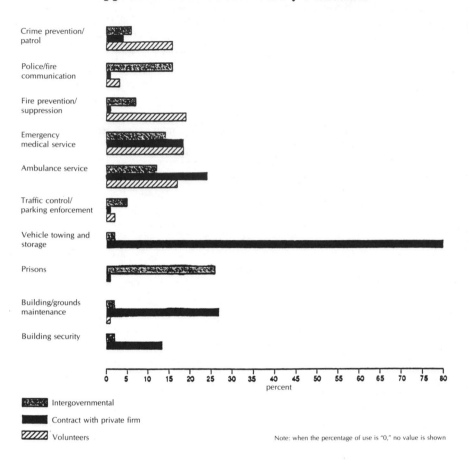

Intergovernmental

Contract with private firm

Volunteers

Note: when the percentage of use is "0," no value is shown

Source: "How Local Governments Are Providing for Our Safety," *The International City Management Association, Special Data,* No. 10, p. 4.

to efficiently manage and continue to use injured or limited-service employees. Obviously, if too many services are contracted out, this flexibility is lost. It is evident that today's police manager has to create a balance between the amount of work that is to be contracted out and how much to assign to officers in the department.

The preparations that a local government must make before entering into a contract with a private firm ultimately will affect the quality and cost of the contract, how well it will be accepted by the existing personnel, and its resistance to corruption. First and foremost is the need to work with the contracted firm and the personnel to ensure that every party understands the role of the firm and the benefit it will provide the police department. Therefore, the police agency should be involved

Table 9.2 How Much Does Government Spend for Justice?

Police and corrections account for a small portion of government spending.
Federal, state, and local spending for selected government functions, 1985.

Purpose of expenditure	Billion dollars*
Insurance trust expenditure Social security; Unemployment compensation; Worker's compensation; Public employee retirement; Veterans life insurance	$328.8
National defense and international relations	288.7
Education	205.9
Interest on general debt	172.7
Environment and housing	107.1
Public welfare Old age assistance; Aid to families with dependent children; Aid to the blind; Aid to the disabled; General relief	94.8
Hospitals and health	63.7
Transportation	57.2
Police, judicial services, and corrections**	48.5
Postal service	28.9
Space research and technology	7.3

*Does not include $187.8 billion in seven additional categories—see source for itemization. Detail by
level of government does not equal totals because duplicative intergovernmental amounts are excluded
from totals. **This is the amount reported in source; it differs from the amount in the primary source
used in the rest of this chapter. Source: *Government Finances in 1984–85*, U.S. Bureau of the Census.
In the National Institute of Justice, *Report to the Nation on Crime and Justice*, March 1988.

in the planning and drafting of the contract, even if some other government agency will actually be signing the contract.

The police must understand how to analyze the Request for Proposal (RFP) to make the bidding process competitive and rewarding for the department. The RFP should clearly outline the requirements for both the firm and the employees that will be expected under the contract specifications. The process of preparing and thoroughly distributing the RFP is in itself a protective measure to reduce the opportunity for corruption on the part of the firm and the awarding agency.

If the police agency is concerned with the wages and benefits that the firm's employees will receive, the police department can specify the wage and benefits to be paid rather than specifying the qualifications or performance standards. Standards tell the bidder what the government agency requires out of the contract.

Another problem that is often overlooked is the nature of private business. Firms can go out of business, leaving the jurisdiction in a precarious position. When a jurisdiction finds that it must remove a contractor or the contractor goes out of business, local officials are often forced to make expensive, interim arrangements. Local governments often find that a contract, originally awarded at an attractive rate, becomes more and more expensive with time. This common practice among contractors called "buying in" is an effort to win the contract to establish a rapport with the jurisdiction and then slowly raise the contract cost in the subsequent years. This practice, relying on one firm to provide services over a long period of time, as it continues, forces the city to become more and more dependent on that one contractor to such an extent that it cannot change contractors or take back that service. This is possible with police support services.

The Limits of Privatization

Because public safety functions are so important and visible to the public it seems unrealistic to assume that these services can or will be passed on to the private sector. A perceived reduced level of accountability associated with private firms providing public services is one factor which greatly discourages public officials from attempting total privatization.

Unions have argued against contracting out since the idea's inception. Police unions and employee associations are likely to be vocal in their opposition to the continued use of contracting. Local governments may also be restricted by union contracts, civil service regulations, or state law from laying off employees. As a result of union requests, employees who lose their jobs to contracting have to be transferred to other positions. Local governments may have difficulty retraining or absorbing all the affected employees (Farr, 1989:87). This reduces the overall value of the contract because the costs of the contract are reassigned to other departments.

When local governments make the decision to contract for private security services, police unions often interpret this as an attempt to shift hiring practices from sworn police officers to inferior civilian security officers. The large number of civilian police personnel hired between 1970 and 1980 did not significantly improve police services (Chaiken and Chaiken, 1987:21). Civilian employees did not actually replace sworn officers, but many rank and file officers saw these civilians as replacements for authentic, sworn officers.

Public police departments were formed primarily to provide equal services for all persons in need of assistance in law enforcement and victim assistance. Privatization is viewed by some civil libertarians as a return to the rejected style of private policing (which existed before the creation of public policing) that served the particular interests of the wealthy. When police services are delivered by sets of personnel with different skills and capabilities, a concern may arise that tasks which involve serving the poorest citizens may be allocated to the least skilled private security personnel. The converse is of equal concern to police officers. They fear that private firms will strive to take over the most popular and profitable services that police departments undertake, leaving the department with the residual tasks that are more expensive to operate and not highly regarded in the public's eyes. City officials are extremely concerned that city service be provided equally for all citizens. Public police services are often subject to equity problems in that most financially depressed areas in a community are those most in need of police services.

This problem has become more difficult to resolve due to the growth of the private security forces. Wealthy individuals are supplementing public police services by contracting with private firms for burglar protection and neighborhood patrols. This practice may release police resources for poor areas but may cause wealthy citizens to view the expenditure of tax dollars for public police as less important.

One of the immediate concerns about the use of contracting for private security is the abuse of power. The powers of public police departments are constitutionally limited, and court rulings have placed specific constraints on police practices. Many private security personnel do not understand the subtleties of the law and may, in many instances, act as if they were sworn officers (Chaiken and Chaiken, 1987:27).

References

Chaiken, J., and M. Chaiken (1987). "Public Policing-Privately Provided." *National Institute of Justice* (June).

Farr, C. (1989). "Service Delivery in the 90's: Alternative Approaches for Local Governments." *International City Management Association* (May).

National Association of Counties Research Foundation (1985). "Interlocal Service Delivery: A Practical Guide to Intergovernmental Agreements/Contracts for Local Officials." National Association of Counties Research Foundation, Washington, DC.

10. Privatization in Criminal Justice: One Perspective in Southern California

Jerry A. Usher

In 1978 the author was recruited to organize and direct the patrol and alarm response division of cssi, later to become Westec Security. The company was beginning to experience substantial success in selling residential security systems to the higher priced homes in the Los Angeles area, as well as San Diego and Palm Springs. The decision was made to build a division to provide the company its own response to alarms due to the uncertainty of a good response time by the law enforcement agencies in some of the market areas. Expensive alarms were difficult to sell without a good response capability.

Start-up Conditions

At the time of start-up there were few private companies providing quality alarm response. Bel-Air Patrol was probably one of the largest and best in southern California at the time. They served primarily the exclusive Bel-Air market, with both alarm response and patrol and other services. One of the largest national security companies had entered the market as a subcontractor for cssi prior to my arrival. This activity was such a small part of their total operation and so different from their normal activities that the operation for cssi was not satisfactory. There were several small companies that performed the traditional "door shaker" patrols and attempted to do alarm response, but they too were generally unsatisfactory.

The cssi wanted a top quality operation and were prepared to pay to get it. Coming from a small police department relying heavily upon preventive patrol and having been a college level instructor of law enforcement subjects, it was natural that the development of our operation paralleled law enforcement more than private security. Our aim was to develop an effective neighborhood "police department" without the "peace officer" status. Care had to be taken not to use the name "police" or to confuse our role due to the state requirements in this regard.

Program Development

Low pay in the industry as a whole and the general poor reputation of "security" required the first step to be attracting and keeping good quality personnel. We

138

established a pay scale well over our competition in the private sector. There was no point trying to compete with local police department wages as a prospect who wanted to go into law enforcement would do so no matter what we paid. We were interested in attracting law enforcement prospects and having them work for us until they were hired by law enforcement.

Very specific procedures were developed and published in manual form. A supervision ratio of one supervisor to each five officers allowed good supervision and close control.

Each applicant underwent a full background investigation. New hires were trained in our academy and careful training records were kept.

The typical negative attitude toward "rent-a-cops" among law enforcement and the public in general, and even in our own industry, required that we take steps to improve our image as something different. This was also important if we were to get the prices we intended to charge. The potential liability also required that we do a better job with our personnel.

Image Enhancement

If a company or industry cannot convince its own employees that they are superior, then the public cannot be convinced. The higher wages helped, but by themselves would have been just more costs. We made it hard for anyone but the best to be hired. Our rules were tough and enforced. This caused the survivors to realize they were something special. We bought the best equipment available and made everything look as much as possible like police units while maintaining our own identity.

Acceptance by law enforcement was critical to our plans. The appearance of our officers was of special importance. The police officers in the Los Angeles area look as sharp as any in the country. At that time at least, one would never see a sloppy L.A. police officer. We were, therefore, careful in the appearance of our officers, provided good uniforms, and provided a generous cleaning allowance. This also gave us the ability to control how an officer looked in his personal grooming at a time when it was becoming out of style to control hair length, facial hair, etc.

There were other "self esteem" steps taken, of which one example was our firearms policy. The state firearms training and qualification standards at that time were totally inadequate and still remain far below what they should be. Due to over thirty years of professional firearms competition experience, beliefs established during my teaching career, and the liability potential, we developed a very firm training, qualification, and rules program. Typical of this was immediate termination of an officer who drew his weapon without a justifiable, lethal threat. The officers who handled their guns carelessly or showed any tendency to rely on the gun instead of good procedures were terminated. In return we developed a training program that produced safe, excellent gun handlers and shooters, comparable or better than any police department of which we were aware. We provided monthly range qualification, practice ammo, and required quarterly qualification on our own course of fire. Officers who did not qualify were disarmed. Our training and qualification stressed decisions, use of cover at all times, drawing from the holster while gaining cover, and "instinct shooting." This allowed fast, effective fire in any light condition without the officer needing to unholster his gun too soon. Twice a year we "qualified" in total darkness. We encouraged our officers to attend local competitions and assisted them financially in doing so. The result was officers who were good and they knew it. At one time we had three world-class shooters who represented the United States in world competition. Our company was actually known better worldwide among shooters than we were within our own locality. In addition to pride, we had no "bad shootings" in ten years. We also had no law suits and no officers injured in the seven shootings that did occur. The suspects who caused the shootings did not fare so well. As another indication of the results of the program, local law enforcement accepted us, several officers went on to law enforcement careers, and the market accepted our prices.

Program Establishment

Within five years we had established twenty-four-hour patrols in many specific areas. In just the Los Angeles market we had over thirty-four units in the field at a time. We were larger than many police departments. Our ratio of officers to customers was far better than nearly any police department could provide for patrol alone. The result was effective patrol deterrent to crime and remarkable alarm response times. It was not unusual in some areas to receive a complaint if the response was longer than three minutes. We made no effort to establish patrol in areas that could not afford us or that already had excellent police response to alarms.

In areas such as Palm Springs, with its large area and many enclosed golf course communities, there was less emphasis upon patrol and alarm response and more on access control and response to those communities. For a period of time until we had taught the industry what was needed to control a market, and until we had a change of owners and management that reduced the emphasis upon patrol, we had things pretty much our own way.

Impact upon Crime

Although the aim was market control, our activities had a marked impact upon where crime occurred and especially upon the type of crime. In many areas where dedicated patrol existed street crime, residential burglaries, and, to a lesser degree, vehicle thefts nearly disappeared.

It is important to note that overall crime itself is not affected by this type of security. Where the crime occurred, however, is impacted. Private security of any kind, if it is any good, will make an area too difficult to "hit" in relation to other areas that are not protected. This benefit is limited in the most part to persons from outside the immediate community who risk being seen and remembered by the security. This area of California has a very mobile criminal population. As long as the criminal has to travel into or through an area, patrol is very effective. When an area has good security the criminals simply work somewhere else. Crooks who live in the protected area, such as the drug dependent youngsters of customers, can also be controlled to a degree, at least within the protected area. Murders and other violent crimes that occur between family members, as so many do, are not affected much by local security. There are plenty of times, however, when the fast response of security can prevent the escalation of a dangerous altercation.

The capability of good security to move crime is very easy to see with the use of crime pin maps. This is especially true if "before and after" information is available. The same number of crimes in a general area will probably occur, no matter if security is present or not. It is easy to see, however, that crimes in protected areas decrease and adjacent unprotected areas experience an increase. This trend is the basis of sound marketing. Once a small area is protected, adjacent areas of the same economic value will soon be receptive to marketing.

Unsatisfactory Experiences

There were factors in the business we had set up that were not totally satisfactory. The attitudes developed in our officers along the lines of law enforcement were sometimes a problem since they had no real law enforcement powers beyond that of a private citizen. This was especially a problem when some of our officers were also part-time or reserve officers in law enforcement. We had to terminate officers who could not make the adjustment between the private and public sector. Some law enforcement practices pose a severe liability threat to a private company. A private company cannot afford to have an employee act like a cop without the training and controls required. There are a small but significant amount of law enforcement officers being a law unto themselves. Even a little of this attitude can destroy a private company. There is also the problem that some officers forget they are working for a private, profit-minded company instead of a tax-supported entity.

Marketing expansion problems resulted from our setup and philosophies. Residential patrol is so expensive when done right that it is difficult to have much of a margin. A single household will pay only so much for patrol. When enough homes are added per officer to make the business profitable, the load increases and the effectiveness decreases. The company with which we started this program had the benefit of income from alarm sales, service to alarms, and monitoring fees. The total operation, therefore, made the program as a whole profitable. Later, when each individual department had to show a substantial profit on its own, patrol expansion stopped and conflicts developed. Due to the company's goal being the sale of alarms to high income homes, certain markets could not be explored. The huge market of commercial locations that certainly are not found in high income suburbia was largely ignored. The middle income and certainly the lower income areas that need patrol the most were not marketed.

There was a school of thought among alarm sales people that the highly successful patrol operation reduced the number of alarm sales even in the high income areas. The facts are, however, that only the combination of patrol, response, and alarms can really have a major effect upon the safety of an area. The fact that only about 40 percent of an area carries the cost for the entire area is perfectly normal. The reason that patrol needs alarms to be really effective is that in many areas patrol simply does not have a good enough view of homes to see enough. The more isolated the homes are, the more high fences and foliage that conceal a house, the less effective patrol can be.

A New Approach

When we started our current company, Golden West K-9, we kept the good things we had learned and adjusted the others. We also were in business now without the benefit of income from alarms and monitoring. We reduced the "police attitude" of our personnel and stressed the business aspects as well as providing a broader security value. We now do very few residential patrols and are heavily into commercial patrols and the patrol of apartment and condo complexes. We do, however, respond to alarms wherever they may be. Instead of concentrating our patrols in only wealthy residential areas, we accept patrols only near main transportation access routes to allow us to reach a much wider geographic area for alarm response. We have found that it takes as long to travel one mile of twisting, turning, and dead-end residential streets in an exclusive neighborhood as it does to travel four or more miles on freeways.

Instead of being limited to the business of only one company and its policies, we now subcontract for nearly 100 companies and charge them for the accounts we serve. The result is no sales cost, a very real advantage of "scale," and a much diversified market.

The good things we learned from quality personnel and service have been increased.

Continued Impact on Crime

Once again in our modified approach we see that the movement of crime continues. Parking areas, recreation areas, etc., of condo homeowner associations experience a very real reduction of problems due to our random patrols. Since criminals, especially drug dependent ones, tend to work in a relatively small geographic area, the movement of crime is easier to track. The heavier the use of drugs and the lower the economic level of the user the smaller his or her area of operation will be. When good security makes it too risky to work one area, he or she will work an unprotected, nearby area.

Open drug dealing requires at least some degree of freedom from interference and a location where the customers know they can find a dealer. Our activities tend to make our customers' locations unprofitable and the dealers eventually move to a nearby area where we will not bother them.

Convenience stores and shopping areas with outside phones always have crime if loiterers are allowed to remain. Street prostitution, drug sales, and gang shootings are all an eventual result of unrestricted loitering in our areas. In addition, there is a major problem with illegal aliens and legal persons unable to find work who gather outside certain locations waiting for someone who wants cheap labor to offer them day work. These people are usually not criminals themselves but are often victims. Their loitering, however, does reduce the normal business at the location. The normal buying public simply will not pass through a group of strangers. The problem for the community is that not all persons have the transportation to go to other, nicer areas to shop. With our armed personnel and large Rottweiler dogs we can be effective in moving unwanted groups, although usually only to a nearby location that is not protected.

Police Relations

The load on local police is difficult to appreciate unless you have some way to know the whole story. Local law enforcement is so understaffed that most of their time is spent running from call to call. Alarm response, of which over 95 percent are false alarms, are a tragic waste of their time. Loiterers and many varieties of street crimes have become so prevalent that, since so much of these problems are seen they simply have become "normal." There is also the problem of report time, no room in jails for minor offenders, the difficulty of convictions, and the "special teams" and "task force" philosophy. I should preface the above with the observation that while drug sales and prostitution may be obvious to us, they are not always so for the police. Such activity can be covered up quickly when the "spotters" see the police coming. They do not bother to do so when our company comes into an area since they know we will not make arrests for such activity. Generally we can talk to them and convince them to move their business elsewhere. On the rare occasion we get into an altercation, we make arrests for the altercation rather than their other criminal activity. In these cases we get excellent backup from the police.

The task force and special team activity needs to be explained. When problems, complaints, and political pressures mount locally, a task force is assembled and an area is "projected" for enforcement. When this occurs mass arrests are made—with few convictions—and the crime moves for a time. The other element is the understaffed narcotic, vice, and gang depression teams that are constantly working areas. The cop on the street tends to leave this enforcement to the special groups. Sometimes it is hard to tell the good guys from the bad guys. Also street cops can get in trouble for interfering in an undercover operation.

Most of the street cops seem to appreciate our activities, especially the older and wiser ones. By moving problems we help in many ways. First, we reduce their call load by clearing false alarms. We respond to many minor problems, freeing them for other activity. Second, in addition to cleaning out a specific area, it also results in concentrating activity elsewhere. The more illegal activity is concentrated the easier it is for special enforcement to deal with it. Finally, the better investigators realize that our officers have valuable information for them to tap.

The result is that in street locations and enclosed condo communities private security can have a very real impact upon the safety of the location. Although there is very little removing of criminals from circulation by private security, the combination of public and private enforcement can have an important overall effect.

Description of Services

Residential Patrol

Residential patrol primarily involves high visibility patrol as a deterrent. Suspicious persons and vehicles can be obviously watched and in some cases contacted. This prevents many possible crimes. By the patrol remaining in a relatively small area it provides very fast response for alarms or even calls from the clients. Visual patrol of the property of contracted clients serves as both a deterrent and a basis of investigation by the officer of anything that looks unusual. Competent, dedicated patrol provides a level of knowledge of the area so that officers soon learn the clients, children, pets, and which vehicle belongs to whom. Open garage doors, strange vehicles, mail and newspapers piling up, etc., all trigger a special check by an officer.

This type of service requires a certain level of participation to be effective and profitable. One of the areas we protect is typical. This area is a delightful residential section that is surrounded on all sides by problems. Before our involvement street prostitutes would pick up their tricks on a nearby main street and then drive into the residential area, in the customer's car, to perform their "service" in the driveways and shaded streets of our clients. Nearby low income apartment complexes were a source of walk-in potential criminals as well as centers for high drug activity. Cruising gangs were also a potential problem. Since we have been contracted to protect the area, prostitutes are seldom seen and unwanted persons and vehicles are no longer a problem. The police no longer spend time patrolling the area. They simply respond when we have someone in custody, pick up the suspect, and book him.

The area is now a much better place to live. Due to its proximity to high income work areas, the property values, or at least the ability to sell homes, has improved. The long-term residents who moved there before the surrounding area deteriorated now feel more secure.

Commercial Patrol

Random patrol of commercial accounts has many benefits similar to residential dedicated patrol. The major difference is the type of problems encountered, the length of time near the scene, and action taken by the officers. Commercial accounts pay for the contracted amount of time per month they wish us to be on the scene. The charges are based on the amount of time required to do what the client wishes us to do times the number of "checks" per month times our charge rate. The client also has the ability to dispatch us to assist him twenty-four hours each day. This expected time is also factored into the rate. The result is that some clients contract for enough time to really do a good job and some do not.

If a patrol contract requires us to make two five-minute checks each shift, that is what we do. This does not include extra time required to deal with a problem found. A typical account would be a convenience store that is having a loitering problem. Each time we patrol the scene we make contact and move the subjects found there. Normally our repeated efforts eliminate the problem. Occasionally arrests must be made of repeated problem persons. Our largest problem on this type of account is the client who believes he does not need us anymore after we clean up the area. Condo homeowner associations usually have different problems. Although the normal security problems exist, more of our problems center on parking problems. We often become involved in giving parking citations on private property and eventually towing away vehicles. The emphasis upon one or the other phase of our service varies from association to association and is due, at least in part, to the location of the property and the income level of the residents. The actual duties performed in these random patrols varies a great deal. In nearly every case, however, this type of service can be eventually effective.

Standing Guards

We call standing guards "sentries" as we do not like the term "guard." Actually this phase of our work here is probably not much different from that in any other part of the country. We do see an eventual increase in "access" control of a much wider variety of stores and shopping areas. In Rhodesia (now Zimbabwe), in 1978 during the height of the terrorist activity, nearly every store had a standing guard to check packages for bombs. While we are not to that point here yet, it may come. We see more and more premises protected by standing guards. Our sentries do a lot of this type of work, the largest part of which occurs in typical commercial and industrial applications. One application that is growing, however, is the assigning of a sentry to do foot patrols in some of the huge condo/townhomes in our area. Police patrols of such areas are impossible due to the garden type of common areas and the distance from any streets suitable for normal police patrol. The major duties in this type of application are to prevent unwanted persons from entering or staying in the complex, enforcement of common area rules including parking, and the fast response to local problems. If the number of times our officers must respond is any indication, a great deal of police time is saved.

There are a few features of our officers that are apparently different from those in other areas. First, is the quality of the officers and the prices we can charge for their service. Second, it appears we have more armed officers than is normally the case. Lastly, our use of K-9 teams is not at all common. By combining our patrol and sentry activities we are able to provide backup and random supervision of our sentries. The job advancement possible for a sentry to move up into the higher paid jobs in patrol and alarm response also makes it possible to attract a level of sentry that might otherwise not be possible.

K-9 Teams

The use of K-9 teams in all of the above operations and in the alarm response activities to follow puts us in a market by ourselves. Los Angeles has far tougher requirements for K-9 operations than the state has. We are currently the only licensed agency with that capability. We are developing a program where a small local police department intends to use us as their K-9 response when needed. This will allow them the ability to have the very real occasional advantage of a K-9 team without the cost and bother of supporting it themselves.

The costs and difficulties of maintaining a K-9 operation is one reason there are so few in existence currently. We expect to see more develop in the future due to the value of such a program. The costs, skills required, licensing, and liability will limit this development to very few companies.

It is important to state the difference between a K-9 team operation and a business that places attack dogs unsupervised in a location. Our dogs are always under close control by a trained handler. The legal and liability risks of unsupervised dogs in California should prevent any responsible business from using them. We are fortunate that my partner, Fred McNabb, is a recognized expert in the field. He does all of the dog and handler training and control. Without him I would not even consider using dogs. Although we have had no civil actions against us from the use of dogs, the costs are very, very high.

The advantages of K-9 teams in the field are very real. Used properly the dogs can make an operation much more effective and efficient. During a recent strike in the movie industry we assigned one armed handler and a dog in each of several key locations at night. It would have taken at least three officers alone in each location to provide the same level of protection. More importantly, in locations protected without dogs there were potentially serious confrontations. Not a single confrontation occurred at any location protected by a K-9 team. The ability of a dog to be aware of a potential intruder is a very real comfort to an officer alone at a post. The presence of a well-trained, impressive dog is also a very real value in preventing an escalation of force.

The normal application of K-9 teams in the field is a standard routine. During each shift we have at least one K-9 officer and his dog in the field on mobile patrol. Often this officer is also a supervisor. When a K-9 is needed for a search at an alarm response or as a backup for a patrol confrontation, the K-9 officer responds. When a K-9 officer is the officer on the initial contact, the dog remains in the unit unless needed.

On a standing post where the client has requested a K-9 team, the team is, of course, on duty for the assigned time. A very common application of this service is at a location such as a lumber storage yard where thefts have been a problem.

By placing a "quiet" K-9 team on the premises, an attempted entry usually results in an apprehension by the dog. The word of these occurrences usually gets around pretty fast and the problem stops. Another application is where a location has become a common drug sales location. A K-9 team tends to reduce the number of potential customers as well as moving the dealers. People are generally afraid of our dogs and as a result confrontations are rare.

Alarm Response

The alarm response business in this area of southern California is apparently quite different from other sections of the country. In many areas of southern California the local law enforcement agency simply cannot provide alarm response on a timely manner to the huge number of alarm activations in their jurisdiction. The false alarm ratio of even the best companies is well over 95 percent, regardless of what they tell their customers. The reasons for these false alarms are not usually the alarm companies' fault directly. The vast majority of false alarms at residences are due to misuse by the client. Probably the next highest category of false alarms is due to systems that were designed without considering the habits and needs of the customer. This is especially noticeable when a home with an existing alarm is sold to a new owner with a different size family or life-style. The number of false alarms due to equipment failure is usually quite small. False alarms at commercial locations usually are employee or cleaning service caused. Poorly designed systems, especially outside protection on fences, storage yards, etc., also cause false alarms. Only about 1 to 2 percent of alarms are due to a verifiable "actual." There is a huge unknown factor involved. It is not at all unusual to have an alarm considered a false alarm by law enforcement or a responding agency but then to find out later that an actual attempt occurred and the alarm did its job. Other causes of false alarms that usually are listed as unknown are due to wind storms, sprinkler systems, or rain.

Regardless of the cause of an alarm, the number of alarms in our area and the number of dispatches are huge. We serve approximately 3,000 alarms and expect to be dispatched on 25 percent of those alarms at least once a month. The dispatch percentage on commercial accounts is closer to 40 percent. Since we serve only a small percentage of the alarms covered by the Los Angeles Police Department, for example, a substantial part of their available officer time can be wasted on alarm response.

TYPE OF ALARM RESPONSE. A few large companies that sell and service alarms also provide response only to their own alarms. It takes a large customer base to make this worthwhile. It also means they either cannot provide response in widely scattered areas or they provide poor response. Some attempt to use a combination of response and service personnel to do both. The result is poor service, and or poor response.

Our function is to provide alarm response to any licensed company that needs it. As a subcontractor to nearly 100 companies we can provide response to small companies that could not possibly provide response on their own. Even the large companies are finding that it is cheaper and more efficient to use us rather than operate their own response teams. By avoiding the costs and liability of armed personnel, not to mention the control problems of a twenty-four-hour operation, the company has more time and resources for the rest of their business.

COMMUNICATING VERSUS NONCOMMUNICATING ALARMS. Alarms that communicate an activation to a central station are becoming a needed item in California. I personally would not want to be without an alarm in my home or business. The alarm has protected us in both locations. In our home the suspect made a successful entry but the alarm sounding apparently caused him to leave before valuables were found or damage done. Fortunately, he did not know that it would take local law enforcement over forty minutes to respond. Our alarm sign stated we had "armed response." Unfortunately, we live outside of the area to which my officers can respond. My dog was also not there at the time. At our office, which is in our area of operation, when the alarm sounded we responded within minutes. One suspect was caught running from the scene and a second suspect was found by the dog of the responding officer. The police, however, refused to take the suspects into custody. At least the suspects were unable to remove any of our property, even though they broke a $300 front window.

Alarms do a great deal more than deal with burglars. We have also had a fire at our home. The fire alarm in this case was not a communicating one. We were, however, home and asleep at the time and the alarm woke us up. We were able to save the house after considerable damage. Had we been away, the noncommunicating alarm would have been of no value and the house would have been lost.

Noncommunicating alarms are virtually worthless except in the case mentioned above. Just as everyone ignores auto alarms these days, few people will call in when they hear an audible alarm. Fewer still would investigate.

A communicating alarm has no more real value than a noncommunicating one if there is no one to respond when it activates. The only exception would be when the sign says there is response but the crook does not know better. When the response is extended the value reduces accordingly.

Very few communities in southern California allow alarms to communicate directly to a police department. The load on public personnel increases to the point where it cannot be handled as alarms increase. The use of private companies to monitor alarms, sort out some of the false alarms, dispatch and respond to the alarms, and then ask for law enforcement when actually needed is an important, valuable, and growing business. The growing tendency of law enforcement to treat alarms as a low priority and the growing false alarm fines will continue to make the industry important.

OUR FUNCTION ON ALARM RESPONSES. On both residential and commercial alarms the first and common procedure for both is to receive the dispatch. The delay of being dispatched can be critical to the response time. Our system allows us to receive a dispatch in fifteen seconds from any monitoring center, including some in other states. The signal goes directly to our mobile units without needing a common radio frequency with the dispatching company. While responding, the officers are provided information via radio.

The first concern of the responding agency is to get there as fast as legally possible. Private companies are not emergency vehicles in California and may not break any traffic laws. In southern California traffic, only having enough personnel scattered around an area can reduce response times. Once the officer arrives on the scene he must park his unit out of direct view of the location and in such a way as not to interfere with police or fire units. Once on the scene he reports in by radio and checks to see that there is no danger to him outside, he then checks for signs of forced entry. If signs of forced entry are apparent he will back off, set a perimeter, and call for backup and, in some cases, police. The only time he would take action against an intruder without backup on the scene, or a dog, would be if that action is required to protect a client or the property. When this occurs, the decision must be tempered with the possibility of escalating the danger to the client and the officer. Our legal duties end with "observe and report." The customer, however, will expect a great deal more. We do not, however, expect our officer to be killed to protect only property.

Should there be no sign of an intruder on the scene but an opening found, the officer will check it out, report, and secure the property before leaving, and leave a card inside.

The only difference between residential and commercial accounts is the amount of time required to check it out and the need to often wait for the owner to arrive to check for a loss.

VARIATIONS ON ALARMS. The type of alarm received and the information available to us varies a great deal. Some alarms are dispatched to us as "unknown cause." Others may provide us more information. Some alarms are sophisticated enough due to sensors, cameras, and microphones that we often know exactly into what the officer is getting. Obviously, the more information we have the quicker and better our job can be done, not to mention the safety aspect.

In addition to a wide variety of entry-type alarms, we may receive "panic," "duress," "armed robbery," "fire," "water flow," and "medical emergency" alarms. In the major jurisdiction we serve, the police will accept only a "459" (burglary), or "211" (armed robbery) alarm. This can cause problems for the dispatching source in order to get a response from law enforcement. In the "panic," "duress," "211," and "medical emergency," someone had to manually set off the alarm. In some jurisdictions the police will not respond to medical emergencies and the correct fire department or paramedic group must be dispatched. On other manually activated alarms the dispatching center must decide to report the alarm as a "211" and risk the dispatch of SWAT or similar special response groups or report it as "unknown" and have a bad response. In most cases, unless it is a clear "211," the dispatching center would rather have us respond before dispatching the police. Our personnel on responding and finding a true problem must be able to deal with it by at least keeping the situation from escalating until the proper authorities can arrive. Fire and medical emergencies almost always receive an excellent response from the fire department and they are usually dispatched before we are.

ADVANTAGES TO PRIVATE RESPONSE. Some of the unique problems in our area which makes a private response of value include the poor response times by some law enforcement agencies to "unknown" alarms, and the "alarm permit" situation. It is not unusual when a monitoring company calls for a police response to be put on hold for several minutes. After it has been reported, the police will ask for the "alarm permit number." No alarm permit, no dispatch. Even when the alarm permit number is given by the dispatching center, it must then be verified on the police computer. Often there is a two-week delay between the time a customer purchases an alarm permit and when it finds its way to the police computer. During that time no dispatch is possible. Many alarm companies pay us to respond until the alarm permit is recorded. Even if the permit is in place and a dispatch is made by some police in our area, the total length of the response is usually over thirty minutes to an "unknown alarm." It is no exaggeration to state that this response is often well over an hour. Obviously at that time it will usually be a false alarm and will result in a false alarm fine.

It is important to note that not all police jurisdictions we serve have these problems. The bulk of our business, however, is in areas where these problems do exist.

A private company such as ours can be of very real value to both the police and our clients. Many monitoring centers dispatch us first without dispatching the police, unless there is information that would cause the police to provide a priority response. The total time involved in dispatching us and our requesting the police when needed is usually much faster than if the police were dispatched in the first place. The client gains protection and the police save hundreds of man hours on false alarm trips.

Other advantages of using a private response includes a better check of the property due to our knowing the location, the layout of the account, where the alarm points are, and because we usually have access to the property. Police officers will seldom climb fences, climb on roofs, or check areas where there is a dog. We have the advantage of keys to fences, knowledge of roof access, and information or personal knowledge about the dog.

We also know when a client is on vacation and know where they can be reached. Knowledge of the client is important in the case of a business. In a large city it can take a great deal of time for the police to discover whom to call to come down to check out a business. They also do not like to waste a great deal of time waiting for the owner to appear. There is also the problem of alarm information and the resulting securing of the property after an activation. We believe many business owners, who usually live some distance from their business, hire us specifically in order to avoid their having to drive to the business several times a month. We often take care of the total check and securing of the property and merely leave a note for the owner to call us in the morning.

RESULTS. The use of private security to respond to alarms adds very real protection to the client, convenience, and peace of mind. The police gain an unbelievable amount of time by not responding to alarms, as well as less time spent on actuals due to the information available to security.

The number of criminals actually arrested by security is small and insignificant by itself. Even one arrest, however, may result in the closing of dozens of past crimes and the prevention of others. Even though few criminals are arrested by security, the number of on-the-scene arrests by security still exceeds the number of the same kind of arrests by the police in some jurisdictions.

The largest crime deterrent value of private alarm response is the fact that a criminal will not usually, knowingly attempt to break in at a location that is alarmed and has a fast alarm response capability. Those who do attempt to make entry usually leave quickly when the alarm sounds without time to take much.

The Security Business in Southern California

The size of the security business in California is so large it is difficult to describe. There are, for example, 8,900 officers in just the Los Angeles area with security firearms permits. This is more than the number of uniformed L.A. Police Department officers that can be put on the street. I would guess that there are nearly as many security officers carrying guns illegally as there are licensed ones. There are at least ten times the number of security officers in California than there are police officers. If one includes all kinds of legal and illegal security personnel, I would guess this difference could be more than doubled.

One security company in the Los Angeles area has a gross income of well over $500,000 per month just from their monitoring fees. Total income of just one branch of this company is well over $1 million a month and it is far from the largest such concern in this area.

The total number of all kinds of security companies in Los Angeles are probably over 400. There are not many patrol companies in the city due to the excellent control of the L.A. Police Department, but these do number about fifty. The actual number of legal and illegal security companies that provide only personnel for standing guards is anyone's guess. Mine is over 200.

The amazing thing to me is the relatively few security guards who are themselves involved in crime, considering the potential. Bearing in mind only those who actually appear in the newspaper, the ratio appears no worse than the ratio of law enforcement officers. One must qualify this, however, with the observation that peace officers who go "bad" almost always hit the papers but similar security personnel may not.

The background checks on security personnel and preemployment screens vary as much as the industry does in other ways. The way it is supposed to work in California is that the prospective officer's application and finger prints are sent to the state bureau for clearance. Even if this is done, however, an applicant can work, without a gun, without clearance. The officer is supposed to work for no more than sixty days without clearance, but there is really no way to enforce this because it can take considerably longer than sixty days for the state to process the application. Many companies with high turnover do not bother to send in the applications at all. The result is that officers could work in security, even though they have a record, unless the hiring company does their own checks. The control of armed officers is much better in that they cannot legally carry a gun without the card having been processed and returned by the state. Unfortunately, it is more usual than not for the state to take three to seven months in processing the cards (the time required is improving). The result is a lot of officers carry guns illegally. There is virtually no enforcement of this item by the state until a case develops and is brought to their attention. Local law enforcement is generally spotty due to lack of time and of knowledge of the laws involved.

One bright spot in the enforcement and quality picture is the Los Angeles Police Commission. While they have no control over standing guards or alarm response, they do license all patrol operations in their city. They do on-the-spot record checks and generally have a very real impact upon the quality of that section of the business.

There are state controls on the licensing of managers and operators of security companies. The requirements and testing, however, do little to prevent marginal operations. With virtually no investigative staff there is really not much more the state can do to upgrade the industry.

It is only fair to note that even with its shortcomings, the state of California is certainly one of the leaders in trying to establish a competent and controlled security industry. The industry is simply growing faster than the ability of the state to keep up. The normal problems of any government body with the budget and legislative process combined with special interest groups slows the process, just as it does anywhere else.

The better security companies in California accept their responsibility to see that their personnel are qualified and safe to be on the streets. Many do not leave background checks to the state, even with the difficulties of getting this kind of information. Some companies, including ours, do preemployment drug screens and background checks. This, combined with good training and supervision, creates an entirely different class of security officer. With good wages to attract quality people there is no reason why private security cannot provide very real value to the public and law enforcement.

Summary

The development and professionalization of private security is the only chance there is of getting public safety under control in some areas of California and I suspect also in other areas of the country. Public law enforcement has lost the war against crime in most large cities. The spread of suburbia into thinly protected areas of unincorporated California also causes problems. Nearly all effective measures are reactive instead of preventive. Real protection and crime prevention seldom occurs. There is little visible evidence that the public will accept the costs and measures needed for law enforcement alone to regain control over public safety. Coordination with effective private security could, however, have an immediate effect in at least certain areas.

An oversimplification would find private security in a growing preventive role and law enforcement in the reactive and investigative functions.

11. A Police Chief's View of Privatization of the Criminal Justice System

Thomas R. Windham

Privatization of portions of the criminal justice system is apparently a highly desirable method of bringing the economy of management and fiscal acumen of private enterprise to a system currently bogged down in bureaucratic and legal entanglements which have virtually destroyed the system as a working entity.

The benefits of privatization come immediately to mind: short, direct lines of management, a minimum of bureaucracy, an economy of fiscal funds directed by the desire for a reasonable profit; in short, making a profitable business of the system.

Privatization should be able to provide much of what is missing in the criminal justice system, but there is a flip side to the question of just how much the private sector can do or should do in the criminal justice system.

The criminal justice system is for the large majority of citizens the only time they are in direct contact with virtually any form of government, and, in reality, the government or governments—local, state, and national—are constitutionally charged with providing for the protection of citizens.

In Texas at this time there is absolutely no doubt that portions of the criminal justice system—due to a series of actions taken at the federal level through court orders and legal findings—are bordering on the brink of collapse. Due to overcrowding of the state penal system there is a backlog of prisoners in the pipeline, which has brought to a virtual halt the incarceration of certain criminal classes. Hot check artists, car thieves, or nonviolent perpetrators are almost guaranteed they will not be incarcerated if apprehended and convicted. The turnaround time—from the time of arrest to conviction—including the time served, amounts to more than the time which would be served if the felon were sent to the Texas Department of Corrections.

Apprehension is not sure, certain, and swift; instead, it is too often slow, doubtful, and muddled.

Clearly the system is in jeopardy and there is a crying need for assistance. If this assistance comes from the private sector, steps should be taken to immediately implement it at all levels—from local to federal.

However, it is of paramount importance that the implementation of privatization on any level includes the controls and guarantees necessary to ensure the protection of each citizen's constitutional guarantees.

The implementation of any privatization program without the installation of systems of accountability and checks and balances for the protection of the citizen would be foolhardy at best and dangerous, if not deadly, at the worst.

Here, in Fort Worth, Texas, there is what may arguably be called one of the finest private security systems in the Southwest, if not the nation. The security operation of Bass Enterprises is a classic example of the heights and quality to which private enterprise may take a security system.

The Bass security operation, entitled City Center Security, was created in 1981 when the Bass brothers tapped Joel Glenn, a secret service agent, to head a state-of-the-art security system to guard and protect not only the brothers' twenty-six-square block area of businesses in downtown Fort Worth, but also to provide personal protection for various members of the family in both domestic and foreign situations.

Glenn, who spent part of his time in the secret service guarding presidents Richard Nixon, Gerald Ford, and Jimmy Carter, accepted the assignment and now runs a security operation second to none in the private sector.

Tommy Brown, security manager, underlines Glenn's statement. "Actually, we've had the very best of everything. We report directly to the [Bass] family and that does away with a lot of the bureaucracy. If we need something, we get it."

Brown said the security employees not only attend to the security needs within the Bass brothers' two tall towers (the first is thirty-four stories tall, the second forty stories tall), but also within the entire twenty-six-block area owned by the Basses in downtown Fort Worth.

The security forces work very much like a police department within their area of responsibility and aid and assist Fort Worth when something that happens is of such a nature that city police need to be called to the scene.

The security officers patrol the sidewalks and streets within the area, performing routine patrols and security checks of property and assisting citizens who need directions and information. The presence of uniformed City Center Security officers has had a noticeable effect on the transient population.

Brown said that in the overall concept the security force has taken "what we learned from the police and we try to get the population of the towers and businesses involved."

Over the past four years Fort Worth has turned to a very vigorous community relations program, holding a forum each month where citizens may voice their complaints and questions to the chief of police and top executives of the police department. Quarterly, in each of the department's four sectors, the mayor, city manager, and other city department heads meet with the police and the citizens.

Such involvement with the public and citizens has had a very noticeable effect on relations between both police and citizens. Brown said the emulation of these strategies has been successful with the tenants and persons doing business in the Basses area.

that need to be addressed before the concept is turned into reality: first response and training.

"The first response to an emergency has to be someone who has been trained to do what needs to be done. If this first responder to a police emergency is not a police person, that person needs to know what the police would do, begin doing it, and simultaneously notify the police," Glenn said.

"Secondly, the state of training for the privatization company engaged in security has to be of an extremely high level to be able to cope with the questions of liability, insurance, responsibility, and other questions of a business nature," he said.

Glenn also said that, in order for privatization of security and police work to succeed, the specifications for the entity have to be drawn so specifically and tightly that even the lowest of the low bidders will be forced to provide an expected high level of security and maintain that same level throughout the duration of the contract.

City Center's security forces mediate disputes within the towers, accidents within the towers' garages and perform other police duties. "We do have a lot of report writing," Brown said, pointing out that every officer undergoes a training session every day on some aspect of police and or security work. "The classes at the start of each roll call range from how to hold a subject for the police to your basic informational report writing."

Working with the best to be the best is a way of life for the security forces of Bass Enterprises. "We know how poor private security has been in some instances in the past. We know what it is today in many instances, and we just don't want to be a rent-a-cop," Brown said.

He is quick to point out "we're not the police, but we take action up to where the police become involved. We try to do what good citizens do. Our job is to be good witnesses, good note takers. We try to train them [the security officers] to assist the police as much as possible."

In listing the array of duties of the security forces, Brown pointed out that the security personnel are responsible for the 6,000 plus residents of the two towers, the 1,000 plus of the Worthington Hotel, and between 8,000 and 10,000 other persons in the various businesses within the area of responsibility. To really get an idea of what the responsibility can entail, the downtown Arts Festival in Fort Worth often brings 250,000 to 300,000 persons into the area over its three-day run.

Brown points with pride to the technological aspects the security forces have available to them and how they enhance the group's ability to provide security. There is a control room with closed channel television monitoring various areas of the buildings and surrounding sidewalks, the officers are equipped with two-way radios and there are various types of alarm systems in the businesses in the towers.

This adds up to the forces providing "real security and also a state of mind for the residents and people who come down here," according to Brown.

The state of mind comes from the training each member of the 164-person force receives. It includes class work, physical fitness training, an indoor firing range, and then working with a field training officer. After the training, each security force member is then on probation for one year.

Brown said that along with the training, the pay, the benefits of working for Bass Enterprises, and accumulated overtime make for good salaries and benefits which attract good quality applicants.

"We feel that by our presence, by the fact of just being there, we benefit the public and the police. We get to know the personnel who work in this area and their routines. This just adds to providing security for them according to Brown. Glenn, who is the creator of the system, is succinct in describing the operation and the bottom line: "Basically, what we've done is become the eyes and ears of the Fort Worth Police Department in the twenty-six-block area. This saves the taxpayer and the police time, energy, and money."

Glenn addressed the question of privatization of the criminal justice system and said, "A lot of people look at privatization as a power grab, I look at it differently . . . that people have to pay for what they get." He said carrying out the privatization is going one step beyond good citizenship, "We have a responsibility for our [clients and officers]. [The officers have] more safety responsibilities. He may act like a good conscientious citizen, but [if a person] is having a heart attack, we can help out."

Perhaps the key phrase is "help out." Privatization of the criminal justice system or portions of it in the final analysis is another way of the system being helped out in one form or another by private industry. Private industry does not tarry with systems that do not turn profits.

There is no doubt that privatization is a viable alternative as far as it can go, but private businesses and organizations are not necessarily bound by the governing strictures of the police departments. No matter how successful a private concern is in adapting to a role in the criminal justice system, unless the public is guaranteed its constitutional rights and in reality can afford them, privatization could become a many-headed Hydra that could present severe problems for police, citizens, and the system.

12. The Starrett Protective Service: Private Policing in an Urban Community

William F. Walsh
Edwin J. Donovan
James F. McNicholas

Since the mid-nineteenth century when American cities created police departments, crime prevention and control has traditionally been considered a governmental function. But in the second half of this century the volume of crime and its cost, budgetary problems of municipal governments, and cutbacks in the services of the public justice system have made it increasingly difficult for government to provide adequate crime control. As a result an explosive growth took place in the use of private protective services (Green, 1987).

The use of private protective services is a growing phenomenon in the United States. They have an annual growth rate of approximately 15 percent and some experts have projected that the private security industry will have 215,000 new positions by the year 1990 (Bottom and Kostanoski, 1983; Cunningham and Taylor, 1985; Stewart, 1985). It has been estimated that there are three times as many private security employees as public police officers in the United States (Naisbitt, 1984; Green, 1987). Recently it has been predicted that both expenditures and employment of private security will continue to increase as resources for public police stabilize (Cunningham and Taylor, 1985). We now encounter the private security officer in such diverse places as apartment complexes, residential communities, retail establishments, corporate facilities, banks, on public transit, at sports events, at work, in universities, or in hospitals.

Private security has two basic goals: the prevention and deterrence of crime or loss (National Advisory Committee, 1976; Cunningham and Taylor, 1985). The public police function has evolved into a reactive service responding to citizens' requests, whether they are of a criminal nature or not (Reiss, 1971:70; Black, 1980; Ericson, 1982:7). Stenning and Shearing (1979:16) claim that private security, unlike the public police, is more accessible to a preventive style of policing. They point out that private security has a client-defined mandate and that this

Funding for the research in this chapter was provided to the Pennsylvania State University by the Starrett Realty Corporation.

157

provides it with access to private places and a relationship to the persons who control activities in these areas. As agents of the property owner they are insiders who are in a better position to control crime, while the public police are outsiders who are often viewed as intruders in the social setting (Bittner, 1970; Rubinstein, 1979; Wiley and Hudick, 1974; Black, 1980).

The premise that private security is in a better position to conduct preventive policing presents several interesting questions. For example, can private security be an effective community crime prevention factor? Sherman (1983:155) claims that there is virtually no systematic evidence about the crime prevention effectiveness of private security. But if private security can succeed at crime prevention, what implications does this have for community crime control and public policing? These questions led to the research described here. This study is not a comparison of private security and public police. Our purpose was to select a private security unit that had the responsibility for providing a safe community environment and analyze whether it was able to achieve that objective.

Research Setting

Starrett City, a self-contained community of 20,000 residents, is set on 153 acres located in New York City. Established in 1974, it consists of 46 buildings containing 5,881 apartment units. The complex includes eight parking garages, one outdoor parking lot, a shopping center, one elementary and one intermediate school, two nursery schools, a power plant, and a recreation complex. In 1984 the median income of Starrett City residents was $24,000. The majority of these individuals are working-class, blue collar, or civil service employees. The ethnic distribution of the population is: 64 percent (N=12,800) white, 21 percent (N=4,200) black, 8 percent (N=1,600) Hispanic, 5 percent (N=1,000) Asian, and 2 percent (N=400) other ethnic identification.

Starrett City is located within the east New York section of Brooklyn. *The Statistical Report: Complaints and Arrest* (1985), of the New York City Police Department indicates that this area has a higher percentage of both personal and property crimes than other areas of the city. The east New York section has a population of about 170,000 ethnically distributed as follows: blacks 42 percent (N=72,000), Hispanics 32 percent (N=54,000), whites 22 percent (N=37,000), others 4 percent (N=7,000). This area of about seven square miles includes five high density public housing complexes, high unemployment, blighted decaying areas depopulated by arson, and is a micro-repository of the ills of urban life. Public police services are provided to this section by approximately 300 employees of the New York City Police Department's 75th Precinct.

In contrast to its surrounding community, Starrett City has the appearance of a safe community. It is an open, accessible area without fencing and security check points. Security officers do not screen individuals entering and leaving the complex. Pennsylvania Avenue, a major thoroughfare in the borough of Brooklyn, used by thousands of vehicles on a daily basis, neatly dissects the Starrett City site.

The open spaces, park benches, etc., receive high utilization by residents, especially the elderly and children. Individuals of mixed racial and ethnic background interact freely. The buildings are free of graffiti, lawns are maintained, trees are healthy, and there is an absence of litter. The schools, recreation, and shopping facilities are used by both residents and nonresidents. It is by all observations a pleasant community surrounded by an area of high crime, urban blight, and decay.

Methodology

A multimethod research design was used to evaluate the relationship between the Starrett Protective Service and the safety and stability of the Starrett City community. We sought to identify the following:

1. the nature and the extent of the services provided by the security department;

2. the level of serious crime in the Starrett community;

3. the residents' assessment of the security department's impact upon their lives and community; and

4. the benefit to New York City derived from the use of private protective services at Starrett City.

Data were collected through the use of Starrett City Security and New York City Police Department's records, self-administered questionnaires for both security unit personnel and residents, interviews of members of the Starrett City business community, security unit, New York City Police Department, and residents; and field observations of residents and security personnel during their daily activities. The research field period encompassed fourteen months during which forty-five security officers were observed performing their daily duties.

Private Policing in Starrett City

Private policing at Starrett City evolved with the development of the community. Initially, private security contract guard services were used to prevent the theft of materials during the development's construction phase. As the complex neared completion the security guards served to protect the site. But the crime generating reputation of the area surrounding the complex became an important variable in Starrett City management's decision to create their own private protective service. Management saw the immediate need to create an environment that would counteract the surrounding community's reputation and establish the complex as a safe and secure community. Thus, following the trend of privatization of schools, hospitals, and prisons that is increasingly evident in many states, Starrett City management set about providing for its own protection in addition to that provided by the New York City Police Department.

Originally, Starrett City's security unit consisted of a director and assistant director, five sergeants, and forty-five unarmed officers. Transport around the site was accomplished by two vehicles and two scooters. Communication between the command base and the officers was by radio. During the early 1980s the security department established its own canine unit and plain clothes anticrime unit.

Today, protective services within the Starrett City community is the responsibility of Starrett Protective Service (SPS) the proprietary security service of Grenadier Reality Corporations, the managing agent of Starrett City. (The SPS serves residential and commercial properties throughout the New York City area.) The security department at Starrett City consists of fifty-nine individuals. The positions and duties of these individuals are as follows:

Position	Number	Duties
Director of security	1	Management
Site manager	1	Operations
Sergeant(s)	7	Patrol supervisor
Sergeant	1	Anticrime supervisor
Security officer(s)	6	K-9 unit
Security officer(s)	5	Anticrime unit
Security officer(s)	38	Patrol

The average age of the Starrett Protective Service officer is thirty-nine years, representing an age range of twenty-one to seventy-one years. The majority of the group (64.8 percent) is between thirty-one and forty years of age. Only five of the security patrol officers are female. White officers comprise 50 percent of the unit, black officers 35.2 percent, and Hispanic 14.8 percent. Educationally, there are thirty-three officers (61.1 percent) who have completed high school, twelve officers (22.2 percent) who have engaged in post–high school education and nine officers (16.7 percent) who have only completed ninth grade. In addition to the director of security, two of the officers hold baccalaureates, and one has an associate degree.

In 1978 the security unit incorporated into its operation the status of special patrol officer. This status under the laws of New York City gave the security unit's officers full police powers when on duty and on site. Starrett Protective Service conducts its own internal training program for all members of the security staff. Certification training for the special patrol officer status is conducted by the Starrett Protective Service at its own expense, using a state certified trainer in compliance with the Bureau of Municipal Police regulations.

The average security officer has been employed at Starrett City for five years. This tenure reflects a range of less than one year to eleven years. The officers are recruited from the New York City area and are not residents of Starrett City.

The residents of Starrett City, like those of the greater New York City area, reflect a heterogeneous assortment of cultures and ethnic backgrounds. Our observation of newspapers displayed at the Starrett City newsstand disclosed twelve foreign language newspapers or periodicals were offered for sale. For many residents English is a second language, used with difficulty. An interesting finding and one that reflects the movement toward more professional status in security

Table 12.1 Languages Spoken by Security Officers*

Language	Frequency	Percentage
Spanish	8	14.8
Italian	3	5.6
French	2	3.8
Yiddish	1	1.9
Total	14	26.1

*One officer indicated he spoke Yiddish and Italian while a second reported he spoke Hebrew and French.

officers is the fact that 26.1 percent of the Starrett Protective Service officers speak a language other than English. This language facility greatly enhances the security unit's ability to break down barriers that are often experienced by non-English speaking citizens in their dealing with governmental agencies. Table 12.1 identifies the languages spoken by the officers.

The preceding description of the Starrett City security officers contrasts the stereotypical image of private police officers drawn from the 1971 Rand Corporation study that still impacts upon public opinion (Kakalik and Wildhorn, 1971:133). "The typical private guard is an aging white male who is poorly educated. . . . His average age is between 40–55; he has little education beyond the ninth grade; he has a few years of experience in private security . . . many are unskilled."

Security Unit Activities

A task analysis questionnaire and participant observation were used to identify the nature and extent of the duties performed by the Starrett officers.[1] The questionnaire instructed the officers to indicate the frequency with which they performed a particular duty during the last twelve months. The frequency range varied in intensity from "never" to more than a "few times" per tour of duty. Each frequency was assigned a score as follows: 0=never; 1=few times per year; 2=monthly; 3=weekly; 4=once daily; and 5=several times per tour of duty. The task frequency items were subdivided into five functional areas. These are:

1. Crime prevention activities;
2. Service to residents;
3. Service for management;
4. Law enforcement activities;
5. Administrative duties.

Table 12.2 contains an index of those tasks that achieved a mean of three or higher. These tasks were the more frequently performed duties, daily, or weekly. The reliability of data obtained from this survey were verified by field observations, interviews of security personnel, and records review.

Analysis of the task frequency data and our observations disclosed that the

Table 12.2 Most Frequently Performed Tasks

Mean	Task	Function
4.4	Checking parking garages and lots	Crime prevention
4.1	Observe for illegal activity	Law enforcement
4.0	Check park and school grounds	Crime prevention
3.7	Follow suspicious persons	Crime prevention
3.7	Request identity of persons	Crime prevention
3.7	Patrol on foot	Crime prevention
3.7	Examine and test doors and windows	Crime prevention
3.6	Talk with people	Crime preventon
3.6	Investigate noise complaints	Law enforcement
3.5	Patrol vertically in buildings	Crime prevention
3.5	Secure buildings and laundry rooms	Crime prevention
3.5	Assist elderly or disabled persons	Resident service
3.4	Patrol areas which are potentially physically hazardous to residents	Resident service
3.3	Check vehicles for parking permits	Management service
3.2	Respond to general information	Resident service
3.1	Conduct security inspections	Resident service
3.0	Respond to sick or injured persons	Resident service
3.0	Give street directions	Resident service

security officers practice a highly visible proactive form of preventive foot patrol. Their operational objective is the prevention of crime within the complex. On numerous occasions they were observed checking buildings, vehicles, places, and events they considered suspicious or potentially hazardous. Occasionally they would stop an individual and in a courteous but firm manner request identification and the individual's purpose for being on Starrett property. When individuals were found in buildings without legitimate reason arrests were made for trespass.[2]

Officers were also observed performing acts of personal service for residents. For example, assisting elderly persons with packages, providing escorts during evening hours, and assisting people in need of direction. During the time of the day when school children entered and left the public schools, security officers were observed taking conspicuous positions near the two schools in the complex. In the community's shopping center officers engaged in friendly conversation with store personnel and shoppers. These activities contribute to the visibility of the security department and enhances the safety perceptions of the residents. They are representations of what Stenning and Shearing identified as the preventive, client directed orientation of private security.

Public Police and Starrett City

The Starrett City community is under the jurisdiction of the 75th Precinct of the New York City Police Department. The complex is situated within one public police sector. A police sector is a patrol service area usually manned by a two-person, motorized unit which responds to citizens' requests within that area. The 75th Precinct is divided into thirteen patrol sectors which, during maximum personnel periods, would each have a patrol unit assigned to it. The experience of the research team, conversations with 75th Precinct personnel, changes in assignments, vacations, sickness, and court appearances led to the conclusion that it is unlikely that every sector is assigned one patrol unit per shift. In fact, doubling up sector assignments is standard practice in the New York City Police Department. Accordingly, Starrett City residents would receive the services of one public police unit if and when it was available to respond to requests within the complex. Criminal investigation and emergency response services are also provided to Starrett City by the public police.

In 1985 the 75th Precinct patrol officers responded to 72,806 requests for service. This service demand amounts to an average 200 requests for service per twenty-four-hour period. Thus making the 75th Precinct police officers among the busiest in the New York City Police Department. The Starrett City security department responded to 13,248 requests for service within the complex during 1985. This service demand amounted to an average of about thirty-six requests for assistance during a twenty-four-hour period.

The research team interviewed a total of ten 75th Precinct police officers, both supervisors and patrol officers who had contact with Starrett City over a period of five years.[3] All of the officers considered Starrett City a low crime area. Initially, they stated that the complex was a problem area demanding their attention but over the years this has changed. They believe that the change is directly related to the development of the private protective services within Starrett City. When asked to define what they thought the Starrett City Protective Service did that made the complex safe, several officers responded as follows: "They're visible. Out on the streets all the time." "If I go in there the first person on the scene to assist me is one of their 'cops.'" "Their 'cops' make good arrests."

In describing the difference between the police/security style of providing protection one patrol veteran of twenty-one years service stated:

> Look all we are [are] recorders in blue. 911 has us running from one job to another. Half the time we don't have enough cars on the street to handle the jobs. Plus, the rookies only care about collars [arrests]. In Starrett, their "cops" are on foot talking to people, patrolling like we did years ago. If they see something or someone that looks dirty they can investigate. Us, the damn radio is always holding another job to respond to.

This statement provides us with a description of the typical mode of urban police patrol found in high service demand areas. It is reactive, after-the-incident investigating. The police patrol unit usually is covering more than one patrol sector. If an arrest must be made or an incident demands an investigation, the patrol unit involved is placed out of service. As a result, the workload of the remaining patrol units increases, especially during periods of high service demand.

During such periods, the remaining units on patrol respond from one radio assigned call to another with little time for preventive patrol or interaction with the public.

In contrast, the security unit uses on-site patrolling which does not have the demanding 911 dispatch system. The majority of the security officers are on foot patrol throughout the complex. Thus the security officer is visible and has the opportunity to engage in more client directed preventive style of policing than the public officers.

During their interviews a number of the public police officers referred to the Starrett City security officers as "Starrett City Cops." The usual term used by NYCPD officers for security personnel is the noncomplimentary "square badge." When asked why they held the security officers in such a positive manner one officer summed it up as follows: "They act like cops used to act in the old days. They're out there on foot keeping the beat clean. We don't have to spend time in there and we can keep outside where the workload is heavy."

In general, within this very busy precinct with its high demand for service, the public police officers interviewed considered Starrett City a separate world, one of low crime and good security, demanding little of their attention. They enter the complex when requested and this occurs infrequently.

Serious Crime in Starrett City

Crime and fear frequently cause individuals and entire communities to change their way of life (Conklin, 1975; *The Figgie Report*, 1980; Haberg, 1981). They determine the character of a community (Auletta, 1987). Official crime rates are the most frequently used measures of the effectiveness of law enforcement. But the reliability of these rates have been challenged by numerous scholars (Wolfgang, 1963; Skolnick, 1966; Biderman and Reiss, 1967; Black, 1970; Skogan, 1974; Maltz, 1975; Seiderlman and Couzens, 1975; Wycoff and Manning, 1983). In this study we sought to identify the level of serious crime in order to have data upon which to access the comparative safety of the Starrett City community.

In order to obtain a comparative understanding of the level of serious crime in Starrett City we identified the rate of felonies reported to have occurred within the residential community, the United States, New York State, and the local precinct per 1,000 residents for the years 1984–85.[4] Table 12.3 contains this data.

The rate of reported felony crime in Starrett City is considerably lower than the national, state, and contiguous community. The difference between Starrett City and its surrounding community is particularly interesting in the areas of assault, robbery, and burglary. The nature of these crimes, more than other felonies, contribute to a diminishing sense of community. Also, it would seem likely that the socioeconomic difference between Starrett City and the surrounding area would make it a likely target for burglars. But the statistics indicate that this is not the case.

Perhaps, a more striking comparison of the safety of Starrett City may be gained

Table 12.3 Reported Felony Incidents
Per 1,000 Residents, 1984, 1985

	United States 84/85		New York State 84/85		75th Precinct 84/85		Starrett City 84/85	
Murder/Non-negligent manslaughter	0.08	0.08	0.10	0.95	0.30	0.22	0.00	0.05
Rape	0.36	0.37	0.32	0.32	0.90	0.83	0.05	0.10
Robbery	2.05	2.06	5.07	5.04	16.00	15.51	3.60	2.75
Aggravated assault	2.90	3.03	3.66	3.84	6.10	6.88	1.90	1.05
Burglary	12.64	12.87	12.57	12.35	15.40	15.26	2.10	0.40
Grand larceny	27.91	29.01	27.55	28.25	12.10	11.64	2.90	1.30
Vehicle theft (felony)	4.37	4.62	6.51	5.99	10.10	9.51	1.80	1.10

from the fact that in New York City there were 83.5 reported felony incidents per 1,000 city residents and 33.9 felony incidents per 1,000 public housing residents during 1985 (*New York Times*, 1986). Analysis of the felonies reported in Starrett City in 1985 disclose a rate of 7.25 felony incidents per 1,000 residents. In light of these comparisons Starrett City must be considered a relatively safe community.

Wycoff and Manning (1983:23) posit that reducing the incidence of crime should not be the only measure upon which to judge the effectiveness of law enforcement. Instead, they believe that citizen opinion of the security of their community is equally important. Effective law enforcement should also help citizens feel comfortable in their communities. Therefore, the study sought the opinions of those individuals who reside and work in the Starrett City community.

Resident Survey and Sample

An optional, self-administered, anonymous questionnaire was distributed to 2,235 apartment units in seventeen buildings in the Starrett City complex. The sampling procedure adjusted for the impact of land mass (153 acres) upon safety perception (e.g., different building location; different safety perception) by a strategy that selected specific residential buildings for the survey, based on their location in the site plan. The buildings surveyed represent 36.95 percent (N=17) of the residential property and 38.40 percent (N=2235) of the occupied apartment units. The final number of residents' questionnaires utilized for this analysis is 644 out of 687 returned. After evaluation, forty-three returns were rejected because they were either improperly filled out or the majority of the items were unanswered. This process yielded a response rate of 30.73 percent.

Table 12.4 Residents' Safety Perceptions in Starrett City

Item	Very Safe	Somewhat Safe	No Opinion	Somewhat Unsafe	Very Unsafe
Living in Starrett	49.7	39.1	4.2	5.4	1.6
Out alone at night	13.5	41.9	3.9	25.0	15.1
Out alone at daytime	49.7	39.3	2.3	6.8	1.9
Starrett shopping center	35.1	49.5	4.0	9.6	1.7
Safety at home	62.1	28.6	0.9	6.4	1.1

The sample population represents 2,862 residents, which is 14.31 percent of the population of Starrett City. The majority of the sample are long-term residents with 62.7 percent (N=404) residing in Starrett City from six to twelve years. This reflects the relatively low turnover rate of Starrett City apartment units which is less than 2 percent per year. The fact that the majority of the respondents are long-term residents enhances their knowledge of the complex and its security. Their responses disclosed that during the two years prior to this survey, 67.7 percent (N=436) of the sample had occasion to use the security services. A majority of these individuals, 64.2 percent (N=280), used the services more than once. Therefore, the major proportion of the sample evaluated the security department from personal experience. It was hoped that this experiential factor would control for any favorable bias created by long-term residency.

The majority of the respondents were former residents of the Brooklyn, New York area (73.3 percent). The data disclosed that 38 percent (N=245) of the respondents moved to Starrett City in search of a safer environment, while 37 percent (N=241) of the respondents were attracted to Starrett City because it was affordable. The safety and affordability features of Starrett City make this residential property an important factor in the maintenance of the population base of this section of New York City.

Residents' Safety Assessment

The respondents' perceptions of their personal safety were evaluated for areas within the Starrett residential complex and outside Starrett City. A scale of five questionnaire items measured respondents' feeling of safety within Starrett City. Table 12.4 contains this scale.

The overwhelming majority of respondents, 88.8 percent (N=572), consider themselves to be safe within Starrett City. While these responses are consistent with the well-established pattern in research that people feel safer close to home, our observations support these findings (Flanagan and McGarrell, 1986:145). During our many visits to Starrett City we found that there was a higher level of social interaction within Starrett City than in communities outside the complex. Senior citizens appeared relaxed and displayed less defensive behavior in the presence of teenagers. In the evening people were out walking and using recreational

Table 12.5 Residents' Safety
Perception Outside of Starrett City

Item	Very Safe	Somewhat Safe	No Opinion	Somewhat Unsafe	Very Unsafe
Outside of Starrett	6.7	34.2	12.0	29.0	18.2
Alone at daytime	7.9	33.2	7.1	34.9	16.7
Alone at night	2.6	17.4	7.9	28.4	43.6
Shopping centers	12.6	43.3	9.2	22.8	12.1

facilities. There did not seem to be an aura of fear within the Starrett community. Individuals of various ethnic and racial groups interacted freely. A visitor sensed a feeling of community which appears lacking in many urban settings today. The responses to the safety inside Starrett City is further highlighted by the comparison to feelings of safety in areas outside of the community reported in Table 12.5.

Only 40.9 percent (N=263) considered areas outside Starrett City safe and the greater proportion of these (34.2 percent) only somewhat safe. Shopping centers appeared to be the only areas outside of Starrett City where the greater proportion of our respondents, 55.9 percent (N=360), felt safe. Our observations revealed that many of the shopping areas near Starrett City employ private security to provide extra protection. In fact, it is not uncommon to observe armed guards and attack dogs in individual stores.

In summary, the data on the residents' perception of their personal safety leads to the conclusion that they believe their community is a safe place to live and shop. But when they leave Starrett City this perception ends, except in the exterior shopping areas. The question that remains is, do the residents attribute their safety to their private policing unit?

Starrett Protective Service and Community Safety

In order to examine the relationship between resident safety and the Starrett Protective Service we included in the residents' survey an eight-item impact scale that measured resident assessment of what effect a lack of private police would have upon their community.

The distribution of responses by scale item, contained in Table 12.6, provides a more comprehensive picture of what the respondents believe life in Starrett City would be without its own security department. The major proportion of the resident sample (89.1 percent) think that Starrett City would not be a safe place to live and that crime would increase (86.6 percent). In particular, residents believe that without their own security robberies will increase. Robbery, a violent predatory crime, is a major contributor to citizen fear. Many individuals prefer to move from areas where high incidence of robbery exist. In fact, 50.7 percent of our sample (N=327) indicate that if Starrett City did not have its own security department they

Table 12.6 No Security: Impact Scale

Effect	Strongly Agree	Agree	Disagree	Strongly Disagree	No Opinion
Not safe	61.3	27.8	2.5	3.3	5.2
More crime	59.6	27.3	3.1	4.7	5.3
Stop shopping in Starrett	25.3	31.2	21.6	5.0	17.0
Move from Starrett City	28.7	22.0	12.7	3.7	32.7
More robbery	55.3	34.6	2.6	1.6	5.9
Not go out at night	43.8	30.0	13.5	3.4	9.3
Change way of living	21.9	30.6	17.9	7.1	22.5
Negative change in Starrett City	56.2	27.3	2.0	4.0	10.4

would leave the community. We believe this is an important result. It is further proof that the Starrett Protective Service is a major stabilizing influence in this community.

One can speculate on the stability of any residential complex if 50 percent of its apartment units became vacant. Those individuals who would remain living in Starrett without its own security unit indicate they would have to adjust their lifestyles to a less open, more defensive pattern. Assessment of these changes are reflected in the finding that 56.5 percent of the respondents would no longer shop in Starrett City if it did not have a private security unit. Also, 73.8 percent (N = 475) would not go out at night and 52.5 percent (N = 338) would alter their current way of life. It is clear that the respondents believe that the security unit is responsible for the greater personal safety they enjoy within Starrett City.

The respondents were also asked to evaluate the Starrett Protective Service performance in general and specifically as a crime prevention factor in the community. For the overall performance evaluation respondents were instructed to rate their private police on a scale of of scale from 0 to 10. Table 12.7 contains the distribution of their ratings. A majority of the respondents, 75.15 percent (N = 484), rated the performance of the Starrett City Security Department above average. A little more than a quarter of the respondents, 26 percent (N = 167), gave them an excellent rating of 10.

The evaluation of the crime prevention performance of the protective service was accomplished by the utilization of a graduated ranking scale that ranged from a very good job to do not know. The majority of the resident sample, 63.2 percent (N = 407) approved of the crime prevention performance of the security department. Table 12.8 contains the distribution of the responses to this questionnaire item.

As an additional measure of resident assessment of the security department, we included in the questionnaire an item that requested the respondents to identify

Table 12.7 Respondents' Rating of Security Department's Performance

Performance Rating	Range	Frequency	Percentage	Cumulative Percentage
0		12	1.9	1.9
1	Below Average	8	1.2	3.1
2		10	1.6	4.7
3		13	2.0	6.7
4		17	2.6	9.3
5	Average	48	7.5	16.8
6		52	11.3	36.2
7		73	11.4	36.2
8	Above Average	158	24.5	60.7
9		86	13.5	74.0
10		167	26.0	100.0

Table 12.8 Respondents' Rating of Security Department's Crime Prevention Performance

Rating	Frequency	Percentage	Cumulative Percentage
Very good	181	28.1	28.1
Good	226	35.1	63.2
Fair	143	22.2	85.4
Poor	22	3.4	88.8
Very poor	20	3.1	91.9
Do not know	5	0.8	100.0

whom they would first request assistance from if they were assaulted. The greater proportion of the sample, 77.5 percent (N=499), indicated that they would call the Starrett City Security Department instead of the New York City Police Department.

In summary, the overwhelming majority of the respondents attribute the safety of Starrett City to the performance of the private Starrett Protective Service. They perceived their private police unit as a major stabilizing force in their community and would request its assistance first before calling the New York City Police Department.

It may be that these findings reflect respondent bias resulting from possible feelings of proprietorship for the private police. As native New Yorkers these individuals know their residential complex would be an inviting target for predatory criminals without the preventive style of policing offered by the security unit. But the low rate of serious crime in Starrett City and the open, less defensive lifestyle existing within the complex supports their evaluation. The majority of Starrett City's residents feel secure and comfortable in their community. Thus, it may be concluded that the Starrett Protective Service has met Wycoff and Manning's standards (1983:23) and may be considered an effective enforcement factor in the community. This conclusion is further supported by the response to a survey item that asked the respondents what would happen in Starrett City if the security department was replaced by the New York City Police. The majority of the respondents (86.9 percent) believe that crime would increase in their community.

Privatization: Public Benefit

For years private security has been viewed as a for-profit enterprise with the client being the sole beneficiary of its services. On the other hand, does a well conceived and managed private police service result in some benefits beyond that derived by the client? One of the major reasons why privatization has become a trend in United States is that municipalities see it as a way of reducing cost and providing taxpayers with a savings. One of the issues examined in this study was whether the Starrett Protective Service saved the city of New York a substantial amount of money in protective service use time. We explored this issue by estimating the costs of the security service to Starrett City and the potential impact upon the New York City Police Department if that agency was required to provide this service.

Analysis of the records of Starrett City disclosed that the hourly cost of one security officer is $15.75. The officers are members of local 32 BJ–Service Employees International and as a result of their union contract receive maximum compensation from their first day of employment. Therefore, when estimating cost for the Starrett Protective Service, we used the same hourly rate for all its officers.

In attempting to gauge an accurate cost estimate of a New York City police officer, we consulted several sources of information. Conversations with ranking officers of the department, union officials, and various documents provided us with a range of costs, per annum, of a base pay of between $30,824 to $46,228, depending upon seniority. We estimated the hourly cost for the police officer to be $22.22. The figures for both the Starrett Protective Service and the New York City Police Department include all personnel costs. The estimated cost of the private/public police officer is displayed in Table 12.9.

Table 12.9 Private/Public Officers' Comparative Cost

Area	Hourly Cost	Weekly Cost	Annual Cost
Starrett City	$15.75	$630	$32,760
New York City	$22.22	$889	$46,228

These figures are based on a forty-hour work week, fifty-two weeks per year.

Service demand was evaluated as part of this comparative cost analysis. Inspection of the Starrett Protective Service daily dispatch logs disclosed that during 1985 the private police officers responded to 13,248 requests for service. The service

Table 12.10 Starrett Protective Service Dispatched Calls, 1985

Month	Crime Calls	Dispute Calls	Service Calls	Average Per Day	Average Per Tour
January	62	39	562	22.10	7.37
February	62	39	546	21.57	7.69
March	86	60	707	28.43	9.48
April	82	58	738	29.27	9.76
May	73	67	916	35.20	11.73
June	69	66	860	33.17	11.06
July	120	48	786	31.80	10.60
August	131	52	1,140	44.10	14.70
September	112	47	1,303	48.73	16.24
October	122	39	1,278	47.97	15.99
November	96	32	1,272	46.67	15.56
December	92	31	1,455	52.60	17.53
Total	1,107	578	11,563		
	(8.36%)	(4.35%)	(87.28%)		

requests were classified into three categories: service, disputes, and crime reports. These classifications are derived from the New York State Penal Law, the New York City Police Department radio dispatch code designation, and the description of each incident in the dispatch log. Table 12.10 displays the classification of the service demand by each month. The majority of the requests for assistance (87.28 percent) were in the service category. Crime reports and disputes each constituted less than 10 percent of the service demand. It should be noted that these data represent resident request for service and not self-generated work by the officers.

The average number of service requests per day and shift were estimated on the basis of thirty work days per month with three shifts per work day. Table 12.11 reflects the cost per shift based upon the numbers of security officers assigned, without including supervisory and dispatch personnel costs. The daily personnel cost multiplied by 365 work days amounts to $1,563,660 per year. This is a very conservative estimate, represents the cost for 1985, and does not include later increases due to contractual arrangements.

Starrett City is currently included as part of one New York City Police Department patrol sector. Table 12.12 displays the estimated cost to New York City for the assignment of one radio motor patrol unit with two police officers to that sector. The cost per twenty-four-hour period is $1,068, which amounts to a yearly cost of $389,890. This figure does not include investigative services, administration, emergency service response or technical police services.

If Starrett City did not have its own private protective service the New York City Police Department would be required to provide full service to that community. This would mean an addition of at least 13,248 calls for service to the 72,806 responded to in 1985 by the 75th Precinct. There would be an 18 percent increase in service demand for the police precinct. The Starrett City work load figures may be slightly inflated by residential management service calls but they do not reflect

Table 12.11 Starrett Protective Service Cost Per Shift

Shift	No. of Officers	Hourly Rate	Cost Per Shift
12 midnight to 8 A.M.	10	$15.75	$1,260
8 A.M. to 4 P.M.	12	$15.75	$1,512
4 P.M. to 12 midnight	12	$15.75	$1,512

Table 12.12 Public Police Service Cost Per Shift

Shift	No. of Officers	Hourly Rate	Cost per Shift
12 midnight to 8 A.M.	2	$22.22	$356
8 A.M. to 4 P.M.	2	$22.22	$356
4 P.M. to 12 midnight	2	$22.22	$356

direct assignment by supervisors nor situations that require attention but with no call made. Starrett Protective Service officers, like the public police officers, are not controlled by the radio dispatch alone. Considering all of these factors, the removal of the private policing service would represent a dramatic increase in the work load of the public police and would require major manpower adjustment at the precinct level.

Our conservative estimate is that the increased demand upon the New York City Police precinct would mean the addition of at least two officers per shift. It is more likely that the total work load increase would require the assignment of four additional officers to each shift. This would mean a per annum cost of $1,169,460. At these figures one realizes that a person-for-person replacement would be impossible.

It is our estimate that the Starrett Protective Service is saving the city of New York a minimum of $750,000. This estimate is derived by subtracting the present cost of $389,820 from projected cost of $1,169,460. It is unlikely that the city can afford to provide the same level of protection and crime prevention services presently provided at Starrett City by the private police service. The use of private police at Starrett City not only saves New York City a substantial amount of money by reducing the number of regular police officers, it also makes this residential property an important factor in the maintenance of a stable population and tax base in this section of the city since a majority of our respondents indicate they would move from the area if their private police force was removed. Thus, by providing a safe and secure community the Starrett Protective Service renders a substantial benefit to the city of New York.

Conclusion

It is our conclusion that without its private policing service Starrett City would not exist as a secure residential community. Also, the loss of the private police would represent an unwanted strain upon the already overburdened resources of the New York City Police Department. The major difference between Starrett City and its surrounding community is that it is protected by a highly visible client-mandated preventive patrol unit. It may not be an inviting target to the predatory criminal because the high visibility of the private protective service patrol unit increases the potential for arrest.

The Starrett Protective Service is successful because it is a well-managed, supervised group that has earned the respect of their public police counterparts. This fact has been formalized by the New York City Police Department who recently presented the Starrett Protective Service with an award in recognition of their service to the city.

Our observations lead us to conclude that the private police officers are a highly motivated group who have internalized management's goals and objectives. They are close to their clients, the residents. In many cases the security officer goes out of his or her way to provide assistance to residents. This type of activity is encouraged by all levels of supervision as well as peers.

Members of the security department appear to treat each other with respect. There does not seem to be a paternalistic attitude expressed toward subordinates by supervisors and or management. This recognition of the officers as adults culminates with an annual "medal day" when acts of intelligence or courage are rewarded with appropriate recognition. This is a major event in the Starrett City community usually attended by elected officials, residents, management, the press, and officer's relatives.

The private police service at Starrett City is an excellent organization composed of individuals who are given the opportunity to work hard and attain a sense of accomplishment. This management style and the environment it creates are important factors in the success of this privatization effort.

Implications

To the best of our knowledge this is the first empirical study to examine the ability of a private security force to provide community protection. As such, there are implications that can be extracted by enforcement professionals and other researchers.

There are at this time a number of police departments experimenting with some form of community policing in United States (Trojanowics, Pollard, Colgan, and Harden 1986). These programs emphasize a style of preventive foot patrol similar to that employed by the Starrett Protective Service. The labor intensiveness and cost factors associated with this style of policing place it beyond the ability of many municipalities.

Perhaps police administrators in these communities may be able to contract out noncrime related services to reliable, well-trained security personnel. This has been accomplished in municipalities in the province of Quebec, Canada (Harris, 1987). If this movement toward the privatization of protection is to continue, then the mechanisms must be found to foster police/security cooperation that is beneficial to both parties. What we are suggesting is that police/security cooperation extend beyond the occasional sharing of information or cooperative policing at a major event. The two types of policing are not mutually exclusive. As we have found in this study, when both types of policing cooperate and support each other the client as well as the municipality derive benefit.

A security department that is well managed, with highly motivated personnel and an appropriate record of performance could serve as a private partner to the public police service. Such a department may be the type to which a municipality would consider "contracting out" certain types of service requests or areas to patrol. Municipalities which do this should maintain quality control over these operations and lend assistance to the security department in the areas of selection, certification, and training. A security department that is contributing to the well-being of a community and working effectively with the public police should be eligible for some form of public police support.

Perhaps, more than anything else, more research into the relationship between the private protective services and community safety should be conducted. Private policing has had limited scholarly analysis. Until this occurs we shall never know to what extent it may be effectively used. The challenge for those individuals who favor privatization is to prove that it is an effective and efficient approach to community safety.

Notes

1. Major source documents for the security officer task analysis were "Peace Officers Task Analysis: The Ohio Report," Office of Criminal Justice Services Statistical Analysis Center, 1983; and "Statewide Job Analysis of the Police Patrol Officer Position," Pennsylvania Municipal Police Officers' Education and Training Commission, 1981. The survey instrument was pretested to evaluate its content and validity as a data gathering device.

2. Starrett City security officers under the laws of New York City and state are designated special patrol officers. This grants them full peace officer powers (e.g., arrest) and special application to the city of New York for the right to carry weapons—when on duty—at their location of employment. Technically they are only responsible for the buildings within the complex. In fact, they patrol the whole complex area. This is partially because of the limited patrol services provided by New York City in the area and by the desire of the Starrett City management for greater protection. New York City Police Department supports the security department with investigative, administrative (e.g., arrest processing facilities), emergency response, and technical police services. It is an excellent working arrangement for both departments with the bulk of day-to-day protective patrol and arrests within the complex performed by the security department.

3. The 75th Precinct has, like the New York City Police Department itself, undergone massive personnel changes. This made the identification of officers that had a contact with Starrett City more than a few months or years difficult to identify. We identified ten officers, both supervisors and patrol officers, that met this criteria. The interviews were free-flowing, unstructured types that ranged from ten minutes to two hours.

4. The analysis of crime within and without Starrett City is based upon several sources of data. We examined crime reports for the years 1985–86 maintained by Starrett City security department, the 75th Precinct, the New York State Division of Criminal Justice Services, the *Uniform Crime Reports*, and the *New York City Police Department's Annual Crime Comparison Report*. The population figures utilized are based on those reported in the 1985–86 *Uniform Crime Reports*.

References

Auletta, K. (1987). "Fear of Crime Divides the City." *N.Y. Daily News* (January 4), 23.

Banton, M. (1964). *The Policeman in the Community.* New York: Basic Books.

Becker, T. M. (1974). "The Place of Private Police in Society. An Area of Research for the Social Sciences." *Social Problems* 21:438.

Bercal, T. E. (1970). "Calls for Police Assistance: Consumer Demands for Governmental Service." *American Behavioral Scientist* 13:681.

Biderman, A. D., and A. J. Reiss (1967). "On Exploring the 'Dark Figure' of Crime." *Annals of the American Academy of Political and Social Science*, 374.

Bittner, E. (1970). *The Functions of Police in the Modern Society.* Rockville, MD: National Institute of Mental Health.

Black, D. (1970). "The Production of Crime Rates." *American Sociological Review* 35:733–48.

_____. (1980). *The Manners and Customs of Police.* New York: Academic.

Bottom, N. R., Jr., and J. Kostanoski (1983). *Security and Loss Control.* New York: Macmillan.

Brennan, D. T. (1975). *The Other Police.* Cleveland, OH: Governmental Research Institute.

Calder, J. D. (1980). "The Security-Criminal Justice Connection: Toward the Elimination of Separate-But-Equal Status." 3 *Journal of Security Administration* 3:33.

Conklin, J. E. (1975). *The Impact of Crime.* New York: Macmillan.

Cunningham, W. C., and T. H. Taylor (1985). *The Hallcrest Report: Private Security and Police in America.* Portland, OR: Chancellor.

Ericson, R. (1982). *Reproducing Order: A Study of Police Patrol Work.* Toronto: University of Toronto Press.

The Figgie Report on Fear of Crime: America Afraid, (1980). Richmond, VA: Figgie International Inc.

Flanagan, T. J., and E. F. McGarrell, eds. (1986). *Sourcebook of Criminal Justice Statistics— 1985.* Washington, DC: U.S. Department of Justice, Bureau of Justice Statistics.

Green, G. (1987). *Introduction to Security.* 4th ed. Stoneham, MA: Butterworths.

Haberg, J. (1981). "Fear of Crime Leads in Survey on Reasons to Leave Big Cities." *New York Times* (May 16), 81.

Harris, L. (1987). "Police Powers for Private Cops: An Arresting Idea." *The Gazette* (March 28), B30:32.

Johnson, P. (1987). "Cities Struggle to Pay Bills: Some Raise Taxes, Dip into Reserves." *USA Today* (June 30), 3A.

Kakalik, J. S., and S. Wildhorn (1971). *The Private Police Industry: Its Nature and Extent.* Santa Monica, CA: RAND Corporation.

Lilly, J. R. (1978). "What Are the Police Doing Now?" *Journal of Police Science and Administration* 6:51.

Maltz, M. D. (1975). "Crime Statistics: A Mathematical Perspective." *Journal of Criminal Justice* 3:177–194.

Manning, P. K. (1977). *Police Work: The Social Organization of Policing.* Cambridge, MA: MIT Press.

Moore, R. H. (1986). "Private Police: The Use of Force and State Regulation." Presented at the annual meeting of the American Society of Criminology (November), Atlanta.

Morris, N., and G. Hawkins (1977). *Letter to the President on Crime Control.* Chicago: Chicago University Press.

Naisbitt, John (1984). *Megatrends.* New York: Warner.

National Advisory Committee on Criminal Justice Standards and Goals (1976). *Report on the Task Force on Private Security.* Washington, DC: Government Printing Office.

New York Times (April 10, 1986). "Public Housing at a Glance," B6.

Raab S. (1984). "Growing Security – Guard Industry Under Scrutiny." *New York Times* (June 4), B4.

Reiss, A. J. (1971). *Police and the Public.* New Haven, CN: Yale University Press.

Rubinstein, J. (1979). *City Police.* New York: Ballantine.

Scott, E. J. (1979). "Calls for Service: Citizen Demand and Initial Police Response." Bloomington: Workshop in Political Theory and Policy Analysis, Indiana University.

Seiderman, D. and M. Couzens (1975). "Getting the Crime Rate Down: Political Pressure and Crime Reporting." *Law and Society Review* 3:457.

Shearing, C. D., and P. C. Stenning (1983). "Private Security: Implications for Social Control." *Social Problems* 30:493.

Sherman, L. W. (1983). "Patrol Strategies for Police." James Q. Wilson (ed.). Crime and Public Policy. San Francisco: ICS.

Skogan, W. G. (1974). "The Validity of Official Crime Statistics: An Empirical Investigation." *Social Science Quarterly* 55:20–38.

Skolnick, J. H. (1966). *Justice Without Trial: Law Enforcement in Democratic Society.* New York: John Wiley.

Skolnick, J. H. and D. H. Bayley (1986). *New Blue Line: Police Innovation in Six American Cities.* New York: Free Press.

Stenning, P. C., and C. D. Shearing (1979). *Search and Seizure: Powers of Private Security Personnel.* Ottawa: Law Reform Commission of Canada.

Stewart, J. (1985). Address to the Annual Conference of the American Society of Industrial Security. Dallas.

Sykes, G. W. (1986). "Street Justice: A Moral Defense of Order Maintenance Policing." *Justice Quarterly* 3:497.

Trojanowics, R., B. Pollard, F. Colgan, and H. Harden (1986). "Community Policing Programs: A Twenty-Year View. National Neighborhood Foot Patrol Center." School of Criminal Justice, Michigan State University.

Vanagunas, S. (1977). "Socioeconomic Class and Demand for Urban Police Services Not Related to Crime Incidents." *Journal of Police Science and Administration* 5:430.

Walker, S. (1984). "Broken Windows and Fractured History: The Use and Misuse of History in Recent Police Patrol Analysis." *Justice Quarterly* 1:75.

Whitaker, G. P., S. Mastrofski, E. Ostrom, R. Parks, and S. Percy (1982). *Basic Issues in Police Performance.* Washington, DC: National Institute of Justice.

Wiley, M. G., and T. L. Hudick (1974). "Police Citizen Encounters: A Field Test of Exchange Theory." *Social Problems* 22:119.

Wilson, J. Q. (1968). *Varieties of Police Behavior.* Cambridge, MA: Harvard University Press.

Wilson, J. Q., and G. Kelling (1982). "Broken Windows." *Atlantic Monthly* 256 (March) 29.

Wolfgang, M. E. (1963). "Uniform Crime Reports: A Critical Appraisal." *University of Pennsylvania Law Review* 11:708.

Wycoff, M. A., and P. K. Manning (1983). *The Police and Crime Control in Evaluating Performance of Criminal Justice Agencies,* 15. G. P. Whitaker and C. D. Phillips (eds.). Beverly Hills, CA: Sage.

13. Private Sector Liaison with Police
Michael G. Shanahan

Beginning with the publication of the Hallcrest Report in 1984 and a concomitant national law enforcement summit meeting held between the leadership of law enforcement and counterparts from private security, some visible steps have been taken toward rapprochement between the two sectors. Given the pressure on the criminal justice system and law enforcement in particular, one would have thought that major progress could be achieved by now; however, for the most part it is not a simple proposition. Those that form police policy do not have direct counterparts in the private sector since company policy, especially relating to community relations, is made at a higher level than corporate security. Consequently, despite huge business losses that dwarf loss figures associated with most state and local criminal investigations, there are only pockets of effective public- and private-sector operational interface. These exist most visibly in the Detroit area and Washington state.

The last six years, however, have witnessed a thawing of attitudes on the part of the public sector and greater interest on the part of private enterprise to explore innovative ventures at the national and local levels. Because ecumenicism generally springs from proven trust relationships, the next several years must reveal major cooperative successes or both sectors will continue to be unnecessarily wasteful of their protective resources. To do this American business must improve its loss prevention strategies through measured use of criminal justice sanctions. Law enforcement must pursue joint operations that lead to measurable results.

The Private-Sector Liaison Committee

One of the direct by-products of the 1984 summit meeting was the creation of the International Association of Chiefs of Police Private-Sector Liaison Committee (PSLC). Its mission is to develop and implement cooperative strategies for the enhancement of law enforcement and private sector security relationships. This is being accomplished best through the combining of resources designed to combat crime and prevent business losses. Secondarily, work of the committee creates an atmosphere of mutual understanding for the challenges facing both sectors. The PSLC members learned early on that if they were to succeed in committee endeavors they must establish alliances with other organizations such as the American Society for Industrial Security and the National Sheriffs Association. To this end committee strategies are constructed to involve as many outside interests as possible. In fact, it has been this networking that has led to coalitions for the production of widely accepted protocols, model policies, and programs. The following are examples of this newly found spirit of ecumenicism which has led to not only visible attitude shifts, but practical contributions.

Operation Bootstrap

The first project to evolve from the 1984 summit meeting, which was sponsored by the National Institute of Justice (NIJ) and hosted by the (IACP) Division of State Associations, was development of a program that trains law enforcement executives in Fortune 500 companies. The concept was originally envisioned as a supplement to the FBI National Academy and shrinking federal training resources. A simple proposition was made to a number of corporate CEOs offering to pay local police travel and per diem costs if the host company would make one seat per session available in various management training classes. While the proposal was made through the Division of State Associations, the newly formed PSLC adopted the program and brokered the classes back to several state chiefs associations which eagerly accepted the donated training. Corporate responses first came from AT&T, Unisys, GTE of California, Xerox, and the Boeing Company. Boeing itself had pioneered the concept by training local police in the Seattle area. With the financial assistance of the NIJ and a series of grants from the Burlington Northern Foundation, the Ben B. Cheney Foundation, and the Medina Foundation, Operation Bootstrap grew in size and scope. A full-time director was hired and headquartered at the University of Washington Police Department in Seattle. Grant administration was provided by the Washington Association of Sheriffs and Police Chiefs.

By 1989 the PSLC established the Operation Bootstrap Steering Committee made up of representatives from AT&T, Metropolitan Life, and Boeing, as well as federal and local law enforcement. The program had reached a production level of placing approximately 1,000 law enforcement personnel per year into corporate training classes in as many as forty-three states. Over eighty Fortune 500 companies support the program. Because the classroom is a neutral setting, it provides an important environment outside of the 911 crisis setting for both sides to develop a better cross-cultural fit. Today Operation Bootstrap is forging healthy relationships among upwardly mobile managers from both sectors. Through time this interface will make a major impact on cooperation between public law enforcement and private industry.

Product Tampering

In 1986 the Southland Corporation recognized the need to develop a protocol for joint management of product tampering threat cases. The nation had been rocked by the 1982 Tylenol incident in which seven people perished. During 1986 the Food and Drug Administration (FDA) received approximately 1,700 suspected tampering complaints and was aware of more than 350 threats to tamper. It was decided that under the leadership of the Southland Corporation the PSLC would develop a document through which agency or company procedures for response to product tampering threats could be written. This was the committee's first venture into the area of joint operations. To assist in that effort W. J. Bud Crow, and Rosemary J. Erickson of the Athena Research Corporation were retained to craft the document. Major players outside of law enforcement included the Food Marketing Institute, the Grocery Manufacturers of America, the National Food Processors Association, the FDA, and the U.S. Department of Agriculture.

A five-page protocol was approved for national dissemination to both sectors, entitled "Product Tampering — A Recommended Policy of the International Association of Chiefs of Police." Over 100,000 copies of the model policy were distributed in all states. This was the first crisis where federal, state, and local public agencies banded together to jointly plan with counterpart interests from the private sector. The document continues to be used as the basic reference in comanaging this area of consumer safety.

Drugs in the Workplace

Generally, the PSLC identifies a biennial project. With modest resources it is difficult for the committee to singularly address national issues that need consensus input. Typically, from conception to implementation projects have required from eighteen to twenty-four months. At its 1988 annual meeting the PSLC identified this thorny area of American life as worthy of focus. Because Chief Cornelius Behan of the Baltimore County Police Department was chairing a statewide task force on this subject it was decided to seek permission to modify the Maryland product into a generic protocol.

Through a series of editings a draft was prepared that met legal reviews of the Justice Department, FBI and the Drug Enforcement Administration. Further, the *Model Policy Manual* was reviewed by various local agencies and corporations. As in the case of product tampering the purpose was to share the instrument as widely as possible in both sectors. Booklet and photo-ready flat copies were circulated throughout the United States. In some areas local officials were encouraged to approach corporate interests for further reproduction. In several jurisdictions drug forfeiture monies were used to print what conservatively has exceeded 150,000–200,000 copies.

As a sequel to the production of the drugs in the workplace protocol the PSLC is in the process of drafting guidelines for local law enforcement agencies, private security directors, and prosecutors to jointly manage drug cases generated in the workplace. While the model manual effort encourages the development of employee assistance programs, the real threat of prosecution is also important. Currently there are no widely accepted guidelines for corporations or units of government to follow in prosecuting drug trafficking or abuse cases that occur within their areas of responsibility. The drug issue is far more troublesome to corporate or government relations than the product tampering question. However, it provides a good test area of how the two sectors will address an issue that impacts workplaces in both camps.

The Future

Especially under the community policing model, law enforcement will continue to follow an open approach to problem-solving. Corporations which are subject to consumer loyalty and the marketplace will remain skittish about trust relationships since many criminal justice issues strike so close to home. However, since 1984 and the issuance of the Hallcrest Report, several useful ventures have been attempted. Most have not fallen apart, but rather have produced recognizable goodwill. For its part the American Society for Industrial Security (ASIS) has also produced a major video documentary, entitled "Operation Cooperation." It is a genuine effort at breaking down the stereotypes associated with contract security to emphasize the positive role that these noncommissioned elements now play in the day-to-day safety of citizens. Research agendas also exist through the ASIS Foundation.

Ever so slowly the ice is melting around the edge of the pond. Jokes about rent-a-cops have less and less of an audience in police circles. In fact, as law enforcement begins to confront the thorny question of white collar crime it has become all too apparent that investigative expertise lies not in the public, but rather in the private sector. If one were to venture a gaze down the confluence between these two huge interest groups it would be safe to predict that law enforcement will come to rely on the talents found in the private sector. Conversely, the private sector will find that there is great loss prevention advantage to be found in a partnership where public authority can be brought to bear on problems which, if left unaddressed, will have a ruinous effect on the bottom line. It is obvious that operational rapprochement is at hand. However, for law enforcement a burdensome workload in other areas will be the driving force. For the private sector it most likely will be large doses of red ink that can be solved in part by use of criminal justice sanctions. Neither sector can go it alone. Neither wants to. Therein lies the difference between relationship issues in the 1980s and the emerging promise of the 1990s.

14. The Reasons for the Inefficient U.S. Justice System and Suggested Remedies

Richard Neely

If the United States can defend the entire free world from aggressors, why can't we also defend ourselves from our own criminals? The answer to that question leads to a discussion of complicated political, social, and economic forces. The bottom line, however, is that lack of money is not the only factor that makes government law enforcement incompetent. America's law enforcement is also incompetent because all of us, at some point in the system, consciously, intelligently, and deliberately want it to remain incompetent. That proposition may be counterintuitive, but it is nevertheless true.

When all of us live in constant fear of violent crime, reasoning would imply that we immediately beef up our engines of enforcement. But protecting ourselves from crime is only one of our political goals; there are many others, such as paying low taxes, minimizing government intrusion into our personal lives, and avoiding close proximity to prisons and other concentrations of the underclass. These types of considerations compete with personal safety for our political support.

The persons who exhaust their anticrime efforts by demanding more police, prosecutors, and prisons would be appalled by a plan to provide those resources through a 5 percent state payroll tax! Similarly they would be less than enthusiastic about living next to a medium security prison or work release center. Thus, higher taxes and facility location are two immediate impediments to beefing up enforcement. We can ask ourselves whether we want to pay for crime control or put up with the pollution of our neighborhoods by prisons; and on those two limited subjects we can obtain a simple up or down vote.

A strong political will and a little creative thinking will usually solve any problem that we entirely understand. The factors that make the expansion of government crime control nearly impossible are not so obvious as funding levels or prison location. For example, insurance companies are unalterably opposed to creating more judgeships because court delay helps insurance companies settle civil cases cheaply. Yet this is not a factor that most citizens concerned with better law enforcement think about and it is not something that the insurance companies talk about.

In politics people are seldom forthright about what they really want or why they want it. What really confounds us, then, in law enforcement are factors related to the *unintended* side effects of government policing that are largely obscure to the

182

man in the street. Government may be rational in some grand way, but it is not rational in a simple way. Unfortunately, the considerations that inform the complex reasoning of government are only dimly understood by the average voter; hence government officials have such low approval ratings.

Certainly insurance companies that want clogged, understaffed, incompetent courts so that civil cases take years to get to trial and businessmen who want prosecutors' offices to be so understaffed that there are no personnel to enforce the environmental laws do not go mouthing these objectives publicly. But it is factors like these that make community self-policing necessary; community self-policing has few if any unintended, adverse side-effects that will enrage powerful interests. Furthermore, community police organizations can bypass the standard political process that will never permit more aggressive *government* policing.

Initially, it is important to emphasize that crime prevention does not involve simply hiring more policemen. Numbers of police are important, but how they spend their time is equally important. When our neighbors are having a late night party upstairs, it is the police whom we call to ask them to turn down the music. When someone is noisily threatening imminent bodily injury to his wife and children, we call the police to quell the disturbance. The police are called out for every traffic accident — no matter how minor — primarily to provide lists of witnesses and reliable reports for later civil litigation. In this last regard, the police spend endless hours, paid for by the taxpayers, in civil courts testifying about what they discovered at accident scenes.

The police organize parades, lecture school children about proper highway safety and the health hazards of drugs, and the police even chauffeur high-ranking public officials around. Finally, in our legalistic criminal law system where civil liberties are correlated with "due process," and "due process" is correlated with meticulously following complicated procedures and providing appropriate documentation, it is difficult to reduce an officer's paperwork load. At the end of the day, therefore, it takes little imagination to understand that for every $100 worth of police man hours we purchase with our taxes, only about $2 or $3 will be spent on active patrolling to prevent crime.

Therefore, accepting that the average uniformed state or local policeman now spends only 2 percent of his or her time patrolling, and that increasing that percentage beyond perhaps 5 percent is nearly impossible, it is easy to recognize the futility of spending more money on additional officers. The average voter simply does not *want* to pay for more paperwork, school lectures, chauffeuring, traffic enforcement, or domestic advice.

Furthermore, additional police are useless without more prosecuting attorneys to prosecute offenders, more judges to hear the cases, more probation officers and social workers to prepare presentence reports and supervise convicts diverted from prisons, and more prisons, mental hospitals, and juvenile schools to receive the offenders we commit to public custody. Yet, there is little enthusiasm for expanding the number of judges available to hear criminal cases. The criminal courts in every major city are so overburdened that defendants are guaranteed favorable plea bargains as incentives not to clog the system by demanding time-consuming jury trials.

The reason for utter incompetence in the judiciary, however, has little, if anything, to do with decisions about the value of trying defendants charged with violent crimes. The real problem is that courts are *not* just *criminal* courts; courts that process criminals are almost always civil courts as well.

One way to decide many issues that arise in the civil courts is to make the courts so clogged, overburdened, complex, expensive, and incompetent that no decision can possibly emerge in any reasonable time. That decides everything in favor of the status quo, and the status quo is exactly what many powerful interest groups really want. Lack of a concerted effort to improve the courts, far from being simply a function of legislative parsimony or governmental inattention, is actually a reflection of general contentment by those with disproportionate political power with a system that does not work very well.

When, for example, civil courts work efficiently, the net result is that plaintiffs as a class prosper to the detriment of defendants as a class. In cases pitting working people against insurance companies, employers, or manufacturers, courts are simple machines that redistribute wealth from those who have money to those who do not. When the machine breaks down, no wealth can be redistributed, and this is obviously a positive economic benefit to individuals and institutions with money.

Civil plaintiffs, such as accident victims, need money today, not money ten or fifteen years from now when the courts get around to disposing of their cases. Therefore, when available judges are so overwhelmed with criminal cases that the civil docket moves at a glacial pace, civil defendants—particularly insurance companies who are regularly sued as a normal part of their business—are able to settle cases for ten cents on the dollar.

But courts are not unique among our public enforcement engines in being the targets of hidden political agendas. The hidden agenda problem is even more prominent with regard to prosecuting attorneys and their staffs. If we create more prosecutors to go after armed robbers, murderers, rapists, and dope dealers, the additional personnel will also be available to go after those who commit consumer fraud, antitrust violations, and political corruption. Although the political establishment in most places is genuinely against murder, armed robbery, rape, and dope dealing, the typical political establishment is minimally enthusiastic about prosecuting its country club friends for white collar crime.[1]

Because prosecuting attorneys are usually elected and have aspirations to higher political offices, they are inclined to play to the press by crusading against white collar crime and political corruption. Efforts to increase staffs for the prosecution of violent crime become impaled, then, on fears that prosecutors will use the larger staffs to torment members of the political elite who engage in an occasional political payoff, rig elections, pollute the air, or perpetrate frauds on consumers. Furthermore, it is not possible to rely on enlightened prosecutorial discretion to minimize this political problem because all of the incentives to any politically ambitious prosecutor encourage white collar, country club prosecutions at the expense of robbery, murder, rape, or drug prosecutions.

The newspapers and TV stations get bored with run-of-the-mill, violent, underclass crime, but they go into ecstasy over the prosecution of the humblest white collar criminal. The reason is simple. Newspapers and television stations are private, profit making companies that are in the *entertainment* business and not the information business. White collar prosecutions are middle-class morality plays that assuage the average reader's or viewer's personal sense of unrequited merit. It's great entertainment to watch Ivan Boesky go down in flames, but not so enthralling to see the mundane armed robber sent up for ten to life.

The upper echelons of American society – businessmen, politicians, lawyers, and government officials – are acutely aware of the extent to which they are the targets of envy. Government regulation now is so pervasive that it is nearly impossible to carry on normal business or government activities without running afoul of some low-grade criminal law. Furthermore, the anticorruption statutes – particularly the federal statutes prohibiting conspiracy, mail fraud, extortion (Hobbs Act), and organized crime (RICO), have been so liberally construed by pro-prosecution federal judges, that an ambitious federal prosecutor can indict a cheese sandwich under one of these statutes and win a conviction. At the state level there are similarly vague statutes presenting opportunities to procure easy indictments and easy convictions.

Statutory "crimes" like conspiracy in restraint of trade, illegal water pollution, running overweight trucks on public highways, or speeding must be distinguished from good old fashioned felonies like murder, rape, and armed robbery. Huge segments of the population favor passive resistance to the newer, statutory offenses that are part of our economic and environmental regulation. Whole towns, for example, may conspire to violate the environmental laws to save an obsolete plant, and millions of motorists now equip their cars with radar detectors and CB radios to violate the 55 or 65 m.p.h. speed limits on interstate highways.

Society is composed of diverse groups with diametrically opposed interests; these groups attack one another viciously in the political process. When one group wins a political battle, a statute is passed prohibiting something that another group wants to do. In turn, the losers continue the political battle by undermining enforcement of the offending statute.[2] Thus, passive resistance to regulatory laws is not always limited to elites: there are big differences in attitude about highway safety, for example, between the jogging, granola-eating, safety conscious yuppies of the Northeast and the smoking, drinking truck drivers of Wyoming.

The attitude of both truck drivers and business elites about the legitimacy of the regulatory laws is neither irrational nor reprehensible. The problem for society as a whole, however, is that the exact same machinery that we use to protect us from violent felons is also used to enforce the regulatory laws that many people like truck drivers and business elites believe are unjust.

At this point it is worth taking into account the different crime related experiences of different social classes. A person's likelihood of being a crime victim is strongly correlated in a negative way with income. In general poor people are victims while rich people are not. Rich people live either in suburban neighborhoods or in well-patrolled, fortified city buildings. The underclass is discouraged from visiting either place by some combination of geographical distance, social distance, private security, and community vigilance.

But because the lion's share of the people who determine how many prosecutors we will hire have more or less solved their own crime problems through private expenditures—buying either geographical distance or armed guards—they perceive prosecutors more as nuisances and menaces than as crusaders against our common enemies. Thus, regardless of what our governing elites say in their public utterances, they are largely content when young, ambitious prosecutors are so busy trying murderers, robbers, rapists, and drug dealers that they have an acute shortage of time and resources to enforce the regulatory laws.[3]

The attitude of America's elite toward prosecutors is the same attitude that the middle and blue collar classes have toward the police. Police are by nature bullies as well as heroes. The average guy on a bar stool intuits that the more uniformed officers we hire to crack down on crime, the greater the likelihood that his civil liberties will be abused. Although the guy on the bar stool may not be able to explain it quite this way, at some gut level he suspects that work in any bureaucracy will expand to fill the time allocated to do it, and that among available work opportunities, public employees will always select the easiest.

If police are not busy with serious crime, they will inevitably meddle in citizen activities like private poker games and speeding on the interstates, where no one wants their "help." Blue collar workers become most aware of the police when officers are enforcing the speed and parking laws. Minor moving violations these days typically cost between sixty and one hundred dollars in fines and court costs. This is no insignificant sum for a working family.

When I was a state legislator I served on a number of conference committees that were banging out differences between the senate and house versions of bills to raise the pay of state policemen and increase the number of officers. Among legislators in both chambers I found that the state police were universally supported by the rural members and universally despised by the urban members. The reason for this strange difference in attitude was that in rural areas the state police spent their time driving pregnant women to hospitals, coming out in the snow to jump-start stalled tractors and trucks, and investigating serious crimes. In the cities, on the other hand, ambulances and garages did the useful things that the state police did in rural areas, so the average citizen's experience with the state police was limited to seeing them set speed traps, ticket vehicles for not having inspection stickers, and roust late night revelers at after hours bars.

The average person is entirely unenthusiastic about a pervasive police presence because he does not want to pay one hundred bucks every time he runs a yellow light or makes an illegal turn. However, what the average person does want is a supremely efficient "reactive" police force that is there quickly and competently whenever needed. This, basically, is what the state police gave our rural residents, which was why the rural residents supported them. In the cities, however, there was too much policing for the average persons' taste. This is why I made the point earlier that it is nearly impossible to change the current reactive model of *public* policing.

How much gambling, prostitution, drinking, and drug selling a particular locale will tolerate is largely a matter of police and prosecutor discretion. This means that what type of police force a particular locale has is a matter of supreme importance to the purveyors of vice. And, for that reason, purveyors of vice have little in common with ordinary criminals like burglars, armed robbers, car thieves, rapists, and arsonists. Ordinary criminals avoid normal social intercourse and stick with the underclass, but the purveyors of vice are surpassingly active participants in the *political* community. In my own experience the purveyors of vice have *much* more political influence than the local chamber of commerce, and the thing the purveyors of vice most want from the political process is bad law enforcement. On many occasions I have seen the vice interests (which, of course, are allied with other criminals like the ones who fence stolen goods) actually elect their own local prosecuting attorney.

Ordinary citizens who simply want honest, efficient, and evenhanded government are numerous, but they are not very active in politics. The people who are active in politics are largely those who want specific policies from government that will benefit themselves. In an election campaign for prosecuting attorney in which the purveyors of vice have a friendly candidate, that fact does not necessarily come to public notice. Today, elections are won with technological firepower like television advertising and direct mail. All that is needed to obtain this technology is money. The purveyors of vice are noticeably more generous campaign contributors than ordinary, honest citizens, and their campaign contributions are funneled through sources that appear legitimate. Furthermore, even city councilors, county commissioners, and state legislators are in regular political contact with the vice interests because the vice interests have street-level, election day organizations. In a pinch local, county, and state politicians can be counted on to lend a helping hand to undermine enforcement machinery.

These organized forces, then, are joined by entirely honest citizens who are cynical about the police's crime fighting abilities (there's never a cop around when you need him!) and are reluctant to be ticketed for parking or stopped for speeding any more frequently than is currently the case. State legislators and city council members can always find more interesting and politically rewarding ways to spend money than on police, courts, and prisons. Finally, none of the resistance to more police is necessarily irrational or reprehensible. As I have already pointed out, a small percentage of the time of any new officer is likely to be spent patrolling neighborhoods, rousting unsavory characters, or protecting persons and property.

I have elaborated on the ironies of local politics at the risk of sounding cynical because it is impossible to make the case for private law enforcement without first showing just how low the political common denominator is in our consensus about public law enforcement. Indeed, the bigger the political subdivision making the decisions about law enforcement, and the greater the class, ethnic, and racial diversity in that political subdivision, the lower the likelihood that any particular neighborhood will be protected without hiring private guards or patrolling itself.

The real value of community crime patrols, then, is that such patrols can devote themselves entirely to the lowest common denominator about which everyone agrees. In this regard community crime patrols (just like private security guards) are not concerned with illegal parking, unauthorized U-turns, private poker games, environmental transgressions, or violated building codes. Therefore, no political interest group perceives community crime patrols as threatening, so community crime patrols have no effective political opposition.

Any augmentation in the official policing apparatus, including prosecutors and courts, will immediately inspire political opposition from those with hidden agendas. But no one will oppose government support of community volunteers as long as they act like volunteer firemen and not like Ku Klux Klansmen. This, then, is the crux of the argument for community enforcement: it is not that community enforcement is the *best* alternative for controlling crime; rather, it is that community enforcement is the *only* alternative for controlling crime.

Notes

1. Rudolph Juliani, a former high profile U.S. attorney for the southern district of New York, narrowly lost the 1990 New York City mayoral election to a black Democrat because his own natural constituency of white, upper middle class Republicans distrusted him at best and roundly despised him at worst. Juliani's high profile prosecutions of financial district inside traders and his street busts of middle class Wall Street cocaine users were praised by the media but left many of the voters whose support he most needed either indifferent or hostile. Of course, without the high profile prosecutions no one would ever have heard of Juliani, and he would not even have got the Republican nomination for mayor.

2. For example, if those favoring temperance among college students succeed in passing a statute prohibiting beer distributors from delivering kegs directly to fraternity houses, then the beer distributors retaliate by having their friends in the legislature cut back the funding for the beer commissioner's enforcement staff. If there are but two beer inspectors for an entire state, distributors can deliver beer to fraternity houses for years without getting caught. When they do get caught, they can take a month's suspension, pay a small fine, and simply write the episode off as a cost of doing business. Such a battle, albeit within the government's regulatory scheme, cannot logically be thought to be about "crime." All the participants, as well as all the spectators, understand full well that this particular battle is only about politics.

3. The portrait that Tom Wolfe draws of his state prosecutor in chapter 29 of *The Bonfire of the Vanities* is not only entirely accurate, but it is also the way most members of the business, professional, and political elites perceive prosecutors.

Part 2: Adjudication

15. Privatization of Justice

Larry Ray

The adversary process works well to determine past events, provided each party can afford skilled counsel. But many disputes, especially those involving long-term relationships, do not lend themselves to resolution by a traditional adversarial proceeding. ADR is still in its early stages, but seems likely to play an increasingly significant role in our legal system.

Justice Sandra Day O'Connor,
Supreme Court of the United States

Private justice as a component of the alternative dispute resolution movement (ADR) is a growing phenomenon. Frustration with public court costs, delays, and rigid processes is propelling this great growth. Another equally important impetus is the burgeoning realization on the part of businesses, lawyers, and citizens that dispute resolution processes need to be better adapted to the dispute. (Columbia University Law Professor Maury Rosenberg has dubbed this phenomenon as "fitting the forum to the fuss.")

Ten years ago there were only one hundred dispute resolution programs throughout the country (ABA *Dispute Resolution Directory—1980*). Today, there are more than four hundred such services (ABA *Dispute Resolution Directory—1990*). Most services are a combination of public and private. Some are distinguishably private. Most receive referrals from the legal system as well as direct private contacts.

Ten years ago practically no for-profit dispute resolution firms existed and possibly there were no national dispute resolution deliverers of private services. Today there are more than fifty private, for-profit ADR firms such as EnDispute, Judicate, the Private Adjudication Center, Judicial Arbitration and Mediation Services, and Judicial Resources. There are also nonprofit private service providers such as the Center for Public Resources. A number of individuals (60,000 in the American Arbitration Association alone) offer private ADR services as well. While most private firms concentrate on moderate-sized, tort-related matters, some firms focus on areas in which they have established expertise, on medium to large multiparty cases, or on small, higher volume cases (Mazadoorian, 1988). Many of the private ADR programs offer the full range of dispute resolution services found in the public court system, including negotiation, mediation, arbitration, and adjudication—such as hearings using private judges (Thompson, 1988).

California was the first state to engage actively in private judging, using a statute that permits public judges to refer cases to a private process. Other states are following suit. Approximately twenty-three other states have discovered similar existing, but yet unused, statutes which permit private judging. Other states, such as Ohio, have recently implemented Supreme Court rules allowing private processes. (In fact, in anticipation of increased use, the Columbus Bar Association designed its new building to include several private courtrooms.)

There is a paucity of data on private justice firms and practices. The impact on the public system, the courts, litigants, and the public at large is unclear. Users of private ADR services are interested in speed, lower costs, creative solutions, and procedural flexibility, including the right to select the third-party neutral and relaxed rules of evidence (Thompson, 1988; Green, 1985).

Need for "Alternative" Dispute Resolution

There are three interrelated reasons for the growth of alternative dispute resolution programs. First, courts are so overburdened that there are long delays in responding to citizen complaints. Second, these programs more adequately perform the informed dispute settlement roles once more fully provided within communities. Third, they are more capable of dealing with the whole conflict rather than a particular legal infraction. As society has become more complex and impersonal, citizens have increasingly turned to the legal system as the mechanism for resolving their disputes, which has placed an unmanageable burden on the legal system. Is the solution to long court delays the hiring of more legal system personnel? Some experts think not. They cite the fact that courts cannot handle all the disputes that citizens bring them because a vast number of cases already await court attention, and there seems to be no indication that there will be any fewer in the future.

Why is the legal system overburdened? Ronald Olson, former chairperson of the American Bar Association's Standing Committee on Dispute Resolution, finds an answer in the ways in which society has changed: "Increased urbanization, broadening government involvement in everyday life, and a waning of non-judicial institutions traditionally engaged in dispute resolution have combined to produce an unprecedented explosion of formal litigation. Judicial institutions have not kept pace." As a result, courts have been congested, filing costs and delay have reduced the effectiveness of the judicial system, and justice as well as mercy has become more remote. These results have especially pertained to the resolution of ordinary problems of consumers, tenants, neighbors, and family members.

Many leaders in the alternative dispute resolution movement seize on the idea that many of the traditional institutions such as the extended family, neighborhoods, churches, and communities have broken down and are no longer as important as they once were in interpersonal quarrels and fights. A grandmother may have intervened in a dispute involving siblings; a priest may have aided communication between parish members. Because alternative dispute programs bring dispute settlement services closer to the parties involved and their communities than does the legal system, they can be seen as a return to "simpler, less complicated times."

However, alternative dispute resolution can have a greater impact on society than remembering the past. The ultimate goal of most individual mediation sessions is to look forward to what will happen if the two parties encounter a similar problem in the future. Ideally, parties not only address the present problem of, for instance, a broken windshield, but also confront the underlying issues of the parties' relationship. This process sets the stage for the parties to resolve future disputes through effective communication.

This type of general conflict problem solving cannot be undertaken in a courtroom.

A judge often cannot deal with the variety of problems presented in a single case: the social problems confronting the disputants have both civil and criminal aspects, and many of them do not involve legal infractions. Unfettered by these limitations, a justice mediation program may be better able to consider the whole problem than a court. Because of this capacity, the alternative dispute resolution movement could aid society to focus on resolving disputes rather than on restraining, or cleaning up after, their manifestations.

Historical Background

The current generation of alternatives to courts has many antecedents. In the 1950s the juvenile court, often a source of innovation, developed some of the first community dispute resolution centers—for example, the New Jersey Juvenile Conference Committee. In the late 1960s the prosecutor's office in Philadelphia, building on a tradition of court-annexed arbitration, pioneered the use of arbitration to resolve relatively minor disputes instead of referring them to formal adjudication.

The theory behind minor dispute mediation programs has been developed by such academics as Richard Danzig, Earl Johnson, Laura Nader, and Frank Sander. Sander's 1976 paper for the Pound Conference Revisited provided a well-publicized model for thinking about these problems. Sander envisioned a panoply of dispute resolution processes ranging from conciliation, mediation, and arbitration to ombudsperson and factfinding. Each process would be used for the appropriate type of complaint.

When Griffin Bell, the former chairperson of the Pound Conference Follow-Up Task Force, became attorney general in 1977, he began a program which included the creation of dispute resolution centers in Atlanta, Kansas City, and Los Angeles. The American Bar Association gave the movement an additional boost by holding an important conference at Columbia University in May 1977 which reviewed a variety of dispute resolution techniques and helped to legitimize and publicize alternatives to courts.

Chief Justice Warren E. Burger, in his "Annual Report on the State of the

Judiciary," which was presented to the American Bar Association on January 24, 1982, urged increased use of alternative methods such as mediation, conciliation, and arbitration in "divorce, child custody, adoptions, personal injury, landlord and tenant cases and probate of estates."

The foregoing does not mean that courts and attorneys no longer have a role in resolving disputes. On the contrary, the alternative dispute resolution movement permits attorneys to define their roles better. Former ABA President David Brink envisions a day when attorneys will be viewed as "counselors, problem solvers, and deliverers of prompt, appropriate, and affordable justice."

At the same time, the legal system must recognize its responsibility in provoking the rise of the alternative resolution movement. Canadian Bar Association President William Cox confronted this responsibility when he said, "We must realize that these centers are being proposed because there is dissatisfaction with the justice delivery system. People are just not satisfied with the means with which they are given access to our judicial system. Accordingly, alternative means of delivering justice and of settling disputes are being requested, in fact demanded, by many of our citizens."

It is thus both opportunity afforded by and responsibility felt toward the alternative dispute resolution movement that has fueled its support from legal agencies and the participation of legal professionals.

Classification of ADR

It has become increasingly difficult to classify ADR. In the beginning most viewed the movement as an alternative to the formal adversarial legal system.

Today, proponents in New Jersey are using the term CDR (complementary dispute resolution); in Los Angeles, IDR (improved dispute resolution); in Canada, BDR (better dispute resolution); and the American Trial Lawyers Association, FDR (flexible dispute resolution). Regardless of the term used, the movement captures a new and different approach to problem solving using a variety of different tools.

One way to classify dispute resolution methods is by the amount of control the disputants have over the process and outcome. Viewed in this way, the processes can be lined up from right (much control) to left (very little control). At the extreme right is negotiation; in the middle of the spectrum is mediation; then, arbitration; and the extreme left is adjudication.

Negotiation is a voluntary, usually informal, unstructured process used by disputants to reach a mutually acceptable agreement. At the option of the participants the dispute may be kept private. There is no third-party facilitator; disputants may appoint lawyers to represent them. No limits are placed on the presentation of evidence, arguments, or interests. In that respect, negotiation is similar to mediation.

In mediation, parties may choose a neutral third party to help them arrive at their own solution. Mediation is usually private, voluntary, and informal. In some jurisdictions parties are required to attempt mediation before they can go to court.

The mediator can hear evidence and arguments, and explore the interests of the parties, but is not empowered to render a decision.

Arbitration typically occurs in two forms: as a private, voluntary process where a neutral third-party decisionmaker – usually with specific expertise – is selected by the disputants and renders a decision that is binding; or as a compulsory, nonbinding process that must be tried before going to court. Each party may present proofs and arguments. The hearing customarily is less formal than court adjudication. Sometimes the decisionmaker supports his or her findings by a written opinion.

In court-annexed arbitration, if the parties accept the award as a judgment, it is entered after the time to appeal has passed and litigation is terminated. If one of the parties rejects the award and demands a trial, nominal sanctions may be imposed on the requesting party, such as payment of the arbitration fees.

In some jurisdictions greater financial disincentives – usually a percentage of the arbitration award – are imposed if the party does not improve its position by a specified amount at trial. These penalties also can include payment of the opponent's trial costs, attorney fees, and experts' fees.

Private ADR processes between arbitration and adjudication are often blended to produce a variety of hybrids. They range from private judging to moderated settlement conferences.

1. Private judging involves the referral of a case by a judge or by agreement of the parties to a party-selected neutral decisionmaker who, under statutory authority, makes a binding decision. The proceeding is usually governed by statutory procedure and is flexible as to time, place, and process. Parties present their proofs and arguments and may appeal the judgment through the regular process.

2. Neutral factfinding may be either voluntary or involuntary under Rule 706 of the Federal Rules of Evidence. It is an informal process where a neutral third party, selected by the disputants or the court, investigates the issue and submits a report or testifies in court.

3. An ombudsman is a third party selected by an institution such as a university, hospital, or government agency to investigate complaints by its constituents, clients, or employees. It is a voluntary, private, and informal process. The report issued is usually nonbinding.

4. The minitrial is a private, consensual proceeding where the lawyers for both parties make shortened presentations of their cases before the person with settlement authority for each side and, often, a neutral third-party adviser. After this exchange (which usually lasts a day or two), the principals try to settle the underlying dispute. If they are unable to do so, the adviser renders a nonbinding opinion as to how he or she expects a court to decide the legal, factual, and evidentiary issues as well as the overall case. Then disputants try again to reach a settlement.

5. A summary jury trial is the equivalent of a minitrial with a jury. It takes place in a courtroom with a presiding judge or magistrate and a mock, six-member jury impaneled by the court from the regular list. The lawyers make expedited presentations, limited to evidence admissible at trial. The jury's advisory verdict helps the

parties build a mutually acceptable settlement. After the summary jury trial, the presiding judicial officer meets with the parties and lawyers to encourage settlement.

6. A moderated settlement can be initiated by counsel or by the court on its own motion. The attorneys present their cases before a panel of impartial third parties, usually lawyers, who evaluate the case and render an advisory non-binding opinion for use in settlement negotiations.

The Public-Private Night Prosecutor's Mediation Program

In 1971 Capital University law professor John Palmer noted the astounding number of criminal misdemeanors which were dismissed each day in the Columbus, Ohio courts. Many of these began as trivial disputes, such as neighborhood driveway disagreements, which had escalated to full-scale battles. Others were between family members who, in the heat of the moment, would call the police and file charges, only to drop them when calmness reigned once again. Professor Palmer felt surely there must be a way to deal more effectively with these situations, possibly even in a preventive way.

After a series of meetings, the city prosecutor's office and Capital Law School combined forces to create the Night Prosecutor's Program, initially, viewed as a diversion program. Assistant prosecutors would process citizens' complaints. If these complaints were classified as minor in nature, a hearing was scheduled.

The university operated the program under a contract with the prosecutor's office. At the outset, law professors served as the hearing officers. The program gained success during its first year, resolving over one hundred cases.

Soon it was determined that law students could hear cases. Before long, the program became the most popular law student activity. Scores of students were volunteering and then were surprised to discover there was pay involved. The program provided opportunities for law students not only to talk with clients but to serve the satisfying goal of helping.

During the late 1970s the program won numerous awards. The Department of Justice designated the program as an exemplary project and promoted its replication. The ABA Law Student Division designated the program as the number one law student activity. The project served as a model for over fifty other similar programs in Kentucky, Indiana, Florida, Illinois, California, and Texas.

Also, during the late 1970s, the project evolved from a prosecutor's diversion program to a mediation program. Instead of merely referring nonprosecutable cases to mediation, a sophisticated intake process began in an attempt to discern whether cases were more appropriate for mediation or prosecution. Law students became the intake counselors. Soon a counseling component was added. Social work, psychology, and seminary students worked side by side with the law students to assist citizens.

Many Capital Law School students declared that this experience changed their approach to law. Kenneth Jaray has incorporated mediation into his private practice

During these years, even though law professors encouraged law student involvement, the project was viewed by many as an extracurricular activity, not fitting within the traditional legal studies. No courses or seminars were offered in this area.

In 1989 Capital Law School Dean Josiah Blackmore legitimized dispute resolution as a mainstream law school study by establishing a course in this field. Several conferences and seminars have now been cosponsored by the law school.

The Public-Private Multidoor Dispute Resolution Concept: Multidoor Courthouse Centers Project

> At present, it is almost accidental if community members find their way to an appropriate forum other than the regular courts. Since these forums are operated by a hodgepodge of local government agencies, neighborhood organizations, and trade associations, citizens must be very knowledgeable about community resources to locate the right forum for their particular dispute.
>
> Earl Johnson, 1978

With these words, California Judge Earl Johnson identified a key problem in the administration of justice in America: the need for systematic methods for screening citizen disputes and assigning them to appropriate forums for their resolution.

Professor Frank Sander of Harvard Law School suggested a solution to this problem. He proposed that experimental Multidoor Courthouse Dispute Resolution Centers be developed in which citizen disputes could be diagnosed and referred to the most appropriate dispute resolution process, including conciliation, mediation, arbitration, and adjudication. The ABA helped to develop such centers in Tulsa, Oklahoma; Houston, Texas; and Washington, DC. Central to this effort is determining effective approaches for screening and referring disputes to the best resolution process.

Although the courts are the most visible dispute settlers, they are supplemented in many American cities by consumer dispute mediation and arbitration programs, ombudspersons, prosecutors' programs for criminal complaints, community agencies, and neighborhood dispute centers which handle domestic conflicts, landlord-tenant problems, and other controversies. Such alternatives to the courts have spread rapidly across the United States in recent years.

The successful effort to develop alternative means for settling disputes led the justice system to take a necessary next step—the systematic screening and referral of disputes to appropriate forums. In most areas, however, dispute-processing programs operate independently of one another. Citizens are seldom aware of the full panoply of community court services available to them, nor are they aware of which one might assist them most effectively. Many agencies view initial intake of cases as a clerical function. Citizens suffer from long waits, few answers, and little assistance. Citizens frequently leave the agency with a feeling of frustration, convinced that they have been victimized by another bureaucratic runaround.

The Plan: "Making the Concept a Reality"

Advocates of Multidoor Courthouse Dispute Resolution Centers wanted to provide a venue where answers to the current confusion of linking cases to appropriate forums might be explored. The ideal dispute resolution model was a center offering sophisticated and sensitive intake services as well as an array of dispute resolution services all under one roof. The screening unit at the center would refer the disputant to the appropriate "door" for handling the case—hence the title "Multidoor Courthouse Dispute Resolution Center."

Development of an effective screening and interviewing method to assign disputants to the proper forums was a necessary first step toward the ultimate development of comprehensive dispute resolution centers.

The multidoor courthouse project was planned in two phases. The first eighteen-month phase would focus on intake and referral; the second phase on filling the dispute resolution gaps identified in phase one by creating new programs and improving existing processes.

The multidoor programs used hundreds of different agencies and organizations for dispute resolution. The number of alternative *processes,* however, was more limited. Mediation was the most common and available alternative dispute resolution process and was used extensively in Washington, DC, and Houston. The Tulsa program made fewer referrals to mediation. Arbitration processes are available there in limited form; their BBB offers arbitration for automotive warranty issues. Washington has a voluntary civil arbitration program which is underutilized. A surprising fact, perhaps, is that the Tulsa and Houston centers relied to a large extent on traditional dispute processing—the courts, prosecutors, district attorneys, police, and private lawyers.

The three centers approached intake a bit differently. The Washington, DC, project focused on those disputes not necessarily suited for traditional dispute resolution processes. In those cases they had a predisposition or preference toward alternatives such as mediation and arbitration. The Houston and Tulsa centers accepted for intake any dispute and did not necessarily stress alternatives over the traditional process.

The connections of the multidoor programs to particular dispute resolution agencies, the housing of intake points within agencies, and the adoption of the agencies' screening functions by intake specialists, appear to influence decisionmaking substantially with regard to referrals.

Summary

Overall, the three multidoor courthouse sites present three variations on the concept. Variations include location of intake sites, background of intake specialists, and referral methods. Tulsa's director concentrated on fund-raising and public relations.

The director emphasized securing judicial support and created structural procedures. Houston's director focused on staff development and the intake process itself. All three took advantage of opportunities as they occurred.

Underlying all these variations is the superordinate goal of improving the methods by which citizens and systems handle disputes. Phase one of the Multidoor Courthouse Centers Project focused on intake and referral as the first step toward this goal. All three centers believe they have accomplished this step. As a result, they have gained a significant amount of information about which dispute resolution processes (doors) are effective, which need improvement of existing processes, and the need for creation of new doors.

It is clear that "in the disputing world, the forum should fit the fuss," but priorities and perspectives complicate establishing a simple classification scheme. The classification of disputes is fragile and may be just beginning. Each path exhibits a dark and light side which may be tested by a series of "what ifs." Much research and study must be accomplished before actual transactional costs can be calculated.

Delivery of Public and Private Legal Services

The ADR techniques are beginning to make inroads in the area of private practice. Whereas ten years ago few, if any, practicing attorneys would have suggested mediation or arbitration to a client, today attorneys are utilizing these and other established techniques in increasing numbers.

Three main fields of practice are showing increased use of ADR. Law firms, corporate law departments, and legal service organizations are, to one extent or another, all experiencing this trend. Though differing in means as well as in application of ADR, lawyers in each area consider it a boon for both their clients and their organizations. In fact, their successful use of ADR indicates that it is being accepted as a legitimate option for clients.

Nowhere could the expansion of alternative dispute resolution techniques take a more significant step than in their accepted use by major law firms. While by no means widespread, a gradual trend toward this sort of acceptance is becoming apparent. Lathrop, Koontz, and Norquist of Kansas City; Steptoe and Johnson of Washington, DC; and Tillinghast, Collins, and Graham of Providence, RI, are examples of large firms which have developed ADR sections and which have designated particular associates as resident ADR experts. These are lawyers designated to advise clients on alternatives and, where appropriate, act as advocates through the process.

Marguerite Millhauser, at Steptoe and Johnson, is the firm's ADR specialist. In her view, while there is a common trend among firms today to expand their range of services, firms with specialized ADR sections are still quite novel. She sees the fact that ADR is advantageous both to the client and to the firm as the reason for its growing acceptance. The trick, she says, is convincing not only your own client to try an alternative but also the other party.

For-Profit Private Judging

Private judging is the fast growing area in the dispute resolution field. Groups offering private judging actually offer the broad panoply of services described above ranging from negotiation assistance to mediation to private judging. Often their clients desire the least formal, of which mediation is the most popular.

Flexibility, saving money, and speed are the usual selling points for corporations, businesses, and other disputants who choose a private dispute resolution service instead of the courts. To demonstrate the contrast in speed, the California situation is most frequently cited.

Presently, more than 10 percent of the filed cases in California take approximately five years to come to trial. In contrast, a typical case in a private dispute resolution firm consumes less than one year.

This delay problem helps explain why the so-called rent-a-judge concept has become so popular. Rent-a-judge was created in 1976 by two San Diego attorneys who rediscovered a California statute which dated back to 1872 (California Code Civ. Proc. Section 638). This California General Reference Statute permits private parties mutually to agree to have their cases decided privately and then to have the decision entered as a decision of the court.

The delay problem and the success of the rent-a-judge program laid the groundwork for creation of the Judicial Arbitration and Mediation Services (JAMS), which is the largest and busiest deliverer of private judging in the nation. The JAMS caseload for 1988 was approximately 6,400 cases. Although significant, this number pales in comparison to the more than 640,000 civil cases filed in the California state court system.

As an increasing number of private judging and dispute resolution services appear throughout the country, an increasing number of concerns are raised.

Private Justice Concerns

We must avoid creating a private system affordable only by a few.
Robert D. Raven, immediate past president American Bar Association

The range of concerns about private programs is broad. Some observers worry that the availability of higher pay will lure many of the best judges from the public to the private bench. So far there has been no evidence, only individual case stories, that this shift is occurring. If this worry proves valid, it may provide the impetus for raising judicial salaries to more acceptable levels.

Others note that a private justice system is just that, private. They feel the public has a right to view both the proceedings and the decisionmaking process. Private justice proponents argue that approximately 97 percent of the civil caseload currently is settled without a public session and without public viewing. Settlement negotiations and conferences are not only a norm within the civil justice system, but are substantially encouraged.

In addition, parties themselves have stated that disputes generally arose from private transactions and contracts, so that solving them privately made sense.

Another argument posed against the private justice system is that it removes the impetus for reform in the public system. Often problems such as caseloads demand set the stage for legal reform. This situation was, in fact, documented early by the creation of the Columbus, Ohio, Night Prosecutor's Mediation Program. The removal of criminal filing fees raised the specter with legal leaders of a caseload flood; thus, they sought and discovered an alternative—mediation. To counter this argument proponents note that the private justice caseload is and probably will remain a miniscule part of the overall filings; thus, the pressure for reform should remain.

The concern raised by many national legal leaders, including Robert Raven immediate past ABA president, is that of establishing a two-tier system of justice—a private, expensive one for the rich and a public, affordable one for everyone else. Proponents point to other dichotomies within the American system, such as the private and public school systems or the differences in fees that well-known, experienced civil litigators and less known litigators are able to charge. The other side counters by distinguishing the free enterprise system from the legal system.

In the legal system they say, "all Americans are supposed to stand equal—where the size of one's bank account is of no account" (Harry L. Hathaway, President, California Bar Association, November 1989).

Conclusion

If your only tool is a hammer, everything looks like a nail.

Unknown

Despite concerns, the future for the dispute resolution field generally and the private justice movement specifically are brighter than ever. Both have spawned a spirit of truly searching for justice, often in spite of procedures and process. Dispute resolution processes such as mediation have proven to be the heart of this enthusiasm because of excellent follow-up results. Users of ADR state that the agreements reached are durable and being fulfilled (85 percent of the time). Users also say they are satisfied (90 percent) and would use the process again (95 percent).

The dispute resolution field is successful because it is calling upon some of society's best resources: citizens' entrepreneurial spirit, retired and experienced citizens, and the desire of most people to settle conflicts peacefully.

Concerns raised by ADR include questions of the need for precedent, the impact of confidential hearings and outcomes, high costs, and the potential for draining judicial talent from the public courts (ADR Reports, 1988). Some are worried about the creation of a two-tiered system of justice: "luxury" justice for those who can afford the private system and second-hand justice for those who cannot (Green, 1985). The "second-hand" justice label has been attached to ADR processes in the past (Marks et al., 1984).

Most believe that our present court system must be improved dramatically or privatization will increase dramatically. The urgency of this need may drive reformers toward a quick fix, without giving adequate consideration to perplexing legal and public issues. Legal leaders must carefully consider and guide the inevitable changes. Justice is not simply a matter of efficiency.

References

ABA Natl D. R. Consumers Conference, 1983, keynote speech.

ABA Standing Committee on Dispute Resolution Survey of Private Providers, December, 1990.

Arons, S. (1980). "This Court for Hire." *Inquiry* 5:11–13.

Austin, R. W. (1989). "Another Look: Private Dispute Resolution—What's Right with It." *Chicago Daily Law Bulletin* (August 21), 2, 14.

Brown, K. (1989). "Retreat from Courtroom Battles Made Phillips Mediation Pioneer." *San Francisco Business Times* (May 30), 12.

Carlen, L. J. (1987). "Arbiter Sees Both Sides from Middle Ground." *The Business Journal* 1 (June 22):30.

Christiansen, B. F. (1982). "Private Justice: California's General Reference Procedure." *American Bar Foundation Research Journal* 79, 1:79–110.

Colino, S. (1989). "Enter the Private Courts of Justice." *Student Lawyer* 4 (April): 35–38.

Coulson, R. (1982). "Private Settlement for the Public Good." *Judicature* 66, 1 (June–July): 7–10.

Cox, G. D. (1987). "The Best Judges Money Can Buy." *National Law Journal* (December 21):42.

Dress, T. (1988). "Mediation: An Ancient Panacea Reexamined." *Daily Journal Report* 88–95 (September 25): 2–9.

Gnaizda, R. (1982). "Secret Justice for the Privileged Few." *Judicature* 66, 1 (June–July):6; 11–13.

Green, E. (1985). "Private Judging: A New Variation of Alternative Dispute Resolution." *Trial* 10 (October): 36–43.

Jaffe, S. M. (1989). "Private Judging—Proceed with Caution." *ADR Report* (BNA) (June 8): 204–6.

Kemper, S. "Donald B. Reder: At Hartford's Dispute Resolution, Inc." (unknown: department, "Conversations").

Knight, H. W. (1981). "Private Judging." *California State Bar Journal* 3 (March): 108–9.

Marks, J. B., E. Johnson, Jr., and P. L. Szanton (1984). *Dispute Resolution in America: Processes of Evolution.* Washington, DC: National Institute for Dispute Resolution.

Mazadoorian, H. N. (1988). "ADR: For-Profit Take Firm Hold on Field." *Bar Leader* (September–October): 22–25.

"Mediation Is a Tool for Managing Litigation" (1985). *Federal Bar News Journal* 32, no. 5 (June): 22–27.

O'Connor, Sandra Day (1983). Keynote speech, Bar National Dispute Resolution Consumers Conference.

Payne, E. (1987). "Don't Litigate, Negotiate!" *Fair Press* (March 26).

Peason, C. (1978). "Justice, Inc.: A Proposal for a Profit-Making Court." *Juris Doctor* (March): 32–38.

"The Private Sector" (1988). *Consumer Arbitrator* (Fall), 8.

Raven, R. (1988). "Private Judging: A Challenge to Public Justice." *ABA Journal* 4 (September 1): 390.

Ray, L. (1989). Tentative list of Private Neutrals, prepared for ABA Standing Committee on Dispute Resolution (August).

"'Rent-a-Judge' Still Generates Conflict" (1982). *California Lawyer* 2 (February): 17.

Ring, L. M. (1989). "Private Dispute Resolution—What's Wrong with It?" *Chicago Daily Law Bulletin* (August 17), 2.

Rosenthal, M. M., and R. M. Shapiro (1984). "Invoking Private-Judge Dispute Resolution." *California Lawyer* 9 (September): 25–27, 74.

Silas, F. A. (1986). "McJustice: Mediation Franchising Begins." *ABA Journal* 72 (January): 17–18.

Stone, C. (1984). "Private Justice: Judicate Promises Speed, Efficiency in Deciding Cases for Profit." *The Pennsylvania Lawyer* 10 (October 15): 7–9.

Thompson, M. (1988). "Rented Justice." *California Lawyer* 3 (March): 42–46.

Wulff, R. W. (1990). "A Shortcut to Settlement." *The Recorder* (August 22, commentary section).

16. Market Failure Versus Government Failure in the Production of Adjudication

Bruce L. Benson

Many advocates of public adjudication simply assert that the private sector would do an inadequate job of providing adjudication services. For example, Bernard Herber, in a typical public finance textbook, wrote, "Since . . . [law and adjudication are] not controversial function[s] of government, . . . [they do] not require a lengthy analysis in the effort to construct an economic case for the existence of a public sector for resource allocation purposes" (Herber, 1975:22). However, there have been a few attempts to provide a systematical analysis of the "market failure" arguments regarding adjudication (Landes and Posner, 1979; Mabry et al., 1977; Christainsen). The implicit assumption underlying such justifications is that when the market fails government can do better, but government is also far from perfect.

Thus, the question that should be posed when deciding whether adjudication should be produced by market or government institutions is which method's failures are likely to generate the most significant misallocations of scarce resources. Therefore, let us bring the relevant historical and current facts regarding both market *and* government failure to bear on the major arguments for public (versus private) provision of adjudication.

There are two basic types of market failure: (1) external costs and benefits (including public goods) whereby the private sector is presumably unable to internalize either some of the costs or the benefits associated with production or consumption of a particular good or service; and (2) monopoly power, whereby the forces of competition are presumably not sufficient to guarantee efficient production. Both types of market failure have been suggested as likely if adjudication is not publicly produced. Consequently, arguments pertaining to each are examined in the following two sections of this chapter. Concluding comments appear in the final section.

This project was conceptualized while I was supported by an F. Leroy Hill Fellowship from the Institute for Humane Studies, and produced with support from the Political Economy Research Center. It draws on and extends material appearing in *Enterprise of Law*, supported by the Pacific Research Institute.

Externalities and Public Goods

The externality argument for public provision of adjudication might be characterized in the following manner: courts generate external benefits for which private suppliers may be unable to charge (Mabry et al., 1977:80). Thus, there are strong free rider incentives associated with adjudication, and a private for-profit judicial industry would under-allocate resources to its production. Perhaps the most widely claimed external benefit of adjudication is the body of precedent law that court decisions generate. Mabry et al., for instance, wrote "the continuous creation of a collection of decisions, interpretations, opinions, and precedents is the production of a collectively consumed service. . . . Since they are available to others at no additional cost, precedents are externalities. Indeed the entire set of law known as common law has developed as an external benefit of past adjudication" (Mabry et al., 1977:80; Landes and Posner, 1979:80; Buchanan, 1971:2). While individuals would be willing to pay for the private benefits they obtain from a private court (e.g., dispute resolution), they would consider only these private benefits. The resulting failure to recognize and capture payment for the additional benefits accruing to the community at large implies that a private market under-allocates resources to the provision of judicial services.

If there is a significant free rider problem it actually means that *too little* private-sector adjudication is purchased and produced. The problem arises because individuals cannot be persuaded to cooperate in buying judge-made law, not because the private sector would not produce it if producers were fully compensated for the benefits they provide. When free riding is prevalent, people will have to be coerced into paying for a service since they cannot be persuaded to cooperate. Government is the only entity that is widely recognized to have the power to coerce. Thus, the free rider problem provides a justification for government collection of taxes in order to subsidize the private producers of precedents; it does not provide a justification for government production of adjudication unless it is combined with other circumstances which imply that private judges are also less efficient producers.[1] But, according to Landes and Posner, "because of the difficulty of establishing property rights in a precedent, private . . . judges might deliberately avoid explaining their results because the demand for their services would be reduced by rules that, by clarifying the meaning of the law, reduce the incidence of disputes" (Landes and Posner, 1979:238; Mabry et al., 1977:82). Thus, private judges presumably have incentives to create uncertainty regarding rules of obligation, in order to create demand for their services.

An even more fundamental externality argument is often put forth by even the most staunch supporters of the market economy. Clearly defined property rights are critical requirements for the operation of a market system. Thus, some system of defining and then protecting and enforcing property rights is needed before a market economy can develop. Enforcement of property rights, it is suggested, requires coercion and, as noted above, only government is widely viewed to have coercive powers (Hayek, 1973:47–48; Buchanan, 1972, 1975). The establishment of laws, including precedents, and a coercive mechanism for their enforcement, including courts, therefore, has the hugely beneficial external effect of allowing the market economy to develop and function.

It could be contended that the existence of nonexclusionary external benefits makes laws and law enforcement "public goods." Indeed, they are, given Samuelson's delineation of the domain of public goods: "A public good is one that enters two or more persons' utility. What are we left with? With a knife-edge pole of the private good case, and with all the rest of the world in the public good domain by virtue of involving some consumption externality" (Samuelson, 1969). However, the theory of public goods "is a dangerous and misleading theory if it suggests to the unwary that government services should be handled *as if* they were public goods" (Goldin, 1977:53). Efficient provision of goods which generate external benefits requires cooperation, but cooperation does not always require government. Whenever external benefits exist there are tremendous incentives to internalize those benefits. Consequently, billions of instances of voluntary cooperation in the private sector occur every day. Every market transaction involves cooperation between the buyer and seller. Virtually every good or service produced requires the voluntary cooperation of numerous input suppliers. Every contract is a formal agreement to cooperate. In fact, such voluntary cooperation to capture reciprocal benefits which would otherwise be external is the essence of customary law — it is the source of the recognition of duty to that law (Fuller, 1981). A major distinction between government and the private sector is the means used to induce cooperation. Government, as noted above, typically is granted (or takes) the right to *coerce* its citizens. Private cooperation, on the other hand, is typically achieved through persuasion. Individuals *voluntarily* enter into cooperative arrangements because they are persuaded that it is in their best interest to do so. Relatively slight modifications to many existing or historical contractual arrangements would go a long way toward internalizing the externalities that advocates of publicly produced law anticipate for the private sector, as explained below.

The Evidence

Landes and Posner contended that "a problem is that a system of voluntary adjudication is strongly biased against the creation of precise rules of any sort," but, despite their relatively careful analysis, they actually cited evidence which contradicted this argument when they observed that "Precise rules are familiar features of primitive legal systems" (Landes and Posner, 1979:239, 245). Primitive law was privately adjudicated customary law (Benson, 1989, 1990b). Landes and Posner criticized primitive law for being too precise. They preferred what they perceived to be the flexibility and potential for precedent setting of modern common law to the inflexible precision of primitive law. In fact, neither a lack of precision nor inflexibility have characterized privately adjudicated legal systems.

The opinion that primitive law tended to be rigid is frequently traced to Sir Henry Maine, who wrote that "the rigidity of primitive law . . . has chained down the mass of the human race to those views of life and conduct which they entertained at the time when their usages were first consolidated into a systematic form" (Maine, 1864:74). However, anthropologist E. Adamson Hoebel maintained that "If ever Sir Henry Maine fixed an erroneous notion on modern legal historians, it was the idea that primitive law, once formulated, is stiff and ritualistic" (Hoebel, 1954:283). *If* a primitive society was actually characterized by very little, very slow changes, the benefits of precision simply outweighed any advantage of extreme flexibility (Benson, 1989b). But when flexibility and growth in the law are vital to facilitate growth and change, privately adjudicated law has been characterized by such flexibility; indeed, flexibility and change clearly characterized some and probably all primitive law systems (Benson, 1989b; Popisil, 1971). It is just that most anthropological studies of primitive legal systems have been short term in nature and not particularly interested in studying legal change, as Popisil explained (Popisil, 1971).

Moreover, witness the rapid development of the privately adjudicated medieval Law Merchant, for example, that was both a consequence of and stimulus for the commercial revolution in Western Europe (Benson, 1989c; Trakman, 1983; Berman, 1983). The number of important precedents set in a relatively short span of history is nothing less than phenomenal. Indeed, the foundation of today's commercial law was established by this privately adjudicated system of law within the eleventh and twelfth centuries (Berman, 1983:530; Benson, 1989c). Furthermore, after common law courts absorbed the medieval Law Merchant it lost a good deal of flexibility, became relatively rigid, and its development slowed (Trakman, 1983:25–26). Similarly, the independent (private) *brehon* in the medieval Irish legal system also established clear rules of law and recorded them for others to use (Peden, 1977). They frequently wrote opinions or legal treatises that explained how their decisions were built on previous precedents.

How can such high levels of precedent creation occur in light of the Landes-Posner argument that judges will "deliberately avoid explaining their results" in order to create demand for their services? They suggested one possible reason when they wrote:

> Competitive private judges would strive for a reputation for competence and impartiality. One method of obtaining such a reputation is to give reasons for a decision that convince the disputants and the public that the judge is competent and impartial. Competition could lead private judges to issue formal or informal "opinions" declaring their interpretation of the law, and these opinions—though intended simply as advertising—would function as precedents, under a public judicial system [Landes and Posner, 1979:238].

Landes and Posner went on to argue that this is an unlikely scenario, contending that in an effort to reduce costs, other methods of advertising would be sought. In this regard, however, contractual organizations and surety arrangements which characterized the historical privatized legal systems alluded to above, as well as others, internalized the benefits of precedents. These organizations either had their own members as judges, or contracted with judges who applied a clear set of rules and provided clear rulings that would reduce future disputes. Under such arrangements, maximizing profit does not involve maximizing the number of cases decided. A judge who provides clear rules and opinions commands a relatively high price for *contracts* with various organizations. Once under contract, the judge actually has incentives to minimize the number of disputes which go to trial by making his rules clear—that is, by setting precedents. Under this scenario, private judges have precisely the opposite incentives to those predicted by Landes and Posner. Those judges who "tend to promulgate vague standards which give each party to a dispute a fighting chance" (Landes and Posner, 1979:240) actually do less business. The point is not that these precise internalization procedures will arise in all private adjudication arrangements (indeed, there are other reasons to suspect that *competitive* judges will be forced to supply clear rulings even in the absence of such institutional arrangements, as explained below), but that institutions can be envisioned which produce incentives to write clear opinions and set precedents. Furthermore, such institutions are likely to arise if they generate substantial benefits. Thus, Fuller contended that "Being unbacked by state power . . . the arbitrator must concern himself directly with the acceptability of his award. He may be at greater pains than a judge to get his facts straight, to state accurately the arguments of the parties, and generally to display in his award a full understanding of the case" (Fuller, 1981:110–11).

Many international (and intranational) industrial and trade groups have their own arbitration systems today (Benson, 1989c), even though various nations' public courts are theoretically available for resolution of their disputes. Indeed, modern commercial arbitration often creates law, in contrast to Landes and Posner who contended that commercial arbitration is "not a source of rules or precedents" (Landes and Posner, 1979:245). When a dispute arises because a contract did not anticipate a change in the business environment, the arbitrator will have to determine what business practice should be under the new conditions based on what custom and practice has been under related but not identical circumstances. When this occurs, as it frequently does, then:

> Even in the absence of any formalized doctrine of state decisis or res judicata, an adjudicative determination will normally enter in some degree into the litigants' future relations and into the future relations of other parties who see themselves as possible litigants before the same [type of] tribunal. Even if there is no statement by the tribunal of the reasons for its decision, some reason will be perceived or guessed at, and the parties will tend to govern their conduct accordingly [Fuller, 1981:90].

In other words, a new law has been created that begins to "govern" the behavior of parties entering into similar circumstances in the future. Such a law is likely to be recognized very quickly when the arbitration involved is internal to a trade association. It may take longer to spread through the entire relevant population if that group is more diverse, but if it is an effective remedy to a now frequent potential conflict it will catch on quite quickly anyway. Indeed, the lawmaking consequences of private arbitration led Wooldridge to suggest that its substantial growth in this century has involved a "silent displacement of not only the judiciary but even the legislature" (Wooldridge, 1970:104).

Actually, despite the claim that modern arbitration does not produce precedents, Landes and Posner recognized that the benefits of precedents could be internalized if the parties "agree on the judge (or on the method of selecting him) before the dispute arises, as is done in contracts with arbitration clauses" (Landes and Posner, 1979:237). But they went on to argue that "this solution is available, however, only where the dispute arises from a preexisting voluntary relationship between the parties; the typical tort or crime does not" (Landes and Posner, 1979:237). They are largely correct in this regard, of course. Under *existing incentives* and *institutions* such arrangements may not provide for judgments of torts or crimes. However, the recent and rapid development of private for-profit courts illustrates that many torts can be privately adjudicated without preexisting arbitration agreements (Benson, 1989c; Pruitt, 1982; Koening, 1984; Meyer, 1987). Furthermore, the current system is far from the historic norm. Primitive societies had very effective, privately adjudicated tort systems of justice (Benson, 1990b) (there was no criminal law, of course, since all offenses were against individuals rather than against a "state" or "society"), as did the medieval Anglo-Saxons (Benson, 1990a), Icelanders (Friedman, 1979), and Irish (Peden, 1977). The medieval Irish system of sureties and independent, private-sector judges, in place as the English system of governmentally adjudicated common law was developing, may have been the most advanced legal system of its time (Peden, 1977; Benson, 1989b). A claim that a modern free-market judicial system would not produce even more advanced contractual arrangements to cope with the added complexities of modern society has no basis in historical fact. We may not be able to visualize the arrangements that would arise, but there is little doubt that what we see today, in a system dominated by public courts, does not correspond at all with what would arise in the process of fully privatizing adjudication. Nonetheless, the preceding arguments are not intended to imply that the external benefits of the judicial process will be entirely internalized by private systems of courts. They only are intended to suggest that the misallocation of resources under private adjudication may not be tremendous. On the other hand, the misallocation of resources by the public courts is demonstrably substantial.

Externalities in Public Adjudication

Court time is presumably available "free of charge," but the underpricing of adjudication creates a tremendous excess demand. The result is that nonprice methods of rationing have arisen. The most obvious is rationing according to willingness to wait. Court congestion and delay is the result. Congestion costs are negative externalities, of course, and court congestion is significant in many states. Indeed, litigants may have to wait as much as four or five years to appear before a judge in places like New York and California. The result is that those with relatively low values of time ultimately get to court, since they are willing to wait, while those facing high time costs opt out. As Fuller explained, when we recognize that "a right decision too long delayed may do more damage to the accused himself [or the accuser] than a mistaken decision promptly rendered, the matter assumes a different aspect. We then perceive that even in this case we are compelled to make a calculation that is in the broad sense 'economic' even though money costs are completely left out of account" (Fuller, 1964:179–80). Furthermore, this system of allocation clearly does not guarantee that those suits which should be considered in order to generate relatively valuable precedents will get to court. In fact, there are reasons to expect that many of those cases never make it to the public courts.

Many very complex commercial disputes are opting out of the public court queues, for instance, and using either commercial arbitration procedures or the rapidly developing system of private, for-profit courts (Benson, 1989c).[2] Pruitt wrote, "Most [private] rent-a-judge cases [in California] involve complex business litigation where lawyers feel the public courts cannot quickly and adequately try complicated civil cases" (Pruitt, 1982:51), and the same appears to be true of most of the growing private court business. If the complex cases are increasingly opting out of the public court system because of the allocative inefficiencies inherent in that system, then the precedents actually produced by the public courts need not be those which would have greatest impact on allocative efficiency. This does not mean that the needed precedent is not established, however, because a private arbitration decision is likely to become part of evolving customary law, as explained below.

Willingness to wait is not the only rationing technique of relevance in the allocation of public court time. Public judges have also been granted considerable discretion over which cases are heard and which are dismissed. The criterion typically used, according to one observer, is that judges "ration justice by turning their backs to comparatively weaker claims and defenses that require additional judicial time to resolve fairly. By dismissing these 'weaker' claims and defenses, the overworked judge disposes of such time-consuming matters and gets on to the stronger (i.e., easier) cases, where the claims or defenses are more obvious and compelling" (Person, 1978:32). Thus, it would appear that those cases which are *not* "easy," and therefore may produce very important precedents were they to go to trial, are less likely to be litigated by public courts. Instead, public judges tend to consider the stronger cases – those which can be judged quickly and easily, and therefore by implication with relatively incidental changes in existing rules and precedents. Judges do so because of the incentives they face. The tremendous excess demand due to underpricing of public judicial services means they face considerable pressure to resolve as many cases as they can. Thus, then tend to avoid the difficult, time-consuming cases that require consideration of complex legal arguments and, perhaps, lead to the establishment of important new legal precedents. Once again, precedents would not appear to be optimally produced by the public courts. Therefore, the potential failure of a private system of courts to internalize all the external benefits arising with precedents is not, in itself, sufficient justification for public production of these services.

Now recall the Landes-Posner argument that private judges have incentives to promulgate vague and confusing rules to create uncertainty and thereby maximize demand for their services, and consider what has occurred with the public courts. The vice president of Control Data, after a privately arbitrated construction dispute stated, "We will use these contractors and architects again. I guarantee that if we had gone to court, there would have been no further business relationships with them" (Henry, 1984:47). The fact is that the public court process is designed to be adversarial. Thus, it "isolates disputants, sets them against adversaries, consigns them to professional specialists [lawyers], and resolves their dispute according to rules and procedures that are remote and inaccessible" (Auerbach, 1983:12). Furthermore, the resulting government court ruling may be made on procedural grounds that have nothing to do with the essentials of the dispute itself and provide no real satisfaction to the parties. Thereafter, the parties remain adversaries. *And,* moreover, future conflicts between these parties or others who face similar circumstances remain possible, because the public court may not have satisfactorily settled the dispute (set an understandable precedent) if the decision was based on a legal technicality. In other words, the public courts' rulings are likely to create uncertainties through their rulings which lead to additional conflict.

Uncertainty is, in fact, inherent in the political arena that influences public court performance. When some court decisions must reflect political considerations, judges must have considerable discretion, and must be able to mask the political nature of the decision with legal technicalities (Benson, 1988, 1990a). Judge Richard Neely pointed out, for instance, that in some jurisdictions trial court judges are liberal while appellate judges are conservative, and in other jurisdictions the opposite occurs. Consequently, lower court decisions are often overturned on "Minor procedural technicalities" because the appellate and lower court judges disagree ideologically (that is, they were appointed at the urging of different interest groups). He concluded that "The net result is that law is a chancy business at best. . . . [M]ore often cases appear to be clear until skilled lawyers begin to manipulate the panoply of half-hidden principles that lurk in [the] body of law . . . to the layperson [a] case would appear open-and-shut, but . . . nothing is open-and-shut once it hits the courts" (Neely, 1982:109). The uncertainty generated by the public court system's myriad of confusing procedural rules cannot be denied.

Lawmaking

Government does not have to assign the private property rights which establish the basis for a market economy. Reciprocities are the basic source both of the recognition of duty to obey law and of law enforcement in a privately adjudicated customary law system (Fuller, 1964:23–24; Benson, 1990a). That is, individuals must "exchange" recognition of certain behavioral rules with one another for their mutual benefit. Individual A must agree (perhaps explicitly as through a contract, or perhaps implicitly through behavioral patterns that establish expectations) to act in a certain way in his relationship with B in exchange for B acting in a certain way in his relationships with A. Since the source of recognition of customary law is reciprocity, private property rights and the rights of individuals constitute the most important primary rules of conduct in such legal systems (Benson, 1990a; Benson, 1989a). After all, voluntary recognition of laws and participation in their enforcement is likely to arise *only when substantial benefits from doing so can be internalized by each individual.*

Individuals require incentives to become involved in any legal process. Incentives can take the form of rewards (personal benefits) or punishments. Punishment is frequently the threat which induces recognition of authoritarian government law imposed form above, but when customary law prevails, incentives are largely positive. Individuals must expect to gain as much or more than the costs they bear from voluntary involvement in the legal system. Protection of personal property and individual rights is a very attractive benefit. Thus, as Fuller noted, "it is clear that property and contract were . . . functioning social institutions before state-made laws existed or were even conceived of" (Fuller, 1981:174). A few examples of privately adjudicated customary legal systems have been referred to above, including the medieval Law Merchant (Benson, 1989c). All of them relied on private property rights as the primary rules of obligation. Other examples range from the complex system of water rights among the primitive Ifugao of Luzon (Benson, 1986, 1989a; Hoebel, 1954; Barton, 1967), to the private holdings of virgin forests among the Kapauka Papuans of New Guinea (Popisil, 1971:66), to the allocation of mining rights in the Western territories of the United States during the 1800s (Anderson and Hill, 1979; Umbeck, 1981; Benson, 1986).

Government Legislation, Including Precedent, Versus Evolutionary Customary Law

Much of common law was simply a codification of the basic norms common to Anglo-Saxon society (that is, from customary law), but common law was also royal law, and therefore, even during its earliest periods of development, some aspects of it were legislated and imposed by authoritarian kings (Benson, 1990a). The basic character of much of common law today can be traced back to such royal legislation which was designed to either enhance the power of the kingship or to increase government revenues. Of course, the portion of the law imposed by government authorities (legislatures, courts, administrative bureaus) has been growing in relative importance in our representative democracy, particularly over the last century. Indeed, the increasing significance of such legislation in almost all the legal systems of the world is one of the most striking features of recent legal history (Leoni, 1961:4; Auerbach, 1983; Berman, 1983). But legislation in a representative democracy is generally designed to meet the demands of special interest groups, not to establish and maintain property rights in order to support a market economy (Benson, 1990a).

Furthermore, it must recognized that the judicial system is also part of the political process. When courts make new law through "creative interpretation" of legislation or setting of a new precedent, it is frequently as a consequence of political considerations rather than of the need for clarifying private property rights. Indeed, as Neely explained, "There are certain classes of cases on the frontier of the law where there are real disputes, but these are political disputes between interest groups where the battleground is a lawsuit. Efforts to change existing laws can be characterized as "disputes," but they are political disputes rather than the factual disputes that courts are theoretically in business to resolve" (Neely, 1982:166–67). There is no reason to expect that the resulting precedents are desirable in the sense that they produce important external benefits. Benefits are likely to accrue to the interest group involved but others can bear substantial costs.

Politically dictated rules are not designed to support the market process; actually, government-made law is likely to do precisely the opposite. Indeed, it appears that the increasing centralization of lawmaking has been associated with increasing transfers of property rights from private individuals to government, or, perhaps more accurately in representative democracies, to interest groups (Anderson and Hill, 1970; Tullock, 1970; Berman, 1983). Beyond this, the continual and growing process of taking private rights creates considerable uncertainty about the future value of those private rights which have not yet been taken (Leoni, 1961; Hayek, 1973).

When resource owners are relatively uncertain about their continued ownership of those resources, they tend to use them up relatively rapidly. When producers of resources (or those who may improve resources to enhance future production) are relatively uncertain about their ability to retain control of those resources, they will produce less (or expend less on improvements). Thus, the government process of taking private rights creates negative externalities for society as a whole in that society's resources will be overused and underproduced.

This does not mean that the law necessarily should be rigid. Law has to grow in the face of changing technology and social norms. This is precisely the characteristic of common law that Landes and Posner and others have found desirable (Leoni, 1961; Rubin, 1977; Rubin, 1980:319–34; Rubin, 1982:203–4; Rubin, 1983; Priest, 1977:65–82; Hayek, 1973:94–103). They attribute this characteristic to the fact that common law is judge-made law. But common law, *assuming away legislature interference by nonjudges,* (e.g., kings, legislation, bureaucratic administration) *and outright authoritarian legislation discretionarily imposed by judges themselves,* would grow gradually. It would, in other words, grow and develop in the same way that all customary law grows and develops. In particular, it would grow as a consequence of the mutual consent of parties entering into reciprocal arrangements. Two parties, for instance, may enter into a contract which creates a new, voluntarily agreed-upon rule of obligation, and if the arrangement proves effective it may be voluntarily adopted by others, thus becoming part of the evolving customary law. But whether a contract creates such a law or simply conforms to existing practices, some unforeseen event may occur which the contract did not clearly account for. The parties then *agree* to call upon an arbitrator or mediator to help lead them to a solution of the resulting conflict. The solution only affects those parties in the dispute, but if it turns out to be an effective one and the same potential conflict arises again for these parties or others aware of their solution, or before the same private adjudicating organization, then it will be voluntarily adopted by others. In this way it becomes a part of customary law and the customary law grows (Benson, 1989b). In effect then, the private arbitrator/mediator has no authority over anyone beyond what individuals *voluntarily* give them by requesting a particular decision and adopting it after it is made. Their decision carries no weight for others unless it is a good one that others find useful in facilitating interaction, and it is likely to be perceived as useful only if it fits well within previously accepted practice and custom.

Indeed, the basic substantive principles underlying the law are not likely to change, nor should they, as Epstein explained:

> The merits of freedom of contract in no way depend upon the accidents of time and place. Acceptance of that basic principle will not however put an end to all contractual disputes. It remains to discover the terms of given contracts, usually gathered from language itself, and the circumstances of its formation and performance. Even with these aids, many contractual gaps will remain, and the [private or public] courts will be obliged, especially with partially executed contracts, to fashion the terms which the parties have not fashioned themselves. To fill the gaps, the courts have looked often to the custom or industry practice. The judicial practice makes good sense and for our purposes introduces an element of dynamism into the system. . . . But it by no means follows that conduct in conformity with the custom of one generation is acceptable conduct in the next. The principles for the implication of terms, I believe, remain constant over generations. Yet the specific rules of conduct so implied will vary with time and with place. At one level therefore, the major part of the thesis is secure. At another level, it is subject to sensible modification [Epstein, 1980:266].

The basic rules of private property and freedom of contract characterized all primitive law systems. As such systems evolve (e.g., in medieval Ireland [Peden, 1977], among the medieval European mercantile community [Trakman, 1983], and today in international commercial law, among many other examples cited above), the need for extensions of these basic principles to cover unanticipated circumstances always arise, however, and the customary law adapts, building on the existing base of substantive principles. But customary law *grows*, it does not change in the sense that an old law is suddenly overturned and replaced by a new law. That growth tends to be gradual but fairly continuous through spontaneous collaboration.

Note that this is very different from the way legislated law grows. Legislation imposed from above by a coercive authority can make major alterations in law (rather than gradual extensions) without the consent of all parties affected. It becomes enforceable law for *everyone* in the society, whether it is a mutually beneficial law or not. And, significantly, the same is true of judge-made, common law precedent. These precedents are backed by the coercive power of the state and therefore they take on the same authority as statute law, whether they are efficiency enhancing laws or not.

The Negative Externalities of Coercive
Legislation, Including Public Court Precedent

When authoritarian legislation or precedent imposed from above makes major changes in property rights assignments that affect many parties, negative externalities are generated. Leoni explained it well when he noted that:

> Legislation may have and actually has in many cases today a negative effect on the very efficacy of the rules and on the homogeneity of the feelings and convictions *already prevailing* in a given society. For legislation may also deliberately or accidentally disrupt homogeneity by destroying established rules and by nullifying existing conventions and agreements that have hitherto been voluntarily accepted and kept. Even more disruptive is the fact that the very possibility of nullifying agreements and conventions through supervening legislation tends in the long run to induce people to fail to rely on any existing conventions or to keep any accepted agreements. On the other hand, the continual change of rules brought about by inflated legislation prevents it from replacing successfully and enduringly the set of nonlegislative rules (usages, conventions, agreements) that happen to be destroyed in the process [Leoni, 1961:17].

When negative externalities arise in the process of production of some good or service, too much of the good or service is being produced. This is the case with coercive government production of laws, including precedent law.

Leoni, despite his strong support for court created law as opposed to legislation, noted that without doubt, judicial law may acquire the characteristics of legislation, including all its undesirable ones, whenever judges have the discretion to decide "ultimately" on a case (Leoni, 1961:23–24). In particular, when "supreme courts" are established, the members of these courts, or a majority of them, can impose law on all citizens concerned. Thus, establishment of a supreme court actually introduces the legislative process into the judiciary, according to Leoni. The fact is, however, that any government court is in a sense "supreme" if its rulings are backed by coercive power. Thus, the tendency for "legal pollution" arises, whether legislation comes from a legislature or from a public court. On top of that, given the allocation mechanism for court time discussed above, it would appear that many of the issues which should get court attention never get through the system. So not only are there too many legislated laws by courts but they are also not necessarily the laws which the court should be making. Thus, even if the private sector would produce too little law, as is implied by the public good externality argument for government provision of law, it does not follow that the public sector does a better job.

Neither system is likely to be perfect. Indeed, the preceding discussion implies that private-sector failures have been substantially exaggerated by advocates of government adjudication while significant government failure has been overlooked. Now we turn to the other major "market failure" justification for government law, monopoly.

Monopoly

Is there a "natural monopoly" in law? There certainly appears to be significant economies of size (or standardization) for some *systems* of law. Still, it is likely that several specialized systems would arise under private adjudication. These specialized systems may have a functional basis and be very extensive geographically (e.g., the international Law Merchant), or a geographic basis and be extensive in terms of subject area or some combination thereof, but it is doubtful that there would be one monopoly system. Consider the evidence.

Berman explained that the development of our present Western legal system really involved several separate law systems. In fact, "Perhaps the *most distinctive characteristic* of the Western legal tradition is the coexistence and competition within the same community of diverse jurisdictions and legal systems" (emphasis added) (Berman, 1983:10). At the outset, during the early middle ages there was the law of the Roman Church—canon law and ecclesiastical courts—and several secular legal systems with their own courts, including the Law Merchant, urban law, manorial law, feudal law, and royal law. Numerous other historical examples of competing law systems could be cited, but competing systems of law are not unique to historical developmental periods. Today, *every country* has its own legal system and even within countries there are competing systems. For instance, in the United States there are fifty state legal systems and that of the District of Columbia besides the federal system, and "each has its own substantive and procedural rules that are often in conflict with one another. Each side of any quarrel rushes to get the case started in that jurisdiction that has the laws most favorable to its side" (Neely, 1982:56–57). Beyond that, there are municipal and county systems, military systems, and the myriad of customary systems with arbitration and mediation arrangements that have their own procedural and substantive rules. In fact, when we define law as "the enterprise of subjecting human conduct to the governance of rules," as Fuller did, "then this enterprise is being conducted, not on two or three fronts, but on thousands. Engaged in this enterprise are those who draft and administer rules governing the internal affairs of clubs, churches, schools, labor unions, trade associations, agricultural fairs, and a hundred and one other forms of human association . . . there are in this country alone 'systems of law' numbering in the hundreds of thousands" (Fuller, 1964:124–25; Popisil, 1971:125–26).

It might be argued that there actually is an hierarchical arrangement of courts in the United States, with the federal system at the pinnacle. Government courts backed by powers to coerce can forcefully overrule the customary systems, and state systems are subject to federal control. These government systems all have their constitutional limitation, of course, including the federal system, which has tended to keep them separable in many areas in the past. In fact, appeal to the federal Supreme Court requires consideration of some "constitutional" issue, so many court cases are outside its jurisdiction. Berman contended, however, that "the plurality of legal jurisdictions and legal systems within the same legal order is threatened in the twentieth century by the tendency within each country to swallow up all the diverse jurisdictions and systems in a single central program of legislation and administrative regulation. . . . In federal systems such as that of the United States, the opportunity to escape from one set of courts to another has radically diminished" (Berman, 1983:38–39). Thus, while monopolization in law and adjudication might arise, it is likely to require coercive government domination.

Of course, the rapid emergence of private systems of dispute resolution such as commercial arbitration and for-profit courts alluded to above may be at least partially explained as an effort to avoid the centralization trend in government law. In this light, note that Landes and Posner contended that the arbitration clauses in contracts are "effective, in a major part anyway only because the public courts enforce such contracts; if they did not, there would often be no effective sanction against the party who simply breach the contract to arbitrate" (Landes and Posner, 1979:247). Thus, courts are not effective without the backing of a monopoly on coercion. This claim is demonstrably false. For one thing the historic development of the Law Merchant demonstrates that a significant boycott sanction can be produced by the commercial community (Trakman, 1983). Beyond that, however, it was during the years prior to 1920 (when the first state statute recognizing arbitration rulings as legally binding was passed in New York) that arbitration really began to catch on, particularly among trade associations (Wooldridge, 1970:99–101). Thus, arbitration was well established and widely used before government coercion was available to back its decisions. Someone who refused to accept an arbiter's decision would find access to his trade association's arbitration tribunal withdrawn and or see his name released to the association's membership: "these penalties were far more fearsome than the cost of the award with which he disagreed. Voluntary and private adjudications were voluntarily and privately adhered to if not out of honor, out of self interest" (Wooldridge, 1970:100–101). This does not mean that the state arbitration statutes have not had an impact on arbitration, however. In fact, the impact is precisely the opposite of that suggested by Landes and Posner. Arbitration became a less attractive alternative to the public courts than it would have otherwise been in the absence of these laws.

How can this be? It seems that such laws would only strengthen arbitration by providing powerful state-backed sanctions? This, of course, is the assumption implicit to the Landes-Posner conclusions. But the problem is that what statute law protected, government also controlled (Auerbach, 1983:109). An enormous number of court cases were filed after passage of the New York statute, for instance, as businessmen tried to determine what characteristics of arbitration would be considered "legal" by the state courts. Cases involved such issues as the appropriate way to select arbitrators, whether lawyers had to be present, whether stenographic notes of the proceedings should be taken, and so on. Businessmen, forced to pay attention to the prospect of judicial review, had to make their arbitration processes compatible with statute and precedent law, including public court procedure. In this way the supremacy of arbitrated commercial law as an independent legal system was undermined and made to appear to be subjugated to government law. A Harvard business law professor who observed the period immediately following passage of the arbitration statutes suggested as much when he wrote, "There is irony in the fate of one who takes precautions to avoid litigation by submitting to arbitration, and who, as a reward for his pain, finds himself in court fighting not on the merits of his case but on the merits of arbitration . . . [this] monumental tragicomedy [demonstrates the success of the government legal process at] thwarting legitimate efforts to escape its tortuous procedure" (Isaacs, 1930:149–51).

Should There Be a Single Legal System?

Now the question becomes, is the trend toward monopolization under government law a necessary, or even a desirable trend? Many argue that it is and Landes and Posner put the case as clearly as any: "there would appear to be tremendous economies of standardization in [law], akin to those that have given us standard dimensions for electrical sockets and railroad gauges. While many industries have achieved standardization without monopoly, it is unclear how the requisite standardization of commonality could be achieved in the [law] without a single source for [law] – without, that is to say, a monopoly" (Landes and Posner, 1979:239). Actually, however, it took privately produced and adjudicated mercantile law to *overcome* the limitations of political boundaries and localized protectionism, thus paving the way for the commercial revolution and development of international trade (Benson, 1989c). In fact, modern international commerce still relies on private customary law and arbitration to adjudicate disputes (Lazarus et al., 1965:29). In other words, where the "tremendous economies of standardization" that Landes and Posner alluded to exist, the private sector will take advantage of them. Government typically cannot because of the artificial constraints of political boundaries. There is absolutely no reason to believe that any particular national government is of the ideal size to take full advantage of the economies of standardization in law. In some areas of law (e.g., commercial law) these economies appear to be greater than any existing nation can encompass. In other areas of law such economies may be considerably more limited, so existing political entities are too large. After all, political boundaries are not drawn for the purpose of establishing efficient sized legal jurisdictions. But a customary system of law would generate efficient sized "market areas" for the various aspects of law – perhaps many smaller than most nations and others encompassing many of today's political jurisdictions. The existence of *economies of standardization* really *provides an argument against government provision of adjudication and law* then, in order to break away from the inefficient artificial political restrictions that exist.

Finally, consider the desirability of a diversified legal arrangement consisting of several specialized but competing jurisdictions and legal systems. As Berman explained so well,

> It is this plurality of jurisdictions and legal systems that makes the supremacy of law both necessary and possible . . . The very complexity of a common legal *order* containing diverse legal systems contributes to legal sophistication. Which court has jurisdiction? Which law is applicable? How are legal differences to be reconciled? Behind the technical questions lay important political and economic considerations:

> church versus crown, crown versus town, town versus lord, lord versus merchant, and so on. Law was a way of resolving the political and economic conflicts. . . . The pluralism of Western law, which both reflected and reinforced the pluralism of Western political and economic life, has been, or once was, a source of development, or growth—legal growth as well as political and economic growth. It also has been, or once was, a source of freedom. A serf might run to the town court for protection against his master. A vassal might run to the king's court for protection against his lord. A cleric might run to the ecclesiastical court for protection against the king [Berman, 1983:10].

Thus, in contrast to those who feel that the entire system of law must be monopolized, there would appear to be substantial benefit from not having monopoly, just as there is for the production of all other goods and services.

Other Monopoly Criticisms of Private Adjudication

There are a number of arguments which have been raised against privatization of adjudication that are commonly raised against market processes in general by people who either do not comprehend the way that competitive markets work or refuse to believe that they work the way they do. Thus, they anticipate abuses which might arise under monopoly but simply cannot arise in a competitive environment.

For example, private courts are expected to produce a lower quality product as they cut corners to save money and increase profits. Thus, Ira Glasser, executive director of the American Civil Liberties Union, expressed a fear that private, for-profit courts will take short cuts and ignore procedures that have been adopted by public courts to guarantee fairness (Tolchin, 1985:38; de Sando, 1986:A2; Landes and Posner, 1979:241).[3] There are a number of problems with using this argument as a justification for public production of adjudication services, however: (1) it is doubtful that sellers in private markets are motivated in the way the argument assumes; (2) even if the private producers of such services are so motivated, market forces will probably prevent such behavior; and (3) even if these predictions are born out, it does not follow that government providers of the services do a better job—in fact, evidence indicates that government provision of such services is far more likely to involve abuses and poor quality than private production. Let us expand on each of these points.

1. Private producers certainly have incentives to minimize the cost of producing whatever quality they produce, and there is clearly a range of qualities available for most types of privately produced goods and services. But neither of these points imply an incentive to cut corners and reduce quality below the level consumers want. The only way that arguments such as those cited above can be valid is if cutting costs by reducing quality below an appropriate level does not generate an offsetting (or more than offsetting) reduction in revenues. But that is precisely what will happen in a *competitive* market as consumers simply buy from alternative high quality suppliers.

2. If a private adjudicative firm's owners want to consider only a few cases and be in business for a relatively short period of time, they may provide very unsatisfactory services, but there are not many firms that can be identified having such narrow goals. Most private courts are likely to hope to consider many cases, and remain in business for a long time. For each case (or each arbitration contract for some group's future cases) the firm will have to compete with others interested in providing adjudication services. If a firm builds a reputation of doing an unsatisfactory job it will not survive for very long in a competitive market. As William Mac-Queen of Judicate, a for-profit court, noted, "If we can't guarantee fair and impartial justice we're a failure. We would put ourselves out of business" (de Sando, 1986:A2). This should be obvious since no one has to use a particular private court firm. In a competitive environment where sellers have long-range profit goals, the incentives are to offer the same quality of services at lower prices (and therefore cost) than competitors, or a superior quality than competitors but at comparable price. Indeed, reputation for providing a good product at a competitive price is a valuable asset in a competitive market – an asset that firms invest in and work to maintain just like any other asset (e.g., capital equipment). Of course, there are con men and hucksters who move into an area for a short period, defraud a number of consumers, and move on. But no matter how ignorant some may consider consumers to be, it is difficult to imagine many of them buying adjudicative services from such fly-by-night operations. A sense of permanence and a reputation for quality services would clearly be a much more important criterion for consumer choice of such services than this "quality cutting" argument assumes.

3. Neely noted that in order to understand why judges act the way they do we must consider the interaction of judges with the structure of the courts; for it is the institutional setting which generates much of the behavior we observe. Indeed, "Certain personal vices are not remarkable in people employed outside the judiciary (immediately arrogance and indolence spring to mind). And if the people appointed to the bench exhibited various qualities to excess before their appointments, they would not have been selected. It is the nature of the judiciary, with its life tenure, or long elected terms, that it can encourage arrogance and indolence as the occupation of a salesperson tends to mask them" (Neely, 1982:35). Judge Neely made a very important point. Many individuals would abuse their position, no matter what the position is, by cutting costs, doing poor quality work, and bullying, *if they could.* However, the institutional arrangements within which people perform their tasks determine whether such abuses can be carried out. Some institutions strongly discourage such behavior while others encourage it. Competitive markets are one of the best (if not the best) institutional arrangements designed to discourage abusive, inefficient behavior. A salesperson can, on occasion, be quite abusive to customers but if they are, those and other customers can go elsewhere to buy the same goods. Before long that salesperson no longer is a salesperson – *competition regulates the behavior of market participants.* A public judge can be abusive to every party in every dispute they adjudicate without much fear of losing their job. But a private judge "needs" litigants to stay in business and therefore must treat litigants with respect.

The differences between public institutions and competitive, private institutions go well beyond the difficulty in firing public officials who do poor jobs. The premise underlying the predictions of much of the abusive behavior that many expect from private judges is that private judges will be rewarded according to the *number* of cases tried. In fact, private producers are rewarded for providing what consumers want—for judges, clear, quick resolution of disputes with opinions based on the commonly held norms of society. Public bureaucrats, however are *not* rewarded on the basis of a market (consumer) evaluation of their performance. Their rewards are obtained through the political process, and those rewards are frequently tied to some measurable representation of the *size* of the bureaucracies' operations, like the number of cases a public court handles. Thus, public judges face similar incentives to those that some have attributed to private judges, but they are not regulated by the threat of competition at anything close to the level that exists in private markets. Consequently, public producers are far more likely to react to those incentives than private producers. The Neely quote indicates that public judges often do react (Benson, 1988).

The argument that a private court will provide poor quality services to enhance profits ignores the revenue consequences of such an action. A related argument focuses exclusively on revenues: "If the rendering of verdicts is to be independent of the relative wealth of the litigants, then the provision of judicial services naturally requires separation of the decison-makers gain from that of each litigant. This fact either requires heavy regulation or it requires public provision of the judge directly" (Mabry et al., 1977:83). Why? Because, according to Mabry et al. (and many others), of the "possible corruption in a private payment system" (Mabry et al., 1977:83)—the wealthy, or the big gainer from a suit can pay the judge more so they will be favored. Private justice will not be impartial justice (Landes and Posner, 1979:254).[4] Are such arguments valid?

Landes and Posner, after arguing that competitive courts should produce biased opinions, admitted some difficulty because "Left unexplained by this analysis is the actual pattern of competition in the English courts during the centuries when judges were paid out of litigant fees and plaintiffs frequently had a choice among competitive courts . . . none (of which we are aware) of the kind of blatant favoritism that our economic analysis predicts . . . emerge[d] in such a competitive setting. Why it did not emerge (assuming it has not simply been overlooked by legal historians) presents an interesting question" (Landes and Posner, 1979:255). But the reason is actually fairly obvious. In a private system, where no state power to coerce exists, a plaintiff cannot force a defendant to submit to trial before a *particular* judge. The defendant must be persuaded that participation is in his best interest. That persuasion may come from some form of ostracism that presumably is strong enough to convince him to submit to a fair trial. However, a defendant is not likely to agree to participate in a trial before a judge who is known to be biased against him, particularly if other (competitive) judges are available. Arbitrators and mediators throughout history who have successfully stayed in business for any length of time and prospered have done so by providing (and building a reputation for providing) fair, impartial judgments (see Peden's discussion of the *brehons* in

Ireland [Peden, 1977] and several examinations of the *mokalun* among the primitive Ifugao [Barton, 1967], for example).

The Comanche (Hoebel, 1967) and the medieval Icelanders (Friedman, 1979) actually had private institutional arrangements to see to it that there was no bias against the poor. For instance, Friedman explained that in medieval Iceland victims were given a *transferable* property right, the right to restitution, which meant that "A man who did not have sufficient resources to prosecute a case or enforce a verdict could sell it to another who did and who expected to make a profit in both money and reputation by winning the case and collecting the fine. This meant that an attack on even the poorest victim could lead to eventual punishment" (Friedman, 1979:406). In addition, the wealthy were not immune from prosecution in Iceland. *Anyone* refusing to pay restitution was outlawed, and an outlaw who defended himself by force was liable to pay for every injury inflicted on those trying to bring him to justice: "every refusal to pay another fine would pull more people into the coalition against him" (Friedman, 1979:407). The point is not that *this* system of ensuring the rights of poor or weak and the culpability of the rich or strong will arise (although *some* facsimile may), but that the private sector will produce some arrangement to prevent the favoritism of some group over another in the justice process.

Might not all the private judges have the same biases because it is the rich who can afford to pay the most? The fact is that in a private system where the rich are not protected by the government, it is doubtful that the rich as a group would want such a biased court system.

First of all, one rich man may at some point have a dispute with an even richer man, so he would be reluctant to support a system where a decision goes to the highest bidder. But more importantly, the poor, in a system of competitive legal systems, would, in all likelihood, simply opt out of such a system and establish their own. Privatization does not just mean private firms *selling* adjudication. It means private citizens freely choosing among competitive options, one of which is the arbitration and or mediation of disputes between some people in a group (e.g., perhaps in a neighborhood) by others in the same group. Participatory adjudication was practiced under the medieval Law Merchant (see Benson, 1989c; Trakman, 1983), for instance, as well as under many primitive societies' legal systems (Benson, 1989a). Of course, the rich may try to force their brand of justice on the poor, thus forming a coercive government legal system, but this outcome simply produces what we now have. After all, as Supreme Court Justice William Rehnquist explained, a great deal of time and money typically must be spent before trial and in appealing cases afterward: "The result is a system ideally suited to a lawsuit by General Motors against IBM — both of which have the resources to accommodate the delay. But how well suited is it for the countless other litigants who are not in that class?" (*Billings Gazette*, 1984:1A). Under the current public system it frequently seems that only the wealthy can afford to use the public courts. This, Rehnquist pointed out, is forcing more and more of the rest of the population to turn to private alternatives like arbitration if they are to get their disputes resolved at all (Benson, 1988).[5]

Conclusion

Some of the arguments against privatization of adjudication may have some validity (others clearly do not), but the answer to the question of whether to privatize or not really must involve an examination of the *relative* performance of private and public systems of law and order. Neither system is going to be perfect. Neely, in discussing the court system, noted that "perfect justice under ideal conditions is illusory. To ask perfect justice of a court system is like asking a skilled surgeon to perform brain surgery with a meat ax. He might be able to do it 5 percent of the time if he is really skilled, but smart money does not bet on it" (Neely, 1982:122). The cumbersome "meat ax" that must be used under the public system of law and order consists of the institutional arrangements that have arisen in the public sector and the incentives that those institutions create. A competitive private sector involves a very different set of institutions and incentives. These institutions are far less cumbersome. They probably should not be likened to a perfect scalpel, but rather, perhaps, to a set of cutlery consisting of several well-sharpened knives with different specialized functions and uses. The surgeon still will not be perfect 100 percent of the time, but the patient's chances are a lot better than when only a meat ax is used.

Notes

1. The "constitutionalist" or "social contractarian" school (e.g., Hayek, Buchanan, and others) asserts that the free rider problem means that defining and enforcing rights requires coercion, and that government should be given a monopoly on the use of force. However, they advocate establishment of a rule of higher law — a constitution — to specify the limited role of government.

2. Auerbach (1983:113) states that the use of commercial arbitration grew quite rapidly after 1900. Accurate accounts of the level of arbitration are not available but it has been estimated that by the 1950s almost 75 percent of all commercial disputes were being adjudicated before arbitrators. Moreover, the estimates in 1965 indicated that the use of commercial arbitration was increasing at about 10 percent per year (also see Lazarus et al., 1965:20). According to Koening (1984), several private, for-profit firms have also entered the justice market during the last few years in virtually every state. One, Judicate, has now gone national, employing 308 judges in 45 states as of March 1987, and handling an estimated 2,500 cases that year (see Meyer, 1987).

3. This type of argument was actually introduced briefly in the articles of Tolchin (1985:38) and de Sando (1986:A2). Landes and Posner (1979:241) (among many others) contended that a private-sector judge "may write confusing opinions that generate unnecessary disputes; he may create unmeritorious rights; he may even . . . promulgate rules that discourage the growth of nonjudicial substitutes for judicial dispute resolution" in order to create as much business and profit as possible.

4. A slight twist on this argument was presented by Landes and Posner (1979:254):

"it might seem that competition would lead to an optimal set of substantive rules and procedural safeguards. But this is incorrect. The competition would be for plaintiffs, since it is
the plaintiff who determines the choice among courts having concurrent jurisdiction of his
claim. The competing courts would offer not a set of rules designed to optimize dispute
resolution but a set designed to favor plaintiffs regardless of efficiency."

5. It also breeds corruption, which means that decisions may be for sale to the highest
bidder (see Benson, 1988).

References

Anderson, T., and P. J. Hill (1970). *The Birth of the Transfer Society*. Stanford, CA: Hoover
Institution Press.

_____. (1979). "An American Experiment in Anarcho-Capitalism: The Not So Wild,
Wild West." *Journal of Libertarian Studies* 3:9–29.

Auerbach, J. S. (1983). *Justice Without Law?* New York: Oxford University Press.

Barton, R. F. (1967). "Procedure Among the Ifugao." P. Bohannan (ed.), *Law and Warfare*.
New York: Natural History Press.

Benson, B. L. (1986). "The Lost Victim and Other Failures of the Public Law Experiment."
Harvard Journal of Law and Public Policy 9 (Spring): 399–427.

_____. (1988). "Corruption in Law Enforcement: One Consequence of the Tragedy of
the Commons Arising with Public Allocation Processes." *International Review of Law
and Economics* 8 (June): 73–84.

_____. (1989a). "Enforcement of Private Property Rights in Primitive Societies: Law
Without Government." *Journal of Libertarian Studies* 9 (Winter): 1–26.

_____. (1989b). "Legal Evolution in Primitive Societies." *Journal of Institutional and
Theoretical Economics* 144 (December): 772–88.

_____. (1989c). "The Spontaneous Evolution of Commercial Law." *Southern Economic
Journal* 55 (January): 644–61.

_____. (1990a). *The Enterprise of Law: Justice Without the State*. San Francisco: Pacific
Research Institute.

_____. (1990b). "The Evolution of Law: Custom Versus Authority." Florida State
University working manuscript.

Berman, H. J. (1983). *Law and Revolution: The Formation of Western Legal Tradition*. Cambridge, MA: Harvard University Press.

Billings Gazette (1984) "Courts Need 'Radical' Ideas – Justice." (September 16), 1A.

Buchanan, J. M. (1971). *The Bases for Collective Action*, 2. New York: General Learning
Process.

_____. (1972). "Before Public Choice." G. Tullock (ed.), *Explorations in the Theory of
Anarchy*. VA: Center of the Study of Public Choice.

_____. (1975) *The Limits of Liberty*. Chicago: University of Chicago Press.

_____. (1977). *Freedom in Constitutional Contract*. College Station: Texas A&M Univer-
sity Press.

Christainsen, G. B. "Law as a Discovery Procedure." Hayward, CA: California State University, Hayward working paper.

de Sando, B. (1986). "Rented Scales of Justice Ends Wait for Day in Court." *Asbury Park
Press* (June 23), A2.

Epstein, R. A. (1980). "The Static Concept of the Common Law." *Journal of Legal Studies* 9 (March): 253–89.

Friedman, D. (1979). "Private Creation and Enforcement of Law: A Historical Case." *Journal of Legal Studies* 8 (March): 399–415.

Fuller, L. (1964). *The Morality of Law.* New Haven, CT: Yale University Press.

————. (1981). *The Principles of Social Order.* Durham, NC: Duke University Press.

Goldin, K. D. (1977). "Equal Access vs. Selective Access; A Critique of Public Goods Theory." *Public Choice* 79 (Spring): 53–72.

Hayek, F. A. (1973). *Law Legislation and Liberty.* Chicago: University of Chicago Press.

Henry, J. F. (1984). "Minitrials: Scaling Down the Costs of Justice to Business." *Across the Board* (October), 47.

Herber, B. P. (1975). *Modern Public Finance: The Study of Public Sector Economics,* 22. Homewood, IL.: Richard D. Irwin.

Hoebel, E. A. (1954). *The Law of Primitive Man,* Cambridge, MA: Harvard University Press.

————. (1967). "Law-Ways of the Commanche Indians." P. Bohannon (ed.). *Law and Warfare.* New York: Natural History Press.

Isaacs, N. (1930). "Review of Wesley Sturgess, Treatise on Commercial Arbitration and Awards." *Yale Law Journal* 40: 149–51.

Koening, R. (1984). "More Firms Turn to Private Courts to Avoid Expensive Legal Fights." *Wall Street Journal* (January 4).

Landes, W. M., and R. A. Posner (1979). "Adjudication as a Private Good." *Journal of Legal Studies* 8 (March): 235–84.

Lazarus, S., et al. (1965). *Resolving Business Disputes: The Potential of Commercial Arbitration,* 20, 29. New York: American Management Association.

Leoni, B. (1961). *Freedom and the Law,* 40 Los Angeles: Nash.

Mabry, R., H. H. Ulbrich, H. H. Macauley, Jr., and M. T. Maloney (1977). *An Economic Investigation of States and Local Judiciary Services.* Washington, DC: National Institute of Law Enforcement and Criminal Justice, Law Enforcement Assistance Administration, Department of Justice.

Maine, H. S. (1864). *Ancient Law,* 74. Third American edition. New York: Henry Holt.

Meyer, J. (1987). "Judicate, Others Provide Novel Alternative." *The Legal Intelligencer* (March 17).

Neely, R. (1982). *Why Courts Don't Work,* New York: McGraw-Hill.

Peden, J. L. (1977). "Property Rights in Celtic Irish Law." *Journal of Libertarian Studies* 1:81–95.

Person, C. (1978). "Justice, Inc." *Juris Doctor* (March), 32.

Popisil, L. (1971). *Anthropology of Law: A Comparative Study.* Harper and Row.

Priest, G. L. (1977). "The Common Law Process and the Selection of Efficient Rules." *Journal of Legal Studies* 50 (January): 65–82.

Pruitt, G. (1982). "California's Rent-a-Judge Justice." *Journal of Contemporary Studies* (Spring).

Rubin, P. H. (1977). "Why Is the Common Law Efficient?" *Journal of Legal Studies* 6 (January): 51–64.

———— (1980). "Predictability and the Economic Approach to Law: A Comment on Rizzo." *Journal of Legal Studies* 9 (March): 319–34.

———— (1982). "Common Law and Statute Law." *Journal of Legal Studies* 11 (June): 203–24.

———— (1983). *Business Firms and the Common Law: The Evolution of Efficient Rules.* New York: Praeger.

Samuelson, P. A. (1969). "Pure Theory of Public Expenditures and Taxation." J. Margolis and H. Guitton (eds.), *Public Economics: An Analysis of Public Production and Consumption and Their Relations to the Private Sector: Proceedings of a Conference Held by the International Economics Association.* London: Macmillan.

Tolchin, M. (1985). "Private Courts with Binding Rulings Draw Interest and Some Challenges." *New York Times* (May 12), 38.

Trakman, L. E. (1983). *The Law Merchant: The Evolution of Commercial Law.* Littleton, CO: Fred B. Rothman.

Tullock, G. (1970). *Private Wants, Public Means: An Economic Analysis of the Desirable Scope of Government.* New York: Basic Books.

Umbeck, J. (1981). *A Theory of Property Rights with Application to the California Gold Rush.* Ames: Iowa State University Press.

Wooldridge, W. C. (1970). *Uncle Sam, the Monopoly Man,* 104. New Rochelle, NY: Arlington House.

17. Private Prosecution

Tim Valentine

During my thirty years in the active practice of law, I handled many criminal cases, misdemeanors, and felonies. I accepted employment on numerous occasions as private prosecution in misdemeanor and felony cases. I always advised the prospective client in these situations that to become involved in private prosecution it was necessary for me to receive the district attorney's approval and be, in effect, welcomed into the case by him. It was my policy to explain to the prospective client the drawbacks of private prosecution, that is to say the possible effect on a jury of too many attorneys at the prosecution table, especially the presence of a private one who was paid by the victim or someone else to help prosecute a particular defendant. I was always keenly aware of the danger in providing the defense attorney a way to present the defendant as a martyr, harassed not only by the power of the district attorney's office but by a "hired gun" brought in by the victim.

With that background information, I present the following in defense of the right to employ a private prosecutor. In many cases the district attorney's office just does not have the time, personnel, or resources to investigate, to gather together, and confer with state's witnesses in advance of the trial date; or even to confer at length with the prosecuting witness or victim. That battered wife needs to have the attention of an attorney in advance of trial. She might not know the importance of a neighbor who saw her bleeding five minutes after the assault and does not think of that person as a witness who would be invaluable in court. The average district attorney's assistant just has not the time to give every case the attention it needs before trial.

In so many cases the best money the victim can expend is for a capable attorney to serve as private prosecution—not to take the case over but to help in preparation and assist in the presentation. In some cases it is equally as important to have a private prosecutor there in court to resist efforts to have the case postponed repeatedly and to acquaint the district attorney with his client's urgent need to have the case tried.

Victims have as much right to a fair trial as do defendants. It is wrong to deny that right to either side. In many situations the only workable solution lies in the availability of private prosecution.

This is not to suggest that private prosecutors should supplant the district attorney's office. Private prosecutors should always work with and under the district attorney. Their interests are the same but the private prosecutor's interest is more personal and active. He is working on only one case or at least only a few cases for trial on a particular day. He has been hired to concentrate on a specific case or cases.

There is no valid reason for any district attorney's office to fear or take umbrage with a privately employed prosecutor who presents himself as a resource. This is gratuitous assistance and, if the district attorney does his part, can make him and his office look better.

Furthermore, the fact should be faced that the employment of private prosecution is in some cases and in some jurisdictions the only way for victims of crime to get justice. You either have a private attorney to assist the state in prosecuting the drunk husband who assaulted you or he just does not get prosecuted. If you hire an attorney and he allows your case to be continued into oblivion (or into the trash can) without putting up a spirited fight in open court, or if he otherwise fails to perform adequately, he can be subject to disciplinary action by the grievance committee of his bar association.

What is wrong with a victim's procuring competent, private legal assistance? Sometimes it is needed even to get a straight answer as to a trial date. Those who call this a dangerous idea just are not familiar with the facts of prosecutorial life in some areas. Victims have rights too.

The practice of allowing private prosecution, limited and restricted as herein set out, helps the victims of crime feel that the system is working for them. Otherwise, they can get lost in the shuffle. Private prosecution makes sense not only from the point of view of crime victims but from the point of view of those citizens who long for a criminal justice system that works. Private prosecutors make sense to citizens who are concerned about the rights of both defendants and victims. Fairness and justice for crime victims should not be something for which one needs to apologize. Fair, aggressive, and timely prosecution of persons charged with crimes does not deprive them of any rights except in the eyes of those who think that defendants have all the rights. Does a defendant have the constitutional *right* to a sloppy, ill-prepared prosecution?

Does a defendant, under any circumstances, have a fundamental *right* to the benefits which might accrue to him as the result of a harried, overworked, understaffed district attorney's office?

I can understand the feelings of a defense attorney who has been paid thousands of dollars by a wealthy defendant charged with manslaughter as a result of the operation of a motor vehicle while intoxicated when an aggressive prosecution, aided by hours of investigation and trial preparation by a private attorney, results in a verdict of guilty. This might be especially true when that defense attorney has been accustomed to facing an unprepared district attorney's office. The private prosecutor, whether his fee was paid by the victim or the victim's family or by a group of outraged citizens, is nonetheless working on a particular case for the state, for the people, for citizens who have a right to a criminal justice system that works. Surely citizens are generally as much entitled to a fair, able, well-prepared, and vigorous prosecution as a defendant is entitled to a fair, able, well-prepared, and vigorous defense? Trial and appellate judges are there to protect against abuses and unfairness. Let each side face the other on something at least approaching even terms.

The system should provide fair and timely trials, freedom for defendants who are acquitted, and punishment for defendants who are convicted. Private prosecutors ensure that result in many cases.

To advocate a system which allows or encourages private prosecutors is not to indict the district attorney's office. The problem with so many district attorneys and their assistants, investigators, and staff is not one of competency, ability, or dedication. It is, in most cases, a problem of workload: too many cases to be handled, not enough judges, courtrooms, or trial preparation and courtroom time. It has been my experience that most district attorneys understand this and realize that they need all the help they can get.

18. *Private Dispute Resolution*
Michael S. Gillie

American institutions are continually evolving. Consider the changes that have taken place over the last thirty years in the role of government, health care, the media, and financial structures. The American legal system has been no exception. Everyone is familiar with the changing nature of case law and statutes. The public is much less aware of changes that have been taking place in legal structures — changes that have been vigorously supported by the courts and legal profession. One such structural change is the topic of this article — the increased use of Alternative Dispute Resolution (ADR) and, in particular, the providing of such services by private organizations.

The two major alternatives to litigation are *mediation*, where disputants work with a neutral expert to explore settlement possibilities, and *arbitration*, where disputing parties present their case to a neutral third party for a legally binding decision.

Mediation

The use of mediation is experiencing a rapid growth rate, probably because most cases settle even though the mediator has no power to force the parties to accept a settlement. Mediation is often more effective than direct negotiations; thus, mediation increases the chances of a timely settlement. Many types of cases are being mediated, including major commercial disputes, automobile accident claims, allegations of medical malpractice and defective products, and construction-related issues.

It is worth noting that such settlements are not necessarily better or worse than "courthouse steps" settlements. However, they are achieved much earlier — often even before litigation — thereby saving all sides litigation expenses and processing costs. It is not uncommon for mediation programs to have a settlement rate of 80 percent or better.

By agreeing to mediate, parties simply are agreeing to take part in a structured settlement negotiation, a "mediation session," with the help of a neutral expert. They are not agreeing that they actually will settle, and the mediator has no authority to force them to do so. Either party may terminate the process at any time without cause.

Usually an administrative agency, such as an office of United States Arbitration and Mediation or the American Arbitration Association, is used. The administrative agency's role is to explain the process and obtain everyone's agreement to mediate, help the parties select a mediator, make arrangements for fees, and generally provide an administrative structure to the proceedings.

All sides to a dispute are present at the mediation session, which is scheduled at a convenient time and place. After introductory remarks by the mediator, each side is given the opportunity to explain its position and describe the evidence it will offer if the matter goes to trial. After the joint meeting, the mediator engages in a series of private meetings with each side, in which he or she discusses the risks of the case: "What is the worst outcome for you on this issue?" "How much is it going to cost you to go to trial?" etc. This discussion helps each party understand the strong and weak points of the case and effectively analyze the risks. The mediator also discusses settlement possibilities. If a settlement agreement is reached, the parties usually will draft formal settlement documents. If an agreement is not reached through mediation, the parties are free to pursue whatever other options are available to them, such as arbitration or litigation.

Example Case

A head-on collision between a truck and a car resulted in the deaths of the driver of the automobile and his three passengers. Wrongful death claims in excess of $2.5 million were brought against the owner of the truck. There was evidence of drinking on the part of the automobile driver and cross-claims were filed between the plaintiffs.

Discovery showed that eyewitness testimony and experts' accident reconstructions were conflicting and contradictory. After the case had been in the court system for three years the defendant's insurance company decided to propose mediation in an attempt to reopen settlement negotiations. The four plaintiffs' attorneys agreed to participate and a mediation session was scheduled. The parties selected a mediator who was also a personal injury attorney.

The mediation session was attended by all the plaintiffs' attorneys and their clients, an insurance company representative, a defense attorney, and the mediator. With everyone seated around the conference table the mediator began the session by asking each side to explain their positions to the other participants. After those presentations, the mediator began a series of private meetings with each party. During these private meetings the mediator discussed the strong points and weak points of the case. He asked the tough, devil's advocate questions to be sure the clients and attorneys fully understood and analyzed the risks of the case. It is important to note that the mediator was not giving his opinion of the case. The mediator then explored with each party what its true settlement position was.

Through this process the mediator was able to achieve a tentative agreement among the plaintiffs as to how the cross-claims would be handled if a settlement could be reached. He was then able to help the plaintiffs and defense agree on a six-figure settlement number. The parties went on to execute formal settlement documents.

Arbitration

Basically, arbitration is a substitute for a court trial. It involves a hearing and an enforceable decision, but the process takes place outside the court system, thus avoiding many of the delays, expenses, and stresses associated with litigation. To use arbitration, all parties to a dispute first must contract to be bound by the arbitrator's decision. This contract has two possible forms: a contract to arbitrate an existing dispute, called a "submission agreement"; or an "arbitration clause," placed in a business contract, lease, etc., that requires arbitration of any future disputes. At an arbitration hearing that is like a less formal court trial, the parties present evidence to the arbitrator, who then renders a legally binding decision that, under state and federal law, can be enforced like a court judgment.

Arbitration is usually much quicker than litigation — in the right case, it can produce a result in a matter of days. It is also much more convenient — hearings are set up at a mutually agreeable time and place, and start when scheduled. Arbitration does not involve the demanding procedures, detailed rules of evidence, and wide-open discovery motions found in the court system. Thus, it is usually much less time-consuming and therefore less expensive than the court system. It also is confidential, which is very important in certain types of cases. In addition, the arbitrator selected by the parties (usually through an arbitration agency) can be a technical expert in the subject matter of the dispute, which aids in shortening the presentations of the parties and in producing a sensible result.

Example Case

A business and one of its major suppliers were unable to resolve a dispute over the specifications of certain goods that had been supplied. Mediation settled some issues and clearly identified that the major disagreement was over the interpretation of a specific contract clause. To avoid litigation, the parties agreed to submit the dispute to arbitration and selected an attorney with expertise in their industry to act as the arbitrator.

At the hearing, each side presented evidence and arguments to support its interpretation of the contract clause. This hearing was much quicker than a court trial because of the lack of formal court procedures and rules of evidence. A day after the hearing the arbitrator rendered her award. The losing party voluntarily complied with the decision. The parties thus used arbitration to resolve the dispute and, by avoiding the expense, antagonism, and delay of litigation, were able to maintain their working relationship.

As shown by the example, the most effective programs use a mixture of arbitration and mediation: mediate first to attempt to reach an agreed-to settlement; then, if unsuccessful, proceed to arbitration and thereby avoid the court system.

ADR and Insurance Claims

The insurance industry has taken the lead in applying alternative dispute resolution techniques. Many major insurance companies—including the Travelers, the Hartford, Maryland Casualty, Chubb, the St. Paul, State Farm, Fireman's Fund, USAA, CIGNA, and others—have undertaken projects to increase their use of ADR. These companies have established home office ADR directors, have set national goals for the number of cases handled by ADR, and actively are submitting large numbers of cases to commercial ADR services. It is worth noting that these companies are not claiming that they are getting lower settlements by using ADR, just earlier settlements, which result in savings of litigation-related defense costs. The companies properly view ADR, particularly mediation, as a new tool available to their claims departments, one that saves litigation costs, helps process claims, and allows companies to keep better control over the outcome of cases.

There are signs that the rest of American industry is moving toward alternative dispute resolution. The Center for Public Resources, a New York nonprofit organization devoted to furthering ADR, has obtained pledges from many major U.S. companies in which they agree to consider using litigation alternatives for their disputes.

These companies are the heart of corporate America—General Motors, IBM, Eli Lilly, 3M, etc. At least one reason for the increased use of ADR is that such companies' foreign competitors do not have the litigation overhead that American businesses do. The increased use of ADR will thus increase America's competitiveness. However, U.S. industry only now is starting to use such techniques, and many companies still have not considered ADR. The major applications of the process are yet to come.

The increasing use of alternative dispute resolution in the commercial area is properly viewed as part of a larger movement throughout American society. Since 1980 numerous ADR programs have been developed to resolve a wide variety of disputes, including family-law matters, consumer complaints, and environmental issues. For example, the Better Business Bureau currently administers a nationwide mediation/arbitration program for business-consumer complaints, and almost every major American city has a dispute resolution center that aplies ADR techniques to landlord-tenant and neighborhood problems. These programs come in all shapes and sizes—governmental, court-annexed, nonprofit, and private business—and almost all are successful at resolving disputes without litigation. Yet, while these programs work well, they are handling only a small percentage of the cases that could benefit from such resolution services.

It is also worth noting that alternative dispute resolution enjoys broad-based support within the legal community, with courts and bar associations sponsoring ADR programs and calling for more. For example, Supreme Court Justice Sandra Day O'Connor recently stated, "The courts of this country should not be the places where the resolution of disputes begins. They should be the places where disputes end—after alternative methods of resolving disputes have been considered and tried."

Issues Raised by "Privatization" of Dispute Resolution

Over the last decade I have heard a variety of concerns expressed about private ADR, some valid, many not. I have categorized these concerns under five headings.

Only Judges Should Resolve Disputes

The argument here is that judges are society's designated resolvers of disputes, and their function should not be diminished. This argument was heard consistently in the early 1980s. It completely ignores a very basic point: the huge majority of disputes are already being handled privately by the disputants themselves. We are all confronted on a daily basis with problems and issues that must be resolved, ranging from family disagreements to misunderstandings with coworkers to complaints about the quality of goods or services (or the bills therefrom). And these problems get worked out, either by agreement or by a determination that they are not worth pursuing. Such matters have always been in the private arena, and always should be.

In a comparatively minute number of instances the situation warrants more formal action; action such as consulting with an attorney about a lawsuit, filing a claim, or contacting a public agency. And here again, most disputes are resolved without a judge's decision—for example, insurance industry statistics show that approximately 95 percent of all litigation will be settled before trial. Courts around the country hold that there is a strong public policy in favor of voluntary settlements of civil lawsuits, and the courts go out of their way to uphold such settlements.

The point of all this is that when we are discussing the privatization of justice as a new phenomenon, we are talking about only a very small percentage of disputes that are now being handled differently. There are legitimate issues here, certainly, but the scope is much narrower than the title implies. And the position that judges should hear every dispute is clearly not realistic.

Disputants Should Not Be Forced to Use ADR

This concern is the result of lack of knowledge about ADR procedures. People have the constitutional right to go to court and no one can be forced to use private ADR. Thus, private ADR is totally voluntary.

The ADR is often called "an extension of the negotiating process," meaning that when the parties reach an impasse during their direct negotiations, they at least are able to agree on a format to continue to work to resolve the matter. Thus, ADR is simply a form of voluntary settlement.

The availability of ADR is changing the role of the attorney. Dispute resolution is now a matter of selecting the right approach for a case, rather than automatically going to court, and it is now the attorney's function to advise their client of these options.

Impartiality Will Be Distorted by the Profit Motive

Sitting judges are elected or appointed, and there is no financial aspect to their activities (although there certainly can be election/appointment influences). There is, of course, a financial aspect to private ADR services. A common example of a potential problem is that a retired judge who acts as an arbitrator might favor the insurance company (or plaintiffs' counsel) that uses the judge's services on a regular basis. The same point can be made concerning an ADR organization that has a long-term relationship with one side of the dispute.

This is certainly a valid area of concern, but it is no different from profit motive concerns in other professions. Some examples:

1. A doctor ordering a course of treatment for a patient which will financially benefit the doctor.

2. An attorney on a contingent fee recommending that their client accept a settlement when by having the case settled the attorney will financially benefit by not having to prepare for trial.

3. A reporter doing a story about an advertiser.

4. A CPA preparing a financial report for a regular client.

5. An escrow agent handling a real estate closing involving one party that is a regular user of the agent's services.

The ability to act objectively, irrespective of personal financial concerns, is thus part of many professions. In ADR services, as in other professions, impartiality becomes second nature and is not difficult to accomplish. The ADR practitioner does not represent any side of a dispute, but *represents the process itself* to ensure that it is an objective one.

Some would argue that there is a distinction between for-profit businesses and not-for-profit organizations. I disagree. Not-for-profit organizations typically pay significant salaries and many charge professional-level fees for their services. Their officers' survival may depend on their ability to generate fees, or perhaps to generate favorable statistics for their grant proposals. They are thus subject to the same or similar financial influences as a private business.

Finally, a related issue concerns the need for *disclosure* of any possible conflicts of interests or financial relationships. Remember that private ADR is voluntary, and if parties proceed after they have been furnished with any relevant information, then they are presumed to have waived any concerns about impartiality. I am aware of court actions by attorneys general in two different states against an organization which held itself out as impartial but, in fact, had a close financial relationship with one side. These types of problems are present in every profession and, as in other professions, the consumer of ADR services should check the background of anyone they are considering doing business with. Stated another way, ethics depend on the person or organization itself, and not the profession itself.

All this is not to say that there is not a need for standards and regulation in the alternative dispute resolution field. As any new profession matures there is naturally a movement toward developing professional standards, once the issues to be dealt with start to clarify. The development of ADR standards is currently in the adolescent stage. For example, Arbitrator Codes of Ethics have long been in place, and a leading mediator/arbitrator professional organization, the Society of Professionals in Dispute Resolution (SPIDR), has enacted a code of ethics for its members. The American Bar Association has model codes of mediator/arbitrator ethics, and numerous governmental agencies are developing standards for such things as ADR training certification, mediator/arbitrator qualifications, etc. All of these approaches address the issues of conflicts of interest and improper influences, and some have enforcement "teeth." But there is clearly a need for such standards of practice to be more comprehensive.

Private ADR Will Injure the Public Court System

The concern here is that private ADR, by taking some of the pressure off of the court system, will result in the public and legislators being less likely to provide the court system with the resources it needs. While there may be some theoretical support for this position, it ignores the realities. Court systems around the country are overwhelmed by ever increasing numbers of criminal filings (which must be given priority) and by the increasing complexity of lawsuits in general. This has resulted in civil litigation being delayed or, in some instances, not being processed at all. Public respect for the court system is diminishing as a result, yet adequate funding is not politically possible. In such a situation, private ADR helps to relieve the pressure from the court system and perhaps avoid an overreaction by the public.

In my opinion the provision of ADR services for such things as family and neighborhood disputes is close to a basic social service that should be provided by government. However, beyond such matters—disputes between businesses, for instance—there is no reason why disputants should not pay their own way. The ADR should thus be a mix of public and private services, with the public sector providing social services and the private sector providing innovative and responsive services for other types of disputes.

A related issue concerns the relationship between the court systems and private ADR organizations. I am aware of one instance in which formal court rules were enacted that ordered litigants to use a private ADR organization's services. The day after the court rules were announced, the president of the local bar association and the chief judge of the court system denounced them and they were repealed. I am also aware of instances in which sitting judges have ordered litigants to use a particular ADR service; a practice which has largely been stopped when it has come to light. These results are absolutely correct. The court system, and government for that matter, should never favor one private ADR organization. If there is a need for outside services, a competitive bidding process should be used; and if the courts refer litigants to mediation or arbitration, a list of ADR organizations should be referenced. To do otherwise would result in a public institution's favoritism for one private ADR organization which will not necessarily provide litigants with the best alternatives, and will injure the public's perception of the court's abilities and impartiality.

Finally, there is one other area of concern. Some private ADR organizations have been identifying the most respected sitting judges and then luring them off the bench with big salaries, with the goal being to privatize and monopolize all the best judges. This approach has proven to be very controversial with both the bench and bar, and there are clearly significant public policy issues here. Perhaps some laws or ethical codes relating to this activity would be appropriate.

Private ADR Will Turn the Court System into "Second-Class Justice"

The argument here is that wealthy litigants will be able to use private ADR firms — "Cadillac justice" — while those that cannot afford it will be forced to use the court system. This is a great oversimplification. In my experience, private ADR programs have helped people in all economic situations. Some examples of the programs U.S. Arbitration and Mediation has been involved with are as follows:

1. Consumer Protection restitution programs for attorney general actions against health clubs, car dealers, etc. that dealt with the public unfairly. These programs returned millions of dollars to consumers — money they would not have otherwise received because so few of them would have used the court system.

2. The Manville Personal Injury Settlement Trust Alternative Dispute Resolution Program, established to compensate, without the need for litigation, shipyard workers and others who were injured by their exposure to asbestos.

3. A mediation program for individual tort and commercial cases such as automobile accident claims, partnership disputes, employment matters, medical malpractice issues, and a wide variety of other cases. People from all walks of life use this program, and mediation helps them achieve quick, inexpensive settlements.

4. State "Lemon Law" arbitration programs for new car buyers to help them settle "lemon" problems quickly, avoid litigation, and give manufacturers an incentive to deal effectively with any problems.

None of the above programs are consistent with the argument that ADR creates Cadillac justice. In fact, they show that ADR provides more access to justice for the little guy.

A corollary of the Cadillac justice argument is that unsophisticated parties will not be able to use ADR effectively. In fact, ADR is much easier for people to use than the court system. The court system is fraught with complicated legal procedures and evidentiary rules, not to mention the obligatory delays in achieving a result. ADR, on the other hand, is simple and fast. There are some exceptions, of course. Certain issues such as child custody protection require court action, and in complex legal situations parties should be required to have legal representation. But overall, ADR is much better suited to the unsophisticated party.

Conclusion

Alternative dispute resolution is a new American profession that is emerging from an evolving legal system. Like every new profession, there are standards to be determined and ethical issues to be resolved, but none that are insurmountable. The ADR holds great promise to improve American society by helping people and businesses settle their disputes as quickly and easily as possible. It has already accomplished a great deal, but the major applications of ADR are yet to come.

19. Mediators: Legal and Practical Profiles

David U. Strawn

Once lawyers, judges, and justices were enough and our rules for their conduct were sufficient. Now lawyer and nonlawyer mediators are involved in helping to manage the caseload of Florida's courts. In the rapid integration of mediation into the work of our courts, insufficient time has been provided to develop a body of precedent, or standards, rules, and statutes to explain fully the legal, practical, and ethical standards which will be applied to judge the conduct of mediators.

Centuries were required to develop standards of conduct for attorneys. The body of law concerning acceptable professional behavior for lawyers is still evolving. Mediators are presently operating with little guidance about their liability, or what practice behaviors will be approved in the professional environment in which they are operating.

Our familiar court system is changing, as new devices for dispute resolution take their place beside the trial.

Why the Legal and Practical Roles of Mediators in Our New System Must Be Examined Together

Mediators must examine their conduct both in terms of professional responsibility as mediators, and in terms of their responsibility within any other profession in which they are trained and in which they offer service. Within the ranks of court mediators we find lawyers, certified public accountants, psychologists, social workers, and any number of other well-educated professionals. The legal and practical profiles of mediators are merged also with their obligations as members of differing professions.

In examining the development of the literature concerning attorney behaviors, we see that some behaviors are described as "actionable" (taking a client's money) and others are seen as "unethical" (advertising and soliciting, at times in our history). How will this dichotomy develop for court mediators? Will representations about "rates of settlement" be appropriate? We can assume that misrepresentations upon which settlements are based will be unethical and possibly actionable as well, depending upon our courts' construction of immunity statutes.

238

What the Mediator Is Not

Mediators are not advocates. Mediation has been defined by statutes and in rules of procedure. We can infer from those definitions that a mediator should not act as an advocate for any party or for any position or set of settlement terms. In other words, advocacy of any specific outcome could be inappropriate conduct for a mediator. "Advocacy" should be contrasted with explaining an objective view of probabilities. Mediators may no doubt offer persuasive reasons for accepting a settlement, while not "advocating" an opposing party's position to the listener.

Mediators do not represent parties. In fact, mediators must be exceedingly careful not to give advice or in any way to take action which would (at least for lawyer mediators) be seen as establishing a lawyer-client relationship. This might most easily arise in a private session or caucus with a party mediating in the absence of counsel who seeks the mediator's advice. Although mediators may seek to couch their advice in terms of being "legal information" it is unlikely that a judge would assume as a matter of law that a lawyer mediator giving such information was not advising. Would a lawyer-client relationship thus develop from the advice which could result in professional liability? If the client is represented by other counsel, the giving of the advice could also constitute a violation of the standards of conduct for lawyers.

Mediators should not make pursuit of settlement their only goal. Ideally, mediators should be guardians of the process of mediation, and should not let settlement itself become the reason for mediation. When mediation is appropriately conducted, a sufficient rate of settlements occur, and occur in an informed and intelligently consensual way. If settlement becomes the goal, the mediator becomes no more than another negotiator at the table, as opposed to acting as the neutral and impartial facilitator envisaged by state (Florida) law.

The Mediator's Role: The Neutral, Impartial Facilitator

Listed below are several criteria with which the practical profile of the mediator might be examined. There are no doubt other criteria, but this list will be adequate for an elementary understanding of a mediator's appropriate role in resolving conflict.

1. A mediator is neutral. Neutrality means not being biased toward any particular outcome for the case. It means a willingness to permit the disputants to select an outcome appropriate to their interests and needs. The neutral mediator should be interested in identifying these interests and needs. Doing so can reveal the lawsuit as no more than a surrogate for some other problem. An example is not having enough money now to pay a settlement but having enough money in three months to satisfy the creditor's demands. The ostensible litigation is over whether the debt is due, but the real issue is financing.

2. A mediator is impartial. This is the sort of impartiality we expect from our judges. It includes a freedom from bias and prejudice to the extent humanly possible.

In striving for impartiality the mediator must develop an increased sensitivity to those whose demographic characteristics differ from our own in ways that subtly tempt us to deal differently with them. The mediator must become conscious of such sly biases and compensate for them.

3. A mediator listens. Listening is a primary skill for mediators. By listening, we mean more than "hearing" alone. Listening involves eye contact, a posture signifying interested involvement, and the use of feedback. The latter technique is one in which the mediator must continually restate important items articulated by the disputants to be sure there is understanding between them, and that subtlety is avoided and candor assured between the disputants.

4. A mediator must be creative. Mediators must deal with their personal frustration as their suggestions are rejected as the parties negotiate the settlement of the dispute. Making suggestions is an essential part of the mediator's role. The mediator's purpose is not to come up with the ultimate answer but to come up with enough solutions that the parties continue to talk with each other about a solution acceptable to them. Unlike the attorneys and their clients, the mediator is free of the emotional and psychological content of the dispute. The mediator should, therefore, be most willing to offer suggestions, even in the face of rejection.

5. Mediators must be thick-skinned and they must be willing to be scapegoats when appropriate. Mediators promise confidentiality about communications made in private sessions with only a party and attorney present. When a party sets nonnegotiable procedures for conduct of the mediation for reasons important to the party, the mediator may be forced to handle the mediation in ways that anger other parties who will never know the nature of the problem. Mediators have to work with what parties are willing to give them, and sometimes parties unwittingly deprive their mediators of useful tools. Mediators can do no more than endure the anger directed at them in these situations however unfair that might be.

6. Mediators must silently accept rejection of their ideas by disputants. It is difficult enough for mediators to withstand the reasoned rejection of many of their ideas for settlement by the parties as the parties move toward a settlement of their own. Some parties add to that difficult behavior which can make mediation an unpleasant event for the mediator. In addition, parties are sometimes unable or are not permitted to express their anger toward an adversary. Mediators must be prepared to act as a scapegoat for anger in private sessions with these parties. If the anger is not ventilated, the case probably will not settle, or the settlement risks later attack or noncompliance. The mediator must be prepared to be a surrogate for the other party, permitting the anger to be aired.

7. A mediator wants settlement. Generally, mediators believe it to be in the best interests of the disputants to resolve their dispute. Although resolution of the case is not the only reason for mediation (emotional conciliation, shortening discovery, cutting legal costs, and preservation of business relationships are a few of the other reasons for choosing mediation), mediators must still want resolution, and must be always mindful of opportunities to bring cases to a close. There are times when mediators might reasonably conclude that lawyers and their clients are relishing the battle, even though they have a subtle sense that it must someday end

and a subtle knowledge of what the ending will be. The mediator's drive toward settlement will help the parties free themselves of energy and capital-consuming battles, which they know will ultimately be ended.

8. Mediators must be principled. Useful standards of conduct are now under consideration by the Supreme Court of Florida and, no doubt, in other states. When available, these standards of conduct will guide us. In the interim we can safely say that there is no lawful basis for a mediator to engage in deceit or fraud of any kind in order to facilitate a settlement. Mediators should not make representations about their beliefs or knowledge of outcomes of cases, unless it is made clear that the mediator's opinion of the outcome is certainly to be given no greater weight than that of the attorneys' representing the clients.

9. A mediator is communication-literate. Knowledge of communication science literature and communications skills is essential to a mediator. Almost all of the communication occurring during mediation sessions is oral. Very little is written, and very little is presented graphically. Speaking well and listening accurately are two very difficult tasks. Mediators should be aware of the trouble that can be caused by spoken human communication. For example, the problems that occur during the serial communications, that occur as the client tells the lawyer of an interest, the lawyer later tells the opposing lawyer of the client's interest, the opposing lawyer tells the other client of the interest, and the process is renewed as the other client responds. Such communications are readily demonstrated to result in change of emphasis, loss, and transformation of information. Serial communication is a dangerous way to try to settle a lawsuit. Even with the great care trial lawyers exercise, information will be transformed as it moves from person to person. Such transformations are largely avoided by a mediation conference.

10. Empathy is an essential quality in mediators. The ability to transfer into a disputant's position, not only in terms of understanding the logic of the position but understanding the feelings of the disputant as well, aids mediators in discovering subtle roadblocks to settlement and eliminating them.

11. A mediator is tolerant of silence. Silence often precedes an announcement of real importance to the disputant; therefore, it is of importance to the mediator. Often when no one is talking, someone is thinking. Mediators unwilling to give people a quiet moment during mediation miss many opportunities to help others settle their disputes.

12. A good mediator understands that about the only people consistently able to persuade any of us to do anything are ourselves. In addition to giving people time to think about difficult decisions, mediators should learn to probe the vulnerabilities of a position by subtle questions asked with kindness. It is easier for me to be critical of myself than to hear another attack my thinking.

13. Mediators must be willing to engage in extended conversations in which they speak far less than those who own the dispute. Mediators must enjoy the give and take of negotiations as disputants work with the mediator to find an answer to their problem. Extroverted behavior is essential, even for introverted mediators. Mediation is an intensive form of communication and can go on for ten or more hours as settlement seems closer and closer!

14. Mediators should keep their judgments to themselves. Parties settle cases, not mediators. It is their judgment that matters. In any event, it is rare that a mediator can leap to a solution that is immediately accepted by all litigants. Judged on the basis of knowledge of the dispute, the mediator is the most ignorant person in the room. Even though a mediator may privately guess at an outcome, it is seldom appropriate to suggest that outcome until the parties have begun to consider something close to it.

15. Mediators manage information in conflict. An ability to think and to deal simultaneously with conflicting propositions is essential to the mediator as it is to the judge. However important thinking may be, a well-developed sense of the feelings and emotions present in the mediation will prove to be as helpful to counsel and their clients. Good mediators not only identify the role of feelings in settlement but also openly discuss feelings about the case during private sessions with a party when acknowledgment of feelings may be essential to settlement.

Despite the reluctance mediators should have to attempt to impose their judgments upon disputants, there are times when disputants will privately seek the judgment of the mediator as a guide to what might be appropriate as an outcome. The mediator must be willing to offer the judgment after determining that the client understands the mediator will defer to the client's attorney in making any judgment about how to settle. A strong base of knowledge about our legal system coupled with high intelligences are important qualities for mediators.

The Legal Profile

The first discriminant in analyzing the legal responsibilities of mediators is whether the mediation is court-ordered or is a private mediation which is conducted under other than the authority of a statute providing for court-ordered mediation.

If the mediation is court ordered, statutes and rules of civil procedure may define the legal role of the mediator and define the mediator's work.

Court-Ordered Mediation

The principal distinction in court-ordered mediation is the legally important fact that the mediator may be given immunity by law (e.g., §44.307, Fla. Stats., 1990, under which the immunity extended is the same as that enjoyed by a sitting state judge in Florida's courts). Immunity from suit may be inferred from case law in many jurisdictions.

Mediation Without a Court Order

To the extent that waivers of liability are possible for any professional, mediators may be able to secure at least partial immunity from suit by contract. In cases where there is no pending lawsuit, entry of a court order is at this time impossible. In the future it is possible the Florida legislature will adopt additional recommendations of its 1984–86 Legislative Study Commission on Alternative Dispute Resolution for the Courts, calling for direct filing for mediation as opposed to first being required to file a lawsuit to obtain mediation.

Mediators will probably be unsuccessful in attempting to persuade people to file lawsuits so that the mediator can gain protection under the immunity statute. Such behavior would probably be unethical for lawyer mediators and perhaps illegal.

Hybrid Forms of Mediation with Arbitration

The lure of efficiency has tempted disputants and mediators to engage in a process described as "med/arb." In this process mediation first occurs. To the extent mediation is not successful in reaching a resolution of a conflict, the mediator is permitted to declare the matter at impasse, and to thereafter act as an arbitrator for the parties in binding arbitration.

There are difficulties inherent in this process. The role of the mediator, and that of the arbitrator (who acts as an adjudicator) are grossly different. The mediator is proactive and encourages the flow of information to the mediator. The mediator also utilizes ex parte communications given in confidence to the mediator as a means for learning information that may aid the parties in reaching settlement. There is no ethical or practical problem with ex parte communication to a mediator, as a mediator does not make decisions about the facts, the law, or the outcome of the case.

An arbitrator is an adjudicator and like judges should behave very differently from mediators. The arbitrator should be more passive, less interactive with the parties, and should not engage in ex parte communications with any party or counsel. Ideally, the arbitrator's decision is based only on the information provided at the hearing. If the mediator seeks confidential information from each party, it is not likely to be given if the parties know that the mediator can unilaterally convert to a judge-like arbitrator at any moment. An essential resource unique to mediation is thus lost and renders the mediation portion of the proceedings impotent. By what insight will the neutral know the moment at which conversion should occur? Will the decision be dictated by frustration with the parties' negotiations or a party's unwillingness to accept the neutral's proposed resolution? It would be more efficient simply to conduct arbitration from the beginning.

Because of the conflicts in the two roles of the neutral the Society of Professionals in Dispute Resolution has been prompted to create a standard of conduct governing these situations.

Mediator Liability: Fundamental Theoretical Bases

In this section theoretical liability will be discussed. The law of liability will develop slowly in states granting immunity from suit to mediators.

Intentional Tort

Misrepresentations by mediators to litigants upon which litigants base decisions to settle or not settle could be the basis for liability of a mediator to the litigant.

The practice of "caucusing," splitting the parties and their respective attorneys into separate groups, rather than having all negotiations face to face requires that mediators serially communicate the bargaining positions of the parties to each other. Serial communication results in changes to information including abbreviations, dropping of information, and transformations of information. Later disputant perceptions of misrepresentation by the mediator may result.

Breach of Contract

Mediators enter expressed contracts and implied contracts logically deduced from the subjects of their agreement, as well as quasi contracts in which liability is assumed because of an appellate court's perception of some public need.

The dearth of cases nationally leaves us in doubt as to court reactions to mediator liability. We can, therefore, only infer that mediators will be held liable as other professionals are, using existing concepts in law.

Expressed Contracts

As mediation continues to grow as an alternative forum for resolution of disputes, mediators will ask for and receive written contracts covering the scope of the mediation work they are expected to conduct. Promises in these contracts, such as one to keep all communications confidential, can be breached. If damage occurs through the breach, which can be measured by traditional standards, mediator liability will result.

Implied Contract and Fiduciary Responsibilities

Where no expressed contract exists, our courts will probably be willing to infer obligations such as confidentiality, competency to handle the work, clear and unambiguous communication of both the information upon which a decision to settle might be based and of the settlement itself, and the like. Such inferences will result in implied contracts for service. Breach of these contracts will be handled by our courts no differently than the breach of implied contracts has been handled historically.

Will mediators be seen as having fiduciary responsibilities differing from and perhaps exceeding those of other participants in the dispute resolution process? An example is the duty to maintain the confidences given to the mediator during mediation. We should contrast the mediator's obligations of disclosure with his duty to maintain confidences. For example, will there be a fiduciary duty to disclose a plan to defraud which the mediator learned of in a confidential setting?

Quasi Contracts

It is quite likely that these obligations may more likely be stated as ethical requirements for mediators. The courts' concerns here will be in assuring the honesty and candor of mediators claiming court certification. We have no court-provided standards of conduct to guide us. Standards are under consideration by the Supreme Court of Florida and may be adopted by the time this book is published. If so, the need for quasi contract contortions by the courts will be avoided.

Negligence

The attorney's first challenge in examining the negligence theory as a possible source of mediator liability will be in determining what duties mediators have which might be breached.

The proposed standards of conduct may provide other sources of duty upon which liability could be based. Once a duty has been found and its breach established, novel questions of what was the proximate cause of financial loss will be raised in mediator litigation. However, precedents for the management of these questions will be found in examining the development of the law of lawyers' professional responsibility to clients. Analogies will be used by lawyers coping with emerging ideas about mediator liability.

Specific Sources of Liability

We can probably identify specific actions and inactions which could result in mediator liability. Some of the following are drawn from information in insurance carriers' claims files. There is very little case law about mediator liability. Claims data has been the major source of information, other than informed speculation by judges, attorneys, and legal scholars.

Giving Legal Advice

Both lawyer and nonlawyer mediators should be liable for giving advice or legal information if the advice or information later proves to be incorrect and damage or loss results. The theory of liability could be negligence or breach of an implied contract or fiduciary duty. Responsible mediators rigorously avoid giving information and advice about the laws that might apply to a case, even while guiding disputants toward legally defensible resolutions. Even if lawyers are not representing the disputants or do not attend the mediation (often true in family mediation), mediators should refer disputants to legal aid and legal referral services or to their lawyers when they are represented.

Unauthorized Practice of Law

For nonlawyer mediators the giving of advice or information about the law might result in liability based upon lack of membership in the local bar. Could "unauthorized practice of law" be a basis for strict liability? Would there be a presumption of causation when it is shown that incorrect information was given, a settlement resulted, and that another, better settlement might have been obtained if the correct state of the law and its application had been conveyed?

Failing to Keep Confidences

Claims against mediators are commonly based upon an alleged breach of promised confidentiality. Aside from possible statutory or court-ruled obligation to keep mediation proceedings confidential, the courts could readily imply a contract when the mediation was not court ordered and when there is no contract calling for confidentiality. Connecting the breach of confidence to ultimate loss and damage will probably be trial counsel's major task.

Misrepresentations to Disputants

Social scientists studying mediation are aware that some mediation practitioners have deliberately engaged in misrepresentation of one party's position to the other in order to stimulate settlement of a case; for example, adamantly representing to one of the parties that the other party will not offer a better settlement and that the settlement is "as good as anyone could get" when none of this is known to be true. Theories of intentional tort and breach of contract are probably appropriate to such situations.

Drafting Documents for Disputants

Mediators may be asked to draft documents for settling parties. The context might be a small case in which neither party has an attorney or only one party is represented by counsel. Other situations include family mediation in which lawyers might choose not to be present during much of the mediation.

If the mediator is a lawyer, questions of attorney-client relationships are immediately raised by the drafting task, implicit within which is the implied giving of advice as well as legal information. Nonlawyer mediators run the risk of being accused of the unauthorized practice of law by drafting documents which are intended to have binding, legal effect.

The best answer is for the mediator to draft a memorandum, including a clause stating clearly that the parties do not intend the document to be binding and that it does not represent the "meeting of the minds" required in contracts. The document should also provide that the parties have been advised by the mediator to seek advice of counsel before a binding agreement is drafted an signed.

If one or both of the parties is represented by counsel, the clause could specify that the agreement will not be valid until approved by counsel. Of course, the parties would be free to strike out these provisions and present the agreement as final and binding if they chose to do so. The mediator has no power to forbid parties to enter into an agreement.

However, the mediator is subject to liability on the same basis draftsmen have been liable for deficiencies in their agreements over the decades. Ample case law precedent is available, by analogy, to pursue such remedies against a mediator.

The employment contract also should specify that the mediator will not be required to prepare any binding agreements for the parties and that the parties will either prepare their own binding agreement or seek the assistance of counsel to do so.

Violation of Applicable Court Rules

A direct violation by a mediator of rules of civil procedure or the provisions of a court order for mediation might be the basis for mediator liability. Theories of liability would include intentional tort, negligence, and in extreme cases, perhaps §1983, U.S.C.A., liability.

The latter liability could develop if the mediator is seen as a state officer by virtue of court appointment and if the mediator uses pretended powers to bring about a coerced settlement.

Incompetent Disputants

If a disputant is mentally incompetent or incompetent by reason of age or other legal disability to enter into a binding agreement, all disputants might seek to hold a mediator responsible if the mediator knew or reasonably should have known about the incompetency and did not call it to the attention of all the parties. Mediated settlements result in contracts of settlement and the usual considerations of competency to contract apply.

Void and Voidable Mediated Agreements

All mediators should be aware of the substantive law concerned with the subjects of mediation. A lawyer mediator might be held liable for permitting a settlement which resulted in a voidable contract. One hopes that the courts would link any resulting dismissals with prejudice to the efficacy of the contract of settlement. If this is not done, certainly damage will result. If parties are represented by counsel, perhaps the mediator's liability will be secondary to that of the responsible attorney. Mediators may have a right of indemnity against the attorney as well, inasmuch as mediators should avoid giving legal advice to disputants.

Here we detect another potential dilemma for mediators. On the one hand, they are wisest to refrain from giving legal advice, or even legal information. On the other hand, if a mediator observes incompetent counsel permitting counsel's client to enter into a settlement which will not be enforceable or in some way will be detrimental to the client, should the mediator have a duty to disclose the state of law to the lawyer? To the client? Should mediators be held liable for money damages resulting from such settlements?

Violation of Applicable Standards of Conduct and Codes of Ethics

Mediators will find that they are governed by multiple codes of conduct and ethics. For example, a lawyer mediator is governed by the standards of conduct for members of the bar. If the lawyer mediator is working on a federal court case, still more rules of conduct directly applicable to attorneys admitted to that court may apply.

The American Bar Association has proposed standards of conduct for lawyer mediators mediating family disputes, and the Society of Professionals in Dispute Resolution has published standards of conduct for mediators.

Nonlawyer mediators will no doubt find that standards of conduct and rules unique to their professions will apply to them in addition to the standards of conduct adopted by courts.

Will the new standards make the same effort as that made in the standards of conduct of bar associations, seeking to avoid the possibility that the standards will become the basis for professional liability?

Mediators will probably be required to determine whether they have sufficient knowledge of the substantive area of law to permit them to intelligently and usefully mediate a dispute. This requirement presently applies to lawyers representing clients. Lawyers who mediate should consider that it applies to them in mediation as well. It is predictable that our courts will insist on such a standard, as the consuming public is entitled to have competent mediators.

Justification for such a standard is found in the practical requirement that mediators be sufficiently informed to successfully test and probe the vulnerability of legal positions taken by litigants.

Immunity

Immunity from liability was seen as needed to encourage the growth of mediation as an additional forum for handling litigants' disputes in Florida's courts.

An encouragement to bright, senior lawyers and judges and other professionals to become mediators was needed. Relief from the prospect of expensive professional insurance is a strong economic incentive for qualified professionals to enter the field of mediation.

Mediators remain liable for acts in excess of their jurisdiction as mediators. For example, if a mediator were to cause a litigant to be incarcerated for some breach perceived by the mediator, the mediator would have clearly exceeded the authority granted by the order appointing the mediator and the statute and rules for court-annexed mediation in Florida.

However, lack of legal knowledge, lack of mediation skill, a failure to conduct mediation in an appropriate and professional way, or other breaches (e.g., failing to appear for the mediation or terminating the mediation before the parties are at impasse) would not be actionable, even though inept, improper, and financially damaging to litigants. Florida law grants judicial immunity to court-appointed mediators.

Nonlawyer Mediators

Standards of Conduct

Nonlawyers performing court-ordered mediation will be subject to the same standards of mediation conduct as lawyers. In addition, standards of conduct unique to their principal professions (e.g., psychology) may also apply.

With regard to the immunity statute, the principal concern of nonlawyer mediators will be with enforcement of the court's adopted standards of conduct for mediators.

Evaluating Mediators: Client and Lawyer Concerns

From a practical point of view clients and lawyers are most likely to encounter nonlawyer mediators only in the area of family law. If knowledge of substantive law and an ability to predict court outcomes is essential to aiding a client and lawyer in determining whether to settle, a lawyer mediator should be preferred. If there is a great deal of anger in the case, or delicate questions of child welfare and development are present, and the case is in its early stages of litigation, nonlawyer mediators trained in mental health should be preferred.

An emerging model for complex case mediation in family law involves using nonlawyer, mental health trained mediators on issues involving the children of the marriage and the couples' emotions, and a lawyer or CPA mediator to aid the couple in dealing with financial issues. Lawyer mediators are used exclusively when the mediation proceeds to writing the terms of settlement. Managed properly, this method of mediation should not result in significant additional cost to the parties, as the mediators are working on different sets of issues with them. There is no duplication of effort by the mediators, as they do their work over time—first the mental health mediator, then the CPA lawyer mediator, and finally the lawyer mediator as draftsperson for the final memorandum from which a marital settlement agreement will be prepared.

Pro Bono and Low Fee Mediation

Mediation promises to become a major forum for resolution of litigants' disputes. Lawyers are offered an opportunity to assist insufficiently financed and indigent clients with dispute resolution services which will result in binding settlements but with far lower costs for attorneys' services and much shortened time spans of effort.

In these cases the cost of the mediator can be an inhibiting factor, although the cost of mediation is seldom a material factor in the total cost of litigation. In such cases low fee or pro bono mediation must be encouraged.

Bar associations can bring about the training of lawyer mediators for pro bono service through local bar organizations. In addition, lawyer mediators who are members of a local bar can offer low fee services similar to the low fee lawyer referral systems now operating in many urban areas.

Lawyer mediators who choose not to practice law will find pro bono mediation a means for satisfying their ethical responsibility to provide services to the part of the consuming public unable to afford "full press" legal services.

Practical Dilemmas in Mediation

Internal Inconsistencies

All written rules of conduct have internal inconsistencies which are best detected by looking at experiences in practice. Practicing attorneys can readily appreciate this problem when considering the conflicting rules of conduct which at once require a trial attorney to be absolutely candid with the court but somehow also zealously to represent a client and to maintain virtually all the confidences given the attorney by the client.

Examples of Mediator Dilemmas

In family cases, mediators often promise absolute confidentiality to litigants. This duty cannot be observed in many states when even so much as a suspicion of child abuse arises.

A mediator may learn in a private session of caucus with a party of that party's attorney's intention to maintain a position which is not supported by any evidence of any kind. If the mediator is a lawyer, does the mediator have any responsibility to disclose this professional misconduct to the court or to the other litigant?

If a mediator sees a party accepting a settlement that is likely to be considered grossly one-sided by a reviewing court, does the mediator have a positive duty to try to prevent the settlement?

If a mediator learns that a party is prepared to accept a settlement which the party would probably not accept if the party knew the correct state of the law, does the mediator have a positive duty to see to it that the client is adequately informed of the law? What mechanisms will be deemed appropriate for carrying out this duty, if such a duty is ever recognized?

Many of these conflicts are resolved by noting that mediators should pursue durable settlements, not settlements that are likely to blow apart or to be criticized or rejected by court. In addition, mediator rationalization for taking action that would be inappropriate for a judge or an attorney representing a client can stem from the fact that mediation is not an adversary proceeding and mediators are not judges or arbitrators. Mediators should seek fully informed, rational settlements. In pursuit of this end, they should suggest areas of legal and factual inquiry to disputants, to assure that pertinent aspects of the dispute and the manner of settlement have been considered by all parties. For example, in family mediation assuring that the parties have considered the tax effects of a settlement proposal.

Conclusion

Mediation is intended to be conducted differently from in-court proceedings. The "adversary assumption" that the parties will be equally informed and equally skilled and given an equal opportunity to exploit each others' weaknesses is the basic rationale for our trial system, but does not apply to mediation. In mediation a mediator should (proactively) assure adequate knowledge of the parties, permitting an informed and durable decision to settle. Unlike judges, mediators should actively raise issues for debate.

The great difficulty for mediators and their attorneys will be in determining which courses of conduct will accomplish these goals without abuse to other desirable standards of conduct? For example, would it be permissible for a mediator to tell the attorney for a party, in a one-on-one conversation, of the existence of case law that could strengthen that party's position?

Lawyer and nonlawyer mediators are charting new territory. Although lawyers know that they can borrow from other experience in dealing with the responsibility of professionals to those they serve, they are aware that there are unique facets of mediation which will cause those principles to be modified and perhaps applied differently. For example, we need only remind ourselves how appropriate it is to have an ex parte (private) conversation about the dispute with a mediator, and how inappropriate it is to have such a conversation with a trial judge or a juror.

Part 3: Corrections

20. Private Corrections

Samuel Jan Brakel

The law enforcement enterprise is composed of three components — the police, the courts, and corrections. Each is a vital link to the other and all are critical to the societal objective of maintaining the public peace through justice.

The vital role played by corrections in this tri-part system is suggested by the amount of public money spent on it. Of all justice system expenditures — federal, state, and local — corrections accounts for 31.7 percent (a comparatively modest 17 percent of municipal and county justice costs, and only 13 percent in the federal system, but a heavily consuming 58 percent of the average state justice budget) (U.S. Department of Justice, 1988:2) The importance of corrections is also reflected in the degree of public and political concern with prison issues. Today, due to the overcrowding crisis and all that comes with it — rising prison violence, unprecedented court intrusion, and the costly but failing efforts of government to build its way out of the crisis — corrections has become the leader among justice system equals in terms of public visibility.

Privatization is one of the key political-economic concepts of the 1980s — a status it is likely to maintain in the 1990s. Vis-à-vis the courts, private enterprise involvement is at this moment a small phenomenon, marginal in scope and thrust, but the prospects for growth are good. Private inroads into the policing function, by contrast, have already attained the level of major avenues. Private security firms are as old as public police departments (with which they subcontract for services on an increasing scale) and today actually exceed the public agencies in terms of total number of people employed and expenditures for services delivered (Chaiken and Chaiken, 1987).

Privatization in corrections, while it too has historical antecedents,[1] is essentially a contemporary phenomenon. Corrections' experience with private-sector participation is, of the three justice system components, also the fastest growing and most controversial. Today, some 35 to 40 sizable correctional facilities are *managed* by private companies under contract to federal, state, and local governments — all but a couple of them were contracts entered into during the decade of the 1980s. A total of some 7,500 beds are involved, a figure that has doubled just in the past two years.

In addition, the private sector's role in *building* the physical facilities has greatly expanded. While construction of the prisons was, in the merciful absence of special government building crews, always contracted out to private companies, the

254

difference today is that the private builders have in an increasing number of instances been given full responsibility for overall *management of the construction enterprise,* including the selection of sites, materials, and architectural design and, in some cases, the financing of the projects. Ownership may be retained by the private builder or the government may purchase the facilities, typically by way of a long-term arrangement whose properties resemble a lease.

Why Privatize Corrections?

> A principal reason for this return to private providers is the convergence of three historic trends: increasing public demand for imprisonment of criminals, increasingly stringent court-imposed standards requiring significant new investments in manpower and facilities, and growing fiscal strain on governments. Simply put, the public demand for quality corrections is outstripping the ability of the public sector to provide them [Grant and Bast, 1987:2].

The specifics generating these pressures on public corrections have been amply documented. Changes in law enforcement practices and sentencing policies have driven up the prison population at an unprecedented rate. In 1977 there were 300,024 prisoners in federal and state facilities. By the end of 1987 the number had risen to 581,609 (of whom 48,399 were in federal prisons)—a growth of 94 percent. County and municipal jails, housing another 300,000-some inmates on any given day and processing as many as 8.5 million per year (1987), have experienced comparable crisis-proportion population increases (*President's Commission on Privatization Report*, 1988:46; U.S. Department of Justice, Prisoners, 1988:2).

In the federal setting, enactment of the Comprehensive Crime Control Act (1984) and the Anti-Drug Abuse Act (1986), plus corresponding policy decisions by the relevant law enforcement agencies to vigorously enforce these new laws, have been among the major events contributing to an overflowing prison system. Today, the federal detention network is reported to be overcrowded by a factor of almost 60 percent, with 44,000 offenders sentenced to facilities whose maximum capacity is only 28,000. The upshot is a situation where half of the federal judicial districts are operating under serious to critical space-availability conditions, and 16 percent are experiencing "emergency" conditions, with detention space simply not available. The U.S. Marshals Service, which is responsible for detaining federal pretrial defendants, has been forced to hold 60 percent of them in state and local jails.[2]

All this comes at a time when the situation for state and local corrections is at least equally alarming. Statutory enactments and enforcement policies on those levels have been comparable in direction and consequence to those of the federal system, with overcrowding a serious problem in all but a handful of favored jurisdictions. Court pressure to alleviate the problem by whatever means available— including imposition of burden-shifting but not burden-solving mandates such as closing prisons to new admissions, population transfers to the facilities of other jurisdictions, and massive "early-release" programs—has been especially pronounced on the state level. As of 1988 thirty-five states plus the District of Columbia were under court order to reduce overcrowding in their prisons or jails, with another five states in which such suits were pending.

Arguments of Proponents of Privatized Corrections

Private-sector participation in the corrections business has been touted as promoting greater efficiency in the construction and management of prison facilities and as improving quality (i.e., "effectiveness") in these same respects.

Greater *efficiency in construction* would include gains in the speed with which facilities are built or renovated as well as savings in costs—both critical advantages in the context of today's crisis. The private sector is also seen to have an edge in terms of the capacity to *finance* major construction projects that governments operating under the constraints posed by annually delimited budgets and overburdened taxpayers would be unable or very reluctant to undertake.

The theory on *management efficiency* is that private entrepreneurs will strive to hold down costs through optimum utilization of staff, reduced capital investments (for example, equipment), and lowest-price purchasing of subsidiary prison goods and services—areas where public management has historically been inefficient.

Improvements in *construction quality* would, according to privatization's proponents, flow from the entrepreneur's comparatively greater flexibility in choosing sites, personnel, and material from the array of such resources available and the concomitant ability to take advantage of the latest innovations in architectural design and building technology. The result would be not only better facilities, but an improved capacity to respond to the specific needs of a varied and often variable prison population.

In addition, better facility design will, it is said, result in significant manpower savings and provide substantial gains in operational efficiency. Each guard *position* eliminated by virtue of improved prisoner oversight and control capabilities—be it through construction of cell tiers and connecting hallways permitting more efficient direct surveillance or via deployment of centralized video technology and computerized locking systems—in effect (over a twenty-four-hour day, a seven-day week) means a reduction of five *guards* and five *salaries* in actual manpower expenditures.

Potential improvements in *management quality*, the supporters of privatization contend, go hand in hand with greater management efficiency. It is argued, for example, that the use of prison staff at optimum efficiency levels subsumes a staff deployment system based strictly on merit, with implications for improved quality over public-sector management under which decisions are influenced by political considerations and civil-service protectionism.

Some Counterpoints

Many observers on either side of the prison privatization debate would concede that private entrepreneurs operating in a competitive environment and driven by the profit motive would be more efficient than their public-sector counterparts functioning in a monopoly setting and encumbered by a politicized bureaucracy. Fewer are inclined to accept as readily the proposition that the private sector's participation would upgrade quality. Indeed, there is a substantial body of opinion—strongly held and not easily dislodged—that in the quest for efficiency, quality will suffer. Given the pervasive shortcomings in the public-prison conditions, services, and procedures, as detailed in the voluminous prison litigation, any general diminution in quality would not be deemed acceptable.[3]

Finally, there is substantial controversy about the "propriety" of private-sector involvement on the scale represented by the recent developments. This is a moral issue, possibly a legal one, only marginally influenced by either theory or facts regarding the efficiency and effectiveness of privatized corrections.

The Empirical Data

What does the recent experience with (re)privatized corrections tell us about the cost, quality, and possibly the propriety of the concept? The facts are at this point scattered throughout the literature—a rapidly growing body of popular magazine and newspaper articles, specialized professional reports, and some broader, academically targeted writings (Logan, 1985). They are subject to the particular caveats with which preliminary data must be evaluated—that is, there are often genuine questions about their accuracy, completeness, and interinstitutional and interjurisdictional comparability. Nevertheless, the available factual information begins to reveal an interpretable picture—a still-frame of usable quality in the developing privatization film.

Cost, Speed, and Quality of Construction

General construction cost estimates derived from the *public*-sector experience range from $50,000 to near $100,000 per prison bed (DeWitt, 1986). More specific computations show the average figure to be $58,000 for maximum-security cells, but a more modest $46,000 and $26,000 for beds in medium- and minimum-security facilities, respectively (Grant and Bast, 1987:5). The amount of time needed to build an institution has been estimated at a fairly uniform 2.5 years (DeWitt, 1986:6; Grant and Bast, 1987:6), although actual experience reveals wide variation depending on the type of facility and various extraneous factors.

Whatever the variation in the cost and time figures, one constant is that they have demonstrably overwhelmed the public sector's capacity to respond. Despite a decade of the biggest construction push in the history of corrections, prison capacities have continued to fall farther behind the accelerating need for space. Between 1978 and 1986, 188,043 beds were added to the state systems, a capacity growth of 77 percent, yet the shortfall in beds rose from 26,525 to 70,708 (167 percent) (Harms and Allen, 1987). The impact of the U.S. Sentencing Commission Guidelines could, according to the commission's own projections, lead to a doubling of the federal prison population over the next decade and triple the overcrowding rate in federal facilities.[4]

There is selective evidence today that private enterprise involvement can help close the gap at affordable costs. For example, Corrections Corporation of America (cca), the leader in the new prison construction and management industry with twenty-one contracts in six different states covering the range of government entities (federal, state, and local) as well as two international ventures (in France and Australia), has developed a record of impressive savings. Five years ago, under contract to the ins, the company built a 350-bed minimum-security facility in Houston for the detention of illegal aliens in the space of 5.5 months at a cost of $14,000 per bed — as against the service's own average of 2.5 years and $26,000 (Grant and Bast, 1987:6).

Comparable gains have been realized at the local government level. In a contract with Hamilton County (Chattanooga), Tennessee, for the management of the county's jail or work-farm, the same cca company has made capital improvements (major renovations and the construction of one new dormitory) to the tune of some $1.6 million at no direct cost to the county (Grant and Bast, 1987:5). The company recoups its outlays in a per diem management charge that is *lower* than the county's rate when it operated the facility.

On the state level one of the earliest privatization experiences in corrections — 1975 in Pennsylvania — points up the quick response capabilities of the private sector.[5] A legal opinion by that state's attorney general to the effect that juvenile offenders could not be incarcerated with adult offenders caused the state to turn to a private firm for the provision of a high-security juvenile facility. In ten days the private contractor (rca Corporation) was able to put into operation its Weaversville Intensive Treatment Unit by converting a building complex already owned by the state (Grant and Bast, 1987:6).

The private sector does not deal in magic. Conversion of facilities is also a public-sector option, though bureaucratic and political impediments will exact their toll. By the same token, the efficient building techniques (prefabrication, modular construction) and building management concepts used by private entrepreneurs in achieving the cost and time savings in new constructions can be and have in some states been used by government agencies (DeWitt, 1986:5). Quality is not compromised in the application of these techniques. To the contrary, the use of design and materials specified to particular security needs constitutes quality improvement over the traditional construction uniformities that have given us the dungeons of the past and some of the monumental health and security hazards of more recent times.

Competition and the profit motive are what drive private-prison entrepreneurs to take advantage of the latest building innovations. Among the potential advantages of private-sector participation in the prison business is that it may accelerate the public sector's motivation to compete with similar efficiencies.[6]

Financing Prison Construction

Government entities have traditionally financed capital improvements in their prison facilities with current operating revenues and or, in the case of state and local governments, via the mechanism of selling general obligation or revenue bonds (Mullen, Chabotar, and Carow, 1985:33). The private sector has at times played a tangential role in the second of these financing strategies—the bond-issue approach—by serving as the underwriter and marketer of the bonds. Recent developments, however, signal the prospect of a substantially expanded private-sector role in financing.

Often with the assistance of financial intermediaries (including corrections-specialized investment banking firms), prison construction and management companies are becoming the primary financiers of prison construction projects in a growing number of instances. They have done so via one of several so-called lease-financing techniques that allow governments to hurdle the increasingly imposing barriers to current revenue, "pay-as-you-go" financing and to avoid both the economic and political costs of the bond-issue approach. Lease financing— including straight leases, lease-purchase, and even lease-back arrangements[7] whereby the government entity rents the prison facility from the private owner-builder, with or without an option to buy,—spreads construction costs over the long term (conceivably the life of the facility), thus avoiding the extraordinary strain on current revenues or the equally large obstacle of obtaining political approval for sudden, huge increases in operating budgets. Leasing arrangements are in many situations[8] also preferable to bond-issue financing—a revenue-raising approach used by state and local governments, but not on the federal level. The lease approach avoids the time delays and costs, including the extra costs caused by lapse of time, that are normally incurred in the process of floating bonds.

Questions have been raised regarding the political and even the legal propriety of lease-type financing arrangements, to the extent that they avoid public participation in approving government expenditures that would otherwise come into play as legislatures appropriate operating revenues and taxpayers vote on bond referenda.[9] In view of the small annual impact of costs spread out over the long term, these concerns may not be of paramount importance. They may be further allayed by pointing out that public oversight is preserved in other ways—most notably via a contract that may be more specific and more "visible" than typical public accounting mechanisms.[10]

The salience of the issue is further diminished when, as in the pattern followed by the CCA company, for example, construction costs are wholly absorbed by the private builder-manager of the prison facility and reflected only in a per diem management fee that actually saves money in relation to the government's own operating-cost experience and projections.

Management Efficiencies

Even with the heavy emphasis on construction during recent years, capital outlays constitute no more than 13 percent of total corrections expenditues (U.S. Department of Justice, 1988:4). The remainder are operational costs. For that reason, any improvement in the efficiency of prison management will have a deep impact on total corrections outlays.

In one sense, the possibility that private-sector prison management can generate cost savings is something that needs to be proved more to the private companies in this business than to the contracting government entities. The reason is that, from the government's perspective, the matter is usually decided a priori: contracts for prison management between government and private entrepreneurs are by and large drawn up at cost rates explicitly pegged *below* what it cost the public entity to run the particular facility in immediately preceding years or to projections of what it would cost the public manager in the immediate future. At least one state (Tennessee) *requires by law* that prison management contracts with the private sector be premised on a fee structure that is at minimum 5 percent below public-sector costs.[11] Thus, even if the contracting private entity proves to be unable to operate within the agreed-upon cost limits, it will simply have to run the facility at a loss, while the government would still receive the benefit of the contractually set savings.

This contractual sleight of hand does not, of course, dispose of the total matter of the cost consequences of private prison management. A priori–set savings that cannot be replicated empirically only postpone the day of reckoning. No private company can or will operate at a loss for long: either it will pull out of the business or it (or its successors) will renegotiate the contract at a higher price, conceivably *exceeding* the costs experienced or projected under public-sector management.

Two sets of figures are available on the cost of *public* management of federal (INS) facilities. One gives the average cost as $38.36 per inmate per day (Grant and Bast, 1987). The other study reports the average to be $31.89 per diem, based on an analysis of seven publicly managed facilities (Massachusetts Legislative Research Report, 1987). This study also provides a comparison with five *privately run* INS facilities, calculating the average per diem for the latter to be $37.26 – higher than the public-sector cost average from the same study, but marginally lower than the $38.36 figure. The averages reported, however, are based on an analysis that lumps together, without weighting for number of beds, facilities with populations as low as 47–50 to one with a population of 668, and per diem costs *per facility* that range from $17.65 to $88.69. No attempt is made to account for the variables that would explain the huge cost differences – for example, differences in the facilities' basic objectives as reflected in the average length of detention of the population, the overall security level, and the available inmate services and programs.

Another unexplored variable influencing management costs is the operational efficiency of the particular government entity or company responsible for managing a given facility. A selective analysis of that factor for the private-sector side is possible. The CCA company—the leader in the private prison industry—has a cost-of-management (efficiency) record that falls roughly in the middle relative to its competitors. Though costs vary widely from facility to facility, CCA operates each of the facilities it has under contract well within comparable public-sector management cost experiences and projections. It runs two INS facilities—one in Houston at $23.75 to $26.84 per diem (the available figures conflict),[12] another in Laredo at $31.00 (Massachusetts Legislative Research Council, 1987). Both facilities were built by CCA and the management costs include construction costs (up to $5 million for the Houston facility) spread out over the term of the contract.

In its state and local contracts as well CCA has been able to make operational savings of significant magnitude.[13] Moreover, in each of its facilities, the company is currently making at least a small profit, showing that the contractual terms are realistic. The CCA's profit margin has increased substantially in its latter contracts as compared to the earlier ones, and the company as a whole has, after incurring losses during the first four start-up (capital acquisition) years, shown a profit during the last two.[14] The record thus demonstrates that, contrary to allegations of the concept's detractors, private corrections makes business sense and that at least one of the industry's bigger and better companies more than equals the government's performance in terms of management efficiency.

Management Quality

If it is true that private-sector management can save costs, do the gains in efficiency come at the expense of effectiveness—the quality of prison conditions and prisoner services and the fairness of prison procedures? A common perception is that efficiency and quality are indeed trade-offs in the (presumably) zero-sum game of prison management.

To date there has been only one detailed, independent study of the quality of private-prison management, of the day-to-day operations of a facility run by a profit-making company. The study, conducted by this author, focuses on the CCA-managed Silverdale Detention Center in Chattanooga (Brakel, 1988a). Its results resoundingly disprove the trade-off assumption. The gains in efficiency yielded by privatizing the Silverdale facility were in fact found to be accompanied by significant quality improvements.

The study examined sixteen major aspects of prison conditions and procedures and concluded that CCA's takeover of the Silverdale facility had resulted in substantial gains in the following areas: (1) the physical plant, including its general upkeep and cleanliness; (2) safety and security, in particular improved classification; (3) staff professionalism and treatment of inmates; (4) medical services; (5) recreation programs and facilities; (6) religious and other counseling services; (7) disciplinary procedures; (8) inmate grievance and request procedures; and (9) legal access. In the remaining areas CCA's performance was roughly equivalent to the county's performance, but in no area was there found to be a diminution in quality.

The study pointed out that the improvements achieved by CCA came in a setting where a great deal of improvement was needed. The county's own management record contained many glaring deficiencies, a fact that figured heavily in the county commissioners' decision to go private in the first place. From one perspective, this might appear to diminish the significance of CCA's accomplishments. On the other hand, it could be interpreted to augment them. The CCA was dealt a difficult hand at Silverdale: a dilapidated facility, with long-standing management problems, situated in a resource-poor environment, contracted out at a per diem fee rate that left the private provider only the slimmest possible profit margin. That the company was able, against these odds, to achieve overall institutional respectability within two-and-one-half years of the takeover can be viewed as strong evidence of the private sector's capacity to contribute to quality in prison management.

Nonempirical Matters: The Propriety of Private Prisons

For many, evidence that private providers are capable of maintaining decent conditions and fair procedures in the prison facilities they manage, or even of achieving adequacy in these respects where the public sector's performance was inadequate, will have a bearing on whether they view privatization as a proper and legitimate response to corrections' problems. For some, however, the propriety issue is essentially a moral issue decided by a priori values and only marginally influenced, if at all, by whether privatization in fact leads to good or bad, efficient or inefficient, prison management.

Legality

Whether privatized corrections is legal may be viewed as one aspect of propriety. The basic, and really the only, question[15] about legality is whether government has the *authority to delegate* correctional responsibilities to nongovernment entities. According to opponents of the concept, overseeing the lot and lives of individuals convicted by the state's justice apparatus and sentenced to involuntary confinement (and its host of concomitant liberty deprivations) is a uniquely state function that cannot be parceled out to private agencies. While this position has a measure of instinctive or emotive appeal, there is more than high legal principle (or for that matter, altruistic concern for prisoners) at issue here. The legal position staked out contains a significant component of self-interest — the desire to protect jobs and turf seem to be threatened by the entry of private vendors on the heretofore securely monopolistic public corrections scene.[16]

This self-interest has obscured the fact that the position is quite tenuous. The delegation of central state authority to subagencies, both public and private, is one of the most common and unavoidable features of modern government. No such delegation has been invalidated by the U.S. Supreme Court in over fifty years, a situation paralleled on the lower federal and state court levels (Robbins, 1986: 329–30). Indeed, there is both statutory and case law that not only supports delegation of government functions to private agencies, but encourages it, including some that speaks specifically to corrections.

On the federal level, the language of 18 U.S.C.A. §4082(b) remands all federal offenders to the custody of the attorney general for confinement in "any available, suitable, and appropriate institution or facility, whether maintained by the Federal Government or otherwise."[17]

Based on an analysis of the legislative history of this law and its amendments, the general counsel to the Federal Bureau of Prisons has concluded in a formal memorandum that "there is authority to contract with private facilities, both halfway houses and traditional prisons and detention facilities" (*President's Commission on Privatization Report*, 1988:147). Beyond that, the federal government has long (since 1955) been under the general mandate via the so-called "A-76 program" (Butler, 1986:4) to compare in-house costs of routine commercial services with those obtainable from private suppliers, and to opt for the least expensive supplier of the appropriate quality of service.

The relevant case law is sparse. However, one of the cases most frequently invoked by privatization opponents—because the facts of it put an early INS contracting experience in a bad light—in the final analysis provides strong support for the legality of government's delegating its corrections responsibility. In *Medina v. O'Neill*,[18] the federal district court of the southern district of Texas unequivocally rejected the INS's defense of no-state action where a guard from a private security company with the contract to run the alien detention facility had accidentally but negligently shot and killed one inmate and seriously wounded another. Under the "public function" doctrine, the court found "obvious state action" and therefore dual liability (on the part of both the government and the private company) for the incident. Thus, *Medina's* resolution of the liability issue—an issue frequently raised in the literature as one of the prime legal obstacles to privatization—in fact serves to strengthen the case for privatization by virtue of its holding that in delegating, government retains ultimate responsibility for proper prison management and liability for instances where the entity to which some of that responsibility is transferred manages improperly.

The conclusion that both the state and the private contracting party are answerable to prisoners' legal claims may comfort prisoners and their advocates. However, it eliminates one of the advantages government entities may seek in deciding to delegate correctional authority—the advantage of avoiding liability. However, this objective can be at least partially recaptured via *indemnification* provisions written into the contract, whereby the private provider obligates itself to reimburse the government for the costs of attorney fees and damages incurred in defending against prisoner lawsuits.

On the state level, there were until recently legal barriers in some jurisdictions to the privatization of ostensibly public functions, including corrections.[19] However, the present trend is toward "clarifying and granting statutory authority to state agencies to permit contracting" (Hackett et al., 1987:17). Such "enabling legislation" specifically authorizing the private provision of prison space and services has in the last few years been enacted in a number of states, including Alaska, Colorado, Florida, Kentucky, Massachusetts, Montana, New Mexico, Tennessee, Texas, Utah, and Wisconsin.

Morality

The other component of the propriety issue entails moral philosophy or even moral symbolism. Charles Logan has addressed the matter with most directness. Invoking political theorists of the stature of John Locke,[20] he argues that the state does not *own* the right to punish, but that its authority to imprison derives, like all its powers and authority, solely from the consent of the governed. It follows, contends Logan, that this authority may, with similar consent, be delegated further to subsidiary trustees "as long as they, too, are ultimately accountable to the people and subject to the same provisions of law that direct the state" (Logan, 1987:36). It is the law, says Logan, not the civil status of the actor, that determines whether any particular exercise of authority—including the use of physical force or other coercive measures[21]—is legitimate.

These points are not persuasive to all. Donahue (1989) and DiIulio (1988:80) have invoked the White House–President analogy to illustrate what they see as the moral or symbolic bankruptcy of the idea that giving private agents control over prisons and prisoners is all right so long as they do the job with reasonable effectiveness and efficiency. Donahue posits the "Who Should Paint the White House versus Who Should Guard the President" dichotomy, finding it self-evident that the former is a job for private business while the latter is a function to be performed by public servants. DiIulio paints a rent-a-president scene in which an actor "president" plus an entourage of musicians and dignitaries of the "Medals Corporation of America" play out on the White House lawn the role of giving out the National Medal of Honor to deserving citizens. According to DiIulio, it is clear that such a scenario would not satisfy us. The appeal is primarily to our moral intuition, though Donahue brings in the complexity of the guard-the-president task as among the more concrete reasons for having a public Secret Service rather than a private protective force.

Whether one is more likely to buy into Donahue and DiIulio's intuitive appeals than into Logan's "rational reasons" is a matter of personal inclination. Two points are worth taking into account, however. (1) The evidence is that the prisoners, as opposed to DiIulio's hypothetical deserving citizens, care little about who is "doing it to them"; and (2) in contracting out for prison management or construction services, the state does not abdicate its responsibility for corrections. It merely relinquishes parts of that responsibility (while maintaining full liability) in a contractually circumscribed partnership with the private provider. The contract provides, as it has been put, "another layer of accountability" (*President's Commission on Privatization Report*, 1988:147).

The Role of Contracts in Securing and Restraining Privatized Corrections

There are four primary interest groups concerned with the prospect of increased privatization in corrections, as there are in any public service industry susceptible to similar developments: the taxpayers as true consumers of correctional services; the prisoners, who are the direct "service recipients" but not the consumers in this case; the new private providers intent on gaining a foothold in the industry or on expanding the one they already have; and the existing public service bureaucracy, anxious to protect jobs and turf it views as its own. Behind these primary groups stands the elected politician whose ostensible mission is to represent the legitimate interests of all and to strike an appropriate balance where they conflict.

The Taxpayers' Interest

By and large, the taxpaying public does not care a great deal about prisons or prisoners, beyond the elementary concern that expenditures for them be minimized. Proof that privatization promotes efficiency in the construction, financing, and management of prison facilities—available on a selective basis today—is thus likely to be the strongest selling point. The existence of a specific performance contract, which underlies all privatization forays into corrections, provides a substantial measure of accountability and visibility and protects the public against unitemized expenditures and unapproved cost overruns.

The conscience of more enlightened citizens, who may express concern about the general treatment of prisoners, can be assuaged by pointing out that, on the evidence, quality in corrections appears not to have been compromised by privatization. Good contract-making and good contractor selection have a great deal to do with assuring quality. The achievement of corrections' larger objectives of rehabilitating prisoners and preparing them for reintegration in the community— ends about which taxpayers as consumers should in theory care a great deal—has foundered for so long in the *public* prison setting that the objectives themselves have ceased to be credible. It is unlikely that privatization can or will have much effect one way or the other on the achievement of these nobler aspirations or on public cynicism about them.

Prisoners' Interests

Though one may encounter on occasion prison inmates who mouth politically inspired views for or against privatized corrections, most of them could not care less about who runs the prisons, under what temporal authority, or by what philosophic mandate. Prisoners' concerns are much more basic: decent conditions, decent services, procedural fairness, and various other rights and privileges of greater or lesser tangibility that they have come to expect as guarantors of their humanity and the limited freedoms they retain despite incarceration. Evidence that privatization leaves these basic things unchanged, or, as in selective cases, improves upon them, suffices to make the privatization proposition acceptable to prisoners.

A number of particular fears about the potential effect of privatization on the management of prisons and prisoners have been raised, however, not so much by prisoners themselves as by various advocacy groups that presume to speak for prisoners' interests.

One of these fears is that private vendors, in an effort to maximize business and profits, will strive to keep the prisons full. On a macro-level, this has been translated into a specter of hordes of private prison lobbyists invading the legislative halls in an effort to persuade lawmakers to enact ever stiffer sentencing policies whose end result would be to keep the prison population volume up even as crime itself goes down (a trend that seems already to have reversed itself in any event). The scenario of the lobbyists, let alone their success in influencing legislation, seems more than a little farfetched.

Somewhat more plausible may be its micro-level corollary that at the facility level prison staff will manipulate the administrative disciplinary process and other discretionary openings to lengthen the inmates' time served. To counter this possibility, the contracts have often left the final authority to take away "good time" with the government entity, which must review all private staff recommendations to this effect.[22]

Another approach, this one more frequently suggested than implemented, is to structure the fee arrangement in such a way as to remove the financial incentive on the part of the private provider to keep the inmates in. Whereas most contracts today provide for per inmate-per diem fees, thus maximizing income to the company when the prison population is at its maximum, the use of flat fees would eliminate this potentially adverse connection, and even serve as an incentive to *reduce* population (and thus costs). Whether the latter is desirable is another matter. The point is that there are a variety of ways to structure the financial terms of the contract to achieve corrections' variable ends and to alleviate stated concerns about management decisions adverse to the prisoners' legitimate interests.

By the same token, fears of abuse by private prison operators of the ultimate authority over prisoners — the authority to use physical force, including lethal force in emergency circumstances — can be dealt with in the contractual arrangement. A proviso that staff shall carry no weapons would give a good measure of assurance against the exercise of lethal force, if not all excessive force. Where weapons are carried or stocked in facilities whose security needs leave little alternative, the contract may provide explicitly for deputization of staff and the necessary training in the use of weapons.

Finally, the contract provides an opportunity to reinforce the general fact that private providers in managing corrections facilities are bound by the strictures of public law, by including relevant portions of it in the specific terms of the contract. In addition, indemnification provisions secure the accountability of both the government and the private provider, giving prisoners a dual target for their legal claims and double protection from being subjected to remediless wrongs.

Private Providers' Interests

Private vendors enter the corrections market to make money, a motive for which they are in this context endlessly, if needlessly, faulted. The evidence, from selective experience of the better established companies, is that this objective can be achieved. Though losses are incurred (and will have to be accepted) in the start-up process of bidding for contracts, staffing facilities and backup service offices, and generally helping to create a legal and political climate that would induce a given jurisdiction to embark on the privatization course, profits can in the long run be realized. It is, however, not a game for the undercapitalized entrepreneur or the fly-by-night company looking for the quick buck.

There are ways to enhance the prospects of success of privatized corrections for the new providers that simultaneously further the interests of the other primary groups. First of all, any bidding and letting of contracts should proceed in a healthy, competitive environment, in which awards go to companies with the best a priori financial and professional credentials and, where applicable, a proven track record. Periodic rebidding, open to the public sector as well as to other private competitors, is essential to the preservation of such an environment. Long-term contracts are anticompetitive. At the same time, agreements of too short a duration only increase instability and costs. For management purposes, a good balance might be contracts that run three or four years. In cases where the private provider has a stake in the financing and construction of the facility, and there is a need for longer-term assurance, the balance can be struck via provisions that allow for a buyout after a set number of years.

The contracts should be adequately specific and tailored to the particular character of the facility in question, so as to promote effective implementation and monitoring. They should not, however, be overly specific in structuring management terms or itemizing costs. Restraint must be exercised in order not to invade the legitimate prerogative of the private provider, which is to save costs (and make a profit) through innovative management and purchasing techniques. Observance of these contracting principles will constrain the potential for unbridled pursuit of profit by unscrupulous entrepreneurs and thereby serve the interests of all parties. In addition, by contractually breaking down prison management into its various component services, the complexity factor that some see as a prohibitive obstacle to the delegation of correctional authority can be substantially reduced.

Public Agencies' Interests

Governmental corrections agencies undoubtedly have genuine, principled concerns relating to the protection of prisoners and the public. But too often, it is self-interest that rules.

Concern over loss of turf can be mitigated by emphasizing that privatization in corrections contemplates a partnership between the public and private sectors, in which public servants will maintain an enduring and important role. Language in the contract on liability and compliance monitoring—that is, on government's retention of both the ultimate and intermediate responsibility for quality corrections—is among the devices available to make this point explicit.

Micro-level concern over loss of line jobs can be alleviated in similar fashion. For example, many of the existing contracts spell out that the private provider must retain all of the public employees who wish to continue working at the facility and that their pension and medical benefits not be reduced. Private companies have been willing to make such strategic concessions for a number of sound institutional reasons. They need to retain a critical mass of the public employees in any event to assure continuity of experience in running the facility. No institution as complex as a prison can be operated by a wholly new staff, no matter how technically competent. Second, initial resignations and subsequent attrition, job reassignments, and the hiring of new employees allow the new provider to mold the staff on the terms it wants and in the image it envisions in comparatively short order.

Finally, unionization and the possibility of employee strikes have been raised as specters clouding the privatization horizon. Two rejoinders are appropriate. One is that public-sector prisons have, as experience shows, not been immune to such eventualities. Second, the contract can be used to deal explicitly with the problem, by way of provisions that strike an appropriate balance between employee rights and institutional imperatives, including the specification of emergency measures in case the worst—a prison employee strike—should happen.

Politicians' Interests

To secure the political feasibility of privatized corrections requires a demonstration of the following: (1) the need for privatization; and (2) its workability in pragmatic *and* political terms.

The need is clear. Public corrections is facing a crisis in space and costs that it is demonstrably unable to solve on its own.[23] The evidence to date, while selective, shows the very real potential for privatization to provide useful solutions to this crisis via improvements in the efficiency and effectiveness of financing, building, and managing prison facilities. These pragmatic advantages are, moreover, matched by the possibility of providing pragmatic assurances—that is, via the contract—that perceived disadvantages to certain of the primary interest groups can be substantially mitigated, if not eradicated. Meanwhile, the legality of involving the private sector in corrections is firmly established in many jurisdictions and is in the process of being secured in others.

There are, however, spokesmen for certain interest groups, as well as independent commentators, who say that the pragmatic gains that may be realized from privatizing corrections are ultimately beside the point—that the real issue is a moral one and that the concept fails by that criterion. Thus, the effort to ensure the political feasibility or salability of private prisons requires participation in the moral debate.[24]

It is difficult to argue against the intuition-centered opposition, such as reflected in the writings of Donahue (1989) and DiIulio (1988). Where the opposition's appeal is primarily to symbols, the seller of privatized corrections may attempt to offer a countervailing symbolism—for example, many special policing functions are performed by private concerns, without apparent objection from the public or public sector; or, citizen participation in crime prevention and crime solving has been touted as a salutary development by people of all political and social persuasions. In other words, privatized security—including punishment, reward and various other pragmatic or ceremonial enforcement trappings—is not inherently objectionable. Also, it would pay to point out that the prisoners themselves do not object, so long as what they regard as their institutional entitlements and privileges are kept intact. Prisoners show little concern about *who* exercises authority over them. What they do not take kindly to is the perceived *abuse* of authority – a perception that does not hinge on the logo on the guard's badge.

Where the opposition essentially reflects an abiding mistrust of the profit motive, some explicit counterarguments are available. The notion that the profit motive and serving the public interest (or running prisons or "doing justice") are fundamentally incompatible is at best naive. It denies the very essence of our political-economic system, of the role of government in our society. It fails to acknowledge that compared to other motives that drive participants in an enterprise – the quest for institutional control, the reach for political power, pursuit of the "convenience motive,"[25] and so forth – the moneymaking motive is among the more benign. It refuses to acknowledge self-interest in all men as economic actors and makes a spurious distinction between economic reward paid out in the form of salaries and that which comes from profit-taking. It even fails, for what it is worth, to account for the reality that many within the profit-taking enterprise – in the prison setting, all operational staff from the lowliest turnkey on up to the warden – are salaried employees. Finally, it is blind to the reality that there are powerful institutional constraints on profiteering at the expense of public values and public service recipients. The costs of mismanaging a prison by undercutting legitimate prisoner rights and services are all too well known from the *non*profit management experience.

Private Management of Secure Prison Facilities: The Final Test?

The large majority of today's private prison management contracts involve facilities of relatively low security. At the same time, a tradition of private-sector participation persists in so-called community corrections – the management of small, decentralized detention centers and homes – that is of substantially longer duration and more widespread.[26] Thus, privatization in the low-security corrections setting is today at the point of becoming an accepted, if not ubiquitous, phenomenon.

As a result, the debate on the merits of the private prisons appears to be devolving into the question of whether entrepreneurs can or should be allowed to meet the real test – the opportunity to manage a large, maximum-security prison.

Opposition to the idea centers on two points. The first is that private companies have shown little interest in managing high-security prisons. The contention is that the leading actors in this new industry prefer to skim the cream off the varying prison population mix. Their motivation – so goes the argument – is that in doing so, they will look good in absolute terms as well as in comparison to the public sector which, left with a rising concentration of hard-core offenders, will look increasingly bad in both the quality with which it performs the task and the costs. The second point is that private companies cannot and (therefore) should not handle the management of high-security prisons.

The opponents are off the mark on both counts. Existing data suggest that government can safely accept private-sector participation in the management of high-security prisons. Experience, though it is limited, shows that the private sector can do it at a cost and quality comparable to that of the government's. And, contrary to the argument that private companies are not willing to enter the high-security prisons' market, several private companies have proposed to do so and in some cases, not all by design, have done so.

Corrections Corporation of America (CCA) proposed to the Tennessee legislature in 1985 that it take over the state's entire corrections system. Earlier, in 1984, the Buckingham Security Company went to the Pennsylvania legislature with a proposal for the construction and management of a 720-bed maximum-security prison at a site near Pittsburgh. Neither of these dramatic proposals survived the legislators' scrutiny.

Nevertheless, a number of privatization instances in situations of comparative high security have materialized. Two large juvenile detention centers housing predominantly hard-core offenders – the Weaversville Intensive Treatment Unit in Pennsylvania and the Okeechobee-Eckerd Youth Development Center in Florida – are today under private management.

In addition, most of the existing county facility contracts obligate the private vendor to accept whatever offenders are brought for detention or incarceration, including dangerous felons. That this can result in substantial numbers of detainees requiring a high level of supervision (i.e., security) as attested to by two facilities managed by the CCA company.

The CCA's Silverdale Detention Center, near Chattanooga, today houses some 120 state felons serving sentences from one to six years among its total population of 360 (33 percent compared to no more than 10 percent at the time of CCA's takeover). Its Bay County Jail in Panama City, Florida, includes a number of prisoners with serious felony charges, including capital crimes. The Butler County Prison in Pennsylvania, formerly managed by the Buckingham Security Company but now back under county control, was specifically designated as a high-security facility and included state and federal prisoners along with local offenders.

The record established by private companies in this setting is by all accounts a good one. Although transitional staffing problems plagued some of the earlier ventures, these have been resolved. Today, the industry has built up a reserve of practical experience and expert personnel that, together with management's practice of retaining the bulk of the facilities' public employees, make it more than adequately equipped to take on the test of high-security corrections.

Lingering doubts about propriety or legality can be dealt with by pointing out that the particular security level of a facility to be privatized makes no difference. If the delegation of correctional authority is proper in Countyville, it cannot be improper in Stateville. Neither are subsidiary concerns about the use of force by private company employees against prisoners any more legitimate when expressed in relation to high-security prisons. The potential for use of force may be greater where the prisoners are more prison-wise and tougher, but the answer to its proper application lies in the experience and humanity of the staff—whether public or private—and in their willingness to submit to the dictates of the law. No one has yet produced evidence that prison employees under private management are deficient in these respects compared to those under public management.

It is thus possible to say today with substantial confidence that the final test of privatized corrections need not come at the expense of the rights and security of the inmates nor of the public.

Notes

1. Imprisonment in this country began as a "private" enterprise, most conspicuously in Pennsylvania where it included the ownership and operation of reformatory facilities by Quaker societies. However, as governments in post-colonial America extended their reach and authority over their populations' social and economic endeavors, the role of private enterprise in corrections correspondingly decreased.

2. Meese, February 1988. The article cites the uprisings at the Oakdale, Louisiana, and Atlanta, Georgia, prisons, the facility damage of which required the transfer of all 2,400 inmates of these facilities, as alone being responsible for a 6 percent jump in the federal overcrowding rate. The 1987 figures have raised the overcrowding rate to 73 percent.

3. There are great differences in the quality of prison institutions both among and within jurisdictions. Some facilities in some states may be quite adequate. Others no doubt continue to operate below minimally acceptable standards. Reductions in quality are not likely to be countenanced in either setting.

4. Meese, February 1988. Estimates have been made that, nationally, prison construction today proceeds at a cost of some $65–70 million *per week* (DeWitt, 1986; Harms and Allen, 1987).

5. Pennsylvania is one of the few states where the side opposing prison privatization has gained the upper hand. The state's legislature three years ago voted to impose a moratorium on further such developments. It also rejected, in 1984, a proposal by the Buckingham Security Company for two regional maximum-security prisons to be built at $21,000 per bed—about one-third the national average for high-security facilities. The legislators' main concern appears to have centered on the question of liability (but see discussion of this issue in this chapter) Grant and Bast (1987:4–5).

6. Privatization in the business of corrections contemplates a *partnership* between the public and private sector, from which both sides may profit. No one has proposed the total abandonment by government of its corrections responsibilities.

7. Under the lease-back method, the government entity sells the property to private investors who then lease it back to the government. This arrangement has been used mainly to finance the renovation of existing facilities. It allows the government to regain its capital investment while providing the private buyers with capital appreciation and federal income tax advantages via depreciation write-offs (Mullen, Chabotar, and Carow, 1985:42).

8. Among the variables influencing the desirability of lease financing over bond-issue financing are interest rates and bond ratings and the fluctuations in these over the time during which the transactions are to occur. See generally, Mullen, Chabotar, and Carow, 1985:33–48.

9. Mullen, Chabotar, and Carow, 1985:47–48, report details of a legal challenge to financing arrangements that seek to avoid public debate and voter approval. The case, a taxpayers' suit, was brought in New York and involved an effort by the state's Urban Development Corporation to circumvent public opposition to increased correctional expenditures (expressed in a failure to support a general obligation bond issue) by resorting to revenue bond financing. (Revenue bonds do not usually require voter approval and, backed by rents paid, are sometimes associated with lease-purchase financing methods.) The taxpayers' challenge was sustained at the trial level, but subsequently dismissed by the state's Court of Appeals.

10. The same point has been made regarding the contract's potential contribution toward increasing accountability/visibility in prison facility management. See Logan, 1987:35, 37.

11. *Tenn. Code Ann.* §41-24-104 (4)(c)(l) and (l)(E) (Michie Co. 1982 and 1987 Supp.). In recently negotiating contracts for the management of 2,000 beds in four new prerelease facilities, the state of Texas required private bidders to submit proposals at 10 percent below public cost projections.

12. The lower figure comes from Grant and Bast (1987); the higher one from the Massachusetts Legislative Research Council (1987).

13. At the Silverdale facility, cca saves the county between $1.00 to $1.70 per inmate per day (depending on yearly fluctuations), which at the full capacity of 360 inmates comes to $130,000 to $220,000 per year on an annual total budget of some $3.5 million. These savings are even more impressive when compared against average regional costs. The cca charges Hamilton County $21.00–$22.00 per inmate per diem, while the average management cost for jails in the Eastern south central states is reported to be $30. [*Corrections Compendium* 11 (November 1986):12]. The manner and extent to which the Silverdale facility deviates from the average jail is not readily determinable. With 30 percent of the facility's population classified as felony convicts, Silverdale's security and inmate services/programming levels are likely to be, if anything, above average. The $1.6 million in renovations and new construction performed by cca at Silverdale also help tip the balance further in the company's favor; it has resulted in what is in all likelihood an above-average physical plant at no capital costs to the county government.

14. This information is from cca news releases and from the company's quarterly reports to its shareholders.

15. The literature identifies other legal issues, such as liability, use of force, and contract specificity, but these are really only subsidiary to the authority issue (see this text).

16. Two of the most vocal groups opposing prison privatization are the American Federation of State, County, and Municipal Employees (afscme) and the American Civil Liberties Union (aclu), in particular its National Prison Project. The self-interest inherent in the afscme's position should be self-evident. The aclu's turf is public corrections, whose deficiencies are the subject of its constant challenge. This posture of legal opposition, however, at the same time breeds a strong identification and binding ties with the public enterprise.

17. 18 U.S.C.A. §4082(b) (West 1985).

18. 589 F. Supp. 1028 (S.D. Tex. 1984).

19. For example, up until recently the law of Maryland provided that "State employees shall perform all state functions within state operated facilities in preference to contracting with the private sector for the performance of those functions" (MD. Ann. Code 21 §18-802 91981), as cited in Hackett, Hatry, Levinson, Allen, Chi, and Feigenbaum (1987).

20. But see DiIulio (1988), criticizing the tactic of invoking in this debate—out of context, he implies—the names or maxims of "some famous, long-dead writers."

21. The possibility that force may be used by private corrections officials against prisoners is often raised by opponents of privatization as a separate legal obstacle to the concept's legitimacy. The matter is, however, essentially inseparable from the primary issue of authority to delegate, which, if resolved in favor of the private prison concept, disposes of the use-of-force issue as well. The behavior of prison officials, public or private, is circumscribed by public law and regulation, private contract, and, where necessary, even by agency law (deputization).

22. This evasion of final authority may be a bit of a charade, as the government reviewers are likely to have little choice but to rubberstamp the disciplinary recommendations. A better safeguard is the reality that private prison staff could not get away with such manipulations, and that it is not in their interest to try. See this chapter on the costs of mismanagement.

23. Some commentators have argued that there is no need and no point to building more prisons, that we need to look to *nonincarceration* alternatives as the solution, since increasing confinement capacities only leads to higher incarceration rates, without relieving overcrowding. The counterargument is that governments of virtually all levels across the nation have decided that the need *is* for more space and that it ought to be met. Given this position, the question is how best to do it.

24. DiIulio (1988) for one, identifies the propriety issue as the "most interesting, challenging and important" in the prison privatization debate.

25. See Logan (1987:39) for discussion of what he calls the "convenience motive," emphasizing its prevalence and its essentially asocial and self-interested character.

26. State and local governments have followed this pattern for decades, and more recently the federal government has joined in this trend. The Federal Bureau of Prisons, which has been hesitant about privatizing its larger adult facilities, has over the last several years contracted out the majority of its 300-plus "community treatment centers."

References

Brakel, S. J. (1988a). "Prison Management, Private Enterprise Style: The Inmates' Evaluation." *N.E.J. on Crim. and Civ. Confinement* 14:175.

_____ (1988b). "Privatization in Corrections: Radical Prison Chic or Mainstream Americana?" *N.E.J. on Crim. and Civ. Confinement* 14:1.

Butler, (1986). "Privatizing Federal Services: A Primer." *Heritage Foundation Backgrounder* (February).

Chaiken, M., and J. Chaiken (1987). *Public Policing—Privately Provided.* Washington, DC: National Institute of Justice, U.S. Department of Justice (June).

DeWitt, Charles B. (1986). "New Construction Methods for Correctional Facilities." Construction Bulletin. National Institute of Justice, U.S. Department of Justice (March).

DiIulio, J. (1988). "Private Prisons." *Crime File Study Guide.* National Institute of Justice, U.S. Department of Justice.

_____ (1988). "What's Wrong with Private Prisons." *The Public Interest* 92 (Summer).

Donahue, J. (1989). *The Privatization Decision: Public Ends, Private Means.* New York: Basic Books.

Grant, J., and D. Bast (1987). "Corrections and the Private Sector: A Guide for Public Officials." Heartland Institute. Policy Study No. 15 (May).

Hackett, H. Hatry, Levinson, Allen, Chi, and Feigenbaum (1987). Issues in Contracting for the Private Operation of Prisons and Jails." *Report of the Council of State Governments and the Urban Institute* (February).

Harms, and Allen (1987). "Privatizing Prisons." *American City and County* (August).

Logan, C. (1987). "The Propriety of Proprietary Prisons." *Federal Probation* 51 (September).

———— (1988). "Privatization and Corrections: A Bibliography." Storns: University of Connecticut.

Massachusetts Legislative Research Council (1987). *Report Relative to Prisons for Profit.* House No. 6225 (July).

Meese, (1988). "Why We Need More Federal Prisons" (February 1988). *Chicago Tribune.*

Mullen, J., K. Chabotar, and D. Carow (1985). *The Privatization of Corrections.* Washington, DC: National Institute of Justice, U.S. Department of Justice.

Pennsylvania General Assembly (1985). "Report on a Study of Issues Related to the Potential Operation of Private Prisons in Pennsylvania. Report of Legislative Budget and Finance Committee" (October).

President's Commission on Privatization Report (1988). (March).

Robbins, Ira P. (1986). "Privatization of Corrections: Defining the Issues." *Judicature* 69 (April–May): 325–31.

U. S. Department of Justice (1988). *Sourcebook of Criminal Justice Statistics.* Washington, DC: Bureau of Justice Statistics.

21. The Privatization of Jails: A Management Perspective

Richard Kiekbusch

In recent years there has been much discussion of privatization as a possible solution to the nation's increasingly severe shortage of jail and prison bedspace. The principal issues have been: (1) whether privatization is cheaper; (2) in given jurisdictions, whether privatization is legal; and (3) whether it is proper for the government to contract its responsibility to operate correctional institutions to private, for-profit companies.

One perspective from which privatization is not often discussed is that of corrections management. By a corrections management perspective I mean a set of beliefs which are held by the managers of a particular jurisdiction in regard to the proper management of correctional institutions and the inmates who reside in them. Can private companies manage correctional institutions and their inmates in accordance with the particular jurisdiction's corrections management perspective? In other words, can private companies do the essential work of institutional corrections the way knowledgeable public-sector practitioners think it ought to be done? This is an issue separate from whether privatization is economical, legal, or proper.

What follows is a discussion of privatization from a corrections management perspective with respect to local jails, as opposed to federal and state prisons. A series of questions are raised which should be addressed by any sheriff's office, Department of Corrections, or other local corrections authority which is contemplating contracting the operation of its jail to a private firm. In the first section the difference between jails and prisons is explained. In the second section the definition and importance of a corrections management perspective are considered. In the third section I define some of the essential elements of a corrections management perspective and pose some questions regarding a private company's ability to address those elements in its operation of a jail. In the final section some conclusions are drawn.

My personal opinions do not necessarily represent the official positions of the Prince William–Manassas (Virginia) Regional Adult Detention Center, of which I am superintendent, or the American Jail Association, of which I am president-elect.

275

Jails Versus Prisons

Jails are correctional institutions used to house two types of persons: (1) those charged with, but not yet convicted of, criminal offenses (pretrial detainees); and (2) those serving short sentences, ordinarily less than a year and usually for misdemeanor offenses.

Prisons, on the other hand, are correctional institutions used to house persons sentenced to longer terms which are ordinarily a year or more and usually for felony offenses. Jails which number over 3,000 are most often county facilities, although some of our larger cities run their own jails. Prisons which number in the hundreds are administered by the states or the federal government. Most jails are run by sheriffs although in some jurisdictions they are run by executive branch correctional agencies independent of the sheriff's office. Prisons are usually operated by executive branch correctional agencies.

Two of the primary differences between jails and prisons are: (1) jails house large numbers of pretrial detainees as well as sentenced prisoners, while prisons house only sentenced prisoners; and (2) jails receive the bulk of their prisoners right off the street shortly after arrest, while prison inmates ordinarily arrive at the prison after they have done considerable jail time as pretrial detainees and after they have undergone at least some diagnostic assessment.

There are many similarities in the management of jail and prison facilities and inmates. Some characteristics unique to jail inmate populations include the presence of large numbers of pretrial detainees (to whom a higher constitutional standard applies), the presence of large numbers of recently arrested inmates about whom relatively little is known, and the relatively short lengths of stay of many jail inmates and the consequent high turnover in jail inmate populations. Because of these unique characteristics, a local corrections authority which is contemplating contracting the operation of its jail to a private firm should pose these questions: How much experience has the firm had in running local jails and how successful has it been? How much successful public-sector jail management experience has the firm's executive and line-level managers had?

Corrections Management Perspective

A correctional organization, public or private, has a corrections management perspective when the following things are true:

1. Priorities: The organization has a set of clearly established priorities. Priorities are simply the purposes for which the organization exists, rank ordered in terms of their relative importance. Some of the purposes for which correctional institutions including local jails exist are institution security, inmate and staff safety, inmate rehabilitation, and public safety.

2. Definition: The organization's priorities are clearly defined. This is very important because something like "institutional security" might mean one thing to the

sheriff or other chief executive, another to the line deputy or correctional officer, and yet another to the legislative funding body or general public.

3. Communication: The established priorities are consistently and repetitively communicated to all staff—executive staff and department heads, midlevel supervisors, and line-level workers (e.g., officers, nurses, food service staff). Vehicles for such communication include pre- and in-service training, policy and procedure manuals, and job descriptions.

4. Decision: All decisions, both those made at the executive level and those made by line staff, are made in accordance with the established priorities.

5. Supervision: The job performance of every staff member is continuously evaluated with respect to accomplishment of the organization's priorities. Did the nursing supervisor or food service director do something to further or compromise institutional security? Did a department head make a decision which unnecessarily interfered with inmate rehabilitative programming? Employees receive feedback on their job performance vis-à-vis the organization's priorities. This takes place on a routine, informal basis and also through periodic formal performance evaluations.

It is particularly important for a correctional organization, including a local jail, to have a clearly conceived and implemented corrections management perspective for the following reasons:

1. Internally, jails are highly interrelated organizations. What goes on in one area or department generally affects all other areas and departments. Unless a carefully articulated corrections management perspective prevails, sections and individuals may wind up working at cross purposes, sometimes with serious and dangerous consequences. The food service or medical department, for example, might unknowingly institute practices which dilute or offset security-related initiatives being undertaken by classification or security staff.

2. Externally the jail is part of the local criminal justice system for which the parts are highly interrelated. In the absence of a clearly articulated and communicated corrections management perspective, the jail's policies, procedures, and practices might interfere with the operations of the other justice agencies and the justice system in general. For example, ambiguities and inconsistencies in the jail's practices regarding inmate visitation and telephone communication might needlessly frustrate pretrial services staff, the prosecution, and the defense bar, all of whom need access to the inmate population.

3. The consequencs of error and confusion in a jail are often very serious and frequently health- or life-threatening. The absence of a well-established corrections management perspective increases the risk of homicides, suicides, assaults, escapes, destruction of property, and other tragedies. It also increases the likelihood of expensive litigation which frequently follows in the wake such tragedies.

Given the above, a corrections authority which is contemplating contracting the operation of its jail to a private firm should pose these questions: What is our corrections management perspective? Does the firm have a corrections management perspective of its own? Is the firm's corrections management perspective compatible with ours?

Some Elements of a Corrections Management Perspective

Every correctional organization must develop its own corrections management perspective, identifying and rank ordering its priorities as the organization's leadership deems appropriate. I suggest that at least four priorities should be included in the corrections management perspective of any local jail, be it publicly or privately run, and that these four priorities be rank ordered as follows:

1. Institutional security;
2. Staff and inmate safety;
3. Institutional and inmate hygiene;
4. Inmate Rehabilitative Programs.

I suggest the above rank ordered jail priorities for the following reasons: (1) Control: In order for a jail to run effectively, the administration must be in control. The administration must have continuous and unquestioned control of the institution and its inmates. The administration is not truly in control unless it can, at all times, ensure institutional *security*, staff and inmate *safety*, and institutional and inmate *hygiene* (priorities 1, 2, and 3 above). Without administration control, nothing else is possible, including the provision of successful inmate rehabilitative programs (e.g., education, substance abuse counseling, vocational training, jail industries). (2) Rehabilitation: Given the fact that a jail's administration has total control over its inmates' existences for extended periods of time, it incurs an obligation to provide those inmates with opportunities to change their behavior and improve their lives, to run rehabilitative programs (priority 4 above). Aside from strictly humanitarian reasons, the provisions of rehabilitative programs makes sound fiscal sense, for well-run rehabilitative programs reduce the likelihood of recidivism, of an expensive return trip to jail, for at least some of the inmate population. I will suggest some questions which should be posed by any local corrections authority which is contemplating contracting the operation of its jail to a private firm. These priorities are, of course, related to one another and some of the questions apply to more than one priority:

Institutional Security

In its simplest terms, jail security means that inmates stay in and contraband stays out. Security is the single most important purpose for which jails exist.

1. How many staff will be employed and what kind of positions will they fill?
2. Specifically, how many will be correctional officers?
3. How will staff, particularly the correctional officers, be recruited and screened?
4. How will staff, again particularly the corrections officers, be deployed in the institution?
5. Will correctional officers receive training and supervision in the proper methods of watching, counting, and searching inmates?
6. How will staff other than correctional officers be trained and supervised with respect to security concerns?

7. How will volunteers be used and how will they be screened and then trained and supervised with respect to security concerns?

8. What kind of classification system does the firm use?

9. Specifically, how are inmates assigned custody levels and housing locations and what provisions are there for periodically reviewing custody levels and housing assignments and reclassifying inmates as necessary?

10. How will inmate housing units be supervised—direct supervision, indirect supervision, a combination of these?

11. What are the rules of conduct for inmates and how will these be communicated and enforced.

12. Will public visitation be contact or noncontact?

13. How about attorney and other professional visitation?

14. Does the firm have its own emergency response unit?

Staff and Inmate Safety

Basically, jail safety means inmates do not hurt staff or each other and staff do not hurt or abuse inmates. It is second in importance only to security as a purpose for which jails exist.

1. How has the firm answered the "institutional security" questions regarding staffing, classification, and supervision of inmate housing units?

2. What means will inmates have to communicate concerns and complaints to staff—formal grievance system, informal communication, or both?

3. In what manner will inmate concerns and complaints be addressed?

4. Will correctional officers receive training and supervision in interpersonal and listening skills?

5. Will correctional officers receive training and supervision in the proper methods of physical restraint and self-defense?

6. How does the firm plan to handle internal affairs investigations?

Institutional and Inmate Hygiene

This means that the jail is kept in a clean and orderly condition and that inmates are required to practice proper personal hygiene. Institutional hygiene is important for the health and welfare of staff and inmates alike and also reflects and instills a sense of pride in the institution among staff and even some inmates. Inmate hygiene, like institutional hygiene, is important for the health and welfare of staff and inmates and also requires the inmates to practice healthful self-care habits which some of them will continue to practice following release.

1. What will be expected of the inmates with respect to keeping housing and activity areas in a clean and orderly condition and how will these expectations be communicated and enforced?

2. What will be expected of staff with respect to keeping the jail in a clean and orderly condition and how will these expectations be communicated and enforced?

Inmate Rehabilitative Programs

These are programs of which the principal objectives give inmates the chance to enhance their skills and improve their lives and to reduce the likelihood of costly recidivism among at least some of the inmate population. Among the secondary benefits of such programs are a reduction in inmate idleness and, where participation is conditioned upon good behavior, an incentive among the inmates to adhere to institutional rules and regulations. Among the more common inmate rehabilitative programs are education, vocational training, and substance abuse counseling.

1. What programs will be offered?

2. Who will offer these programs — staff, volunteers, community agencies, or a combination?

3. How will the scheduling and delivery of these programs be coordinated with other routines and activities in the institution, particularly these related directly to security?

4. How will those persons who deliver the programs be trained and supervised with respect to security concerns?

5. How will inmates be selected for participation and what will be required of them to remain in the programs?

6. What will be the relationship between program participation and inmate behavior?

Conclusions

As we move into the 1990s, privatization continues to be examined as a possible solution to the growing national need for more jail and prison bed space. As local jail officials consider the privatization option, they should not confine themselves to the more frequently discussed fiscal, legal, and philosophical considerations. Local officials should also purposefully articulate their respective corrections management perspectives and then attempt to determine whether the private firms with whom they are talking or negotiating can operate their jails in a manner which is compatible with those management perspectives. At a minimum, the corrections management elements to be addressed should include institutional security, staff and inmate safety, institutional and inmate hygiene, and inmate rehabilitative programs.

22. The Public Sector's Responsibilities in Privatizing Court Related and Correctional Services

Robert J. Gemignani

The increasing involvement of business and industry in government programs is a growing phenomenon in American society. Advocates for increased business involvement argue that private-sector/public-sector collaboration to remedy pervasive social problems, such as crime and delinquency, is needed because these problems have proven to be resistive to change, and because government increasingly lacks the resources (tax dollars) to deal with them. The opening of a partnership with the business community expands the resources available to combat these problems. Private-sector resources include management skills, planning and information technology, budget and accounting skills, and pools of potential volunteers. Private businesses can also be called upon to manage and operate government services. This latter use of the private sector is most often referred to as *privatization* or *contracting out*.

Successful privatization of government services depends on government's awareness and knowledge about the intricacies of contracting out services heretofore performed by public employees. If privatization is to be a successful experience, government must pay particular attention to the critical detail involved in the privatization process. This critical detail is discussed below as it affects the three major phases of privatization.

Preparation Phase

Public administrators are advised to focus particular attention on this initial phase for privatizing government services. A *rush* to contract should be avoided at all costs. This is difficult advice to heed since public administrators may feel forced to contract when faced with growing pressures to provide effective human services while cutting costs. Converting specific public services to private-sector operations is an option available to them. How does the public administrator know that privatization of a specific service will result in increased efficiency at a lower cost? What types of data and information can be used confidently to decide to contract?

Services to be contracted must be subjected to careful and thorough analysis. Problems inherent in the way the services are currently provided must be identified and remedied to enable improved service delivery at a favorable cost.

As every good manager knows, a decision is only as good as the data upon which it is based. The writer studied the data-gathering experiences of several probation departments wrestling with the possibility of contracting in response to shrinking budgets and to political demands for increasing the effectiveness of services. This experience revealed that successful privatization of government services hinges on the ability of government to obtain and to use effectively five distinct types of data: (1) cost; (2) organizational and service; (3) legal and liability; (4) procurement; and (5) environmental.

Cost Data

Ask a chief probation officer what it costs for his or her department to provide intake services. Ask a corrections administrator what it costs to operate a specific treatment facility. Ask a sheriff to give you the costs associated with transportation of prisoners. More often than not, they will be unable to identify the *real* costs of these services. The best they can offer is the line item in their budgets which reflects these particular services. But each service incurs costs which are often contained in the budgets of other agencies. For example, a separate department of general services may be responsible for some or all overhead expenses associated with a particular service. Consequently, the chief probation officer's budget for providing intake services may not include costs associated with telephones, duplicating equipment, automobiles, rent, etc. There are also other less visible costs such as those involving employee benefits. These costs can be both direct and indirect. A major problem, for instance, is the cost of nonfunded benefits such as the department's pension plan.

The contracting of specific government services, such as the ones noted above, requires accurate knowledge of what the service currently costs to operate. This is important for the following reasons:

1. It is needed when drafting a request for proposals. Unless the *real costs* of the services to be contracted are known and used in the RFP (Request for Proposal), unrealistic expectations may be asked of potential contractors. For example, if a corrections administrator plans to privatize a treatment facility under the premise that the cost of operating the facility should not exceed the level of funding for that facility in the department's budget, unrealistic expectations may be created. This would be particularly true, for instance, if some of the costs of operating the facility are subsumed in another department's budget. Failure to use precise cost data discourages capable private contractors from submitting proposals, and results in government and contractor conflicts when contracts are awarded under unrealistic cost constraints.

2. It assists in conducting cost comparisons. Good cost data allow precise comparisons of what it costs government to provide a specific service vis-à-vis what it costs the private sector to provide the same service. Cost data also allow a com-

parison of the current costs of services with the cost of the same services redesigned to enhance their performance. Finally, precise cost data allow for cost comparisons to be made in respect to specific elements within a contracted service. For example, if a detention center were privatized, it would be possible to isolate and compare public-sector versus private-sector costs associated with such elements as food service and general maintenance.

3. It assists in identifying issues/problems relative to cost. Cost data highlight problems on how resources are currently allocated. For instance, the costs for food services in a detention center may be inordinately high. The causes may be varied, such as purchasing from high-priced vendors or buying small quantities of staples, when purchasing in bulk may be more cost effective. Potential contractors should be asked to specify, for instance, their anticipated costs for providing such things as food services in a privatized detention center. Knowing what government is currently paying for this service and being aware of any cost problems will assist in constructive negotiations with the potential contractor and ultimately result in an efficient and cost-effective service.

Organizational and Service Data

In planning to remodel a house the characteristics and qualities of the present structure are first assessed. So should it be when planning to privatize a government service. A review of the existing system is basic to any consideration of its alteration. What are the strengths of the current system? What are its weaknesses? Who are its employees and what roles do they play? Who are its clients and what does it provide them? Answers to questions such as these will yield the data necessary to understand the elements of a specific service and the scope of its operations. These data, together with the cost data, begin to paint a comprehensive portrait of the service considered for contracting. Possessing such knowledge is important for the following reasons: (1) It assists in identifying critical organizational and service elements involved in privatizing. For example, the data not only will reveal the specific staff positions which will be directly affected but also will identify those staff within the larger department who provide indirect support or ancillary services. While general administrative support from the parent agency may not be an appropriate function to contract, the contractor should still be asked how his operation intends to acquire such support services and the costs involved; and (2) it offers a glimpse of the strengths and weaknesses of the current system. Having such knowledge is important whether or not a decision to contract is ultimately made. Together with other data elements, this information is useful when considering improvements in how the services are provided. Certainly it is important to eliminate the weaknesses early and not perpetuate them when the service is privatized.

Legal and Liability Data

State penal codes, welfare and institutions codes, and other state and local ordinances may impact on attempts to privatize correctional services. Such laws and regulations must be analyzed, including their legislative history and interpretation. It is not uncommon to find the *intent* of a statute misinterpreted, resulting in a barrier to privatization. Questions relating to public-sector liability for harms resulting from actions by private contractors also must be clearly answered. Legal and liability data are important for the following reasons:

1. Data assist in identifying barriers to privatization. Early identification of such barriers is important, so that they can be removed before a decision to privatize moves blindly ahead. Some barriers may be difficult to resolve. This is true, for example, when there is legislation specifically prohibiting contracting certain types of government functions. On the other hand, policy and administrative barriers are easier to resolve.

2. Data assist in identifying support for privatization. Laws, regulations, policies, and procedures may also exist which will facilitate a decision to privatize. Knowing what these are will be an advantage to government when arguing for privatization.

3. Data assist in identifying liability issues. What types of liability will government assume when it privatizes a particular service? This is a question which must be addressed head-on. Understanding potential exposures helps to determine what should be asked of a contractor to insulate government from the possibility of lawsuits. It also helps to determine the nature and size of the bonding to be required of the contractor.

Procurement Data

It is surprising at times to note the chasm which exists in a corrections administrator's knowledge between program issues and business issues, such as those related to procurement policies and procedures. In one privatization experience a probation administrator had planned to contract a specific function within six months. When it took eighteen months to conclude the process, problems began to ensue. The administrator had little knowledge of the many hoops he would have to jump through to effect a contract. In this case procurement activities for his agency were mostly the responsibility of a separate office over which he had no control. Knowing how one's procurement process works and identifying issues in the mechanism for contracting is critical. Obtaining such data will:

1. Provide assistance in the process for contracting. How long does it take from the time one decides to contract to the actual execution of the contract? Who is responsible for the development of the request for proposals and for the RFP's statement of work? Who is responsible for inclusion of standard "boiler plate" language required in a jurisdiction's RFPs? Who is responsible for advertising the solicitation and what procedures must be followed? Questions such as these must be answered early in the procurement process. Many jurisdictions have complex and slow procurement procedures which can affect the process of privatization. It is important for a corrections administrator to understand what he or she faces in order to make realistic time-line decisions and to short-cut identified bottlenecks in the process.

2. Help identify procurement barriers. A good example of a procurement barrier is a policy that a contract must be awarded to the lowest bidder. Such a policy may be acceptable when shopping for janitorial services. However, in the provision of human services such a policy could be disastrous. Identifying procurement barriers early on will provide an opportunity to remedy them before it is too late.

Environmental Data

Privatization stirs deep emotions in many individuals. Oftentimes these emotions are founded on unrealistic fears. Employees fear loss of jobs. Administrators fear loss of turf and influence. Most fear change itself. Such fears are the biggest barriers to privatization. Most fears result from misinformation and or lack of information and data. Consequently, it is important to obtain sound environmental data. Individuals and groups favorable to privatization must be identified and enlisted. Individuals and groups who hold unfavorable views should also be identified and should be given information and data to allay their fears. Environmental data will:

1. Prevent corrections administrators from being blindsided. Good environmental data will identify individuals and groups opposed to privatization and will reveal the nature of their opposition. This will allow an opportunity to provide them with relevant information to diffuse their concerns.

2. Identify centers of support. Environmental data will also reveal individuals and groups who are supportive of contracting government services. Their assistance may be needed.

3. Anticipate positive and negative fallout. The environmental data should determine the political and administrative ramifications of privatization. For instance, in a strong labor community, privatization could result in a negative reaction toward elected officials. On the other hand, privatization can result in positive political benefits for elected officials. Being able to gauge the political impact will enable the public administrator to make the proper decisions and to confront opposition with reason and with appropriate data.

A final step in the preparation phase for the contracting out of government services is to consider the redesign of those services prior to their being privatized. One does not have to mirror in an RFP how a service is currently being provided. Contracting offers an opportunity to change things which may have been difficult to change earlier due, in part, to the intractability of government bureaucracy. Armed with the data elements discussed above, a redesign of the function to be contracted can result in its being operated with increased efficiency and cost effectiveness, once it is privatized.

Contracting Phase

The second major phase in the privatization process involves the actual contracting of the service to the private sector. If sufficient attention has been paid to those steps discussed above under the preparation phase, contracting should run smoothly. Unfortunately, attempts at privatization too often move immediately into the contract phase with almost no preparation. Such abrupt attempts at privatization have a high potential for failure. Since opposition to the concept of privatizing government services is often an emotional subject, failures merely fuel irrational fears. This is unfortunate, particularly when such failures can be avoided.

The contracting phase begins with the issuing of a request for proposals, continues with the review of proposals, moves to developing and negotiating the contract document, and concludes with the steps involved in an orderly transfer of functions to the private sector. Each element of the contracting phase is discussed briefly below.

Request for Proposals

The RFP is the instrument by which a governmental agency solicits private-sector contractors who possess the capability to provide the services to be privatized. The RFP is the initiating document which sets in motion a series of events in the contracting phase of the privatization process. The ability to draft a comprehensive and logical RFP is essential to successful contracting. An inferior document will only elicit inferior proposals. The data elements discussed earlier in the preparation phase provide the knowledge needed to draft a good RFP.

The RFP will attract or discourage potential contractors. Therefore, it must clearly state the services desired and the contractual terms and conditions related to the function to be privatized. The RFP establishes the legal framework within which the contract must be fulfilled. It assures that each potential contractor has the same understanding of the nature and scope of the services to be privatized, and has the same information as to what a potential contractor is required to furnish the government.

Review of Proposals

State laws and local ordinances vary in their provisions concerning criteria for evaluating a potential contractor's services. Regardless, an expert review of proposals, submitted to the government for the privilege of operating what is currently a public service, is an essential part of the process toward successful privatization.

All proposals should receive an objective and technical review. A major principle for reviewing contract proposals is that merit is best determined by expert reviewers from relevant disciplines and professions. Yet, government too often relies on reviewers who lack the depth of knowledge and experience in the service to be privatized.

A second major principle is that effective proposal review procedures which ensure the integrity of the review process should protect against information being provided to any potential contractor which may place that contractor in a preferential position.

Developing and Negotiating the Contract Document

Once a contractor has been chosen to operate the privatized function, a binding agreement (contract) between the government and the private-sector operator must be developed. This binding agreement is usually in the form of a contract. The contract document is a technically drawn and legal record to evidence the terms and conditions to be established between the concerned parties. The ability to draft a thorough and comprehensive contract document is paramount to a successful contracting phase of the privatization process.

A second major activity, once the contract document has been drafted, is negotiating its terms and conditions. The government must protect itself by assuring that the contractor agrees to perform the privatized function as envisioned. The terms and conditions of the contract specify the general parameters within which the contractor agrees to abide. In some instances the terms and conditions will also detail specific program agreements. However, government should refrain from too much specificity that it constrains the private-sector contractor from using its ingenuity to provide an appropriate level of service. In the negotiating process the private contractor seeks to assure itself that all terms and conditions are realistic and do not place an undue burden on its operations. A successful privatization experience must guarantee that the legitimate concerns of the public are safeguarded, and that the creativity and the operations of the private-sector contractor are not stifled.

Transfer of Functions to the Private Sector

The orderly transfer of functions previously performed by government to the private sector is the final step in the contracting phase of the privatization process. It is a step which is too frequently ignored. All too often government takes on a surreal posture and assumes that things will take care of themselves. Failure to pay attention to the details involved in transferring personnel, materials, and responsibilities to the private contractor will inevitably result in confusion and in loss of momentum.

Decisions on personnel, for instance, need to be made quickly and wisely. Which government personnel will be affected? For those that are, will they be offered the *right of first refusal,* early retirement, or transfer within the government? Will the contractor be required to pay those government employees it hires the same salaries they are currently earning? These are only some of the questions about personnel that must be addressed.

There are additional concerns that need to be dealt with. Clients must be made aware of the change in service provider. Other agencies and the general public must be notified of the change. Case files and other confidential information may need to be transferred and safeguarded. If government property is involved, the proper procedures must be established for its transfer or its use by the private contractor. And staff training must be conducted to familiarize everyone with the new policies and procedures.

Monitoring Phase

The final phase in the privatization process is monitoring contract performance. Unlike many other public functions which have been privatized, court related and corrections services require continuing governmental responsibility. For instance, when a local unit of government privatizes trash collection or public transportation services, tax dollars are no longer used to finance the service. The private provider charges the individual household to pick up the garbage, and the local private transportation service ultimately realizes its profits entirely from rider revenues. On the other hand, corrections programs continue to be primarily financed by public funds. What has changed is how the service is being delivered, not how it is being paid for. Consequently, government is still intimately involved in safeguarding the tax payers' dollars. Also, under our form of government the ultimate responsibility for arrestees, defendants, probationers, prisoners, and parolees remains with the government. Nothing prohibits the government bureaucrat from contracting with a private agency to provide housing and services for these individuals. However, it is doubtful that government can also relinquish responsibility and the ultimate liability for individuals enmeshed in our court and correctional systems. Therefore, the public sector must also be able to monitor program performance, as well as monitoring cost containment.

At issue is the ability of the public sector to assume contract monitoring functions. Experience shows that local and state governments vary substantially in this critical capability. Few are adept at it. Yet failure to monitor effectively shortchanges the judiciary and the profession of corrections. More so, it shortchanges taxpayers, victims of crime, and the perpetrators themselves. Government, therefore, must learn to establish realistic standards and measurable indicators for monitoring the performance of the private contractor. It must be able to do so without undue interference in the affairs of the private contractor and without imposing unnecessary and bureaucratic red tape.

Conclusion

Is the privatization of court related and correctional facilities and services an accepted concept, and will the involvement of the private sector continue to grow? The answer to both parts of this question is *yes*. But not because government has become enamored with the concept. The private sector will continue to make headway because government can no longer provide adequate services on its own. As state and local coffers increasingly resound with a hollow thud, government must scramble to provide an acceptable level of services with little or no increase in tax revenues. More and more the answer is to *redesign* public services and to *reallocate* existing resources. The private sector offers a vast reservoir of opportunities to provide public services in new and innovative ways. As government learns to use these new opportunities better, it will convert rapidly from the *provider* of services to the *monitor* of private-sector service providers. Privatization, however, is not an easy task to do well. Careful attention must be paid to each phase in the privatization process discussed earlier. When it is done well, the resulting public/private partnership improves America's ability to provide court related and correctional services of which it can be proud.

23. The Economics of Privatizing Criminal Justice Facilities

Robert S. Guzek, C.M.C.

This chapter describes the three general types of privatization transactions and the savings which may be associated with them. The transactions are differentiated by the sector which assumes responsibility for the ownership and operation of the assets. If the assets are owned by the public sector but operated by the private sector, an Operations and Maintenance (*O and M*) Contract would describe the transaction. If the assets are owned by the private sector but operated by the public sector, a Lease Contract would result. Finally, if the assets are both owned and operated by the private sector, then the transaction would be characterized as a Service Contract.

Transfer of facility operations responsibility to the private sector under an operation and maintenance contract has been successfully carried out in a variety of infrastructure areas in communities across the country. The key economic advantage of this type of transaction is that the private-sector firm can spread overhead costs over a network of facilities, which can lower the unit cost of service in individual communities. In addition, profit-motivated private managers tend to devote extra attention to operational efficiency which results in sustained pressure on cost reduction and containment. Communities which have entered into operation and maintenance contracts with reputable private-sector firms can typically secure significant reductions in the unit cost of service.

The second type of privatization transaction, namely, the transfer of facility ownership to the private sector under a lease contract, introduces certain tax advantages which can be evoked by profit-making, private-sector firms. Depending on the type of assets involved, there are prescribed periods and methods for depreciation which, together with other permissible tax deductions, create legitimate tax shelters which can be used to defer tax payments to later years. It should be pointed out that amendments to recent federal tax legislation have impacted the economic advantage of this type of transaction. Under current tax law, leases of assets to nontaxpaying entities cause the depreciation period to be lengthened as compared to the typical periods and force the use of straight line depreciation as compared to accelerated methods.

The third type of privatization transaction which involves private-sector ownership and operation under the terms of a service contract offers the greatest

Table 23.1 Comparison of Public and Private Ownership

	Public Ownership of Facility	Private Ownership of Facility
Cost of construction	$100,000,000	$ 80,000,000[1]
Engineering/legal cost	7,500,000[2]	6,000,000[2]
Contingency cost	5,375,000[3]	4,300,000[3]
Cost of land acquisition	5,000,000	5,000,000
Underwriters fees	8,094,000[4]	4,573,000[4]
Debt service reserve	16,488,000[5]	13,427,000[5]
Interest cost during construction	19,426,000[6]	13,718,000[7]
Total project cost	$161,883,000	$127,018,000
Total debt	$161,883,000	$114,316,000
Total equity	–	12,702,000
Construction period	3 Years	2.4 Years[8]
Term of bonds	20 Years	20 Years
Interest rate on bonds	8% (tax exempt)	10% (taxable)
Targeted annual after tax rate of return on equity investment	–	10%
Depreciation period	–	31 1/2 Years
Depreciation method	–	Straight line

[1] Construction savings of 20 percent reflect a more "modular" design approach and a reduction of public sector administrative requirements.

[2] Represents 7.5 percent of the cost of construction.

[3] Represents 5 percent of the sum of construction and engineering/legal costs

[4] Represents 5 percent of issued debt.

[5] Represents 1 year's debt service on issued debt.

[6] Based on assumed interest rate of 8 percent (tax exempt) and 3-year construction period.

[7] Based on assumed interest rate of 10 percent (taxable) and 2.4-year construction period.

[8] Reduction in construction period of 20 percent reflects fast-tracking of construction by private-sector firm.

economic advantage to a community. In the first instance, all of the operational cost savings described previously under the operations and maintenance contract would apply. Secondly, unlike the lease contract, a service contract permits the use of advantageous depreciation periods and methods (provided tax-exempt financing is not utilized to finance the facility which, from a practical perspective, is increasingly unlikely in light of the restrictive caps which have been imposed on such financing under recent federal tax legislation). The bottom line impact of a properly structured service contract is typically a significant reduction in the unit cost of service.

The benefits of permitting private-sector ownership and or operation of criminal justice facilities via privatization fall into two categories: (1) needed criminal justice facilities can typically be brought on-line more expeditiously than under the traditional public ownership/operation approach; and (2) the annual cost

The results of the case study analysis in terms of estimated annual cost to the community for each option are shown in Table 23.2.

Table 23.2 Estimated Annual Costs
for Public and Private Ownership

Option	Cost to Community
Option 1: Public-sector ownership of facility	$16,488,000
Option 2: Private-sector ownership of facility	$15,088,000

Based on case study assumptions, cost savings of $14 million or 8.5 percent would result from the privatization of this hypothetical criminal justice facility.

to the community in terms of capital and labor to house prisoners can be substantially less.

The economics of privatization which generate the above benefits include the following elements:

1. Private-sector firms as facility owners will typically emphasize a more modular design approach, which may result in a lower cost for construction of as much as 25 percent;

2. Private-sector firms as facility constructors will often fast-track the construction, which may reduce the cost of interest during construction by as much as 25 percent;

3. Private-sector firms as facility financiers can utilize creative financing approaches such as variable rate instruments, which can minimize the interest cost over the term of the transaction;

4. Private-sector firms as facility operators will attempt to minimize operational expenses; and

5. Private-sector firms as taxpaying entities can take advantage of available tax benefits.

As an example of the "economics" of a privatization transaction, consider the following case study which compares the estimated annual cost to a community for a hypothetical $100 million criminal justice facility based on the following options in Table 23.1:

Option 1, Public-sector ownership of the facility; and Option 2, private-sector ownership of the facility. The question of public- versus private-sector operation of the facility is not considered, only the question of ownership.

The purpose of the case study was merely to illustrate the economic potential of privatization for an hypothetical transaction. Obviously, the assumptions for each proposed project must be carefully evaluated in order to develop valid cost comparisons between public- versus private-sector options.

It is important to recognize that privatizing criminal justice facilities can take place at any stage during their evolution. The most advantageous point at which to consider privatization is prior to construction of new or expanded facilities, whereby the private sector can be mobilized to own, finance, design, construct, and operate/maintain the facility. On the other hand, existing on-line facilities can be sold to the private sector as the front end to a lease or service contract. The only difficulties associated with the sale of existing facilities relates to whether or not the construction of these assets was originally funded through the use of federal grants; if federal grant monies were involved, then federal regulations generally require that the facility be sold at fair market value and a prorata share rebated to the U.S. Treasury.

It is also important to recognize that privatization can apply to a full range of criminal justice system assets depending on their individual depreciation characteristics based on the Federal Tax Reform Act of 1986. For example, police headquarters buildings, police stations, police vehicle fleets, and computer equipment are all potential candidates for privatization.

To the extent that privatization proves to be economically viable, a detailed implementation process should be utilized in selecting the preferred private-sector firm. This implementation process typically entails completion of the following steps: preparation and issuance of Request for Qualifications (RFQ); evaluation of qualifications; preparation and issuance of Request for Proposal (RFP); evaluation of proposals; and finalization of contract negotiations with preferred private-sector firm.

Once the privatization contract is negotiated and signed, the private-sector firm and the community begin a long-term working relationship. This relationship should be based on mutual trust and respect and should be directed at achieving maximum benefit for all parties to the transaction.

24. Privatization of Corrections: Two Canadian Perspectives

Daniel Hawe
Howard Sapers
Paulette Doyle

The purpose of this analysis is to examine the recent process of organizational transformation of the Correctional Service of Canada and the John Howard Society of Alberta as they renegotiated their structures and operations within the larger political and economic environment. Their transformation will be presented as one accelerated by a set of significant policy initiatives undertaken by the Canadian federal government.

The particular conceptualization of organization/environment relations that will be emphasized is the political-economy perspective which stresses the basis of relationship control within and between organizations as a function of resource management. A discussion of how environmental constraint, stress, and uncertainty have shaped the management strategies perceived as necessary to negotiate as favorable a position as possible for the two organizations will be presented.

The political-economy perspective on organization/environment relations portrays the environment as a source of scarce resources and hence one filled with stress and uncertainty for organizations which must compete with one another, either directly or indirectly, for a share of the allocation of resources as well as the maintenance of control over their functions (Aldrich and Mindlin, 1978). Political-economy considerations, particularly control and influence based on resource-dependent relationships, are primary factors resulting in specific organizational arrangements. In other words, political considerations compete with efficiency and effectiveness in shaping the structure of organizations (Wamsley and Zald, 1973; Edwards, 1979; Burawoy, 1979).

Organizational analysis through the application of case study methodology will be employed. This method emphasizes process and change through the interpretive perspective of those studying and experiencing the phenomenon. Norman Denzin (1978) notes that the natural life history of an organization is a particular form of the case study method. "The life history presents the experiences and definitions held by one person, or group, or one organization as this person, group or organizations interprets those experiences" (Denzin, 1978:215).

294

This chapter will apply the natural life history method of case study analysis to the recent historical experiences of the Correctional Service of Canada and the John Howard Society of Alberta. The strategy used in this historical explanation and review of organizational transformations will focus on the sequential ordering of events in order to make probabilistic statements about casual links. This chapter, therefore, is an attempt at theory building in the area of organization/environment interaction and is not presented as a test of some preexisting set of hypotheses. The views expressed here are those of the authors and by no means may be stated and or inferred as being those of the government of Canada, government of Alberta, the board of directors of the John Howard Society of Alberta or any other organization or individual.

The significant policy initiatives to be discussed all revolve around the privatization of public services. Privatization itself is not a new concept in the Canadian criminal justice context. Throughout the past century, individual volunteers and not-for-profit organizations have participated with both federal and provincial governments in efforts directed toward the rehabilitation of offenders. In addition, numerous services such as those provided by counselors, psychiatrists, and consultants have all been privately contracted. Within this evolving political-economic environment, a debate about the growth of privatization has centered on traditional issues of quality, accountability, security, costs, and power.

The environment context in which both the Correctional Service of Canada (a federal government department) and the John Howard Society of Alberta (a not-for-profit volunteer organization) find themselves will be presented. This is followed by a description of the organizational context of each organization and how each have negotiated as a result of federal government policy initiatives regarding privatization.

Environmental Context

Political Economy "Reality"

On September 17, 1984, a Progressive Conservative government was sworn in after a landslide victory in a Canadian federal election. The major objective of the new government was stated to be sustained economic growth and productive job creation through economic renewal of the business sector. The policy agenda to achieve this objective was contained in the Economic and Fiscal Statement of November 1984. This document identified the following essential thrusts toward economic renewal:

1. Get the budget deficit under control;
2. Give business a new boost; and
3. Make government more efficient in its own operations and less obstructive to the work of the private sector.

Economic renewal was directly linked to federal government fiscal responsibility. With this specific target in mind, a five-year fiscal plan was established based upon the following principles:

1. To reduce the growth in the national debt to less than the growth in the economy by the end of the decade;

2. To achieve continuing, sizable year-over-year reductions in the federal deficit;

3. To ensure substantial year-over-year reductions in the size of the government's financial requirements; and

4. To ensure that the primary means of achieving these objectives is through expenditure restraint and tight management.

Consistent with these principles and in response to the government's concern about waste, duplication, and red tape, a ministerial task force on program review was immediately initiated. The task force was created in response to two major objectives: (1) better service to the public; and (2) improved management of government programs. The new government believed strongly that an efficient government would improve economic productivity as well as eliminate systemic barriers to economic growth.

In announcing the project, the prime minister stated he was asking the task force to overhaul government programs so they would be "simpler, more understandable and more accessible to their clientele" and that decisionmaking should be "decentralized as far as possible to those in direct contact with client groups."

The task force selected 989 federal programs and services for review, reflecting annual federal expenditures of more than $92 billion. Individual study teams were established with representatives from the federal government, the various provincial governments, and the nongovernment sector. A total of 221 members spread over nineteen study teams were grouped around three major themes as follows:

1. Management of Government
> Procurement
> Regulatory programs
> Regulatory agencies
> Real property
> Major surveys

2. Service to the Public
> Canada Assistance Plan
> Veterans
> Education and research
> Job creation, training and employment services
> Housing

3. Improved Program Delivery
> Citizenship, labor, and immigration
> Health and sports
> Justice system
> Environment
> Indian and native programs

The recommendations relating to the area of corrections that were put forth by the study team on the Justice System were as follows:

1. The Government of Canada, while remaining responsible for offenders sentenced to two years or more, should deliver programs primarily for the safe custody, control and humane management for long-term dangerous inmates.

2. The Government of Canada should seek to integrate its community-based release services with provincial correctional delivery systems.

3. The Government of Canada should continue to be responsible for establishing national standard for case supervision and criteria for conditional release of federal offenders and provide an audit capacity to monitor levels of service to maintain the integrity of service delivered nationally.

4. The preferred means of providing opportunities to offenders is to be found in their own community using existing social service support systems rather than duplicating such services.

5. While constitutional change is anticipated, the Federal Government should undertake to negotiate the resolution of certain jurisdictional irritants of concern to both the Federal and Provincial levels. Central to such a negotiation strategy would be a commitment to make the necessary legislative and regulatory changes to:

(a) accept federal fiscal responsibility for offenders upon their sentencing to federal jurisdiction (Section 16(1) et al. of the *Penitentiary Act*).

(b) establish full jurisdiction by the provinces for the conditional release of their own provincial offenders, thereby removing the involvement of the National Parole Board in release decisions for provincial offenders;

(c) eliminate the present *Prison and Reformatories Act* without removing federal authority to set national standards within its own jurisdiction or co-operatively with the provinces.

6. The Government of Canada should establish a moratorium on further federal prison construction beyond its current plan. It would seek a range of alternative means of managing offenders, including:

(a) transfer of offenders to provincial jurisdictions under *Exchange of Service Agreements*;

(b) direct placement of non-violent offenders to lower levels of security to reduce supervision costs and enhance release potentials;

(c) accelerating the release of non-violent offenders;

(d) development within the Correctional Service of Canada and National Parole Board a more comprehensive client-specific planning system;

(e) development of more specialized community residential centres operated by private agencies to improve release prospects;

(f) development of related initiative to improve the prospects of released offenders in the community;

(g) development of more intensive supervision and surveillance programs for offenders in the community;

(h) initiate a program of "halfway-back houses" that are used to prevent the return of potential parole violators to a "full" penitentiary environment where such a return is not warranted;

(i) decentralization of Temporary Absence authority to penitentiary Wardens rather than the National Parole Board; and

(j) development of further longer-term strategies to prevent the growth of penitentiary populations beyond their present level.

7. The Government of Canada should remain committed to its present level of service to offenders in terms of opportunities to rehabilitate themselves, and accom-

modation standards that include one cell to one offender within a ten percent margin of temporary double-bunking thereby accommodating unplanned population surges.

8. The Government of Canada should pursue a policy of incarcerating offenders in prisons within their own regions, thereby alleviating the dislocations caused by national transfers far from the community to which the offender would eventually return.

9. The Government of Canada should adopt a policy of decentralization of the accommodation of female offenders working in conjunction with the provinces, seeking to house female offenders as close as possible to their homes and families. It is recognized that there may remain a long term need for a centrally operated federal facility for females, but this scan can only be determined upon the conclusion of federal-provincial negotiations in this area. The government would remain fully committed to providing female offenders with the same program opportunities as their male counterparts.

10. The Correctional Service of Canada should pursue its present policy of privatization of services where costs and benefits can be proven to be beneficial. The use of community-based private organizations to provide a significant portion of community supervision and residential services will be given priority.

Although the recommendations of the Task Force on the Justice System are the product of the study team itself and do not reflect any decisions or policies of the federal government, they are reflective of a broad-based federal government, provincial government, and private-sector consultation process providing a policy framework for bureaucrats and politicians alike. The rationalization of Canadian corrections was based on a fundamental belief that through a federal, provincial, and private-sector negotiation process, duplication between jurisdictions and sectors could be significantly reduced. This process would go a long way in ensuring that offenders and the general public receive a reasonable quantity and quality of service and, hence, a return on investment.

The direction indicated by the Task Force on the Justice System in combination with the November 8, 1984, Economic and Fiscal Statement, the May 1985 budget, and the September 18, 1986, Update of the Economic and Fiscal Situation, certainly present a political-economic environment within which the Correctional Service of Canada must operate. As Graham Allison (1971:144-45) notes:

> government decisions are made, government actions are taken, neither as the simple choice of a unified group, nor as a formal summary of leaders' preferences. Rather, the context of shared power but separate judgements about important choices means that politics is the mechanism of choice. Each player pulls and hauls with the power at his discretion for outcomes that will advance his conception of national, organizational group and personal interests.
>
> Note the environment in which the game is played: inordinate uncertainty about what must be done, the necessity that something be done, and the crucial consequences of whatever is done. These features force responsible men to become active players.

Correctional Milieu Reality

The Constitution Act, 1867, formerly known as the British North America (B.N.A.) Act, divides the jurisdiction for criminal justice between the federal and provincial governments. The federal government is responsible for all criminal law legislation and for the establishment, maintenance, and management of penitentiaries, while the provinces have the authority to legislate in relation to the establishment, maintenance, and management of public and reformatory prisons in and for the province and have exclusive responsibility for probation and young offenders (seventeen years of age and under). Adult offenders sentenced to terms of two years or more are the responsibility of the federal government. The Correctional Service of Canada (csc) under the auspices of the federal ministry of the solicitor general provides services to federal offenders.

Prior to Confederation (1867) and the signing of the Constitution, the provinces were responsible for administering sentences in penitentiaries, prisons, and reformatories with the two-year split demarcating differences between a prison and penitentiary. Statutes of the Province of Canada (6 Victoria, 1842, C.S., ss. 3, 4) stipulate "that for each and every offence, for which . . . , the offender may on conviction be punished by imprisonment for such term as the Court shall award, or for any term exceeding two years, such imprisonment, if awarded for longer than two years, shall be in the Provincial Penitentiary."

The Charlottetown and Quebec conferences of 1864 proposed that the administration of penitentiaries remain with the provinces and a resolution passed at the London conference of 1866 placed penitentiaries under provincial jurisdiction. Nonetheless, the B.N.A. Act of 1867 divided the jurisdiction between the federal and provincial levels of government. The rationale behind this last minute reversal was never clearly enunciated nor understood, although there are speculations that it may have been related to the following practical and economic considerations:

1. To alleviate the financial burden on the provinces for the care and maintenance of offenders serving more than two years;

2. To separate "serious" from "ordinary" offenders (Ouimet, 1969); and

3. To cater to the mood of the times which leaned toward centralized authority (Federal-Provincial Task Force, 1976).

The Constitution does not define the terms "penitentiary" or "prison," nor does it divide the line between prisons or penitentiaries. The Criminal Code of Canada (1892, sec. 659), the Penitentiary Act, and the Prisons and Reformatories Act define these terms such that a "penitentiary" holds a person serving sentences of two years or more, and a "prison" holds persons serving less than two years.

The shortcomings of the "two-year rule" and the pragmatic problems arising from this arbitrary division of constitutional authority have been the target of much criticism by those working within the criminal justice field. Numerous commissions, inquiries, conferences, and agency and government reports have addressed the issue over the years; however, despite a consensus that a problem exists, there is no consensus as to the solution.

There have been four major inquiries over the last fifty years that addressed the "two-year" jurisdictional split and offered varied solutions:

1. The Archambault Report (1938) suggested that the best method of protecting the public and rehabilitating the offender was to bring corrections under a single, centralized authority, that is, the federal government.

2. Fauteux (1956) commented on the chaos created by a fragmented system but, curiously, the solution to the problem was simply to alter the dividing line from two years to six months.

3. Ouimet (1969) concluded that Archambault's recommendation for a single correctional system was unworkable and recommended options for jurisdictional change. Fragmentation of the Canadian correctional system was intensified with the passing of the Parole Act in 1958 and the formation of the National Parole Board in 1959. Flowing from the act, the National Parole Service (federal) was formed and was made responsible for the supervision of all (federal and provincial) parole cases released by the National Parole Board. Ouimet more or less rationalized the two-year split and sought to correct some of the anomalies. The recommendation states: "The Committee recommends that the federal government retain responsibility for parole as it affects all inmates of federal penitentiaries and that the provinces assume responsibility for parole as it affects all inmates of provincial institutions" (Ouimet, 1969:238). The three most populated provinces, British Columbia, Quebec, and Ontario, established their own provincial parole boards in the 1970s and proceeded to develop their own supervision programs; for federal inmates and provincial inmates in other provinces, however, the National Parole Board retained responsibility for release decisions and csc continued to supervise these offenders. Ouimet's report further recommended that the Canadian Penitentiary Service and the National Parole Board be drawn together administratively under a director of corrections. This recommendation was implemented in 1978 when the two services were amalgamated into an integrated organization, the csc, under a commissioner of corrections.

4. The Report to Parliament by the Sub-Committee on the Penitentiary System in Canada stated that "one of the major problems facing criminal corrections in Canada is the jurisdictional split between the provincial and federal penitentiary systems" (MacGuigan, 1977:39). MacGuigan further comments on the problem and identifies three major problem areas:

(a) The inability of the provinces to allocate equal amounts of financial and human resources, hence the quality of treatment varies widely;

(b) The recordkeeping is made complicated, impeding the development of statistics; and

(c) The split impedes the development of a coherent system of correctional treatment.

The split in responsibility for corrections between the two levels of government has been criticized since its inception. The following brief "Problem Statement" was agreed upon by the Federal-Provincial Task Force in 1976 and summarizes the essential aspects of the problem which, in most respects, still applies today.

> In contemporary corrections, the federal/provincial division of responsibility (essentially embodied in the B.N.A. Act and in the Criminal Code of Canada) appears to

have little rational basis. This has resulted in duality in a number of areas of corrections, including institutions, paroling authority, community supervision and administrative and managerial processes.

It is clear that corrections is characterized by isolation, duplication, inconsistencies,
gaps, lack of continuity and limitations in terms of relative efficiency and effectiveness. The existence of different perspectives on Canadian corrections com-
plicates the evaluation of these characteristics since that which may appear
detrimental from one perspective may be viewed positively from another. Thus the
assessment of value of these characteristics is very difficult.

Additionally, confusion exists concerning respective correctional responsibilities in
the public eye, political forums, offender clientele and among administrators of the
criminal justice system.

For these reasons, alternative possibilities for the future division of correctional
responsibilities must be examined in order to assess how this situation can be improved [Federal-Provincial Task Force, 1976:1].

Organizational Context of Correctional Services of Canada

Organizational Milieu

On December 11, 1984, the Treasury Board of Canada directed the Correctional Service of Canada to review its operations in terms of the treatment of
offenders, scope of programs, and approach to resources in fulfilling its legal
mandate.

Subsequent to this direction by the Treasury Board, a number of other important issues and events occurred:

1. Recommendations were issued by the Advisory Committee to the solicitor
general on the Management of Correctional Institutions;
2. The solicitor general requested that the Correctional Service of Canada conduct an operation management review;
3. A comprehensive audit by the auditor general of Canada of the Correctional
Service of Canada was undertaken;
4. A new commissioner for the Correctional Service of Canada was appointed;
his duties were to commence February 1984;
5. The Carson Report was issued in November 1985; and
6. A Treasury Board announcement was issued that the 258,220 person-year
federal civil service would be reduced, over a five-year period commencing
1986–87, by 15,000 person-years. (A person-year is equivalent to one full-time individual working twelve months of the year.)

In response to the complex nature of the above and in consideration of the
points noted in the Political-Economy "Reality" section above, the commissioner
of the Correctional Service of Canada initiated in May 1985 some twenty-one
reviews on various aspects of csc's operations and activities. These individual
reviews are collectively referred to as the Operational and Resource Management
Reviews (o.r.m.r.) and are entitled as follows:

1. National Headquarters/Regional Headquarters
2. Review of the Accountability Mechanisms
3. Review of the Institutional Organization

4. Review of Budget Development and Control
5. Improved Control over Contracting
6. Review of csc Direction/Anticipated Results
7. Privatization
8. Review of Offender Support Programs
9. Review of Capital
10. Review of Population Management
11. Review of Mental Health Services
12. Review of E.D.P. Priorities
13. Review of Staff Training and Development Requirements
14. Review of Recruiting Policies/Requirements
15. Offender Forecasting
16. Review of Human Resource Forecasting
17. Review of Accreditation Process
18. Violence Research
19. Review of Electronic Surveillance
20. Native Institutions and Work Camps
21. Review of Long-Term Offenders.

The objectives of each review were to reassess the policies and programs concerning the treatment of federal offenders and to refine the link between resource requirements and objectives. It is not possible to comment on each of the reviews. However, the Privatization Review in conjunction with an overview of federal and provincial agreements will provide significant insight into the Correctional Service of Canada's position on a negotiated, contractually based relationship with its environment in order to maximize resources in a more rationalized organization/environment context.

Privatization

Privatization of government services is viewed, by the Correctional Service of Canada, as one of the methods of organizational structuring and rearrangement to address the larger political-economy considerations as well as to meet the specific goal of person-year reduction (see Table 24.1) dictated by the Treasury Board of Canada. As a result of the review on privatization, the Correctional Service of Canada adopted the following definition: "Privatization is the contracting of programs and services, either wholly or in part, from For-Profit and Non-Profit organizations, including service contracts with individuals but excluding contracts with Federal government jurisdictions" (O.R.M.R., 7)

Correctional Service of Canada also adopted a set of principles and guidelines governing any future privatization initiatives undertaken by the Service. These are set out as follows:

Principles of Privatization

1. For-profit organizations include nonprofit charitable organizations, as well as individuals contracts with doctors, dentists, and teachers, including contracts with other levels of government but *not* with the government of Canada.

Table 24.1 CSC Workforce Adjustment

In his letter of June 10, 1985, to the commissioner of corrections, the secretary of the Treasury Board wrote that the csc should aim for reductions from 1985–86 Main Estimates person-year levels in the order of:

–1 percent for 1986–87 (this means a level of 10,994 person-years as the 1985–86 person-year complement was 11,105);

–a further 1 percent in 1987–88 over previous year (i.e., a level of approximately 10,884 person-years); and

–at least, an additional 0.5 percent in each of the next three years (this represents levels of approximately 10.830 person-years in 1988–89 and 10,776 person-yeras in 1989–90).

The Treasury Board reductions targets for csc are indicated below. The approved reference level represents a 7.4 percent decrease by 1990–91 from the previously approved reference level for 1987–88 of 11,697 person-years.

	1986–87	1987–88	1988–89	1989–90	1990–91
T.B. target	10,994	10,884	10,830	10,776	10,772
Port cartier		+33	+107	+107	+107
Approved reference level	10,994	10,917	10,937	10,883	10,829
Impact of New Initiatives on Person-Years					
Fed/prov agreements		−76	−76	−76	−76
Inmate pay		−30	−30	−30	−30
Privatization		−19	−19	−19	−19
csc target	10,994	10,792	10,812	10,758	10,704

2. Final decisions on what services will be privatized will be made by the commissioner of corrections in consultation with the regional deputy commissioner and national headquarters.

3. Further initiatives will be in areas such as service delivery, internal services, and community release programs.

4. A cost-benefit analysis must be submitted with each proposal indicating the real cost and listing the social benefits, if applicable, as well as those of an economic nature.

5. The operation of an entire institution at this time is not being considered.

6. Consultation with interested employee bargaining groups and other parties will be coordinated through national headquarters.

Guidelines for Privatization

1. The guiding principle in contracting out for programs and services should be that the quality of service be protected above all considerations.

2. The csc should continue to contract with nonprofit agencies those services that have as their primary objective the rehabilitation of offenders for the following reasons:

(a) It is felt that, because voluntary agencies in general are community-based, socially motivated nonprofit organizations, using their services enables csc to involve the community more effectively in the offenders' reintegration into society;

(b) It is also suggested that contracting with nonprofit agencies is viewed in a more positive fashion from a union perspective, thus allowing for an easier transition in service delivery;

(c) Unlike csc whose mandate ends with the expiration of a parolee's terms of supervision, voluntary agencies can provide a continuum of service to certain parolees beyond that date; and

(d) Finally, voluntary agencies bring an independent viewpoint when assisting the offenders' reintegration that can assist csc in developing and improving community programs.

3. For-profit organizations viewed as efficient and business oriented may be used for those programs and services that are operational in nature (e.g., laundry and food services, administrative services, etc.).

4. The csc should retain those services over which it has quasi-judicial authority. The chairman of the National Parole Board has stated that the board is willing to entertain proposals for delegation of "authority to suspend" to qualified agencies.

5. Funding of nonprofit agencies can take different forms:

(a) Purchase of unit service from an agency where the volume of work is too small to warrant total funding;

(b) Block funding where the agency can provide total service for csc clients only;

(c) Shared funding with the provinces where it is appropriate; and

(d) Total funding of experimental projects.

6. The csc standards should be in place prior to contracting for services.

7. Accountability procedures should be an integral part of the contract, including provision for the continuity of service and for contingency plans. Although multiyear contracts assist in this area, it will be necessary to ensure in the contract that such elements are clearly enunciated.

8. As much as possible, providers of service should be drawn from the local community.

9. A comprehensive evaluation mechanism should be in place to look at the benefits of having privatized services with the following criteria:

(a) The philosophical orientation of the government;

(b) The implication of cost-reduction and person-year savings; and

(c) The degree of "spin-off" to the economy through private-sector involvement.

It should be noted that the definition of privatization and the documentation of principles and guidelines simply reflects new terminology for an old concept in federal corrections. Virtually every aspect of the csc has been involved in contracting out elements of the operation for many years. The following list will give some indication of services currently provided under contract to the csc:

1. Organizational Support
   Administration
   Planning

Evaluation and special projects
Systems
Legal services
2. Offender Programs
Parole supervision
Counseling, life skills
Chaplaincy
Native resources
Recreation
Social community affairs
Community residential centers
3. Health Care
Regional hospitalization (per diem)
PINEL (Quebec Psychiatric Treatment Facility)
4. Education, Training, and Employment
Post-release employment
Industries, agribusiness
5. Technical Services
Repairs and renovations
6. Security
7. Communications
8. Staff Training and Development

As an indication of the level of csc financial commitment to privatization, the 1985–86 fiscal year realized approximately $60 million in contracting out arrangements, and the 1986–87 figure exceeded $81.5 million (a 35.8 percent increase over the previous year). The additional $21.5 million in contracts for fiscal 1986–87 is represented by an approximate $16 million increase in federal-provincial agreements; an approximate $3 million increase in contracts with the voluntary-based, nonprofit sector for provision of community corrections services; and an approximate $2 million increase in contracts primarily for such institutional services as food services and medical care. Thus far, privatization initiatives will result in the planned reduction of approximately 100 person-years from the csc complement commencing fiscal 1987–88. Approximately 25 person-years were converted to contract dollars for service provision in the community corrections, food services, and health care areas, whereas approximately 75 person-years have been converted to contract dollars under the federal-provincial agreement mechanism, specifically for the arrangement whereby the province of Alberta assumed responsibility for supplying all federal community corrections services (parole service activities) as well as administering all federal contractual relationships with the voluntary sector within the provincial boundary.

It is noteworthy that in the process of privatizing the activities resulting in the deletion or conversion of approximately 100 person-years from the csc complement, not one job was lost for an employee. Individual employees so affected had the option of being placed within csc in another equal-level position or were presented with, in the majority of cases, the opportunity of becoming employees of the organization receiving the contract, once again with the guarantee of no loss of salary or benefits.

The definition of privatization that the csc adopted did not differentiate between voluntary, nonprofit organizations, for-profit organizations, or "other" governments (provincial, municipal, or territorial) in respect to service supplied to either the csc or directly to federal offenders under its care and custody. However, for the purpose of this study, the difference in "form" and "nature" between the various nonfederal government service suppliers will be noted and delineated under the subheadings of Private Sector Agreements and Federal-Provincial Agreements.

PRIVATE-SECTOR AGREEMENTS. The federal political environment in Canada (since 1984) parallels that of the U.S. federal political environment at least insofar as promotion of greater private-sector involvement in service delivery is concerned. Support for and promotion of the free market model of service delivery is directly linked with a perceived, more efficient level of service, at less cost, with a concomitant reduction in the role and hence size of government.

In corrections the federal and most of the provincial corrections bureaucracies have adopted a wait and see approach in response to interest in the larger political-economic arena for mass privatization of services. The choice has been to build upon historical relationships with the traditional, voluntary based, nonprofit sector for the supply of community programs to offenders and limited expansion of for-profit contracts for service supply in the organizational support, health care, education, training, and employment, technical services, security, communications, and staff training and development areas. Although there has been a modest amount of discussion within the Canadian correctional context about private-sector (for-profit) management of correctional programs (institutional and community), the absence of rigorous cost-benefit analysis and or properly documented research to definitively answer the question, "Can the private sector provide either a higher quality of programming for the same cost or an equal quality of programming for less cost than the government?" has resulted in the current position.

There are also the complex issues for legislators, policymakers, and correctional administrators as to the proper role of the private sector (for-profit and non-profit) in the delivery and supply of correctional services in respect to "peace officer status"; specifically just how far should government go in delegating quasi-judicial and law enforcement functions to nongovernment organizations. This issue is made particularly difficult by the relative absence of realistic goals and objectives of correctional activities and programs, thereby impeding the development of objective, measurable standards for which the organization can be held accountable. The history of accountability between government and the private sector in contracting for the supply of human services has been primarily limited to financial accountability. The difficulty in establishing goals that can be operationalized and measured has plagued the human field and resulted in endless debate on accountability. Added to the major problem of monitoring contracts in order to determine what was delivered (due to the lack of performance or output criteria), and the intensity of debate surrounding contracting out of quasi-judicial or law enforcement functions, the degree of privatization has found what some would assert is a natural and reasonable limit. There is the same inherent difficulty of accountability and monitoring of quasi-judicial activities when they are supplied by government; however, when the issue is raised about moving service supply of such activities to the nongovernment sector, these factors are presented as if they have been satisfactorily resolved with the government operation of them.

With respect to overt social control activities relating to the supervision of federal offenders (parole, mandatory supervision, community assessments, temporary absence supervision) in the community, the csc has for many years contracted with voluntary based organizations to assist in this function. Although these organizations do not have the delegated authority from the National Parole Board to suspend a parolee (quasi-judicial function), and although the csc parole officer maintains ultimate authority over the case, the day-to-day involvement with the offender is the responsibility of the organization. The organization, under contract and paid on a case-by-case, month-by-month basis, is responsible for supervising the offender in the community under the direction of the csc *Case Management Manual,* which outlines the appropriate process and procedure under general conditions of supervision. This overt social control function represents another example of "public agent" contracting which increased from a contracting expenditure level of approximately $2 million in 1985–86 to an expenditure in 1987–88 of over $3 million.

In noting the nature, form, and financial extent of private-sector agreements and contracts between csc and the for-profit and nonprofit sectors, it is important to realize that all contracts between csc and the for-profit sector are conducted under competitive, tendering processes, whereas contracting by csc with voluntary based, nonprofit organizations for the provision of community correctional services is noncompetitive in nature.

FEDERAL-PROVINCIAL ACCOMMODATION ARRANGEMENTS. Formal federal-provincial agreements (Exchange of Service Agreements, ESAs)[1] providing for the interjurisdictional custody and transfer of offenders were originally executed between 1973 and 1975 following the provision of the requisite statutory authority through the enactment in March 1973 of a legislative amendment to the Penitentiary Act and the Prisons and Reformatories Act. Provision for interjurisdictional contracts for services was initially recommended in 1969 by the Canadian Committee on Corrections as a reasonable and flexible response to the divided responsibility for corrections (the two-year rule) in Canada.

The original agreements were of two main types: (1) to enable the transfer of sentenced offenders, and (2) to provide for compensation to the provinces and territories for custody in provincial and territorial facilities of offenders arrested under a warrant of suspension of parole or mandatory supervision.

The objective of transfer of sentenced offenders under the agreements was to afford conditions more conducive to the rehabilitation of the individual.

The objective of the parole and mandatory suspension aspect of the agreements was operational efficiency as suspended offenders would otherwise be transferred to the closest federal penitentiary at great cost and administrative inconvenience. As well, since suspensions can be and are removed during the initial fourteen days prior to referral to the National Parole Board, local custody of a suspended offender in a provincial or territorial facility provides the supervising federal parole officer the opportunity to conduct the necessary case investigation.

During the same period, the ministry of the solicitor general attempted to negotiate forensic custody agreements with all provinces. These negotiations were unsuccessful, with the exception of an agreement signed in 1977 with the province of Quebec for the custody and treatment of federal offenders at l'Institute Philippe Pinel de Montreal. The failure to negotiate such agreements with the remaining jurisdictions resulted in the establishment of the csc regional psychiatric and treatment centers at a considerable capital expenditure.

In 1982 these original agreements were supplemented by the "Tanguay" Agreement with Quebec, under which francophone female offenders sentenced in the province of Quebec to more than two years are housed in the provincial female offender facilities. Given that the sole female offender facility is located in Kingston, Ontario, the Tanguay Agreement enabled the csc to provide a francophone environment for the forty to sixty francophone female offenders. This agreement represents the first time the csc purchased guaranteed accommodation for a period of five years with the option of an additional five years from a province through a capital contribution, in this case approximately $1 million for required renovations to the provincial facility, Maison Tanguay.

Historic growth in transfers under the early federal-provincial agreements as measured by payments to the provinces, via an agreed upon per diem, was at most minimal and variable, depending upon whether provincial populations were high or low (with the exception of the Tanguay Agreement) and therefore were not a significant accommodation factor with respect to the male offender population.

This situation was to change when the csc 1985 Multi-Year Operational Plan and Long-Range Accommodation Plan indicated substantial levels of double bunking, caused by cell shortfall, if:

1. A planned moratorium on penitentiary construction is a reality;

2. The person-year reductions (see Table 24.1, page 303) specified by the Treasury Board are to be met; and

3. The decision by the Treasury Board ministry for a 4 percent reduction in csc's capital expenditure budget is to be continued.

The csc population forecast predicts that by 1994–95, the end of the planning period, accommodation will be required for 15,110 inmates. The capacity of the current inventory of csc institutions and those projected for completion during the period, as well as trailer facilities, is 12,012, requiring a double bunking of 19.7 percent (1,492 cells; 2,984 inmates) by 1994–95 (see Table 24.2).

At the direction of the solicitor general, the deputy solicitor general undertook to examine alternative sentence management strategies that would alleviate this crowding. One of the alternatives put forward was the use of the federal-provincial agreements to transfer federal offenders to the provinces. Preliminary discussions indicated that sufficient capacity could be provided through such agreements to resolve the accommodation shortfall in the short run (1986–87). The breathing space provided by this initiative would allow the full range of alternative sentence management strategies identified in the discussion paper to be developed, tested,

Table 24.2 The CSC 1987 Long-Range Accommodation Plan

Forecasted inmate population (1994–95)	15,110
Planning forecast adjustment	+ 368
Total accommodation required	15,478
Single cell capacity	−12,012
csc beds	− 558
Shortfall	2,908
Existing and planned ESA's	− 745
	2,163
Sentence management strategies	− 194
	1,969
Minus special purpose cells not suitable for general populations use	− 59
New csc accommodation	− 447
Total needs	1,463
Double bunked cells	1,492*

*Number approximately equal to total needs

Cell Shortage by Year

	1987–88	1988–89	1989–90	1990–91	1991–92
Cells	610	718	846	1,105	1,264
Percentage	9.1	10.4	11.9	15.3	17.0
Inmates	1,220	1,436	1,692	2,210	2,438

	1992–93	1993–94	1994–95
Cells	1,219	1,454	1,492
Percentage	16.5	19.3	19.7
Inmates	2,438	1,454	2,984

The result is that 2,984 offenders or 20 percent of the population will be double bunked in cells constructed for single occupancy, more than double the current percentage of double bunking.

and implemented in a planned fashion. It was in this context that the csc negotiated the group of agreements (B.C., Alberta, Saskatchewan, Nova Scotia, Yukon, and the Northwest Territories) submitted for Treasury Board approval in March 1986. These agreements can be considered reactive in that they represent a response to a particular situation: an acute federal accommodation shortfall coinciding with either planned or already initiated provincial construction.

Prior to the negotiation of the expanded federal-provincial agreements, levels of transfer of federal offenders to provincial facilities were neither significant nor dependable enough for including as a factor in csc accommodation planning. The principal difference between the initial federal-provincial agreements and the 1985–86 agreements is the federal purchase through a capital contribution of a specified number of guaranteed beds for federal offenders and guaranteed per diem payments for these beds. The latter guarantee was considered appropriate since the guaranteed units had to be fully budgeted for and staffed, whether csc ultimately utilized them or not. Significant and dependable expansion of transfers to provincial facilities is possible only through this type of guarantee.

In January 1986 a study, *Financial Implications of Issues Related to Federal-Provincial Exchange, Agreements,* was completed under contract for the csc. The study attempted to assess the financial aspects of the agreements in comparison to other alternatives: double bunking, trailers, expansion of existing facilities, and permanent construction. It was concluded that double bunking and trailers were not valid comparisons in that they represent temporary or emergency accommodation versus the semipermanent accommodation provided under the accommodation agreements with the provinces and territories. The csc agreed with this distinction.

The data contained in this study indicates that when compared to expansion of existing institutions or construction of new facilities, the capital cost of accommodation provided under the agreements is approximately equivalent. The average annual operating costs per inmate under the agreements is also comparable to the csc's average costs for operating its low-medium– and minimum-security facilities.

As of January 1987 (one year after the study), and after a further round of agreements had been negotiated with the provinces, a total *capital* contribution of $33,236 million was made toward a total of 499 guaranteed beds (cells) within the provincial network of facilities, or $66,605 per bed. (Temporary custody for suspended parolees is in addition to the guaranteed beds.) Per diem rates on the guaranteed beds vary province by province, with the general male rate in the mid–$80 range, while the general female rate is between $120 and $150. These figures compare most favorably to the $159,000 per bed cost of csc adding 77 beds (cells) to the La Macazza Institution between 1982 and 1985 as well as the csc per diem figure which for 1984–85 averaged $110 for adult male institutions. Given the favorable comparability of costs, the primary benefit of the agreements negotiated in 1985–86 is the fact that beds provided under the agreements would be available to the csc either immediately or within a few months of signing, compared to the two- to three-year period (at a conservative estimate) associated with expansion of csc facilities. This permitted the csc to respond quickly to the acute shortfall identified in the 1985 Multiyear Operational Plan given that the only other response, double bunking up to 20 percent, was considered unacceptable by the solicitor general. As stated previously, these agreements also provided time for csc to analyze the impact of the full range of alternative sentence management strategies identified as potentially viable partial responses to the long-range accommodation shortfall.

Beyond this immediate and situation-specific benefit, the csc has identified the following administrative benefits:

1. The accommodation provided under these agreements has no person-year growth implications;

2. Greater flexibility in managing offenders is provided, federal offenders classified for protective custody can often be integrated into the general population in the provincial system;

3. Geographically dispersed capacity provides greater federal offender access to his or her home community and cultural milieu, thereby enhancing the potential for effective release planning and reintegration into the community;

4. Pooling of small population groups such as female offenders and chronically mentally ill offenders is achieved so that the numbers are sufficiently large to justify a dedicated facility and development of special programming; and,

5. The continued availability of provincial accommodation for temporary detention related to suspension of parole and mandatory supervision and panel hearings is provided, thereby facilitating administrative efficiency.

As well as identifying the administrative benefits of federal-provincial accommodation agreements, the CSC has also identified several principles which will be used in assessing and initiating custody proposals:

1. The cost shall be comparable to equivalent accommodation alternatives;

2. The guaranteed accommodation shall address an identified accommodation requirement and may be used to alleviate overcrowding;

3. It shall provide accommodation in a particular cultural milicu (for example, native culture) or shall be closer to a home community in order to facilitate family contact while in custody and prerelease planning (for example, Manitoba inmates will not be housed in Alberta provincial facilities under an agreement);

4. While capital contributions will be site specific, not all guaranteed beds need be so; and,

5. Capital contributions will be a proportional share of the total cost of constructing the facility to which the contribution is made.

In 1987 a figure of 900 provincial beds (cells), under the accommodation agreements, has been identified as the upper limit of what could most reasonably and predictably be made available to CSC.

DEPENDENCY CONSIDERATIONS. A potential concern identified by the Treasury Board is the overall effect of the accommodation agreements in increasing the CSC's dependence on the provinces for the legislatively mandated provision of accommodation services to federal offenders. The agreements implicitly acknowledge this dependence by making provision for several safeguards:

1. There is a penalty clause for termination prior to ten years under which the province or territory must reimburse a proportionate amount of the capital contribution;

2. The duration of the agreement is specified: ten years minimum with the option to renew at Canada's discretion for two additional five-year periods; and,

3. Termination requires two years written notice at the ministerial level.

The CSC is satisfied that the notice period provides sufficient response time to develop and implement temporary alternative accommodation, such as trailers or expansion of facilities. It is also highly unlikely that all provinces would terminate their respective agreements simultaneously, so that the potential additional offenders to be dealt with at any given time would not be extreme. It also should be recognized that these accommodation agreements are not an entirely new activity but rather an expansion of an existing mechanism which has a relatively long and cooperative history.

FEDERAL-PROVINCIAL COMMUNITY CORRECTIONS AGREEMENTS. In the 1985 review of program delivery options, the Correctional Service of Canada concluded that many of its small parole offices were not cost efficient. Also, geographic distances and the need to maintain a community presence for supervision purposes presented equally strong arguments against greater internal consolidation of resources.

It was believed that provincial delivery of all community corrections, through a contract format, would address the area of administrative overlap and duplication between the federal and provincial systems. Provinces and territories are extensively involved in community corrections and have developed a wide range of programs delivered through a network which is more expansive and geographically dispersed than the csc parole office network. The provinces are also jurisdictionally responsible for the social support services used by offenders on conditional release. Provincial correctional services have established close working relationships with the provincial departments responsible for many such services. Therefore, the provincial corrections administrative structure, by facilitating caseworker access to supporting community services and knowledge of the local community, will serve the objective of federal offender reintegration into the community.

In this regard, and in consideration of the larger political-economic context, the csc and the province of Alberta underwrote a joint study, Review of Alberta-Canada Community Correctional Services (Hawe, 1985). The study identified several areas of administrative overlap and benefits to the community and the offender of the vastly more expansive infrastructure of the Alberta provincial government community corrections system. In addition, this mode of program delivery was considered particularly appropriate in Alberta since the province had for several years administered supervision contracts on behalf of csc and under the expanded custody agreement noted above would house a significant number of federal offenders within the institutional setting.

This study resulted in the first noteworthy noncustodial federal-provincial agreement, the Alberta-Canada Community Corrections Agreement which became effective July 1, 1986.

The agreement states that Alberta will provide the following for federally sentenced offenders:

1. Community supervision for all inmates granted a duly authorized release to the community in Alberta;

2. Case preparation (for conditional release) in accordance with the Parole Act, and for continuous temporary absence conditional release for federally sentenced inmates held in correctional centers;

3. Case preparation for offenders on day parole in Alberta;

4. Community assessments and community investigations for inmates; and

5. Accommodation for inmates on duly authorized release with a residence requirement.

It is also stipulated that Alberta has to establish contracts with nongovernment organizations for the provision of community assessments and parole supervision at not less than 20 percent of the community correctional service caseload.

This agreement requires Alberta to provide services in accordance with the administrative agreement between the Correctional Service of Canada and the National Parole Board. Alberta must also comply with the requirements of the Parole

Act with respect to delegation of authority for suspension of parole and to seek this authority from the National Parole Board as required.

This agreement states that the Correctional Service of Canada will conduct an annual audit of the delivery of services to ensure compliance. It was also stipulated that the audit would be reviewed by the Tripartite Committee (Alberta, Correctional Service of Canada, and the National Parole Board).

As of September 1989 this agreement has been in effect for more than three years. A third audit recently completed by a team comprised of four members – two from Correctional Service of Canada, one from the National Parole Board, and one from the Alberta solicitor general's office. Preliminary findings indicate that Alberta is meeting standards in all areas of service delivery.

The existing and planned federal-provincial community corrections agreements will not reduce the level of resources currently allocated to community corrections; however, the agreements do present, in individual circumstances, the potential for some federal cost avoidance as the economy of scale of provincial community corrections operations allows for a less costly per unit of service. What the agreements do result in, with respect to a federal resourcing, is a reduction of existing person-years.

Just as in the case of contracting with the provinces for the supply of institutional cells, the federal government is still legislatively responsible for the provision of service to federal offenders within the community setting and has simply chosen the vehicle of the provincial government community corrections network (under contract) for the supply of this service. Discussions are under way with other provinces to explore the feasibility of similar contractual arrangements for the supply of federal community corrections services.

Organizational Context of the John Howard Society of Alberta

Organizational Milieu

The utilization by the federal government of the not-for-profit private (voluntary) sector for the provision of community corrections has had a long history in Canada. The voluntary sector possesses many unique characteristics which make significant contributions to the quality of the justice system. The participation of small groups and individuals in the daily machinations of justice stimulate the public's interest and its empathy for the plight of individuals who are in conflict with the law. This contact also fosters a better understanding of the concept of justice itself. The involvement of the voluntary sector is felt to complement and balance the dominance of government. The voluntary sector provides an alternative framework for the delivery of a wide range of social services.

The following are several advantages to the voluntary sector providing government services:

1. The voluntary sector can provide a competitive challenge, motivating government to offer a high quality of service as well as an impetus for reform and evaluation.

2. The voluntary sector can extend their reach to areas where government may not have the resources or capability.

3. The voluntary sector can provide "service delivery" mechanisms independent of government, enhancing the neutrality and independence which must form the hallmarks of a judicial system.

4. The voluntary sector is in a position to question, investigate, and discuss issues and problems that are difficult for government officials to address.

5. The voluntary sector can be more flexible in its development of programs, thus enabling a more individualized and humanized approach.

Hand in hand with the advantages of the voluntary sector providing services in corrections, critics have reported the following disadvantages:

1. Ultimately more expensive because of:
   (a) Possibility for corruption;
   (b) Natural motivation for high profits;
   (c) High social cost because of government layoffs;
   (d) Costs and difficulties of monitoring;
   (e) Government marginal costs low; and
   (f) "Cost plus" provisions in some contracts—no motivation to save.

2. Inequality of accessibility to services due to user fees and the possible elimination of universality.

3. Demoralizing to government departments.

4. Adequate contracting control difficult to achieve due to a growth in the political power of some contractors and a concomitant government dependence on the contractor.

5. Loss of autonomy on the part of private contractors.

6. Private contracting is not necessarily responsive to the needs of recipients. Government capacity to provide human services may be diluted. There is also an inherent tension between the profit-making goal (and in the case of nonprofit organizations, an avoidance of deficits) and human service delivery which adversely affects the quality of the latter.

The claims and counterclaims that abound within any discussion of privatization are not easily resolved. Private contracting is said to both enhance and dissipate economies of scale. Flexibility may or may not be increased. Government may escape accountability through contracting, and contractors may lose autonomy through the same process. Fraud, inefficiency, exploitive labor practices, and other abuses are not exclusive to either sector. Evidence on both sides of the argument is plentiful, and resolution of these conflicts is beyond the scope of this study. For now, it is enough to note that not all parties affected by voluntary sector involvement in the provision of social services agree on its merits.

Despite the controversy over the voluntary sector providing services in corrections, it is commonly held that the state gains an enormous economic benefit from volunteers. Four commissions mandated to study the criminal justice system in Canada support volunteers in the correctional system.

1. Brown Commission (1849).

This commission proposed that a board of visitors be created to oversee discipline in the prisons. This board was to "be of a purely philanthropic character, designed to protect the prisoners from any excess of authority."

2. Archambault Royal Commission (1938).

This commission called for "co-ordination of the efforts of prisoners' aid societies in accordance with principles applied in England and Wales."

3. Fauteux Commission (1955).

This commission was mandated to develop a parole system and its report supported a strengthened role for the voluntary sector in this system.

4. Ouimet Commission (1969).

This report was the first government study to address the question of volunteer or nongovernment roles on a broad basis. It supported the use of the voluntary sector in corrections.

Throughout these years of studies by royal commissions, development was made in the number of voluntary sector agencies becoming involved in corrections and the variety of services being provided by them. In 1905 a Salvation Army worker by the name of Brigadier Archibald became the first Dominion parole officer. By the 1930s the John Howard Society was making direct overtures to the Remission Service of Ottawa in respect to parole decisions. In the 1940s a John Howard Society worker from British Columbia became the first Western representative of the Remission Service. The 1950s brought an expansion of private aftercare agencies, with the Remission Service allotting an increased number of cases to the voluntary sector for supervision.

However, following the establishment of the National Parole Board in 1959, government officials tended to stress the public servants' responsibilities for parole supervision. The voluntary sector pressed for additional government funds and a continuing, if not increased share of the supervision. The National Parole Board countered by expanding its services and insisting that ultimately parole supervision was the responsibility of public servants. The aftercare agencies were urged to devote their energies to the needs of voluntary clients and to continue to seek financial support from the community.

In the early 1970s, the development of community-based residential centers (CRCs) or halfway houses was largely a private-sector thrust. A government report completed by Bill Outerbridge in 1973 identified 156 CRCs in Canada which accepted adult ex-offenders. This report influenced Solicitor General of Canada policy revisions of 1974 in which it was directed that government look first to the voluntary sector for these services. By 1977 meetings between government officials and the John Howard Society led to agreements to contract for parole supervision and community assessments on a local basis.

Political-Economy Context

With respect to government funding of nongovernment organizations, a first grant of $10,000 was awarded by the Penitentiary Service to the Canadian Penal Association for distribution to agencies across Canada in 1947. Since that time, several developments have greatly changed the nature of the relationship between the private and public sector, as well as the manner and extent to which the government is funding the private sector.

The Sauvé Report (1977) on the role of the private sector in criminal justice reviewed the relationship between the private sector and government and stated that the working relationship should be negotiated rather than imposed by government. It reported a "funding crisis" among nongovernment organizations and recommended increased government financial support.

The increase in government funding called for did in fact occur. By 1983 the total dollar amount of services purchased by the Correctional Service of Canada was $228,280,000. Of this amount, approximately $128,280,200 went to the private sector (Canadian Centre for Justice Statistics, 1984).

Since the publication of the Sauvé Report (1977), the issue of funding has grown from a concern about grants and contributions to include questions about amounts of funds available and funding being tied to government priorities (Solicitor General of Canada, 1982). All of the voluntary sector is vulnerable in this situation, but the agencies not providing services wanted by governments, such as policy analysis, independent criticism, public education, or volunteer programs, are most in jeopardy. They hear demands from government to develop a base of community funding support as a precondition for government funding when that community funding source is rapidly disappearing.

The voluntary sector claims that the ever more demanding and complicated funding process imposed upon them by the government in the name of accountability increases their administrative costs, undermines their independence, and diverts their energies away from their main purpose, which is to assist offenders.

Despite these complaints, the voluntary sector has appeared to be a willing partner with government. The general boom in criminal justice spending and the specific growth of community corrections has not occurred without the active participation and cooperation of a large number of voluntary agencies. Tables document this growth as a subset of spending within the larger criminal justice complex.

Table 24.3 shows that while the volume of spending on the protection of persons and property has grown, this growth does not appear to be out of proportion. Between 1983 and 1987 approximately 8 percent of all government expense was for the maintenance of the Canadian criminal justice system. When we examine federal government spending only, this trend is more or less reinforced.

Table 24.4 shows an increase of about 0.5 percent in federal spending between 1983 and 1987. However, Table 24.5 portrays a slightly different picture. Between 1983 and 1987 contracts between the Correctional Service of Canada and not-for-profit agencies grew to number 180, representing over $13 million. This year-over-year growth of approximately 13 percent nearly doubles the average growth in criminal justice spending generally.

Against the backdrop of increased spending on crime control and the expansion of community corrections, the John Howard Society of Alberta had been evolving. The John Howard Society takes its name and spirit from the eighteenth-century humanitarian, John Howard (1726–90) whose name has become a symbol of humane consideration of the incarcerated individual.

Table 24.3 Total Expenditure of All Levels of Government on Protection of Person and Property as a Percentage of Total Consolidated Spending by All Levels of Government (x $1,000)

Year	Total Government Spending	Total Spent on Protection of Persons and Property	Percentage Spent on Protection of Persons and Property
1983	194,543,728	15,251,107	7.84
1984	210,503,135	16,567,136	7.87
1985	226,592,865	17,992,710	7.94
1986	237,047,923	18,671,797	7.88
1987	251,990,574	20,136,394	7.99

Table 24.4 Gross Federal Government Expenditures on the Protection of Persons and Property as a Percentage of Gross Total Federal Government Expenditure (x 1,000,000)

Year	A Total Government Expenditures	B Protection of Persons and Property Expenses	Percentage B of A
1983	95,130	8,645	9.09
1984	104,976	9,866	9.40
1985	117,391	10,854	9.25
1986	120,440	11,876	9.86
1987	125,046	11,986	9.59

Table 24.5 Value of Contracts between CSC and Voluntary Agencies for the Provision of Community Corrections Services

Fiscal Year	Spending
1982–83	$ 6,437,364
1983–84	$ 8,364,754
1984–85	$ 9,938,696
1985–86	$11,686,740
1986–87	$13,000,000 (estimated)
1987–88	$19,000,000 (estimated)

Creation

The John Howard Society of Alberta was formed on September 15, 1947. Its formation was influenced by the late George B. Henwood, O.B.E., W.C., who saw a need for such a society from his personal experience as the former deputy attorney general of Alberta. With the organizational support of the Edmonton Council of Social Agencies, the society chartered under the Companies Act of Alberta and was incorporated on April 11, 1949.

The Society's primary goal was to relieve the stress of ex-prisoners in reestablishing themselves in the community. Secondary goals were: (1) to reform justice legislation; (2) to provide assistance to the families of prisoners; (3) the removal of criminogenic conditions; and (4) prison reform.

At the time of its formation, the John Howard Society of Alberta operated entirely through the support and work of volunteers. In later years the demand for professional counseling forced the hiring of professional staff.

Evolution

The original goals of the Society remained intact throughout the 1950s. During this decade there was a constant struggle to obtain and maintain professional staff.

During the 1960s the nature of the organization's programs and services were to take a new direction. In 1960 the board of directors made an executive decision to focus on personal client counseling. Thus the services of the Society became more intensified with the majority of the staff dedicated to rehabilitation services.

In the 1970s, the Society expanded its services in the areas of employment search, public education in schools, and crime prevention education. The 1970s also brought the creation of community residential centers with the John Howard Society of Alberta operating four such facilities by 1977.

The 1980s saw the Society realize its goal of expanded public legal education with the assistance of a grant from the Alberta Law Foundation. In 1983 a new set of bylaws and goals were adopted, marking the beginning of an era. The adopted objectives are the prevention of crime through the following:

1. The development and implementation of improved policies and techniques within the criminal justice system;

2. The provision of services to those in conflict with the law, including the provision of community and residential services to ex-offenders;

3. The promotion of awareness within society of those circumstances that contribute to crime; and

4. The promotion of acceptance of responsibility and accountability of society to change those circumstances that contribute to crime (John Howard Society of Alberta, 1983:1).

Present Organization

Today, the John Howard Society of Alberta is essentially a federation of six local societies (Calgary, Edmonton, Grande Prairie, Lethbridge, Medicine Hat, and Red Deer). Each district operates whatever programs they feel are required in their local community as long as they are consistent with the provincially held objectives, and each is responsible for securing its own funding through a combination of United Way, fee-for-service work, memberships and donations, fund-raising projects, and any special funding (e.g., from a foundation for a demonstration project). There is no centralized funding for the society, although the provincial organization will provide developmental funding under certain circumstances.

Table 24.6 John Howard Societies in Alberta: Revenue by Source in Dollars (Canadian), 1983–87

Funding Source Year	Prov. Govt Fee for Service	Fed. Gov't Fee for Service	Prov. Gov't Grant	Fed. Gov't Grant
1983	340,192	489,288	116,396	115,977
1984	778,510	272,176	160,759	120,210
1985	1,397,665	245,331	154,526	205,896
1986	1,708,268	376,818	122,459	548,116
1987	1,775,256	168,458	124,714	637,443

Funding Year Source	United Way	Alta. Law Foundation	Misc.*	Total
1983	357,715	541,044	119,493	2,080,105
1984	402,462	570,870	185,158	2,490,145
1985	427,760	443,490	299,443	3,174,111
1986	460,969	431,923	326,037	3,974,590
1987	464,549	1,419,841	424,552	5,014,813

*Includes interest, membership fees, donations, municipal government grants, fund-raising, minor contracts, and donations from foundations.

The Provincial Board is composed of two representatives from each district, a past president, an honorary president, plus six members at large. It determines overall coordination, general procedure and policy in administrative and personnel matters, and it also assumes limited financial responsibility for the Society. The working arm of the board is the provincial executive director and the provincial office. This office is basically administration and research oriented and is funded through a combination of federal and provincial government grants, fund-raising, private-sector money, and annual support from each district society.

This structure assumes that each district remains responsive to the local community and, at the same time, prevents duplication of certain administrative functions and provides guidance and assistance as needed.

The John Howard Society of Alberta serves as a good example of a private-sector criminal justice agency. It has been a stable provider of services within the mixed economy that supports criminal justice in Canada.

Funding

The society's primary financial support is obtained from three basic sources: nongovernment funding, government grant revenue, and government fee-for-service contracts (see Table 24.6).

NONGOVERNMENT FUNDING. Nongovernment funding has traditionally represented approximately 50 percent of the total funds obtained. It provides the most direct evidence of community support for the work of the Society; presumably, the greater the community support, the greater the income derived from this source. The Society values this source of funding most highly since nongovernment money is rarely tied to the provision of direct services and, when it is, the services expected are rarely sanction oriented. As revenues from nongovernment sources increase, the autonomy of the Society also increases. In 1987 this source accounted for 33 percent of total funding, down from 49 percent in 1983.

GOVERNMENT GRANTS. Government grant revenue is viewed as the least restrictive form of government support. In 1983 this source of revenue accounted for approximately 11 percent of total revenue. By 1987 this source had grown to just under 19 percent. Grants are often made to "core fund" an organization, as opposed to supporting a specific service or program. This type of funding is coveted as a means which allows agencies to determine the best manner in which to apply funds.

GOVERNMENT FEE-FOR-SERVICE CONTRACTS. Government fee-for-service contracts are one of the most restrictive means of funding. In 1983 fee-for-service contracts accounted for almost 40 percent of the Society's total revenue. By 1987 over 48 percent of the society's income was derived from this type of contract. These contracts receive close scrutiny from government officials in order to ensure that funds are properly allocated, and instead of being assessed according to client impact, they are audited according to established, rigid procedural criteria. Fee-for-service contracts are generally used to fund programs such as parole or probation supervision. These programs are sanction based and are overtly social control oriented.

The Impact of Funding Sources on the Direction of the John Howard Society of Alberta

Since 1983 the total revenue of the society has grown almost 100 percent (in real terms; see Table 24.7). In 1983 the total from all sources was $1,772,274. By 1987 this amount had increased to $3,016,388 (in adjusted 1980 dollars).

In recent years, there has been a general decrease in nongovernment funding in relation to government funding. Both government fee-for-service and grant income have grown (see Table 24.8).

This trend toward less discretionary government funding means more accountability to government on the part of the society. The overall growth in the society's revenue indicates an attempt to negate the impact of less discretionary government funding. As government funding leads the society toward becoming an overt agent of social control, the society must, in turn, search for ways to escape this end if it is to remain true to its origins. The primary means of escape is through the increased development of nongovernment funding. Secondarily, the society must solicit and receive nontraditional, nonsocial control government income.

Table 24.7 John Howard Societies in Alberta: Real Terms in Dollars (Canadian), 1983–87

Year	CPI*	Total Revenue	Total Revenue (Adjusted)
1983	117.20	2,077,105	1,772,274
1984	120.20	2,492,145	2,073,332
1985	123.70	3,174,111	2,565,975
1986	128.00	3,974,590	3,105,148
1987	133.10	4,014,813	3,016,388

*Consumer Price Index as published by Statistics Canada. Base year is 1981.

Table 24.8 John Howard Societies in Alberta: Total Government Revenue in Dollars (Canadian), 1983–87

Year	Total Revenue	Government Revenue	Percentage Government of Total	Government Grant Total	Percentage Grant of Total
1983	2,077,105	1,061,853	51.12	232,373	11.19
1984	2,492,145	1,331,655	53.43	280,969	11.27
1985	3,174,111	2,003,408	63.12	360,422	11.36
1986	3,974,590	2,755,661	69.33	670,575	16.87
1987	4,014,813	2,705,871	67.40	762,157	18.98

As previously indicated, the society's nongovernment income had remained stable at approximately 50 percent of total revenue until the mid-1980s. As the society realigned itself within the current political-economic environment, it became necessary to make a conscious effort to maintain community roots. If nongovernment income could not expand, the society could change its approach to government. This development of two large-scale Basic Job Readiness Training programs accounts for almost all the growth in government grant revenue. This grant money comes from a new, nontraditional government funder which is not concerned with social control.

The community roots of a volunteer driven social service make it unique and valuable and this cannot be ignored. If governments truly wish to reward community enterprise through the provision of funding to autonomous groups so that local needs can be met quickly and efficiently, the base of these groups should not be threatened through over-regulation or by muzzling the criticism they often voice. Both of these points have been raised by many observers who feel that privatization may well lead to nothing more than the growth of for-profit human services at the expense of traditional, voluntary, and charitable institutions. The John Howard Society of Alberta has sought funding arrangements with government which minimize this danger.

If an organization such as the John Howard Society of Alberta undertakes a new program, it must now be asked why. Previously, programs were always viewed as a response to client needs. Today, programs may result simply from the availability of money being supplied to meet a funder's need. While these two sets of needs are not necessarily incompatible, there is no reason to assume that they are congruent. If a government, for its own benefit (such as the weakening of a union's membership), decides to shift service delivery to the not-for-profit private sector, how should that sector respond? If the service to be shifted is compatible with the organizational aims of the agency in question, then no problem exists. However, if the new program is one of social control introduced into an agency that had previously dealt only with voluntary clients, major philosophical and practical concerns must be voiced. It will no longer be sufficient to speak only of efficiency, effectiveness, and equity when discussing privatization, for the politics of service delivery must also be discussed. The political economy will dictate the extent to which private social services will be available.

The implications for program and service delivery are serious. Do private social services do what they want to do, or do they do what the funders want? Does the private voluntary sector attempt to meet perceived client need, or does it act in response to available money? Is privatization a humanitarian reform or a calculated effort to simply reduce government cost?

One fact which is clear is that the voluntary sector, as evidenced by the John Howard Society of Alberta, is not autonomous in the sense that it cannot make decisions about direction and growth exclusive of today's political and economic environment. Voluntary sector organizations must continuously be on guard against the possibility that external economic and political issues will determine their course of activity, as opposed to the identifiable needs of their clients. While no programming is possible in a vacuum, ignorance and or worship of the political and economic reality can spell doom for voluntary initiative.

Conclusion

The elements of the approach used in this chapter are somewhat innovative in that the recent historical, economic, and political "views" and "actions" of two organizations (csc and the John Howard Society of Alberta) have been combined in one single analytical framework within the larger environment. The csc has been examined as an open political and economic system that is embedded within its political and economic milieu. Likewise, the John Howard Society of Alberta has been described as an evolving charitable organization, the values of which have been tempered by the political economy in which it finds itself. The range of choice open to organizational members has depended on their ability to perceive, control, maintain, and negotiate organizational influence through formal alliances with the environment. Privatization and federal-provincial agreements have been noted as two distinct strategic initiatives used by the federal government to address internal and external issues and factors, thereby changing relationships between and amongst both government and nongovernment correctional agencies.

The two views of privatization noted in this chapter can best be described as mere framework considerations on a topic that is not new to the Canadian criminal justice milieux. What is new is the scope and volume of contracting out initiatives of the Federal Correctional Service of Canada over a relatively short three-year period. However, whether one focuses on the expanding emphasis on the process of privatization and provincialization within the civil service or upon the traditional and ongoing angst of the nongovernmental sector over the nature of accepting fee-for-service government service contracts, there is a distinct absence of discussion on the issues of quality of service insofar as achieving the main objectives of corrections is concerned.

There has been a long tradition within Canadian corrections of quietly debating who has more heart when it comes to offering service to offenders. This debate has consistently been carried on in the absence of objective, quantifiable analysis as to what distinguishes government versus nongovernment delivery methods. More importantly, there has not been any quantifiable evidence to demonstrate that the goal of impacting on offender recidivism has been achieved any more or any less by one approach or the other. In fact, there have been few, if any, credible efforts within the Canadian context to document any cause and effect relationship between correctional programming (institutional or community, government or nongovernment) and impact on recidivism rates.

While federal government corrections officials are fine tuning the process by which privatization initiatives will be considered, it is safe to speculate that the primary concern will focus on the superficial issue of whether or not it costs less. This will be particularly evident in the area of community corrections due to the dearth of quality research to establish a link between programming and the impact on offenders.

Until such time as there is greater understanding of the complex relationship between programming and recidivism, the debate as to what gets delivered and by whom will remain in the realm of political ideology and administrative perception.

Whether one talks to government or nongovernment corrections professionals or volunteers, the overriding approach to the task at hand is the creation of a safe community through humane intervention with those individuals violating the laws of society. However, if one examines the foundation upon which humane activities (i.e., programming) are based, it becomes clear that personal and political ideology, administrative cost-saving, dogma, and blatant and unfounded bias seem to determine the modus operandi, irrespective of organizational setting. One thing is certain, it certainly has not been based on research.

Notes

1. The ESAS have a reciprocal element to them as federal offenders may be placed in a provincial facility and a provincial offender may be placed in a federal facility.

References

Aldrich, H. E. and S. Midlin. "Uncertainty and Dependence: Two Perspectives on Environment." In *Organization and Environment*. Ed. Lucien Karpik. London: Sage, 1978, pp. 149–170.

Allison, G. (1971). "Model iii: Governmental Politics." M. Zey-Ferrell and M. Aiken (eds.), *Complex Organizations: Critical Perspectives*. Glenview, IL: Scott, Foresman.

Archambault, J. (chairman) (1938). *Report of the Royal Commission to Investigate the Penal System of Canada*. Ottawa: Government of Canada, King's Press.

Brown, (secretary) (1849). *Report of the Investigation into the Administration of the Kingston Penitentiary*. Ottawa: Dominion Canada, King's Printer.

Burawoy, M. (1979). *Manufacturing Consent: Changes in the Labor Process under Monopoly Capitalism*. Chicago: University of Chicago Press.

Canadian Centre for Justice Statistics (1984). *Adult Corrections in Canada, 1982–1983*. Ottawa: Ministry of Supply and Services.

Denzin, N. (1978). *The Research Act: Theoretical Introduction to Sociological Methods*. Chicago: Adline.

Edwards, R. (1979). *Contested Terrain: The Transformation in the Twentieth Century*. New York: Basic Books.

Fauteux, G. (chairman) (1956). *Report of a Committee Appointed to Inquire into the Principles and Procedures Followed in the Remission Services of the Department of Justice*. Ottawa: Government of Canada, King's Printer.

Federal-Provincial Task Force (1976). "Bilateral Discussions on the Division of Correctional Responsibilities Between the Federal Government and the Government of British Columbia." Document 830-38/003.

"Financial Implications of Issues Related to Federal-Provincial Agreements" (Sealey Report) (1986). Correctional Service of Canada.

Hawe, D. (1985). "Review of Alberta/Canada Community Correctional Services." Unpublished.

John Howard Society of Alberta (1983). *Minutes, Annual General Meeting*. Edmonton: John Howard Society of Alberta (Alberta April 22).

MacGuigan, M. (1977). *Report to Parliament by the Sub-Committee on the Penitentiary System of Canada*. Ottawa: Minister of Supply and Services.

*Operational and Resource Management Reviews. (*o.r.m.r.*) (1985–86). Nos. 1–21, Ottawa: Correctional Service of Canada.

Ouimet, R. (chairman) (1969). *Report of the Canadian Committee of Corrections*. Ottawa: Information Canada.

Sauvé, R. (chairman) (1977). *Community Involvement in Criminal Justice: Report of the Task Force on the Role of the Private Sector in Criminal Justice*. Ottawa: Government of Canada.

Solicitor General of Canada (1982). "National Voluntary Funding Debate." *Liason* 8, no. 9.

Wamsley, G., and M. Zald (1973). *The Political Economy of Public Institutions*. Lexington, MA: Lexington Books.

25. Barriers to Entry of Private-Sector Industry into a Prison Environment

George D. Bronson
Claire S. Bronson, Ph.D.
Michael J. Wynne
Richard F. Olson, Ph.D.

High fences, guard towers, and razor ribbon are distinguishing fixtures in what has come to be recognized as the face of a contemporary maximum-security prison. Each presents a barrier to secure the perimeter from unauthorized exit by the inmate. Such barriers are an obvious and necessary part of prison structure.

However, many more subtle barriers exist which block entry, not exit, of private-sector industry programs to the prison. These barriers to entry require resolution before such a concept can become a reality. Private-sector industry is not new to prison society.

In fact, the Connecticut Prison at Wethersfield, which opened in 1827, enjoyed several profitable years through such a system as did many such facilities in other states of the Union. These programs were successful because of perceived propriety on the part of the government, a casual attitude toward the inmates' civil or property rights, and absence of government standards in the workplace. Also, success was fostered by the absence of major labor union resistance and less pristine perception of liability on the part of workers, civil authority, and entrepreneurs.

Due to increased influence of these forces, privatization of inmate labor fell into disuse. Now being given a second look, privatization may hold the answer to issues such as inmate idleness, employment, training, decreased costs, community partnership, victim compensation, and dignity of the inmate.

Who benefits from a privatization experience inside a prison? The quick answer is that everyone does. First, the public is rewarded through offender payments of victim restitution, as well as payment for room and board. Also, the public is served through reduction of inmate idleness. Second, the business community is well served by access to an unlimited work pool of offenders. Further, the type of work space may itself be attractive to the business. Moreover, the space may be free of charge with perhaps some reimbursement for utilities.

Third, the inmates receive positive gain by such an experience. They are able

325

to learn work skills, earn additional income, and are given an opportunity to take responsibility for their actions by paying room, board, and restitution.

Inmate idleness is a major issue in most prisons, and many feel that it is usually a precipitant of violence or vandalism. Moreover, inmates are a large, untapped labor pool that an industry can use. Both variables can be addressed with a partnership, between industry and the prison; yet, caution must be exercised. Many constraints must be overcome in order to reap the aforementioned rewards.

The following points will focus upon these constraints, based on an experiment to implement such a project at the maximum-security institution in Connecticut. Attention will be directed to those issues which are unique to the prison environment. Barriers presented to the project will be identified as well as recommendations for eliminating such barriers.

Exploitation

Each state has an obligation to protect inmates from exploitation, particularly to benefit a private-sector corporation whose existence relies on profitability. This motivation poses two immediate cautions. First, there must be assurances that the wages paid to inmates are competitive with the wages that would be paid if the industry were to remain in the community.

Second, to gain community support, there must be assurances that jobs are not taken away from civilians. It is critical, therefore, that a relationship be developed with representatives from organized labor, to ensure that the industry planned for a prison setting is not taking away viable employment from the community. As an administrator, to seek out an industry which has a sweat-shop mentality may have the potential for exploiting labor. Yet, if you choose a skill shop making sophisticated widgets, you may be depriving the free community of jobs. Caution must be exercised to avoid a negative public response.

A planning committee with substantial representation of management and labor can be of great assistance. With the input and concurrence of this committee, many roadblocks will be avoided or minimized. Committee support of a possible private-sector industry will also add credibility to the effort in the eyes of the community.

Liability

In an era plagued by quality control of products and equipment, prisons are not exempt from scrutiny. In fact, this issue is exacerbated in a prison because of the nature of the environment and past behavior of the clientele. Therefore, it is critical that a prospective industry be aware of this risk. It should be clear contractually that the jurisdiction will not be liable for losses or damage. Because such risk is a negative to private industry, the administration must market its resources—the positive aspects of the privatization program. It must clarify the labor advantages:

the availability of in-house labor and control over productivity. It should be pointed out that workers can be easily replaced and that this system can control absenteeism.

Fringe-benefit and retirement packages, as well as in-house special services — such as education, medical, and dental — are not necessary. Such costs remain the responsibility of the state and are not borne by the entrepreneur. In addition, cost breaks on rental space and utilities can be negotiated.

It is imperative that potential private employers understand all existing advantages and restrictions to be encountered. Otherwise, the project may be doomed from its inception.

Equipment Storage, Contraband Control and Searches

In a traditional industry, equipment storage and tool control are necessary to run an efficient business operation. Likewise, proper storage discourages petty theft by employees. In a prison, however, these activities require an additional, yet, very important function — contraband control.

Inmates are ingenious individuals. They can take the simplest object and fashion it into a homemade knife, a handcuff key, or some other object that could jeopardize the safety and security of the institutional community. Accordingly, most prisons have detailed policies and procedures to account for equipment, tools, and parts inventory. Properly locked cribs and storage boxes must be maintained on a shift basis, thus increasing security needs and costs.

Inmates also know how to hide contraband, and industrial areas offer excellent places to secret such items. Therefore, these shops must be subject to inspections by institutional staff. Conversely, security staff must understand how these searches can impact detrimentally on plant operations; therefore, prudent thought should be given before initiating a search that effectively shuts down production.

A further problem is presented by the movement of new materials into the facility, and the transfer of completed products outside of the fence. Special arrangements to make these operations occur without delay, extra cost, or undue interference must be made. "Just in time" input replacement may be desirable. The rationale for emphasizing these special needs is that inmates could use an industry to arrange an escape by having a prisoner hide in a box destined for the outside. This may be construed as alarmist, yet we have noted that similar escapes have occurred, even when the industry supervisors were correctional personnel. When dealing with prisoners who have little or no hope of release, never underestimate their ingenuity.

Orientation and Training

It is assumed that private industry supervisors will manage operations on site, and that they know little or nothing about correctional supervision. It is the facility's responsibility, therefore, to ensure that adequate screening occurs followed by training. It is not necessary to transform private industry foremen into correctional industry supervisors. It is appropriate, however, that they be schooled in basic procedures related to safety and security issues, that is, fire and emergency procedures, tool control, and hostage survival, etc.

Training and orientation should be designed to meet the needs of the institution and the manufacturers. The unique and special circumstances of a prison environment make it imperative that all who work inside are held to certain standards. This is only accomplished by a documented training commitment on the part of the facility and industry.

On-Site Supervision

Most inmates like to work, some for avowed reasons, others to meet a less obvious purpose. Their supervision as employees must follow the same principles and practices accorded similar employees in the community.

The initial contract must clearly explain the wage structure, including bonus opportunities and salary increments. Guidelines must be established on performance reviews and handling of work-related disciplinary situations.

It is the employer's responsibility to take corrective or disciplinary action, yet the prison's rules cannot be abridged even though the inmate worker is in a private industry setting. This is true, notwithstanding most inmates' views that such a work program is a privilege—one which they do not want to lose.

An important aspect of the on-site supervisor's job is to instill or to reinforce the proper work ethic in their inmate work force. Leadership and discipline will prove to be the key ingredients in transforming the criminal to an individual who follows society's norms and mores.

Classification

This term is not used in industrial management. It is, however, an important function of correctional management. Classification is the mechanism by which an inmate's custody level, housing, work assignment, and programming are determined. It impacts upon private industry operation in the following ways.

1. Tentative assignment to the industry (the final review and placement rests with private industry);

2. Inmates may be transferred from the facility, thereby leaving the private industry with a sudden vacancy; and

3. Inmates may have their custody increased because their behavior jeopardizes the safety and security of the institution or their own safety. Again, the industry forfeits an employee without notice.

Such variables in a prison's operations could prove a barrier to finding an industry willing to accept unpredictable change. However, no industry should want to open shop at a facility in which classification procedures were not present. Such changes can be minimized by maintaining a waiting list of employable inmates, creating a labor pool in training, and informing the industry supervisor of an inmate's custody status review in a timely fashion.

Other barriers or constraints related to safety and security include inmate work strikes, riots, and lockdowns. Fortunately, such incidents do not occur at regular intervals. The employer must know and understand that operations will not be interrupted routinely but that under certain conditions such interruptions may occur.

Other barriers exist to private-sector programming beyond those addressed. Their number and complexity may daunt the most forward-thinking penologist; yet, what may at first seem overwhelming can, with thoughtful action and commitment, be overcome. With sound negotiations and with the willingness of both partners to compromise, a privatization experience can prove to be a fruitful partnership between public and private resources.

With such effort, a concept couched in antiquity may emerge to form an effective link in the bonding of society to those written off as lost. If so, it will be a concept in which profit is not counted merely in the realms of cost effective only. Rather, it will, in some measure, assist in changing the view of prisons as the great wasteland to that of a resource for productivity while training future employees.

References

Auerbach, B. J., G. E. Sexton, F. C. Farrow, and R. H. Lawson. (1988). "Work in American Prisons. The Private Sector Gets Involved." *Issues and Practices in Criminal Justice.* Washington, DC: National Institute of Justice.

Boellstorff, L. (1988). "Private Industry Goes to Prison." *Corrections Compendium* 131 (November), no. 4.

Olson, R. F. (1978). "A Study of Formal Academic Education Programs in Connecticut's Correctional Institutions 1968–1975." Dissertation. University of Connecticut (unpublished).

26. More Warehouses, or Factories with Fences?

Warren E. Burger

During my tenure in the federal judiciary I have spoken often on the subject of penal and correctional institutions and the policies and practices which ought to be changed. People go to prisons only by way of the judicial process and every judge should be concerned with the effectiveness of the correctional process, even though we have no responsibility for its management. Based on my observations as a judge and my visits to prisons in the United States and most countries of Europe over the past twenty-five years, including the Soviet Union and the People's Republic of China, I have long believed that there are better ways to accomplish the desired objective.

We should change our approach to the problem and make the public aware why the subject has special relevance — even urgency — to every American.

Our country is engaged in a multibillion-dollar prison construction program. The question I raise is this: are we going to build more "warehouses" or should we change our thinking and build factories with fences around them, where we will first train inmates and then have them engage in useful production?

One thoughtful scholar of criminal justice described the state of affairs in harsher terms than I have used. More than a decade ago he wrote: "Criminal justice in the United States is in a state of spreading decay . . . the direct costs of crime include loss of life and limb, loss of earning(s) . . . physical and mental suffering by the victims and their families" (Gorecki, 1979).

Direct losses, he said, run into many billions of dollars annually; indirect losses, vastly more, approximate the astonishing figure of $90 billion a year. In the immediate future this figure can be reduced only by more effective law enforcement, which in turn will produce a demand for more correctional facilities.

Whether more prisons are the solution is open to question, but I leave to another occasion to discuss the merits of more mandatory minimum sentences or more use of probation and parole. Both of those courses fail to treat the fundamental issues. Today, I want to emphasize that over the next decade it is likely we will spend from $5 to $10 billion in new prison construction. Plainly, if we can divert more people from lives of crime we would benefit both those who are diverted and the potential victims. Yet all that has been done in the correctional systems up to now has not prevented the appalling increase in reported crime rates.

For many years I shared the optimism and hopes of rehabilitation programs with such distinguished penologists as the late James V. Bennett, long the director of the Federal Bureau of Prisons, and the late Torsten Eriksson, his counterpart in Sweden. Those hopes now seem to have been based more on optimism than reality. We now see that even with the enlightened correctional practices of Sweden and other North European countries, the result in terms of rehabilitation have fallen short of expectations. We know that those countries have long done much more than we do in the education and training of prison inmates. The fact that the problem is far more difficult than we had thought is the very reason we must consider changes and enlarge our efforts.

On several occasions I have laid down one proposition to which I adhere today. It is that when society places a person behind walls and bars it has an obligation – a moral obligation – to do whatever can reasonably be done to change that person before he or she goes back into the stream of society. This is more emphatically so with respect to the repeat or recidivist prisoner. If we had begun twenty-five, thirty-five, or fifty years ago to develop the kinds of programs in correctional institutions that are appropriate for an enlightened and civilized society, the word "recidivist" might not have as much currency as it does today. This is not simply a matter of human compassion. It is a hard matter of our own protection.

I have urged in reports to the American Bar Association and on many other occasions that prisons be made places for basic education and vocational training – as only a few prison systems now are. A specific proposal which I first advanced in 1972 is that a national academy of corrections be created to focus on the training of prison personnel beginning with the guards and security level. Soon after that, Attorney General William French Smith announced the creation of the National Corrections Academy at Boulder, Colorado, under the auspices of the National Institute of Corrections and the Federal Bureau of Prisons.

It is none too soon, for during the past ten years the prison population in the United States increased from less than 200,000 to over 350,000. In part this reflects the increase in crime and probably in far longer sentences. It probably also means that a larger proportion of criminal acts are being detected and result in convictions of those who are guilty.

The reality is that if we are to fulfill one of the most fundamental obligations of government – the protection of people and homes – there must be both more effective law enforcement and drastic changes in our prison systems. Just more stone, mortar, and steel for walls and bars will not solve or even improve these dismal conditions. If we are to make progress and protect the persons and property of people and make streets and homes safe from predators, we must consider changes in our approach to dealing with the people in prisons that offer some hope of changing at least some of those who are confined. It is often said that our prisons are just human warehouses and, although there is a measure of truth in this, the connotations of the bare term "warehouse" overstate the case. Many prisons deserve that name but not all. Enlightened administrators, with funds available, have demonstrated some success in vocational training of prisoners to give them a marketable skill to sell when they are released. These are all too few.

The Federal Bureau of Prisons under excellent leadership has performed very well, given statutory restraints on production of goods in prisons—and archaic public attitudes.

It is predictable that a person confined in a penal institution for two, three, five, or more years, who is then released without being able to read, write, spell, or do simple arithmetic, and who is not trained with any marketable skill will be vulnerable to returning to a life of crime. Very often the recidivism commences within weeks after release. What job opportunities are there for unskilled illiterates with criminal records? What business enterprise could conceivably continue with the rate of "recall" of its "products" that we see with respect to the "products" of our prisons?

The best programs in the world will not cure all of this dismal problem, a problem that the human race has struggled with almost since the beginning of organized societies. Improvements in our prison systems can be made, and the improvements will cost less in the long run than the failure to make them.

One possible source of billions of dollars to the states is federal grants, but it is important that such grants be predicated on standards, including:

1. Conversion of prisons into places of education and training and into factories and shops for production;

2. A repeal of statutes which limit prison industry production;

3. An affirmative limitation against any form of discrimination against prison-made goods; and

4. A change in the attitudes of organized labor and the leaders of business toward the use of prison inmates to produce goods or machine parts.

New standards, such as these, are crucial and they should be developed with the participation of the state and federal prison administrators who deal face to face and day to day with the problems and with representatives of labor and management. In the closing decade of the twentieth century I am confident that the enlightened leaders of labor and business will not support restraints on production of goods in prisons and the movement of such products in commerce.

Of course, prison production programs will compete to some extent with the private sector, but this is not a real problem. With optimum progress, it will be three to five years before programs of this kind have a market impact, even then only a small impact. I cannot believe that this great country of ours—the most voracious consumer society in the world—will not be able to absorb the production of even as many as 100,000 prisoners without injury to private employment. That production would be hardly a "drop in the bucket" in terms of the Gross National Product, but the benefit to the inmates—and to society—would be incalculable in the long run.

Most prison inmates, by definition, are maladjusted people. Whatever the cause—whether they suffer from too little discipline or too much, too little security or too much, broken homes, or whatever—they lack self-esteem, they are insecure, and they are at war with themselves as well as with society. They do not share the work ethic concepts that made this country great. They were not taught at home—or in the schools—the moral values that lead people to have respect and concern for the rights of others. Place that person in a factory, whether it makes ballpoint pens, hosiery, cases for watches, parts of automobiles, lawn mowers, computers, or parts of other machinery, pay that person reasonable compensation, and charge something for room and board, and keep, and we will have a better chance to release from prison a person able to secure gainful employment. In addition, that person's self-esteem will have been improved so there is a better chance that he or she can live a normal life.

There are, of course, exceptions. The destructive arrogance of the psychopath with no concern for rights of other people may well be beyond reach of any programs that prisons or treatment can provide. Our prison programs must aim chiefly at the others.

There is nothing really new in this concept. In my native state of Minnesota and in neighboring Kansas there are important beginnings. Special legislation authorized pilot programs involving contracts with private companies to fabricate machinery parts. On my first visit to the Stillwater Prison in Minnesota nearly sixty years ago, guiding boys from a summer camp, prisoners were producing parts of farm machinery for nearby factories.

On my first visit to Sweden's prisons over twenty-five years ago, I watched inmates constructing fishing fories and other products. On my most recent visit several years ago, prisoners were making components for prefabricated houses under the supervision of skilled carpenters. Those components could be assembled at a building site by semiskilled workers under trained supervision. In the People's Republic of China 1,000 inmates in one prison I visited made up a complete factory unit, producing hosiery and what we would call casual or sports shoes. That was truly a factory with a fence around it.

It is not necessary that prisons be self-contained factories capable of producing complete finished products. In terms of production equipment and the probable skills of most prison inmates, it makes more sense—and involves far less capital investment—to have prisoners produce machine parts rather than completed products. This can be done under contracts with private industry, as the Minnesota prison produced parts for farm machinery sixty years ago and produces parts of computer units for Control Data Corporation today.

We need not try in one leap to copy the Scandinavian model of producing prefabricated houses, nor do we need to go to the extent of some of the Scandinavian models and pay the regular union scale of wages, with a deduction for room, board, and keep. We should, however, consider paying some wages for the hours worked, with bonuses based on quality and volume of production, and then, of course, deduct some reasonable amount for room and board.

We do not need the help of behavioral scientists to understand that human beings who are producing useful goods for the marketplace—who are being productive—are more likely to develop the self-esteem essential to a normal, integrated personality. In place of the sense of hopelessness that is the common lot of prison inmates, this kind of program could provide training in skills and work habits that could make many prisoners better able to cope with life on their return to freedom.

In one prison in Europe—one for recidivist juveniles aged fourteen to eighteen who had committed serious felonies involving violence—the wall at the entry had four statements in large, bold script with letters one foot high. Translated they read about like this:

> You are here because you need help.
> We are here to help you.
> We cannot help you unless you cooperate.
> If you do not cooperate we will make you.

Here was an offer of a compassionate helping hand, coupled with the kind of discipline that, if missed early in life in homes and in schools that ignore moral values, produces maladjusted, incorrigible people.

My references to this prison for juveniles may have inspired one witness who testified before a Senate committee to disagree. He said that prisoners either could not or should not be "coerced" into taking training. Depending on what that witness meant by "coerced," I might be able to agree. I would say that every prisoner should be induced to cooperate by the same methods that are employed in many areas. Life is filled with rewards for cooperation and penalties for noncooperation. Prison sentences are shortened and privileges are given to prisoners who cooperate in prison programs.

Rewards and punishments permeate the lives of all free people and they should not be denied to prison inmates. Central to the American system is the idea that good performance is rewarded and poor performance is not. We can induce inmates to cooperate and I suggest only that they should not be made to study more, or work more or longer hours than, for example, the cadets at West Point and the Air Force Academy or midshipmen at Annapolis. I can hardly believe that anyone would seriously suggest that prisoners incarcerated for crimes should be treated with less discipline than those young men and women.

To maintain a prisoner in American prisons costs the taxpayers—in the form of a subsidy—from $10,000 to more than $25,000 per year, without taking into account the large capital investment in the physical facilities. That load should be lightened, if not taken off the backs of overburdened American taxpayers. We will help both the inmates and all of society if we make it feasible for prisoners to help support themselves.

Creating prison industries, with incentives for good performance, would accomplish the dual objective of training inmates in gainful occupations and lightening the enormous financial burden of maintaining the prison systems of this country.

We are at a crossroads on what kind of prisons we are to have as we get ready for the tax collector to reach into our pockets over the next few years for as much as $10 billion or more for new prisons. We can continue to have largely human warehouses, with little or no education and training, or we can have prisons that are factories with fences around them. That is what I propose today.

This almost intractable problem of criminal justice has baffled the human race since the beginning of the recorded history of organized societies. It is plainly in our own interest to try to make every prisoner a better human being who can cope with life when the prison term is over. If we do that more intelligently, there is some chance that we can, in the long run, reduce the tax burden and improve the chance that released prisoners will not renew their warfare with society.

There are no guarantees of success in dealing with prisons and prisoners, but the course we have been following has not worked out. On the contrary, the situation grows worse.

What I propose is that, as we embark on this massive prison construction program, we try a new approach—convert our warehouses into factories with fences around them. To do that we must change our thinking and change the reactionary statutes that stand in the way. I believe the American people are ready to do that.

References

Criminal Justice Construction Reform Act, S. 186.
Federal Prison Bureau Task Force on Training and Selection (1981).
Gorecki, J. (1979). *A Theory of Criminal Justice.* New York: Columbia University Press.

The Editors and Contributors

Bruce L. Benson: Professor of economics at Florida State University. Research fellow of Pacific Research Institute

Ronald L. Boostrom: Director of the Criminal Justice Administration Program and professor of public administration and urban studies at San Diego State University, CA

Gary W. Bowman: Associate professor of economics at Temple University, with research in applications of microeconomics including public and managerial decisions and policy

Samuel Jan Brakel: Professor of law and director of research of the Health Law Institute, DePaul University, Chicago. Senior Consultant, Isaac Ray Center, Chicago

Claire S. Bronson: Associate professor of finance, Western New England College, Springfield, MA

George D. Bronson: Warden, Carl Robinson Correctional Institute, Enfield, CT

Warren E. Burger: Chief justice of the United States (retired)

Roland C. Dart, III: Professor of criminal justice, California State University, Sacramento

Edwin J. Donovan: Assistant professor, Administration of Justice Department at Pennsylvania State University, University Park

Paulette Doyle: Office of Solicitor General, Alberta, Canada

Corina A. Draper: Graduate research assistant in the School of Public Administration and Urban Studies, San Diego State University, CA, and research associate for the San Diego Association of Governments

Philip E. Fixler, Jr.: (Deceased) Former director of local government at the Reason Foundation, Santa Monica, CA

Mike Freeman: Administrative assistant to the city manager, City of Thornton, CO, and former assistant director of the International City Management Association's FutureVisions Consortium

Robert J. Gemignani: President and founder of the National Office for Social Responsibility, Alexandria, VA, and former U.S. commissioner of youth development

Michael S. Gillie: Attorney and founder and executive director of United States Arbitration and Mediation, with 48 offices in the United States, Canada and Europe

Rodolfo A. Gonzalez: Professor of economics, California State University, San Jose

337

Robert S. Guzek: Vice president of Hill, a Willingboro, NJ, consulting firm

Simon Hakim: Professor of economics at Temple University. His work centers on analysis of criminal behavior, police operations, and privatization of justice institutions

Daniel Hawe: Director of intergovernmental affairs, Correctional Service, Canada

Richard G. Kiekbusch: Superintendent, Prince William–Manassas Regional Adult Detention Center, VA

Robert D. McCrie: Assistant professor, Department of Law and Police Science, John Jay College of Criminal Justice, City University of New York

James F. McNicholas: Director of security, Starrett Protective Service, Brooklyn, NY

Dolores Tremewan Martin: White House Office of Policy Development

Stephen L. Mehay: Professor of economics, U.S. Naval Postgraduate School, Monterey, CA

Richard Neely: Chief justice, Supreme Court of Appeals, West Virginia

Richard F. Olson: Assistant superintendent of schools, Unified School District #1, Connecticut Department of Corrections, Hartford

Robert W. Poole, Jr.: President of Reason Foundation, Santa Monica, CA, and editor of *Reason* magazine; White House consultant on privatization

Larry Ray: Executive director of the American Bar Association Standing Committee on Dispute Resolution

Howard Sapers: Provincial executive director, John Howard Society of Alberta, Canada

Paul Seidenstat: Associate professor of economics and director of the graduate program at Temple University. His research is in government finance and management and urban and environmental economics

Michael G. Shanahan: Chief of police, University of Washington, Seattle

Robert M. Stein: Professor of political science, Rice University, Houston, TX

James K. Stewart: Principal with Booz, Allen and Hamilton, Washington, DC, and former director of National Institute of Justice

David U. Strawn: President of Dispute Management, Orlando, FL

Jerry A. Usher: Chairman of the board, Golden West K-9, Pacoima, CA

Tim Valentine: U.S. congressman, Second District of North Carolina

William F. Walsh: Assistant professor, Administration of Justice Department at Pennsylvania State University, University Park

Thomas R. Windham: Chief of police, Fort Worth, TX

Michael J. Wynne: Correctional director of private sector industries, Connecticut Department of Corrections, Hartford

Edwin W. Zedlewski: Scientific adviser to director of National Institute of Justice. Scientific editor of *NIJ Reports* and consultant to the President's Commission on Organized Crime and the U.S. Sentencing Commission

Index